Basic Geometry
of Voting

Springer
Berlin
Heidelberg
New York
Barcelona
Budapest
Hong Kong
London
Milan
Paris
Tokyo

Donald G. Saari

Basic Geometry of Voting

With 102 Figures

Springer

Professor Donald G. Saari
Northwestern University
Department of Mathematics
2033 Sheridan Road
Evanston, IL 60208-2730, USA

Cataloging-in-Publication Data applied for

Die Deutsche Bibliothek - CIP-Einheitsaufnahme

Saari, Donald G.:
Basic geometry of voting / Donald G. Saari. - Berlin ;
Heidelberg ; New York ; Barcelona ; Budapest ; Hong Kong ;
London ; Milan ; Paris ; Tokyo : Springer, 1995
ISBN 3-540-60064-7

ISBN 3-540-60064-7 Springer-Verlag Berlin Heidelberg New York

SPIN 10507193   42/2202-5 4 3 2 1 0 - Printed on acid-free paper

In memory of
Gene A. Saari
and for
Martha M. Saari

*A dedicated team of idealistic, pragmatic radicals
who made a difference by improving the lives of many!*

Happy 78th Birthday!
Much Love,

Don

PREFACE

A surprise of this book is how the well-known intricacies and complexities of elections can be identified and resolved with the comfortable geometry of our three-dimensional world. This allows previously unpublished results and/or new explanations for old assertions to be included. So, even though this book is directed toward students and others interested in learning about the field, experts will find much that is new. To help test understanding and to facilitate using this material in a course, exercises follow each section.

As an introduction to what can go wrong, Chap. 1 catalogues the woes of the Chair of a hypothetical academic department. (These examples are used throughout the book.) The second section builds on this fable to raise issues; this is followed by a selective history. The last section reminds the reader of useful mathematical properties. The actual geometry starts in Chap. 2 where standard terms are introduced with a geometric formulation.

The results of Chap. 3 directly contradict commonly accepted notions. Here it is shown why the standard used by most of the field to judge procedures is highly flawed. In this critical analysis of pairwise voting, foundations are developed to analyze the debates central to this field since the 1780s. New approaches include the "profile coordinate representations" and the "profile decomposition" which make it almost trivial to construct examples illustrating all sorts of voting behavior. The chapter ends by showing that Arrow's Theorem is not as disturbing as commonly believed; instead, as I show, the conclusion is to be expected.

In Chap. 4, geometric methods are developed to analyze positional procedures (generalizations of our standard plurality vote) which make it easy to understand why different methods can lead to different outcomes. Indeed, deriving certain new conclusions now is as simple as drawing lines on a triangle. As part of this discussion, new sets of profile coordinates and decompositions are given which allow us to quickly analyze almost any three-candidate example. For instance, from this description we discover that pairwise and positional rankings can differ because they rely on different kinds of information about the voters. Then the fundamental properties of Borda Count are introduced.

While Chaps. 3 and 4 emphasize single profile issues, Chap. 5 describes those fascinating scenarios involving several profiles. The first three sections, for example, show what can happen when subcommittees join, voters abstain or change their opinions, or the procedure is manipulated. As a sampler, associated with a new, elementary proof of the Gibbard-Satterthwaite Theorem is a technique to analyze how susceptible a procedure is to being manipulated. In the last two sections, which emphasizes proportional voting, new ge~~~~~ techniques explain the serious problems of apportionment methods. As most procedures admit reasonable outcomes only through a fortuitous balance of compensating errors, we must anticipate problems. Indeed, legal issues raised about the current apportionment of Congressional seats for the USA, issues that reached the US Supreme Court, are mentioned.

This book started as a "student" version of *Geometry of Voting*; I dropped those sections primarily of interest to experts, reorganized the presentation to represent how the material would be taught (the ordering of *Geometry of Voting* is dictated by the mathematical development), and added exercises. However, I could not resist adding several recent results. Thus, while portions of this book overlaps material first developed in *Geometry of Voting,* it also contains many previously unpublished conclusions. Some of these new approaches, for instance, eliminate the two-century old challenge of analyzing the profiles from the Condorcet – Borda debates of the 1780s.

When writing a book, one appreciates the critical importance of colleagues and friends! This is particularly so when a computer program doesn't work and I'm rescued by my colleague Clark Robinson. If you like the computer generated pictures, thank Hollie Howard, a Northwestern University undergraduate who worked with me for three delightful years; she programmed them with PiCTeX. Thanks for encouragement, suggestions, corrections, comments, references, information, critiques, etc., etc., go to Roko Aliprantis, Jean-Pierre Aubin, Steve Brams, Len Evens, Eric Friedlander, Hollie Howard, Ehud Kalai, Jerry Kelly, Vincent Merlin, Ken Mount, Diana Richards, Clark Robinson, Stan Reiter, Katri Saari, Maurice Salles, Mark Satterthwaite, Carl Simon, Maria Tataru, Arnold Urken, Steve Williams, our Thursday afternoon discussion group on the "mathematics of the social sciences," and several others. Particular thanks go to my former NSF project director Larry Rosenberg who, right up until he died, was most supportive.

Donald G. Saari
Northwestern University
Evanston, Illinois
May, 1995

Typeset with $\mathcal{A}\mathcal{M}\mathcal{S}$-TEX

CONTENTS

CHAPTER I

FROM AN ELECTION FABLE
TO ELECTION PROCEDURES

What could be easier than interpreting an election? You just count to determine which candidate receives the most votes. What can be difficult about something so elementary? After all, even nursery school children know how to vote to select their juice of choice before nap time.

There is no mystery about two-candidate elections, but the story changes radically with three or more alternatives. Here, as anyone who has followed elections might suspect, if something can go wrong it probably will. Multicandidate elections admit all sorts of paradoxes (counter-intuitive conclusions) that must be taken seriously; they can generate doubt about the meaning or even the integrity of an election. While a selection of these problems is outlined in the introductory electoral fable, it describes only a small portion of what can go wrong. Outcomes can be manipulated, a candidate can lose by receiving more support, procedures don't do what we expect them to do. Nevertheless, even this sampler suggests why this research area is fascinating, essential, and complicated.

The fascination derives from the paradoxes that plague commonly used procedures. Underscoring the essential nature of this topic are actual troubling election outcomes; e.g., the conservative Buckley won the 1970 New York senatorial election even though over 60% of the voters preferred either of the two more liberal candidates. Indeed, it is not difficult to find "real world" paradoxes where it is arguable that the election ranking contradicts what the voters want. With the accompanying shift in power, such outcomes can cause unpopular and unintended changes in policy, differences in the allocations of resources, and even the fundamental direction of a society. More bothersome are those situations where a "voting paradox" leads to violence, death, and even the loss of democracy.[1] There is no debate; the goal of understanding and deriving the properties of voting procedures is an important topic with significant consequences.

"Voting" is not new; it has been around at least for a couple of millennia. While there is a more worthy claimant for "the world's oldest profession," voting theory qualifies for the "top ten list." Yet, in spite of its lengthy history,

---

[1] Marxist Salvador Allende won the 1970 election for President of Chile even though the polls indicated that most voters preferred either of the two more moderate candidates. (See [Fr].) No excuse can justify the action precipitated by the American CIA leading to the overthrow and death of Allende, nor for the dark period of dictatorial abuse occurring in a country justifiably proud of its democratic traditions. Yet, one must wonder whether these events would have been possible had the election outcome better reflected the voters' wishes.

much mystery remains due to hidden technical difficulties. I eliminate these complexities by identifying them with simple geometry.

1.1 An Electoral Fable

Anyone who has tried to coordinate the decision making for a group knows it is an hair-losing proposition. For the uninitiated, let me describe the woes of a conscientious, hardworking chairman from a mythical academic department.

Start with the annual departmental fall banquet where, to save money, one beverage was to be served. In this hypothetical 15-member department:

A. Six told the chair that they preferred milk to wine to beer (denoted by milk $\succ$ wine $\succ$ beer).

B. Five specified beer $\succ$ wine $\succ$ milk.

C. Four specified wine $\succ$ beer $\succ$ milk.

The department's choice was obvious; using the standard *plurality vote* – where each person votes for her or his favorite beverage – the group's ranking was

$$\text{milk} \succ \text{beer} \succ \text{wine}$$

with a tally of 6:5:4. Scrupulously following the departmental wishes, the chair announced that milk, their beverage of choice, would be served at the banquet. For unexplained reasons, milk was not available, so the chair did the obvious; he ordered the department's second choice of beer.

During the banquet, the naturally inquisitive wine lovers discovered that beer was *not* the department's second choice; two-thirds of the faculty (ten to five) actually preferred wine to beer!

Voters	Wine	$\succ$	Beer
A	6		–
B	–		5
C	4		–
	—		—
Total	10		5

With suspicions aroused, the meddling wine lovers continued to compile information about their colleagues' preferences. By the end of the evening, they learned that contrary to the announced decision milk was *not* the departmental top-choice – instead, it was crystal clear that wine was the beverage of choice! In fact three-fifths of the faculty (nine to six) preferred wine to milk and three-fifths preferred beer to milk.

Voters	Wine	≻	Milk
A	–		6
B	5		–
C	4		–
Total	9		6

Voters	Beer	≻	Milk
A	–		6
B	5		–
C	4		–
Total	9		6

What was going on! These results distinctly indicate the department's "true ranking" of

wine ≻ beer ≻ milk.

Why, then, was the "false" ranking of milk ≻ beer ≻ wine announced? The next morning rumors floated that the chair reversed the department's ranking to have a beverage that would favor his overly aggravated ulcer. But once impugned, trust is lost and suspicions grow. In practical terms, our chair's previous announcements became suspect. After all, only he counted the ballots; only he knew how the department really voted. Questions were raised.

Was Bob the departmental choice for the one vacant tenure track position, or did the chair reverse the election outcome so that Bob, his brother-in-law, finally would have a job?

Who really got elected to the departmental Budget Committee?

The unrest in our hypothetical department resulted in a clamor for a departmental meeting where, to ensure honesty, all votes must be by a public show of hands. In this meeting they would decide among the competing proposals:

1. *"The chair is to be commended for his efforts."*
2. *"So that future elections are accurately tallied, the chair must teach remedial math."*
3. *"The dean must take immediate steps to replace the chair!"*

After far too many corridor debates, the opinions within the department split evenly among the three rankings:

a. Five for 1 ≻ 2 ≻ 3.
b. Five for 2 ≻ 3 ≻ 1.
c. Five for 3 ≻ 1 ≻ 2.

To preserve what remained of our worried chair's tarnished reputation, he wanted a meeting agenda to ensure a fair hearing for his case. Now, an *agenda* specifies the order in which the alternatives are compared. With the agenda [1, 2, 3], for instance, the majority winner between 1 and 2 is advanced to be compared with the third listed alternative 3. To provide a full hearing for his case, the Chair decided to stress the positive by focusing the initial debate on his preferred choices; the first vote would be between proposals (1) and (2). Then, the winning alternative would be matched against the dreaded (3). Thus the Chair put forth the agenda [1, 2, 3].

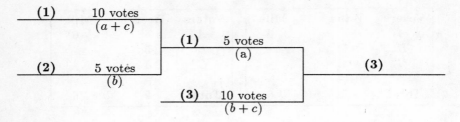

Fig. 1.1.1. The agenda [1, 2, 3]

His strategy failed miserably! As Fig. 1.1.1 shows, where letters indicate how each set of voters voted, the feared (3) was overwhelmingly adopted. The faculty left the meeting satisfied that the department had spoken; both votes were decided by decisive 10:5 tallies.

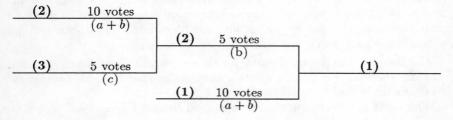

Fig. 1.1.2. The agenda [2, 3, 1]

What a blown opportunity! With a Machiavellian attitude, our chair could have left the meeting with substantial "proof" that his colleagues sincerely appreciated him. With even minimal knowledge about voting procedures, not only would his preferred choice of (1) have been selected, but the accompanying decisive votes would "prove" that any departmental dissent must be due to a small, dissident minority. The outcome of the [2, 3, 1] agenda pairing the winner of (2) versus (3) against (1) is in Fig. 1.1.2.

1.1.1 Time for the Dean

Even before she was approached, the Dean of the College seriously questioned our chair's integrity. Her suspicions were aroused earlier when he chaired a committee to choose a student representative for the Dean's Council.

When assigned to this post, our chair inherited an unwieldy committee of 26. In the name of efficiency, he created two smaller subcommittees of 13 each. To ensure a fair hearing for the three finalists — Ann, Barb, and Carol — our chair asked each subcommittee to conduct an unofficial preliminary vote – a *straw ballot* – with a *runoff procedure*. A runoff involves two votes: the two top-ranked candidates from the first election are advanced to the second ballot — the runoff election — where the majority winner is the selected candidate.

Ann won with both subcommittees. Of course, even though everyone was
carefully instructed to keep all results strictly confidential, Ann's good fortune
was headlined on the front page of the student newspaper. A victory party was
thrown for her that evening.

After the straw votes, our chair convened the full committee to reach the
formal conclusion with the same runoff procedure. Everyone knew about Ann's
victorious straw ballots, so it was commonly accepted that the full committee's
vote was a mere formality – Ann would be the student representative. But,
after tabulating the secret ballot, our chair had the temerity to announce that
Barb, who just happened to be his department's candidate, won by a substantial
margin!

(The 13 voters of the first subcommittee split their rankings as:

a. Four had the ranking Anna ≻ Barb ≻ Connie.
b. Three had the ranking Barb ≻ Ann ≻ Carol.
c. Three had the ranking Carol ≻ Ann ≻ Barb.
d. Three had the ranking Carol ≻ Barb ≻ Ann.

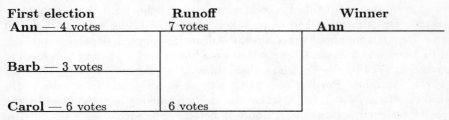

First election	Runoff	Winner
Ann — 4 votes	7 votes	**Ann**
Barb — 3 votes		
Carol — 6 votes	6 votes	

Fig. 1.1.3. The first subcommittee runoff

For this subcommittee, the outcome of the first election was Carol ≻ Ann ≻
Barb by a 6 : 4 : 3 vote. In the runoff, Ann beat Carol by a 7 : 6 vote.

The 13 members in the second subcommittee split rankings so that

a. Four had the ranking Ann ≻ Barb ≻ Carol.
b. Three had the ranking Barb ≻ Ann ≻ Carol.
c. Three had the ranking Carol ≻ Ann ≻ Barb.
d. Three had the ranking Barb ≻ Carol ≻ Ann.

Here the three-candidate outcome was Barb ≻ Ann ≻ Carol by a 6 : 4 : 3 vote.
In the runoff, Ann beat Barb by a vote of seven to six.

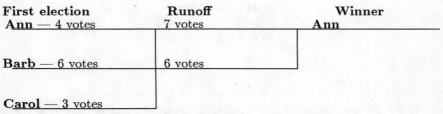

First election	Runoff	Winner
Ann — 4 votes	7 votes	**Ann**
Barb — 6 votes	6 votes	
Carol — 3 votes		

Fig. 1.1.4. The second subcommittee runoff

Ann, the winner of both subcommittees, was *bottom-ranked* in the first vote of the joint committee of all 26 voters with the ranking Barb $\sim$ Carol $\succ$ Ann by a vote of 9 : 9 : 8. In the runoff, Barb decisively beat Carol by a 17 : 9 vote.)

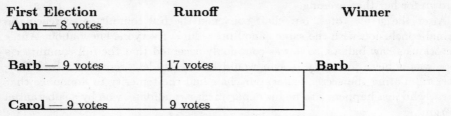

Fig. 1.1.5. The full committee runoff

1.1.2 The Departmental Election

During this autumn of his discontent, our chair's reputation suffered serious blows – the scandal associated with the Dean's Council election, the beverage brouhaha, and the devastating "no confidence" vote from the department. Across campus it was accepted that his reckless, unethical behavior no longer could be tolerated! Drastic action had to be taken. After consulting with the Political Science Department about procedures, the dean announced a departmental election to select a new chair. This election would be tallied according to a method proposed in 1770 by the French mathematician J. C. Borda.

The n candidate *Borda Count* (BC) assigns $n - i$ points to a voter's ith-ranked candidate, $i = 1, \ldots, n$ where the election ranking is determined by the totals of assigned points where "more is better." So, with $n = 5$ candidates, 4, 3, 2, 1, 0 points are assigned, respectively, to a voter's top, second, third, fourth, and bottom-ranked candidates. For $n = 3$ candidates, 2, 1, 0 points are assigned, respectively, to a voter's top-ranked, second-ranked, and bottom-ranked candidates.

After intense campaigning in the department, a coffee-room survey showed that

- 7 members preferred Abbott $\succ$ Boyce $\succ$ Chair,
- 7 preferred Boyce $\succ$ Abbott $\succ$ Chair, and
- only our beleaguered chair preferred Chair $\succ$ Abbott $\succ$ Boyce.

In this de facto two-person race, the tally would be

	Abbott	Boyce	Chair
	$(7 \times 2) = 14$	$(7 \times 1) = 7$	0
	$(7 \times 1) = 7$	$(7 \times 2) = 14$	0
	1	0	2
	—	—	—
Total	22	21	2

Thus, Boyce would lose with the election outcome Abbott $\succ$ Boyce $\succ$ Chair and the tally of 22 : 21 : 2. (The first row are the Abbott supporters where the

$14 = 7 \times 2$ points reflects the seven first-place votes, the $7 = 7 \times 1$ reflects the seven second-place votes, and $0 = 7 \times 0$ are the last-place votes. Similarly, the second row are the tallies from the seven Boyce supporters, while the last row reflects the Chair's ballot.)

To prevent Boyce's defeat, Boyce's supporters decided to be "strategic" by voting as though each preferred Boyce $\succ$ Chair $\succ$ Abbott. In this manner, where each voter provides Boyce with a two-point, instead of a single-point, differential over Abbott, the election ranking would be Boyce $\succ$ Abbott $\succ$ Chair with a $21 : 15 : 9$ tally.

	Abbott	Boyce	Chair
	14	7	0
	0	14	7
	1	0	2
	—	—	—
Total	15	21	9

As Abbott's supporters suspected this would happen, they decided to mark their ballots Abbott $\succ$ Chair $\succ$ Boyce to give Abbott an edge. *The chair was re-elected.*

	Abbott	Boyce	Chair
	14	0	7
	0	14	7
	1	0	2
	—	—	—
Total	15	14	16

1.1.3 Exercises

1. Change the "beverage" preferences so that only the "beer–wine" ranking is reversed – all other rankings remain the same.

2. The beverage example uses 15 voters. Create a similar nine voter example. Can you do this for eight voters? How about 33 voters? (Hint: $10 + 11 + 12 = 33$.)

3. A plurality election ranking of Anni $\succ$ Bev $\succ$ Candy $\succ$ Deanna with the $9 : 8 : 7 : 6$ tally indicates the number of voters with each candidate top-ranked. Suppose Deanna drops out of competition. Show that the new election ranking could be the reversed Candy $\succ$ Bev $\succ$ Anni. To do so, recognize that Deanna's voters can't vote for her, so they vote for their second ranked candidate. Therefore, divvy up these voters to cause the indicated three-candidate outcome. Next, if Bev, instead of Deanna, drops out, we must worry about who her supporters rank in second place. Choose their preferences so that the new outcome is Deanna $\succ$ Candy $\succ$ Anni. Complete this extension of the beverage example so that if any candidate drops out of the race, the three-candidate outcome reverses the four-candidate conclusion. The adventurous reader should create a five-candidate example where, should any candidate quit, the four-candidate outcome reverses the five-candidate ranking. (Hint: Start with a $16 : 15 : 14 : 13 : 12$ tally for the five-candidate election.) How would you create a six (or seven, or eight, or ...) candidate example?

4. To understand the preferences for the departmental meeting, label the vertices of an equilateral triangle in a counterclockwise direction. Now, define an ordering of the labels by starting with one vertex and, in a clockwise direction, read off the names of the vertices. Use each of the next two vertices as starting points and do the same. What you obtain are the departmental preference. Generalize this procedure to four candidates by labelling vertices of a square. The same scheme gives four kinds of preference rankings. With these preferences, compute the election outcome for the agendas $[1, 2, 3, 4]$, $[2, 3, 4, 1]$, $[3, 4, 1, 2]$, $[4, 1, 2, 3]$. Create such an example for five candidates. What happens in general? (These *Condorcet preferences* are named after Condorcet who discovered the three-candidate example.

5. Find the BC ranking for the beverage example; for the departmental meeting.

6. Suppose before the departmental meeting, the five voters with preferences $1 \succ 2 \succ 3$ realized that, with the sentiments of the faculty, "3" would win with the agenda $[1, 2, 3]$. What strategic voting action could these voters have used to thwart this result? (Hint: They cannot get "1" as the outcome.)

7. For the agenda problem, it is not necessary for an equal number of voters to have each of the three types. In fact, show that it is possible for there to be only one person with preferences $3 \succ 1 \succ 2$ for this outcome to occur. With insight from this computation, create an example where "3" wins even though *nobody* has alternative 3 top-ranked.

8. To capture the spirit of the Dean's Council example, suppose there are two fifteen member subcommittees where the preferences for the first subcommittee are evenly split among Anna $\succ$ Toini $\succ$ Connie , Toini $\succ$ Connie $\succ$ Anna, and Connie $\succ$ Anna $\succ$ Toini. (Using Prob. 4, these ranking are obtained by giving the correct labels to the vertices of an equilateral triangle and going around it in a counterclockwise fashion.) Suppose the preferences for the second subcommittee also are split where each of the three choices is the exact opposite of what is given in the first subcommittee. For each subcommittee, find the election outcome for the same agenda $[A, C, T]$. Next, find the election outcome for this agenda when the full group votes. Now, suppose you, one of Anna's good friends, can persuade some voters from each subcommittee to resign. Find who should leave so that the election outcome for each subcommittee remains the same as before, but now Anna is the winner when the full group votes.

1.2 The Moral of the Tale

Although the dean of our far-fetched story was misinformed, she was correct in taking decisive action once she suspected that our chair was changing election outcomes. Elections play a central role in the everyday decision processes of modern society. We use them to choose our leaders, to determine the outcome of primary elections, to select from among legislative proposals, to accept members for professional organizations, to choose the winners of prizes, fellowships or scholarships, to fill scarce tenure track positions in academic departments, to invite potential members to join fraternities, sororities, and other social organizations, to resolve a family debate over what to name a pet mongrel, to coordinate our more pedestrian daily choices ranging from the selection of a dinner beverage to whose car will be used to go to the theater, and even to crown the MVP and the mythical national champion for certain sports.

Elections form such an integral part of our daily life that there is a critical obligation to preserve faith in the process. This concern is manifested on election day with the armies of poll watchers fighting to thwart that age-old charge of *"Vote early, vote often!"* to guarantee that the ballots counted are the ballots cast, and to ensure that a voter is not really an eternal resident of a local cemetery. We see this concern reflected through the outrage generated by stories about "ballot stuffing," even with a popularity contest to choose an "All Star" sports team. At all levels and in all contexts, it is natural to insist on preventive actions to ensure honest elections. This is rightfully so. Elections are treated seriously; they form an important class of group decision instruments to replace might in battle with the right of the ballot.

Elections are useful only if we trust them; e.g., an outcome not to our liking is more palatable if we believe it reflects the sincere wishes of the people. Consequently, our mythical dean correctly took prompt, direct action to ensure her colleagues of the integrity of the process. But, we have an advantage; we know that the chair of our fable was an honest, naive person who did nothing whatsoever to vitiate the electoral process. The true culprits were hidden mathematical subtleties exercising their pernicious effects upon the election procedures. This raises an important challenge; does our concern for the sanctity of elections, does our desire to ensure the "best candidate wins" extend beyond guarding against human malfeasance? If we honestly want elections to reflect the "true beliefs of the people," shouldn't we worry about those mathematical peculiarities that can do more to frustrate this lofty goal than the craftiest actions of a cigar chomping precinct captain?

To stop humans from stealing elections, we first learn how they do it. Similarly, to prevent election procedures from selecting an alternative we view as being decidedly inferior, we first must discover what can go wrong and why. We need to understand the mathematical sources for the various paradoxes and undesired election outcomes. We need to understand the structural reasons why certain procedures are more easily manipulated than others. The development of a mathematical theory to provide the structural foundation for these procedures is the basic theme of this book.

1.2.1 The Basic Goal

Our ultimate goal is to choose a procedure that always honors the voters' beliefs. This sounds simple, but, what are these "true wishes?" After all, *each* method is intended to provide an accurate measurement. But, if different procedures yield different conclusions for the same preferences, which "correct one" is correct?

The complexity of this issue is illustrated with the beverage example. For instance, rather than a plurality vote or basing the decision on the majority votes, use a runoff election. Beer and Milk are advanced to the runoff where Beer wins by a vote of 9 : 6. Thus, for the beverage example:

Election Method	Winning alternative
Plurality election	Milk
Pairwise comparison	Wine
Runoff	Beer

So, each alternative can be touted as the "sincere" choice for the same people. Namely, *the chosen beverage depends more on choice of the decision procedure than on the voters' wishes.* So, which beverage should be selected?

This same difficulty occurs with the departmental election. Had our chair wished to teach remedial mathematics, he could have ensured this outcome with the agenda $[3, 1, 2]$. This remaining agenda pitches (1) versus (3) in the first vote, and the winner against (2) in the second. Here, alternative (2) is selected by such landslide proportions that the legitimacy of the outcome probably would not be questioned by any reasonable observer.

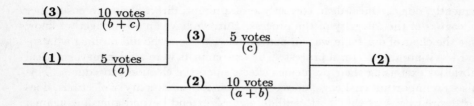

Fig. 1.2.1. The agenda [3, 1, 2]

In words, this division of voter preferences has the curious characteristic that whoever is voted on last in the agenda wins, and all votes are decisive. Again, we encounter the disturbing conclusion that the election outcome depends more upon the choice of a procedure (the agenda) than the voters' views.

Agenda	Winning Alternative
$[2, 3, 1]$	1
$[1, 3, 2]$	2
$[1, 2, 3]$	3

This serious problem is resolved here by decomposing profiles into parts to determine which procedures may frustrate the voters' actual beliefs.

1.2.2 Other Political Issues

The mathematics of voting and other political science issues is an old, yet a relatively new topic. The rich supply of important topics that almost beg to be analyzed with mathematical techniques ensures that this area is ready to explode with activity! It is easy to make this prediction; when almost daily seismic readings of the literature prove the existence of growing activity coming from various locations, "The Big One" has to be expected. It is not clear when it will happen, but it will.

A glance at the daily newspaper furnishes a ready list of issues. Immediately after the 1992 USA Presidential election, for instance, pundits, politicians, spin artists and academics tried to interpret the election outcome. Did Clinton receive a mandate? If so, to do what? What did the election outcome really mean? The initial reaction of Republican Senator Dole was to combine the Bush and Perot vote to argue that 57% of the voters were against Clinton. A familiar Democratic response was that the combined Perot and Clinton vote of 62% created a clear mandate for "Change." Polling services offered their instant analysis by claiming that about 34% of the Perot voters had Clinton as second choice, and 34% preferred Bush.

The 1992 election is typical; elections are followed by a careful analysis of the vote. At times, the goal is propaganda to put a "spin" on a negative outcome. More often, because "voting" is a crude communication procedure, the object is to understand the voters' aggregated message. Whether an election is for a chair of a department, a congressman, or a President, the vote often is and should be interpreted as reflecting the will of the people. So, if reelection is intended, it is worth deciphering the message hidden behind the vote.

Further support for this comment comes from the Peruvian election in mid-November, 1992. The outcome was carefully watched by the international community as a barometer about how the Peruvian people were accepting President Fujimori's extreme actions. At balance was restoration of much needed foreign aid and investments that were suspended in April, 1992, after President Fujimori seized near dictatorial powers. (He justified his drastic action as necessary to effectively combat the Shining Path terrorist group; by 1994 the leaders of this group were captured and its power declined.) Presumably because Fujimori's allies won a majority of seats in congress, the election was interpreted as indicating a wide-spread support for the President. Indeed, the Japanese agreed to give Peru $100 million of new loans and the USA announced that Peru was back on the path toward democracy. But, did Fujimori's allies really receive a majority support of the people? That his allies won a majority of the seats in congress could reflect properties of the voting procedure because, in fact, they received only about 38% of the vote. (In 1995, Fujimori easily won reelection.)

This inverse problem of using the election tally to decipher the intent of the voters is sufficiently critical to qualify as an important theoretical question. What we need, then, is a tool to extract from a given procedure all possible divisions of voters' preferences leading to a specific conclusion. How does the answer vary with the choice of a procedure? These kinds of issues can be answered; as part of our mathematical development of voting procedures, "coordinate representations" for profiles are introduced to allow us to "see" all possible profiles that support a given election outcome.

1.2.3 Strategic Behavior

"Strategic behavior" is an academic growth area that weds game theory with decision analysis. Be careful; it is easy to get hooked by the seductive charm of this area with even a brief exposure to its powers. This is because it offers insight into a vast number of critical issues using only basic mathematical techniques.

Strategic voting is not new; often it is encouraged with the admonition, "Don't waste your vote; vote for –." In the 1988 Democratic Party Presidential primaries, candidate Jesse Jackson tried to counter this threat to his candidacy by encouraging his Black and liberal supporters to vote their convictions. Such counter reactions are common in multicandidate elections; they were expressed by the third party Presidential candidate Anderson when he urged his supporters to send a message to Washington and by Perot's wishful claim that votes for Bush or Clinton would be "wasted."

Actually, "strategic voting" to avoid wasting your vote is a version of informed voting; after all, why not vote only for candidates you believe can be elected. The dark side of strategic action is when advantage is taken of the peculiarities of a procedure to force an unwanted outcome upon the electorate. While it is not clear whether this is a serious practical problem, the issue is so attractive to academics that it has spawned numerous research papers. New questions can be generated just by changing the identity of who is trying to manipulate the system and who is not, who has certain information and who does not. In the departmental meeting from the fable, for instance, what would happen if some of the faculty voted strategically? How should they vote to succeed? In the departmental election, what is the best response of Boyce's supporters once they discovered that Abbott's fans would vote strategically? What if they did not have this information?

My analysis of strategic behavior differs sharply from standard treatments; I believe the real issue is to understand the structures of voting procedures. From this perspective, strategic action is an embellishment; it is an action taken to exploit the structure to obtain a personally better conclusion. So, by unraveling the structure of procedures, it becomes possible (Chap. 5.) to determine all possible ways paradoxes occur and procedures can be manipulated.

A word of caution. Manipulative behavior is important, but it must never be the single deciding factor in choosing a system. As an analogy, we can prevent "carjacking" by driving a beat up, rusted, uncomfortable automobile wildly belching smoke, but few people do so. Precautions are necessary, but extremes are stupid. Similarly, corporations with decentralized decision activities provide opportunities for manipulation, but few embrace a Stalinist, or even more severe approaches to solve this difficulty. Precautions are necessary, but extremes can be counterproductive. All election methods can be manipulated, some more than others, but it is unrealistic to select a procedure just on its manipulative features. Precautions are necessary, but adopting a method which seriously distorts the voters' true intentions even with sincere voting is total nonsense!

1.2.4 Some Procedures Are Better than Others

Some procedures are better for certain purposes than for others. But, based on the mathematical development that follows (and as indicated by the exercises of the last section), the commonly used plurality vote is a very bad choice. Yet, mindful of the importance of being positive, nice things can be said even about this maligned procedure. In fact, for any method, arguments can be advanced, situations created, criteria imposed to "prove" that that procedure is "optimal." (See Sect. 5.3.) Then, by emphasizing a different, carefully edited set of arguments and criteria, it is possible to discredit "competing" methods.

This observation has a corollary; exercise caution and skepticism when encountering a "salesman" from academics or a political party selling election reforms – particularly around election time. Accepting an election reform should be treated like the selection of a major purchase, such as an used car from an unknown dealer – be sure to learn what really is being sold. We recognize the danger of buying a flashy car complete with the latest electronics and sex appeal only to find that it won't run. Similarly, it is not hard to be enticed by flashy, positive attributes of a voting procedures that disguise the simple fact that it does not work – its election outcomes can abuse the intent of the voters. For instance, while being reasonably immune to manipulative strategies, a procedure may produce outlandish outcomes. While being promoted in terms of properties that promise to promote democratic principles, the outcomes of a reform procedure may violate the intent of the voters. In light of this realistic concern, hopefully the theory developed here will assist in a more informed consumer selection of voting processes.

After these warnings, it is reasonable to wonder what method I think is best. Based on what follows, the Borda Count appears to be optimal.[2] It has flaws; I indicated one of them in the fable with the manipulation of the election for a new chair. However, because the Gibbard-Satterthwaite result (described in Sect. 5.3), asserts that *all* non-dictatorial methods involving three or more alternatives can be manipulated, *all procedures join the BC in this hall of shame.*

Why the BC? As the properties indicate, the BC appears to be the unique method to represent the true wishes of the voters. As a preview of its properties, consider what happens when the BC is used with the beverage example. Here, each voter with the preference Milk $\succ$ Wine $\succ$ Beer contributes two points for Milk, one point for Wine and zero points for Beer. Continuing this process for each voter, the final tally is

	Wine	Beer	Milk
	6	0	12
	5	10	0
	8	4	0
Total	19	14	12

The BC election ranking of the beverages *reverses* the plurality ranking to become consistent with how these voters majority rank the three pairs! (As explained later, this consistency of the BC and pairwise outcomes is no accident.) Consequently, had our chair used the BC, he could have avoided all of his difficulties within the department.

---

[2] A silly argument occasionally used against the BC is that it was born in the imagination of a member of nobility. Hey, just because someone is born in a manger doesn't mean he is an ass!

The consistency extends; had the BC been used with the runoff procedure, then wine would win the runoff election between wine and beer. The following table indicates what occurs with the beverage example when the BC is used with the different procedures.

Borda Count outcome	
Election method	**Winning alternative**
Borda election	Wine
Pairwise comparison	Wine
Runoff	Wine

Among other positive BC features, it is the unique method to minimize the number and kinds of paradoxes, to minimize the likelihood of a paradox, to minimize the likelihood that a small group can successfully manipulate the outcome, to minimize the possibility of voters' errors adversely changing the outcome, and so forth. All of this is described in Chap. 4.

When I discovered these results (and rediscovered others that were known, but not by me) I was confused why the BC kept emerging as the best method. So, I searched for "natural" settings where the other procedures do better than the BC. (They exist.) By doing so, the source of the BC properties became evident; they are caused by its symmetry. By this I mean that when a procedure assigns points to a voter's first, second, etc. place candidate, only the BC keeps the point spread between adjacently ranked candidates fixed. Now, a lesson learned early in mathematics is that "optimal" solutions normally are associated with symmetry. Suppose, for instance, that with a fixed amount of fencing, we want to fence in a rectangular region with the largest area. The answer is a square. Conversely, among the rectangular regions with a fixed area, which one has the minimal perimeter? (A square.) Posing these questions with triangles, the answer is an equilateral triangle; for ellipses the answer is a circle. The same phenomenon occurs when we seek the election procedure to optimize a particular "desired feature;" we must expect the "optimal" answer to be the most symmetric one – the BC. (By inventing stories where the "optimal" outcome is "bad," "negative" BC features are found.) Of course, by imposing conditions to destroy the natural symmetry of the problem, other procedures emerge. Using the fencing problem as an example, when one edge need not be fenced because we can use a wall or river, then the square no longer is the optimal answer; similarly, by concocting settings where no person would assume a particular rankings of the candidates,[3] the BC must drop from its central and optimal position.

Even through strong arguments prove that the BC is "optimal," it need not be everyone's "best" choice. As a personal example, I'm interested in the mathematics of these procedures, rather than advocating their adoption – even in my own academic department. However, right after I gave a colloquium lecture

---

[3] The principal role of many of these artificial conditions is to justify publishing another paper.

to my colleagues on the mathematics of voting, they adopted the BC for our important elections.[4] The result is that our elections more accurately reflect the general views of the department. In retrospect, had I thought of it, this would have been an excellent reason for my reluctance to promote the BC; the previously biased outcomes were personally more favorable. In other words, the choice of a procedure can and must be treated as an important strategic variable.

1.2.5 Exercises

1. The two extreme ways to tally ballots are the plurality method, where one point is given to a voter's top-ranked candidate and none to the others, and the *antiplurality method* where a point is given to a voter's top- and to his second-ranked candidates with no points for the bottom-ranked candidate. Find an argument showing that the BC is the midpoint between these two procedures. Find the antiplurality outcome for the beverage example.

2. In the beverage example from the first section, find a strategic way for certain voters to vote so that instead of milk being the top-choice, a more preferred outcome would occur. Do the same for the same example if the method is a runoff.

3. Using the *profile* (the listing of voter preferences) for the beverage example, create the *reversed profile* by reversing the preferences of each voter. For instance, the voters with the Milk, Wine, Beer ranking now are assigned the Beer, Wine, Milk preference. This reversal should, of course, reverse the plurality ranking for the beverage example. Compute the election outcome to see if this is true. (This phenomenon is described in detail in Sect. 4.4.)

4. In Prob. 3, Sect. 1.1, it is shown how to extend the beverage story to a four-alternative setting. Complete the preferences for these voters by adding what they want for third and fourth place. Now, find both the plurality and antiplurality ranking for this profile. Next, find the plurality and antiplurality rankings for the reversed profile. Are there any patterns? Any suggested explanations?

1.3 From Aristotle to "Fast Eddie"

This book is about the theory, not the history of voting. Yet, as the history provides fascinating stories that motivate certain topics, a selective description of the early years of voting theory is outlined. Hopefully this sampler will encourage the reader to refer to the references for a complete account.

Voting probably predates written history. For the same reason that boys in a school yard squabble over how many players are on each team, one can imagine competing prehistoric tribes quickly assessing the strength of the opposition to determine whether action or diplomacy would serve best – this count is a crude form of voting. The same tense connection using a vote count to assess the opposition's strength continues throughout history. Problems can arise when a majority vote does not mean that the "winning side" enjoys a superiority in exercising power. When this happens, the balance between might and right can tilt – even in holy places such as the Catholic Church.

---

[4] To minimize the temptation to manipulate when k out of n candidates are selected, we occasionally use the weights $(k, k-1, \ldots, 1, 0, \ldots, 0)$.

1.3.1 Selecting a Pope

During the period of time often identified with the controversy between King Henry II of England and Thomas Becket, precise procedures for the election of a pope had yet to be established. Not only was there a lack of agreement about what constituted a winner and who was a voter, but a form of "weighted voting" was used where the votes of the wiser, spiritually more meritorious cardinals received added importance. It is not clear, however, how wisdom and holiness were measured. With all of the ambiguity, it is no wonder that two popes – a Pope and an Antipope – were elected in 1130 creating a schism within the Church. The election of 1159 was no better. Even though Roland received a majority vote of the Cardinals, he was hesitant to accept the papacy without the unanimous vote that seems to have been tacitly expected. Finally he was persuaded to accept the decision and become Pope Alexander III.

Controversy often accompanies debated elections, but not necessarily of the wild type witnessed in 1159. At reluctant Roland's investiture, jealous competitor Octavian "snatched the mantle like a robber, tore it with his own hands from Alexander's shoulders, and attempted among cries and confusion to carry it off. But one of the Senators ... was moved to anger, and throwing himself bodily on the ranting man, seized the mantle from his hand." Perhaps anticipating such an event, Octavian enrobed himself with a second mantle supplied by a confederate. Alas, in the excitement he put it on backwards and upside down – definitive proof to Cardinal Boso that "just as [Octavian's] mind was twisted and his intentions devious, he wore his mantle awry in testimony of his own condemnation." Then, for political reasons rather than to shield his embarrassing attire, Octavian quickly was surrounded by his armed supporters; in the resulting violence many of Roland's allies fled for their lives. Following this period of confusion between might and right, Roland became Pope Alexander III with Octavian serving as the competing Pope Victor IV.[5] So, who was the real pope?

What more proof is required about the need for carefully established election procedures? Procedures are needed to spell out who can vote and what it takes to be a winner. The Catholic Church recognized and resolved this problem during the Third Lateran Council in 1179 by creating the method still in use. The qualitative ("who is holier than whom?") weighted voting approach was abandoned; the new rules specify that only cardinals can vote and each cardinal has a single vote. Anyone – even the reader of this book – could be the new Pope, but to win you need one more than two-thirds of the vote. Compliance of the faithful with the election result is ensured by invoking the threat of swift excommunication.

Why a two-thirds vote? Why not, say, 63%? As my colleague R. Kieckhefer speculates, "My own hunch is that the clever folk who devised these procedures

---

[5] Most of this material comes from Cardinal Boso's delightfully biased account of his friend Pope Alexander III. See, for example, *Boso's Life of Alexander III*,[E] (the quotes are from page 44) and the important reference [U]. I also had informative conversations with Prof. R. Kieckhefer from the Northwestern University Department of Religion.

were less concerned about the fairness of the outcome than about its stability. They were sick and tired of malcontents changing their minds after an election and claiming that for one reason or another the election hadn't been proper, then setting up a rival candidate as antipope and producing a schism. So the question was: how can we devise a procedure that will minimize the risk of there being an effective rival claimant after the election has taken place."

The stability ensured by the "two-thirds plus one" rule follows from simple arithmetic. (For a game theoretic explanation, see [S22]). In order to successfully create a schism, a competitor needs to convert to his side a majority of the pope's original supporters. In other words, "For really serious problems to arise now, a newly elected pope will have to be so clumsy as to alienate more than half of the cardinals who originally elected him. That, of course, did happen – whence the Great Schism of 1378. Which is only to say that mere mathematics can never ensure against disaster when it's pitted against human nature. But at least now there's a greater safeguard against foreseeable damage."

1.3.2 Procedure Versus Process

This connection between power and vote is natural. Through time the disenfranchised have gained the vote primarily through might rather than by appealing to justice or reason. History is full of examples where the king, emperor, dictator, or the group in power, after a realistic assessment of the costs, opted for diplomacy over defeat by offering the right to vote to a select group. This natural phenomenon ranges from the formal voting methods offered to the aristocrats in Sparta around 750 BC, to the suffrage movement of the twentieth century and on to numerous examples in contemporary society with changes in developing countries and former dictatorships. But once the vote is granted, how is it conducted? The earlier processes typically involved voting either *yes* or *no*.

One fifth century BC approach, an obvious precursor for the mindless early morning TV game shows, is where each candidate appeared in front of an assembly to be judged by the crowd's level of approval as demonstrated by shouting. In lieu of the electronic sound meters, that required another couple of millennia to be invented, a small group of men would sit in a nearby building charged with ranking the relative loudness of the shouts. Thus, this approach constituted an early form of our computerized tallying of ballots to offer quick conclusions. A difficulty with this counting method, however, is the obvious incentive it provides a candidate to court big-lunged supporters. Aristotle joins many of us in viewing this procedure as childish; presumably his opinion would extend to the morning game shows.

Among the many other processes was the traditional show of hands and the Athenian move toward an added degree of anonymity by dropping pebbles into different containers. ([St] is one of several excellent references about the early history of voting.) What we find throughout the early history of this subject, starting from the Greek and Roman Forums through the seventeenth century, is an emphasis on process – who can vote, how they cast their vote, who can be a candidate, who is a winner, and how to avoid fraud and manipulation. While there are comments already in Aristotle's *Politics* about legislative procedures, not much is expressed about voting methods. In fact, what differences arise in the elections involve for the most part the setting of various quotas, different kinds of runoffs, and establishing the thresholds levels required for victory.

1.3.3 Jean-Charles Borda

The mathematician Jean-Charles Borda appears to be the first to recognize that while the mathematics of voting seems to be trivial, it is not. He was the first to formally investigate the subtle effects of using various voting methods. It is worth noting that his attempts to find a method to capture the true views of the voters were first advanced on June 16, 1770, and then again in 1784. These are the years building toward the French revolutionary period, and this theme supporting the voter was pioneered by a person born to nobility. The Borda Count plays such a central role in voting theory that it is worth spending a couple of paragraphs to say something about the man.[6]

J.-C. Borda, the tenth of 16 children, was born on May 4, 1733, to parents of nobility – Jean-Antoine de Borda and Jeanne-Marie-Théré de Lacroix. That he was an accomplished, influential scientist during those eventful days of the late 1700s is attested to by his election to the Académie des Sciences in 1756 at the age of 23. Readers of this book probably associate Borda with voting, but this work was such a minor portion of his contributions that his biographer Mascart devotes less than seven of 636 pages to it. Instead, most of Borda's research involved the mathematical and experimental investigation of fluid dynamics. To provide a feeling for his work, a small sample of his varied contributions follows.

On the theoretical level Borda critiqued Newton's theory of fluid resistance arguing that, contrary to Newton's belief, the resistance is proportional to the square of the fluid velocity and the sine of the angle of incidence. He made many contributions to the modern theory of physics. He introduced the Borda mouthpiece, or "Borda harp," and then he computed the "jet" properties for the associated fluid contraction. He wrote on the calculus of variations, developed trigonometric tables to accompany his development of a surveying instrument – the *cercle de réflection*. The role of this instrument in astronomy adds to his role as a founder and first President of the Bureau des Longitudes in June, 1795. The list goes on, but the point is made; Borda was an accomplished scientist, physicist, and mathematician.

---

[6] Previously there has been very little in the literature about Borda except where his name is attached to developments in fluid mechanics. This scarcity of reliable information reflects the lack of readily available biographical material about Borda. This situation is changing with the work of A. Urken and I. McClain; e.g., for a start see [Mc, MH, MU, Ur1, Ur2].) The best Borda reference I found – the source for most of my comments – is Jean Mascart, *La vie et les travaux du Chevalier Jean-Charles de Borda* [M]. (The quote given below from this book (page 128) and the material I used was translated for me by K. Saari.) In addition to Mascart's reference, see Duncan Black's classic *The Theory of Committees and Elections* [Bl], and [D].

Admit it. With his important contributions to weights, the pendulum, navigation, geodesy, scientific instruments, fluid flow – both theoretically and as applied to ships, serving on the commission to establish the metric system, his work earning his reputation as one of the founders of modern French mathematical physics, and on and on, it is easy to conjure an image of an introverted, absent-minded, sedentary academic balancing his time between a quiet study surrounded by books and a lab where he shuffled around attired in a stained lab coat. Contrast that image with Borda's active role in the French navy where he attained the rank of *capitaine de vaisseau* on March 13, 1779. Remember, the period of the 1770s and 1780s was not a time where the occasional summer vacation warrior could enlist in a national guard; these were years of active naval conflict between England and France. In addition to his normal military duties, Borda took part in scientific voyages and he even participated in the American War for Independence! Indeed, for his actions in the American war, he was in the short lived "Order of Cincinnatus."[7] Then, in 1782, Borda was captured by the English while in charge of a flotilla of six ships in the Antilles. Although the subsequent English imprisonment broke his health, he remained intellectually active until his death on February 19, 1799, as evidenced by his presentation on voting theory in 1784. So, in addition to his valued contributions to mathematics and physics as well as to voting theory, Borda is treated as an important figure in the history of the French navy. With his many contributions, he can give anyone an inferiority complex.

Back to voting theory. Borda's biographer Jean Mascart starts his brief description of this work by describing Borda's 1784 paper which was based on his much earlier 1770 presentation and that, to escalate the confusion, is published in an Academie volume dated 1781 (but, of course, published years later). Mascart says:

"It is truly remarkable to see a noble, whose family was dispersed by the Revolution, preoccupy himself since 1770 with the correct means to assure the loyalty and sincerity of a vote. 'It is a generally held opinion,'[Borda] says in starting and against which I don't know if anyone has ever made an objection, 'that in an election, the plurality of votes always indicates the desires of the electors; in other words, that the candidate who has obtained the plurality is necessarily the one that the electors prefer to his opponents. But, I will show that this opinion, which is true if the election is held between only two subjects, can infer an error in all other cases.'"

To support his insightful claim, Borda [Bo, D] develops an example similar to the beverage example from the fable. The thrust of his argument is to use the example to show that the candidate who beats all other candidates in pairwise contests can be plurality bottom-ranked, while the candidate who loses all pairwise contests can be plurality top-ranked. Clearly, such a procedure is flawed. Then Borda demonstrates the superiority of his 3, 2, 1 point system by showing

---

[7]In personal correspondence, A. Urken states his suspicion that Borda was an honorary, rather than a full member.

that, at least for this example, the "correct" candidate is elected. His argument must have been persuasive because the Borda Count was adopted by the French Academy until the 1800s when Napoleon Bonaparte exerted his influence to have it overturned.

When an opportunity for a debate exists, it usually generates one – particularly in academic circles. Borda's method begs for controversy to answer the questions: "Why these particular choices of weights?" "Why not use, say, 4, 1, 0, or 5, 4, 1?" Justifications for the BC weights were offered by Borda and by Laplace, but their philosophical responses are not satisfying; the questions remain. Another fault of Borda's method, as shown in the fable, is that the BC can be manipulated. The reported reaction from Borda asserting that his method is intended only for honest people is lame (Chap. 2 of [Bl]); anyway, we now know that all methods can be manipulated. Thus, the debate continues. These questions, which have remained open for the last couple of centuries, are answered here.

1.3.4 Beyond Borda

The next person to become involved was an impressive intellectual of that time and a fellow Academie member and Borda adversary, M. Condorcet. (With Condorcet's better press, there is no need to describe his fascinating contributions. See, for instance, [B, MH].) Condorcet argues that a candidate who wins all pairwise elections should be selected; an argument that remains central to this field. Observe that Condorcet's concept is an immediate extension of the election phenomenon developed, used, and illustrated in Borda's earlier lecture and publication. Presumably following the occasionally accepted scientific protocol whereby credit and the naming of a process is awarded to a popularizer rather than the discoverer, this solution concept is called a "Condorcet winner." (See Sect. 3.1.) A new concept introduces a new issue: which is the more natural, representative solution concept – the Condorcet or the Borda winner? The debate continues; so how can I resist entering? The answer is unexpected.

An important insightful Condorcet contribution, which he used to prove that a Condorcet winner need not always exist, is the disturbing example from the departmental meeting. This division of the voters, which proves that sincere pairwise elections can create cycles, has been rediscovered many times since by important contributors to this area. (See [Bl].) In fact, this election paradox plays an important role motivating Arrow's theorem (Sect. 4.4) where Arrow proves the impossibility of ever constructing a method for three or more alternatives that satisfies certain desirable, yet seemingly innocuous properties. The geometric implications of this paradox are described in several sections; an informational explanation is given in Sect. 4.4.

Once history moves beyond those creative, influential days of Borda and Condorcet, there exist several excellent descriptions about the development of this subject chronicling who did what and why. From these accounts, we learn about Lewis Carroll's contributions, presumably developed between reporting on Alice's exciting and delightful adventures, the debates of proportional voting (see

Sect. 5.4), etc. Moreover, surveys of modern work (e.g. [F1, NiR, Nu, Mo1, Pl, Se2]) are easily found. Indeed, this intellectually attractive subject which now is a couple hundred years old has attracted the imagination of large numbers of researchers, so it has spawned an incredibly large literature! This underscores the value of J. Kelly's compilation [K3] of publications.

So far, perhaps reflecting a natural academic arrogance, I have emphasized theoretical developments. What about the practicing politicians? Do the clever, successful politicians know about the various voting paradoxes? Of course they do, and probably long before us academics! In fact, a case can be made demonstrating how this knowledge has served them well. (However, Riker [R1-2] is among the few scholars who has studied how "paradoxes" have been converted to political advantage.) Indeed, I suspect that some of the voting paradoxes discovered by academics are restatements of properties already being used to the advantage of clever politicians.

Where can illustrating examples be found? Anywhere where smart politicians are in conflict with one another, or decisions have to be made. My favorite political dig, and the source of several of my examples, is the city of Chicago where politics has been elevated to a popular spectator sport. Indeed, it is probably the only major metropolitan area where opposing alderman are sufficiently known to become the featured stars of a popular commercial depicting a "Council Wars" debate over the merits of an advertised food product. Many of these politicians form colorful character studies. For example, while disagreeing with much of his politics, one of my favorites is Edward Vydolyak, whose alleged attempts to manipulate the system through clever "reform movements," political action, coalition development, and even changing and creating political parties earned him the title of "Fast Eddie." Academics have much to learn about voting procedures from the "Fast Eddies" of the world.

1.4 What Kind of Geometry?

The beverage example exhibits voters' preferences where milk, the winning alternative, loses when compared with each of the other choices. If this were the only division of voters' preferences causing such a troublesome outcome, the example could be dismissed as a curious anomaly. The discomforting fact is that such election behavior is not exceptional.

If the beverage paradox is not unusual, it should be easy to construct many different illustrating examples. Try it; you won't like it. Try, for instance, to create a different example of voters' preferences where the plurality election ranking is $c_1 \succ c_2 \succ c_3$ even though the pairwise election results are $c_2 \succ c_1$, $c_3 \succ c_1$, $c_3 \succ c_1$. Or, try to create an example involving n_1 voters with the ranking $c_1 \succ c_2 \succ c_3$, n_2 voters with the ranking $c_3 \succ c_1 \succ c_2$, n_3 voters with the ranking $c_3 \succ c_2 \succ c_1$, and n_4 voters with the ranking $c_2 \succ c_1 \succ c_3$. Finally, try to construct such an example using just the three rankings $c_1 \succ c_2 \succ c_3$, $c_2 \succ c_3 \succ c_1$, $c_3 \succ c_1 \succ c_2$.

This challenge makes it clear that analyzing voting procedures by creating concrete examples can be difficult. The complexity is due to the combinatorics of the many available options. To further illustrate, often near election day the radio and television airways are clogged with advice to *"Have your say! Vote!"* The reason is clear; by not voting, a voter risks an election outcome he doesn't want. But, is this always true? Are there situations where by not voting a voter ensures an election outcome that he prefers to what would have occurred had he voted? Is it possible to argue to a particular voter, *"Don't vote! Only by staying home can you win!"* Procedures admitting such situations exist. (See Sect. 5.2.) But, to verify the existence of such perverse, counter-intuitive behavior is not obvious. If you don't believe me, try to find one. Moreover, "paradoxes" are counter-intuitive, so what does one look for to find new ones? This underscores the major problem – where does one start?

The same is true for manipulative strategies. We know from the startling Gibbard-Satterthwaite Theorem that, with three or more alternatives, all nondictatorial procedures admit situations where a voter can force a personally better outcome by voting strategically. Why is this true? How can these manipulative situations be identified? We saw from the fable how to do this with the BC, but how is this done with the plurality vote? Does the agenda example from the departmental meeting allow such opportunities? If so, for whom? How does one start the analysis?

What we need is a systematic way to explore, discover, and prove the existence of new voting properties. We want an analytic method where the basic ideas become sufficiently transparent so that us mere mortals can hope to discover theoretical advances. In order to create such techniques, we need to avoid the difficult, frustrating combinatorics that traditionally accompany the development of voting theory. This is done here where much of this heavy computational work is palmed off onto the related geometry.

Somewhat surprisingly, for three-candidate problems the mathematical entry requirements to achieve these goals are realistic. (The mathematics involves reasonably standard mathematics known to most readers but in different and new contexts.) To assist intuition, much of the discussion is accompanied by familiar two and three-dimensional geometric figures. What follows is a brief outline of some of the needed mathematical tools. The reader familiar with the connection between convexity and linear mappings (or those willing to return later) should move on to Sect. 2.1.

1.4.1 Convexity and Linear Mappings

An important geometric concept used repeatedly throughout this book is *convexity*.

Convexity. A set is convex if for any two points in the set, the straight line connecting these points also is in the set.

As examples, the first two sets in Fig. 1.4.1 are convex. Intuitively, convexity is ensured because all "bulges" are outwards. Consequently, for any two points chosen in a set, the connecting straight path also is in the set.

The third set in Fig. 1.4.1 fails convexity because the line connecting the two points is partially outside of the shaded region. So, refining the above intuition, a convex set can't have an inward dent. With a dent, as in the third figure, it is easy to find two points near the indentation where part of the connecting line falls outside of the set.

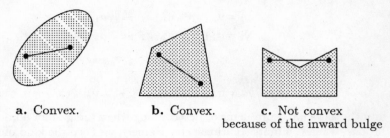

a. Convex.   **b.** Convex.   **c.** Not convex
                                                because of the inward bulge

Fig. 1.4.1. Convex and non-convex sets

A common technical problem for what follows is to divide a convex set into convex subsets. By experimenting with the regions of Fig. 1.4.1, it becomes clear that the boundary between two subsets must be a straight line. If it isn't, then a bulge benefiting one subset causes an indentation for the other.

Linear Mappings. Because it is frequently used in this book, I recall how to algebraically represent the line segment connecting two given points, say $x_1 = (3,2)$ and $x_2 = (6,4)$. Let t, $0 \leq t \leq 1$, represent the position on the connecting line segment that is the proportion t of the distance from x_2 to x_1, or $1-t$ of the distance from x_1 to x_2. Combining these facts, the representation for the line is

$$t x_1 + (1-t) x_2 = t(3,2) + (1-t)(6,4) = (6-3t, 4-2t), \quad t \in [0,1] \quad (1.4.1)$$

So, with the interpretation of t, when $t = 0$ we should be at x_2, which is what Eq. 1.4.1 yields. Similarly, when $t = 1$, we are at x_1. Other t values extend the line beyond these defining points.

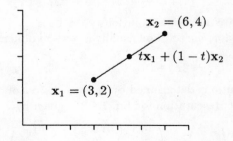

Fig. 1.4.2. The representation of the connecting line

More general than a straight line is a linear mapping – it generalizes the single variable equation $y = ax$ where a is a given constant, x is the input, or independent variable, and y is the output, or dependent variable. In voting, the inputs often correspond to how many voters have each of the possible rankings of the candidates, and the outputs represent the election tallies. The algebra, then, is the set of linear equations defined by specified constants $a_{i,j}$

$$y_1 = a_{1,1}x_1 + a_{1,2}x_2 + \ldots a_{1,n}x_n$$
$$y_2 = a_{2,1}x_1 + a_{2,2}x_2 + \ldots a_{2,n}x_n$$
$$\ldots$$
$$\ldots$$
$$y_m = a_{m,1}x_1 + a_{m,2}x_2 + \ldots a_{m,n}x_n \tag{1.4.2}$$

and the associated problems of determining when the system admits unique solutions, when it admits solutions, etc. Namely, we need the kind of mathematics associated with the familiar phrase "m equations in n unknowns."

As an illustration, by specifying the y_j values, the problem is to solve the system of m equations in n unknowns. If $m > n$, then, in general, there are no solutions. The system of three equations and two unknowns

$$2 = 2x_1 + 3x_2$$
$$6 = 2x_1 + 3x_2$$
$$4 = 3x_1 - x_2$$

demonstrates the difficulty; it is impossible to simultaneously satisfy the first and second equations. A solution is possible only should the y values lie in the n-dimensional image set defined by the equations.

With $m = n$ equations and unknowns, we should expect an unique solution except for the rare choice of $a_{i,j}$ coefficients where no solution exists. To illustrate a setting where the unique solution assertion does not hold, no solution exists for

$$4 = x_1 + x_2, \quad 5 = x_1 + x_2,$$

while the system

$$4 = x_1 + x_2, \quad 8 = 2x_1 + 2x_2$$

admits the infinite number of solutions $x_1 = 4 - x_2$.

Finally, if $m < n$, the solution usually is a $n - m$ dimensional set. For instance, the system

$$3 = 2x_1 + 3x_2 + 4x_3, \quad 2 = 3x_1 - x_2 + x_3$$

has a line of solutions determined by various choices of x_3.

The matrix representation for Eq. 1.4.2 is given by

$$\begin{pmatrix} y_1 \\ y_2 \\ \ldots \\ y_m \end{pmatrix} = \begin{pmatrix} a_{1,1} & a_{1,2} & \ldots & a_{1,n} \\ a_{2,1} & a_{2,2} & \ldots & a_{2,n} \\ & \ldots & \ldots & \\ a_{m,1} & a_{m,2} & \ldots & a_{m,n} \end{pmatrix} \begin{pmatrix} x_1 \\ x_2 \\ \ldots \\ x_n \end{pmatrix} \tag{1.4.3}$$

where the solution properties are expressed in terms of the properties of the matrix $((a_{i,j}))$.

Properties of Linear Mappings. An important (and the defining) property of a linear function f is

$$f(a\mathbf{x}_1 + b\mathbf{x}_2) = af(\mathbf{x}_1) + bf(\mathbf{x}_2) \qquad (1.4.4)$$

where a and b are scalars. This powerful property asserts that a linear combination of inputs is transferred into the same linear combination of outputs. Consequently, a linear function maps a straight line to a straight line because

$$f(t\mathbf{x}_1 + (1-t)\mathbf{x}_2) = tf(\mathbf{x}_1) + (1-t)f(\mathbf{x}_2) \qquad (1.4.5)$$

There is an immediate, useful consequence of this delightful separation property of Eq. 1.4.5 that is enjoyed by linear mappings.

Convexity Property. *If $\mathcal{A}$ is a convex set in the domain and if f is a linear function, then the image of $\mathcal{A}$ is a convex set in the image space. Conversely, if f is a linear mapping with a convex domain and if $\mathcal{D}$ is a convex set in the image set, then $f^{-1}(\mathcal{D})$ is a convex set.*

Outline of the proof. The assertion holds because the $\mathcal{A}$ convexity ensures that the line segment connecting any two $\mathcal{A}$ points must be in $\mathcal{A}$. According to Eq. 1.4.5, the connecting straight line must accompany the image of the two points in $f(\mathcal{A})$. But, every point in the image set $f(\mathcal{A})$ has a preimage, so the conclusion follows.

In the other direction, if $\mathbf{q}_1, \mathbf{q}_2 \in \mathcal{D}$, then by the convexity of this set, the line segment defined by these points also is in $\mathcal{D}$. Now, suppose $\mathbf{p}_i$ are such that $f(\mathbf{p}_i) = \mathbf{q}_i$, $i = 1, 2$. As the domain is convex, the line segment defined by these two points is in the domain. By linearity, this line segment is mapping to the line segment defined by $\mathbf{q}_1, \mathbf{q}_2$. Consequently, the line segment defined by $\mathbf{p}_1, \mathbf{p}_2$ is in $f^{-1}(\mathcal{D})$. $\square$

For reasons made apparent in subsequent chapters, convex sets play an important role in the analysis of election procedures. The natural relationship – connecting the number of voters that have each ranking of the candidates with the election tallies – is a linear function. (The $a_{i,j}$ coefficients reflect the choice of the voting system and the preferences of the voters; the x values represent the number of voters.) As linear functions map convex sets to convex sets, for many procedures the convexity of sets of preferences ensures the convexity of sets of election outcomes.

1.4.2 Convex Hulls

Many convex sets are defined by specified vertices $\{\mathbf{v}_i\}_{i=1}^n$.

Convex Hull. *The convex hull of the vertices* $\{\mathbf{v}_i\}_{i=1}^{n}$ *is the smallest convex set containing all vertices. A way to represent the convex hull is*

$$\mathcal{CH}(\{\mathbf{v}_i\}) = \{\sum_{i=1}^{n} \lambda_i \mathbf{v}_i \,|\, \lambda_i \geq 0, \sum_{i=1}^{n} \lambda_i = 1\} \qquad (1.4.6)$$

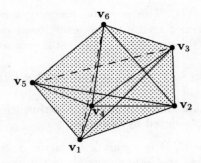

Fig. 1.4.3. The convex hull of the vertices $\{\mathbf{v}_i\}_{i=1}^{6}$

Equation 1.4.6 generalizes the straight line representation of Eq. 1.4.1. The t values from Eq. 1.4.1 provide all possible linear combinations between the two defining points. More vertices offer more possible locations given by the wider choice of λ values. Because the definition in Eq. 1.4.7 includes all possible choices of λ values, it includes choices where only two of the λ_i values are not zero, say λ_1 and λ_2. Here, $\lambda_1 = 1 - \lambda_2$, so Eq. 1.4.7 becomes $\lambda_2 \mathbf{v}_2 + (1 - \lambda_2)\mathbf{v}_1$; this is the equation of a straight line connecting the two vertices $\mathbf{v}_1$, $\mathbf{v}_2$. This description leads to the geometric construction of the convex hull. Just connect all of the vertices with straight lines, and then shade in the resulting figure. A two-dimensional example is given in Fig. 1.4.3.

The Mapping of Convex Hulls. By combining the separation property for linear mappings along with the geometric construction of a convex hull defined by the vertices $\{\mathbf{v}_i\}_{i=1}^{n}$ we have a simple way to construct the image of a convex hull. First find the images $\{f(\mathbf{v}_i)\}_{i=1}^{n}$ and then find the convex hull defined by these points. For example, the convex hull for the four points $(0,0), (1,0), (0,1), (1,1)$ is the square on the left-hand side of Fig. 1.4.4. Suppose the linear mapping is given in matrix form by

$$\begin{pmatrix} y_1 \\ y_2 \end{pmatrix} = f(\begin{pmatrix} x_1 \\ x_2 \end{pmatrix}) = \begin{pmatrix} 2 & 1 \\ 1 & 3 \end{pmatrix} \begin{pmatrix} x_1 \\ x_2 \end{pmatrix},$$

which represents the equations

$$y_1 = 2x_1 + x_2, \quad y_2 = x_1 + 3x_2.$$

To find the image set, just find the image of each vertex, or

$$(0,0) \to f(0,0) = (0,0), \quad (1,0) \to f(1,0) = (2,1)$$
$$(0,1) \to f(0,1) = (1,3), \quad (1,1) \to f(1,1) = (3,4).$$

The image set is the convex hull of these image points, as illustrated in Fig. 1.4.4.

This illustrates a common geometric theme used in this book. When dealing with a convex set of profiles defined by certain vertices, the election outcomes of the vertex profiles are determined. In this manner, the convex hull of all possible election outcomes can be constructed.

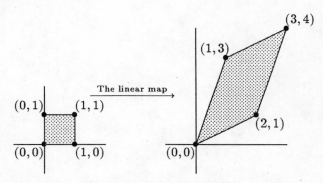

Fig. 1.4.4. Transferring a convex hull

1.4.3 Exercises

1. Find the equation of the straight line connecting the two points $(1,-1,2)$ and $(2,1,3)$. Suppose the first point is mapped to $(3,4)$ and the second to $(2,-1)$ by a linear mapping, find the image of the line.

2. Find the *convex hull* defined by the points $(0,0)$, $(2,4)$, $(0,6)$, $(1,1)$, $(8,0)$.

3. Demonstrate with examples that if a convex set is divided into convex subsets, then bulges are not permitted.

CHAPTER II

GEOMETRY FOR POSITIONAL
AND PAIRWISE VOTING

It is trivial to tally a plurality election; just count how many voters have each candidate top-ranked. Surprisingly, when this elementary description is used to analyze the procedure, it quickly introduces mathematical complications that severely limit what can be learned.

How can this be? In part, the difficulty is due to the enormous number of ways voters' preferences can be arranged. With the beverage example, for example, a voter can rank the three choices in six ways. So, two voters generate $6^2 = 36$ possible arrangements. Already with 15 voters, as in the example, the number of possible assignments grows into the hundreds of billions – $6^{15} = 470,184,984,576$. Try to count to 6^{15}, but expect it to take about 14,899 years. Indeed, a printed listing just for these 15 voters would require a library to hold the more than $340,000$ books of 500 pages each.[1] And, an enterprising reader who maintains interest in this series to the last page of the last book will find that much more is required. After all, to develop a theory, we need to consider all possible arrangements of voters' choices for any number of voters.

Thus, even for three candidates, the overwhelming numbers of possible voter arrangements prohibit anyone from developing an accurate intuition of what can happen based just on experience or by constructing examples. Bluntly, the complexity associated with three or more candidates defies a simple analysis of voting; new approaches must be developed.

Part of this complexity involves the "gaps" separating integers. Without gaps, calculus techniques apply; with the spaces the more difficult techniques of combinatorics and discrete mathematics are required. So, to minimize complexity we should use a model that fills the holes. But, which one? The problem is that there are too many choices. As an analogy, as anyone rushing to clean a room before a dinner party learns, the empty spaces in a hall closet can be filled in highly imaginative, unexpected ways. Many of these clever space-filling

---

[1] This 6^{15} value is correct but misleading; it is the number of rankings preserving the identity of a voter. But, if only Carl and Martha interchange preferences, no change occurs in the election outcome. Thus *anonymity*, where the identities of the voters are irrelevant, reduces the number of rankings. When it only matters how many voters have each ranking, 15 voters generate $14,484$ different profiles. But, where did this value come from? This computation, in itself, underscores the complexities associated with a discrete analysis. Moreover, when one considers what happens with 1, 2, ..., 15, 16, ... voters, millions upon millions of different voter arrangements emerge.

techniques are counter-productive – as when a collapsing shelf dumps dirty underwear, several partially completed manuscripts, and an unstrung tennis racket upon a stunned guest. Similarly, mathematical structures can fill the spaces between the integers in highly imaginative ways. Some are useful, but others share striking similarities with the closet shelf; they can dump irrelevant, unwanted structures on us. Thus, we need to filter out those mathematical structures that are, at best, redundant.

The representation developed here is a natural, geometric one where the number of candidates is identified with the geometric dimension of a space. In this manner the mysteries of election paradoxes and the properties of election procedures are explained with simple geometric constructions and elementary mathematical arguments. In fact, in this manner we discover that the confusing differences between two and three candidate elections are reflected by the geometric differences exhibited by different dimensional spaces.

In this short chapter, the appropriate notation and geometry for voting procedures are introduced. Related results about other procedures are in the exercises. Starting with Chap. 3, the power of this geometric approach is flexed to show how election outcomes over different subsets of candidates have unexpected outcomes.

2.1 Ranking Regions

With two candidates, a voter votes for his top choice. This "count the number of hands" approach seems to be a reasonable way to rank any number of candidates. Is it?

Definition 2.1.1. A *plurality election* is where each voter casts one point for his top-ranked candidate; each candidate's ranking is determined by the number of points assigned to her. If candidate c_i receives more votes than c_j, then the ranking is denoted as $c_i \succ c_j$. If both candidates, c_i, c_j, receive the same number of votes, their tied ranking is $c_i \sim c_j$. □

The vote totals for the candidates $\{c_1, c_2, c_3\}$ define the array (n_1, n_2, n_3) where n_j is the number of points assigned to candidate c_j, $j = 1, 2, 3$. By exploiting our familiarity with the three-dimensional world, treat (n_1, n_2, n_3) as a point in the three-dimensional space $R^3 = \{(x_1, x_2, x_3) \,|\, -\infty < x_j < \infty, j = 1, 2, 3\}$. Namely, identify values on the x_j axis of R^3 with the election tally for candidate c_j; $j = 1, 2, 3$. As each component of (n_1, n_2, n_3) is non-negative, it is a point in the *non-negative orthant* of R^3,

$$R_+^3 = \{(x_1, x_2, x_3) \in R^3 \,|\, x_j \geq 0\}$$

In the obvious manner, (n_1, n_2, n_3) determines the rankings of the candidates. For instance, $(45, 75, 80)$ indicates that c_1 receives 45 votes, c_2 receives 75 votes, and c_3 receives 80 votes leading to the election ranking $c_3 \succ c_2 \succ c_1$. Because an ordinal ranking of the candidates depends only on the relative sizes of the coordinates of a vector, any positive multiple of the tally preserves the election ranking.

So, although a multiple of 1000 separates $(3, 5, 2)$ from $(3000, 5000, 2000)$, both totals define the same election ranking $c_2 \succ c_1 \succ c_3$. There is nothing special about three candidates; with five candidates the election tally is given by $(n_1, n_2, n_3, n_4, n_5)$ which is a point in the five dimensional space R^5. So what if some of us have yet to experience the thinner atmosphere of higher dimensional spaces; if we can decipher the geometry, we can exploit it.

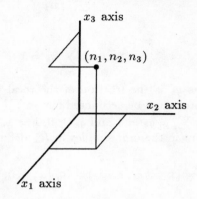

Fig. 2.1.1. The election tally

2.1.1 Normalized Election Tally

A useful technique is, "When in doubt, exploit a mathematical invariance." Our first invariance is that the election ranking for (n_1, n_2, n_3) agrees with the ranking for the *normalized election vector*

$$\mathbf{q} = \left(\frac{n_1}{\sum_{j=1}^{3} n_j}, \frac{n_2}{\sum_{j=1}^{3} n_j}, \frac{n_3}{\sum_{j=1}^{3} n_j} \right) \tag{2.1.1}$$

Here, q_j specifies the portion of the total tally received by the jth candidate, $j = 1, 2, 3$. Indeed, the components of the normalized election vector,

> **HATFIELD WINS $\frac{2}{3}$ OF THE VOTE!!**
> McCoy refuses to concede;
> clan will fight on!

rather than the actual tallies, dominate the morning headlines after election night.

Example 2.1.1. The ranking for the normalized election vector $(\frac{1}{6}, \frac{1}{2}, \frac{1}{3})$ is $c_2 \succ c_3 \succ c_1$. A common denominator for these fractions is any multiple of 6, so the normalized vector represent an election involving six or 12,000,000 voters. In the former case, the integer tally is $(1, 3, 2)$, and in the latter case it is

$(2,000,000,\ 6,000,000,\ 4,000,000)$. Similarly, the election ranking assigned to the six-candidate normalized tally $(\frac{1}{12}, \frac{3}{12}, \frac{4}{12}, \frac{2}{12}, \frac{3}{24}, \frac{1}{24}$ is $c_3 \succ c_2 \succ c_4 \succ c_5 \succ c_1 \succ c_6$. $\square$

The definition of the normalized election vector $\mathbf{q} = (q_1, q_2, q_3)$, where

$$q_k = \frac{n_k}{\sum_{j=1}^{3} n_j} \tag{2.1.2}$$

requires that

$$q_k \geq 0 \text{ and } \sum_{k=1}^{3} q_k = 1$$

This makes sense; as q_k is the fraction of the total vote received by c_k, it is non-negative. All votes must be accounted for, so $\sum_{k=1}^{3} q_k = 1$.

These properties, $\sum_{k=1}^{3} q_k = 1$ and $q_k \geq 0$, $k = 1, 2, 3$, allow the tally to be identified with a point in the *unit simplex* in R_+^3 defined by

$$Si(3) = \{\mathbf{x} = (x_1, x_2, x_3) \in R_+^3 \mid x_j \geq 0, \sum_{j=1}^{3} x_j = 1\} \tag{2.1.3}$$

and illustrated in Fig. 2.1.2. This simplex, the *representation triangle*, is the equilateral triangle passing through the three unanimity outcomes $\mathbf{e}_1 = (1, 0, 0)$, $\mathbf{e}_2 = (0, 1, 0)$, $\mathbf{e}_3 = (0, 0, 1)$. Each point in the representation triangle, $Si(3)$, uniquely defines a particular ranking of the candidates.

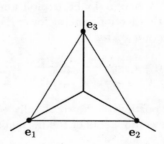

Fig. 2.1.2. The simplex of normalized election outcomes

Only the representation triangle is needed, so suppress the coordinate axes in what follows; this creates Fig. 2.1.3.

Example 2.1.2. In Fig. 2.1.3, each of the three identified points represents a normalized election vector.

Point	Coordinate	Ranking
1	$(\frac{7}{20}, \frac{4}{20}, \frac{9}{20}) \in Si(3)$	$c_3 \succ c_1 \succ c_2$
2	$(\frac{2}{5}, \frac{2}{5}, \frac{1}{5}) \in Si(3)$	$c_1 \sim c_2 \succ c_3$
3	$(0, 1, 0) \in Si(3)$	$c_2 \succ c_1 \sim c_3$

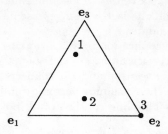

Fig. 2.1.3. Normalized election outcomes

Point 3 at $\mathbf{e}_2 = (0, 1, 0)$ requires c_2 to receive an unanimous vote. □

As in love, where "closer is much better," the ranking assigned to $\mathbf{q} \in Si(3)$ (the representation triangle) is determined by how close $\mathbf{q}$ is to each vertex; the closer $\mathbf{q}$ is to vertex $\mathbf{e}_k$, the better c_k fares in the election. This "closer is better" relationship is easy to understand. If c_k receives a large vote relative to the other candidates, then q_k has a large value, so $\mathbf{q} = (q_1, q_2, q_3)$ is closer to the vertex $\mathbf{e}_k$. (Remember, $\mathbf{e}_k$ represents an unanimous vote for c_k.) Conversely, the closer $\mathbf{q} = (q_1, q_2, q_3)$ is to $\mathbf{e}_k$, the larger the vote proportion, q_k, received by c_k.

With four or more candidates it is difficult – alright, impossible – to draw pictures. Here the normalized tally for n candidates is a point in the simplex

$$Si(n) = \{\mathbf{x} = (x_1, x_2, \ldots, x_n) \in R^n \mid \sum_{j=1}^{n} x_j = 1, \, x_j \geq 0\}$$

Just as $Si(3)$ is an equilateral three-gon (i.e., an equilateral triangle), $Si(n)$ is an equilateral n-gon which lives in a $(n-1)$-dimensional space. For instance, $Si(4)$ is an equilateral tetrahedron. (This is where the four vertices are chosen so that all edges have the same length and the faces are equilateral triangles.) Even though these representation simplices reside in higher dimensional spaces, we use their geometric properties to analyze elections.

2.1.2 Ranking Regions

The "closer is better" relationship divides $Si(3)$ into "*ranking regions*" where each geometric region is identified with a unique election ranking. To illustrate this simple idea with the election ranking $c_3 \sim c_1 \succ c_2$, notice that it occurs only if the election tally is $q_3 = q_1 > q_2$. As such, the $c_3 \sim c_1 \succ c_2$ ranking region is the set of all such election tallies; it is

$$\mathcal{R}(c_3 \sim c_1 \succ c_2) = \{\mathbf{q} \in Si(3) | q_3 = q_1 > q_2\}$$

All possible inequalities involving q_1, q_2, q_3 partition the representation triangle $Si(3)$ into 13 ranking regions. Six regions correspond to election rankings without

ties between candidates, six represent election rankings with a tie vote between
a pair of candidates, and the last region represents the election ranking with a
tie among all three candidates.

To see the geometric connection between ranking regions and the rankings of
pairs of candidates, start with a tie $c_j \sim c_k$ region. For instance, the line $q_1 = q_2$,
indicating a tie vote between c_1 and c_2, connects the mid-point between the
vertices $\mathbf{e}_1$ and $\mathbf{e}_2$ with the remaining vertex $\mathbf{e}_3$ and it is the "c_1, c_2 *indifference
line*." (See Fig. 2.1.4.) This line consists of all points equal distance from the
two vertices.

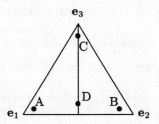

Fig. 2.1.4. The $c_1 - c_2$ indifference line

Just as a tie vote is the division between one or the other candidate winning,
the $c_j \sim c_k$ line separates the $c_j \succ c_k$ region from the $c_k \succ c_j$ region. In particular, a point to the left of the $c_1 \sim c_2$ line, such as point A in Fig. 2.1.4, is closer
to $\mathbf{e}_1$ than to $\mathbf{e}_2$, so it is in the binary ranking region $c_1 \succ c_2$. Correspondingly,
a point to the right of this line, such as B in the figure, represents $c_2 \succ c_1$.
However, further refinements of the rankings is not delineated by the $c_1 \sim c_2$
line. For instance, while C clearly is close enough to the vertex $\mathbf{e}_3$ to define the
relationship $q_3 > q_1 = q_2$ it is not obvious from Fig. 2.1.4 what other points are
in the same ranking region $c_3 \succ c_1 \sim c_2$.

To find all ranking regions, draw all three $c_i \sim c_j$ indifferent lines to obtain Fig.
2.1.5. (From now on, $\mathbf{e}_j$ is replaced with the candidate's name, c_j, $j = 1, 2, 3$.) So,
the intersections of the large "binary relations" triangles create the six smaller
triangular ranking regions defining strict rankings. This process of intersecting
the larger binary triangles (of the type in Fig. 2.1.4) to obtain the smaller triangle
ranking regions of Fig. 2.1.5 is a geometric representation of how the binary
rankings of pairs define a transitive[2] ranking of the candidates.

The six small triangles of Fig. 2.1.5 represent the strict rankings with no tie
vote or indifference among candidates. As the remaining election rankings involve
a tie vote, the associated ranking regions are on indifference lines. One ranking
region, for instance, is where all three indifference lines intersect at $(\frac{1}{3}, \frac{1}{3}, \frac{1}{3})$. This
barycentric point defines the ranking region of *complete indifference*, $\mathcal{I} = c_1 \sim
c_2 \sim c_3$, and it divides each indifference line into two segments – one segment

---

[2] This means that if $c_i \succ c_j$ and $c_j \succ c_k$, then $c_i \succ c_k$. So, with "transitivity" the binary
rankings of certain pairs of candidates imposes a particular ranking on other pairs of candidates.
These ideas are described in Sect. 3.1.

ends in a vertex and the other ends at the midpoint of a leg of the equilateral triangle. The first segment is the ranking region where the tied pair is bottom-ranked (and the vertex identifies the top-ranked candidate), while the second segment has the tied pair top-ranked. In this manner, the six line segments and $\mathcal{I}$ account for the seven rankings with a tie vote among two or more candidates.

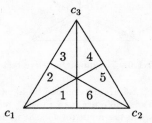

Fig. 2.1.5. The representation triangle

Example 2.1.3. In Fig. 2.1.5, the line segment separating the regions labeled 3 and 4 is the ranking region $c_3 \succ c_1 \sim c_2$. The line segment separating the regions 2 and 3 is the ranking region $c_1 \sim c_3 \succ c_2$. $\square$

The above provides a geometric representation for the "transitive rankings." Geometric representations for other kinds of binary rankings are developed in the exercises.

2.1.3 Exercises

1. Compute the normalized tally for the election outcome $(100, 200, 400, 300)$ and find the election ranking. For the normalized tally $(\frac{1}{3}, \frac{2}{9}, \frac{4}{9})$ find the election ranking and an integer election tally involving over a thousand voters.

2. Geometrically, show that the intersection of the binary ranking regions $c_1 \succ c_2$ and $c_3 \succ c_2$ contains three ranking regions. Show that the intersection of the binary regions $c_1 \succ c_2$ and $c_2 \succ c_3$ defines a unique ranking region. The flexibility admitted by one situation, but prohibited by the other, plays an important role in proving Arrow's Theorem in Sect. 3.4.

3. The geometry for other binary rankings uses objects other than the simplex $Si(3)$. For instance, with the candidates c_1, c_2 and the interval $[-1, 1]$, let positive values represent $c_1 \succ c_2$ while negative values represent $c_2 \succ c_1$. Three candidates define three pairs of candidates, so we need three intervals to represent the different binary rankings. This is given by the cube defined by placing an $[-1, 1]$ interval on each of the three coordinate axes of R^3 where points on the x, y, and z axis correspond, respectively, to a binary ranking for $\{c_1, c_2\}$, $\{c_2, c_3\}$, $\{c_3, c_1\}$. (So, a positive value means that the first listed candidate for the pair is preferred.)

a. Show that the intersections of the binary relationships define 27 ranking regions in the cube. Which ones are *not* transitive?

b. A set of binary rankings is acyclic if $c_i \succ c_j$ and $c_j \succ c_k$ hold, then $c_k \not\succ c_i$. Find the cube regions that need to be excluded to ensure that the remaining binary relationships are acyclic.

c. Find a two dimensional plane that passes through the origin of the cube so that all of the ranking regions on this plane are transitive and all transitive ranking regions are included.

4. Show that if each q_j of $\mathbf{q} = (q_1, q_2, q_3) \in Si(3)$ is a fraction, then $\mathbf{q}$ corresponds to a normalized plurality election tally. How can you use the q_j values to find the numbers of voters

needed for a supporting example?

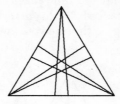

Fig. 2.1.6. The quasitransitive regions

5. The ranking regions of Fig. 2.1.5 are determined by identifying $c_1 \sim c_j$ with $q_i = q_j$. By changing the definition of binary indifference, new ranking regions may emerge. For instance, say that c_i is indifferent to c_j when the point totals are *"almost the same."* More specifically, let $\epsilon > 0$ be a specified constant, say $\epsilon = \frac{1}{16}$. Say that $c_i \sim_q c_j$ iff

$$\frac{1-\epsilon}{1+\epsilon} \leq \frac{x_i}{x_j} \leq \frac{1+\epsilon}{1-\epsilon};$$

and $c_i \succ_q c_j$ iff $\frac{x_i}{x_j} > \frac{1+\epsilon}{1-\epsilon}$.

a.   Prove that " $\sim_q$ " is symmetric; i.e., if $c_i \sim_q c_j$, then $c_j \sim_q c_i$.

b.   Prove that $\succ_q$ is transitive; i.e., if $c_i \succ_q c_j$ and $c_j \succ_q c_k$, then $c_i \succ_q c_k$. Show that $\succ_q$ is asymmetric; i.e., if $c_i \succ_q c_j$ then $c_j \not\succ_q c_i$..

c.   On $Si(3)$, graph the $c_1 \sim_q c_2$ indifference region. (You should get a triangle with vertex at $\mathbf{e}_3$ that straddles the $c_1 \sim c_2$ line from Fig. 2.1.5.) Next, by computing all $c_i \sim_q c_j$ regions, show that Fig. 2.1.6 geometrically represents how the binary relationships interact. Identify all nineteen regions. In particular, identify the six rankings that are not admitted by Fig. 2.1.5.

d.   Use Fig. 2.1.6 to prove that this binary relationship allows the rankings $c_1 \sim_q c_2, c_2 \sim_q c_3, c_1 \succ_q c_3$; i.e., "$\sim_q$" is not transitive.

e.   Identify the regions of Fig. 2.1.6 with corresponding regions of the cube from Example 2.1.3. Which cube regions are *not* in the quasitransitive triangle?

To use this *quasitransitive* relationship with the normalized tally of a plurality election, the election ranking is given by the ranking region that contains the normalized election tally.

6. A normalized election ranking (q_1, q_2, q_3), $q_1 > q_2 > q_3$, defines the ranking $c_1 \succ c_2 \succ c_3$ even should c_1 beat c_2 by a single vote. As an alternative, suppose that to be top-ranked, the candidate with the most votes must beat the candidate with the second highest tally by a specified fractional amount. This motivates the following threshold method.

The *"Distinct winner"* threshold procedure is determined by specified values $\gamma_2 \geq \frac{1}{2}$, $\gamma_3 \geq \frac{2}{3}$. For c_i to win:

1.   She must have the most votes.

2.   If c_j has the second highest vote, then $\frac{q_i}{q_i + q_j} \geq \gamma_2$.

For candidates c_i, c_j to be tied for top-ranked:

1.   There must be no single winner.

2.   Each of c_i, c_j must have more votes than the remaining candidate.

3.   The normalized vote tallies must satisfy $\frac{q_i + q_j}{\sum_{k=1}^{3} q_k} = q_i + q_j \geq \gamma_3$. Otherwise, the three candidates are in a three way tie.

a.   Show that the associated ranking regions are transitive and that they admit a representation of the form given in Fig. 2.1.7. By use of elementary trigonometry of the 30°–60°–90° triangle, describe what happens if $\gamma_3 = \frac{1-\gamma_2}{\sqrt{3}}$ and if $\gamma_3 \geq \frac{1-\gamma_2}{\sqrt{3}}$.

b. What happens to the representation for $\frac{1-\gamma_2}{\sqrt{3}} > \gamma_3 \geq \frac{1}{3}$? In particular, describe the regions where no election outcome is defined. Change the definition distinguishing between whether two or three candidates are top-ranked to handle this situation.

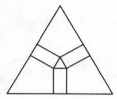

Fig. 2.1.7. The distinct winner threshold method

7. The *"Universal"* threshold method requires the winning candidate to receive a certain fraction of the total vote.   The threshold values are specified numbers $\delta_2 \geq \frac{1}{3}$, $\delta_3 \geq \frac{2}{3}$. For candidate c_j to win, she must have the largest normalized vote tally and $q_j \geq \delta_2$. If no winner exists, then the two candidates with the largest number of votes, c_i, c_j, are tied for top-rank iff $q_i + q_j \geq \delta_3$. Otherwise, all three candidates are tied.
a. Show that for one particular choice of δ's, the ranking regions are as illustrated in Fig. 2.1.8.

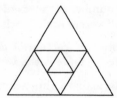

Fig. 2.1.8. The universal threshold method

b. This threshold method becomes what method if $\delta_2 = \frac{1}{3}$? What happens if $\delta_2 \geq \frac{1}{2}$?
c.   Find the relationship between δ_2 and δ_3 to ensure that an election outcome always is defined.

8. Recall: the rational points in the representational triangle are *dense*. This means that if $\mathbf{q}' \in Si(3)$ has components with irrational values, then arbitrarily close to $\mathbf{q}'$ are choices of $\mathbf{q} \in Si(3)$ where all the components are rational numbers. Equivalently, there exists a sequence of points in $Si(3)$ with rational components, $\{\mathbf{q}_n\}_{n=1}^{\infty}$, such that $\mathbf{q}_n \to \mathbf{q}'$ as $n \to \infty$.
a. The components of

$$\mathbf{q}' = (\frac{\sqrt{2}}{4}, \frac{\sqrt{2}}{4}, 1 - \frac{\sqrt{2}}{2}) \approx (0.3535538\ldots, 0.3535538\ldots, 0.2928932\ldots) \in Si(3)$$

have irrational values. Find a sequence of rational points in $Si(3)$ that approach $\mathbf{q}'$.
b. Argue that all points in $Si(3)$, whether the components have rational or irrational values, can be viewed as being the limit of a sequence of normalized election tallies.

9. For $n = 4$ candidates, the *representation simplex* is an equilateral tetrahedron. This region can be divided into $4! = 4 \cdot 3 \cdot 2 \cdot 1 = 24$ little tetrahedrons – each representing one of the possible ways the four candidates can be ranked (without ties). This is done in much the same way as the equilateral triangle is divided into $3! = 3 \cdot 2 \cdot 1 = 6$ small ranking regions. Namely, all of the

binary ranking planes are drawn. Do this. (Hint: in the c_1, c_2, c_3 face of the tetrahedron, the plane showing a tie vote between c_1 and c_2 must appear exactly as it does in the representation triangle.) From this crude drawing, determine how many regions allow only one tie vote, and this is between a pair. Where is the region representing $c_1 \sim c_2 \sim c_3 \sim c_4$?

2.2 Profiles and Election Mappings

To create a geometric representation for voters' preferences similar to that developed for election tallies, assume each voter has a *strict linear ordering* of the n-candidates; i.e., each voter compares each pair of candidates in a transitive manner without registering indifference between any two candidates. A voter's *type* is his ranking of the candidates; the $n! = n(n-1)\cdots(2)(1)$ ways to strictly rank n candidates define $n!$ voter types. For three candidates, denoting each of the $3! = 6$ types by the identifying numbers from Fig. 2.1.5, we have:

Type	Ranking	Type	Ranking
1	$c_1 \succ c_2 \succ c_3$	4	$c_3 \succ c_2 \succ c_1$
2	$c_1 \succ c_3 \succ c_2$	5	$c_2 \succ c_3 \succ c_1$
3	$c_3 \succ c_1 \succ c_2$	6	$c_2 \succ c_1 \succ c_3$

An *"integer profile"* lists the number of voters of each type. Alternatively, we could specify what fraction of all voters are of each type.

Definition 2.2.1. Let p_j denote the fraction of all voters that are of the jth type, $j = 1, \ldots, n!$. A (normalized) *profile* is the vector $\mathbf{p} = (p_1, \ldots, p_{n!})$. $\square$

Vector $(\frac{1}{6}, 0, \frac{1}{3}, 0, \frac{1}{2}, 0)$ is a normalized three-candidate profile where $\frac{1}{6}$ of all voters are of type-one, $\frac{1}{3}$ are of type-three, $\frac{1}{2}$ are of type-5, and there are no voters of the remaining three types. As the smallest common denominator is six, the total number of voters for an associated integer profile is a multiple of six.

As the definition requires $p_j \geq 0$ and $\sum_{j=1}^{n!} p_j = 1$, a profile is a (rational) point in the unit simplex

$$Si(n!) = \{\mathbf{y} = (y_1, \ldots, y_6) \in R^{n!} \,|\, y_j \geq 0, \sum_{j=1}^{n!} y_j = 1\} \qquad (2.2.1)$$

The host space $R_+^{n!}$ has dimension $n!$, so the restricting equation $\sum_{j=1}^{n!} x_j = 1$ reduces $Si(n!)$, *the space of normalized profiles*, to a $n! - 1$ dimensional geometric object.

We have a serious problem. Already with three candidates we need a $3! = 6$ dimensional space where the profile space is five-dimensional. With a few more candidates, say $n = 10$, we must deal with a $10! - 1 = 518,399$ dimensional space of profiles! Now, it is trivial to draw one-dimensional objects, a bit harder to draw a two-dimensional figure, and, with practice, artistically talented people can create a recognizable two-dimensional drawing of a three-dimensional figure.

But trying to draw a four or higher dimensional object explains the frustrations of citizens from Abbott's *"Flatland"* ([Ab]); how can we visualize objects from an unknown higher dimensional world? I cannot; there is no way I can provide a simple sketch for the five-dimensional simplex of profiles $Si(6)$ leave alone trying to image the fascinating directions and by-ways admitted by the half-million dimensions needed to appreciate a ten-voter setting. Nevertheless, the geometric properties of $Si(n!)$ are critical for an analysis of voting, so we need to find ways to exploit and understand them.

Actually, we know just about as much about a five-dimensional space ($Si(6)$) as about the $518,399$ dimensional space $Si(10!)$ (i.e., nothing), so we might as well study both at the same time. (Anyway, it is more impressive in casual conversation to express concerns about the geometry of a half-million dimensional space.) Some properties easily follow from our intuition of our familiar three-dimensional world. For instance, a point $\mathbf{q} \in Si(3)$ is on an edge of the representational triangle if and only if one of the $\mathbf{q} = (q_1, q_2, q_3)$ components is zero if and only if some candidate receives no votes. Similarly, a profile $\mathbf{p} = (p_1, \ldots, p_6) \in Si(6)$ is on a $Si(6)$ edge if and only if some p_j components are zero if and only if there are no voters of certain voter types. Restricting a profile $\mathbf{p}$ to the boundary, then, means it has special, restrictive properties. The same statement holds for a profile in $Si(10!)$.

The *unanimity profile* $\mathbf{E}_i$, where all voters are of the ith type, $i = 1, \ldots, n!$, plays an important role. (For a three-candidate example, $\mathbf{E}_3 = (0, 0, 1, 0, 0, 0)$ requires all voters to have the type-three ranking $c_3 \succ c_1 \succ c_2$.) Just as the normalized outcome $\mathbf{e}_j$ serves as a vertex for $Si(3)$, the six unanimity profiles, $\{\mathbf{E}_i\}_{i=1}^6$, are the vertices for $Si(6)$. That is, $Si(6)$ is the convex hull defined by these vertices (see Sect. 1.4). This fact is underscored by the obvious relationship

$$\mathbf{p} = (p_1, p_2, \ldots, p_6) = \sum_{j=1}^{6} p_j \mathbf{E}_j, \text{ where } \sum_{j=1}^{6} p_j = 1. \qquad (2.2.2)$$

Consequently, *the p_j values are the convex weights defining the profile* $\mathbf{p}$. A similar statement holds for any number of candidates.

In general, two points define a line, three points define a two-dimensional plane, and k points define a $k - 1$ dimensional surface. Using the convex representation Eq. 2.2.2, if k of the six components of $\mathbf{p} \in Si(6)$ are non-zero, then $\mathbf{p}$ belongs to a $k - 1$ dimensional boundary of $Si(6)$. For example, the profile $(\frac{1}{6}, \frac{1}{3}, 0, \frac{1}{6}, \frac{1}{6}, \frac{1}{6})$ is in the four-dimensional surface of $Si(6)$ defined by the vertices $\mathbf{E}_1, \mathbf{E}_2, \mathbf{E}_4, \mathbf{E}_5, \mathbf{E}_6$, while $(\frac{1}{2}, 0, 0, \frac{1}{3}, 0, \frac{1}{6})$ is relegated to the even more restrictive two-dimensional edge of $Si(6)$ defined by the unanimity profiles $\mathbf{E}_1, \mathbf{E}_4$ and $\mathbf{E}_6$.

So, even though we cannot draw these surfaces, we do know some of their properties. Still, until we can "see" profiles and their relationships with other profiles, it is difficult to understand what is going on. Starting in Chap. 3, this is accomplished by introducing geometric coordinate systems for three-candidate profiles which allow us to "see" these profile sets. Until then, a primitive yet useful representation of a profile is to list the components of a profile in the appropriate ranking region of the representation triangle.

Example 2.2.1. The profiles from the introductory fable can be expressed as normalized profiles in $Si(6)$.

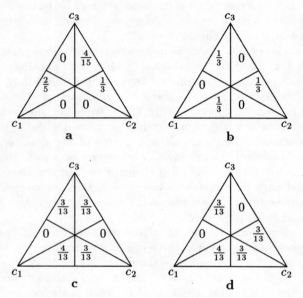

Fig. 2.2.1. Representations of four profiles

- For the beverage example, if c_1 is milk, c_2 is beer, and c_3 is wine, then the beverage profile $\mathbf{p}_b = (0, \frac{6}{15}, 0, \frac{4}{15}, \frac{5}{15}, 0)$ is given in the representation triangle of Fig. 2.2.1a.
- For the contentious departmental meeting, if c_j represents the jth alternative, the profile is $\mathbf{p}_m = (\frac{1}{3}, 0, \frac{1}{3}, 0, \frac{1}{3}, 0)$. This profile is represented in Fig. 2.2.1b. Some consequences of the obvious geometric symmetry arrangement are discussed in Sect. 3.1.
- For the selection of a member to the Dean's Council, let c_1, c_2, c_3 be, respectively, Ann, Barb, and Carol. Thus the profiles $\mathbf{p}_{DC(1)} = (\frac{4}{13}, 0, \frac{3}{13}, \frac{3}{13}, 0, \frac{3}{13})$ (Fig. 2.2.1c) and $\mathbf{p}_{DC(2)} = (\frac{4}{13}, 0, \frac{3}{13}, 0, \frac{3}{13}, \frac{3}{13})$ (Fig. 2.2.1d) represent, respectively, the profiles of the first two subcommittees. Observe the geometric similarity between these two profiles. The (normalized) profile for the committee of the whole is $\mathbf{p}_{DC} = (\frac{8}{26}, 0, \frac{6}{26}, \frac{3}{13}, \frac{3}{13}, \frac{6}{26})$. $\square$

2.2.1 The Election Mapping

The voters and candidates are here, so let's hold a three-candidate election. As an election converts a profile into an election tally, it defines a mapping from the five-dimensional space of voters' preferences, $Si(3!)$, to the two-dimensional space of election outcomes, $Si(3)$. The definition is immediate. For instance, with the profile $(\frac{1}{6}, 0, \frac{1}{3}, 0, \frac{1}{2}, 0)$, c_1 is top-choice for $\frac{1}{6}$ of the voters, c_3 is top-choice for $\frac{1}{3}$ of the voters, and c_2 is top-choice for $\frac{1}{2}$ of the voters, so the normalized election vector is $(\frac{1}{6}, \frac{1}{2}, \frac{1}{3})$. As $(\frac{1}{6}, \frac{1}{2}, \frac{1}{3})$ is in the ranking region $c_2 \succ c_3 \succ c_1$, this is the election ranking.

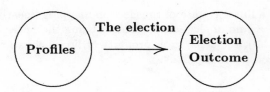

The election mapping is a geometric version of counting. In a plurality election, a type-one voter votes only for his top-ranked candidate c_1, so this is equivalent to registering the voter's vote with the *vector ballot* $\mathbf{e}_1 = (1, 0, 0)$ to indicate that one point is tabulated for the candidate c_1 and none for any other candidates. Similarly, as a type-4 voter has c_3 top-ranked, the associated vector ballot is $\mathbf{e}_3 = (0, 0, 1)$. Re-expressing the plurality outcome for profile of $(\frac{1}{6}, 0, \frac{1}{3}, 0, \frac{1}{2}, 0)$ in this notation, the outcome of the election mapping is

$$\frac{1}{6}\mathbf{e}_1 + \frac{1}{2}\mathbf{e}_2 + \frac{1}{3}\mathbf{e}_3 = (\frac{1}{6}, \frac{1}{2}, \frac{1}{3})$$

We need to be picky about the notation in order to avoid problems when analyzing voting processes. What is wrong with a vector ballot is that it does not identify the voter type; e.g., both type-5 and 6 voters have c_2 top-ranked, so their vector ballot is the same $\mathbf{e}_2$. To indicate the voter type of a vector ballot, observe that each vector ballot $\mathbf{e}_j$ is a permutation of $\mathbf{e}_1$; e.g., $\mathbf{e}_2 = (0, 1, 0)$ is obtained by interchanging the first and second coordinate of $\mathbf{e}_1 = (1, 0, 0)$ while $\mathbf{e}_3 = (0, 0, 1)$ is found by interchanging the first and the third coordinate of $\mathbf{e}_1$.

Definition 2.2.2. Let $[\mathbf{e}_1]_j$ denote the permutation of $\mathbf{e}_1$ that represents the vector ballot for the jth voter type. $\square$

Example 2.2.2. The top choice of a type-four voter is c_3, so the vector ballot is $\mathbf{e}_3$; i.e., $[\mathbf{e}_1]_4 = \mathbf{e}_3$. Similarly, to reflect that a type-5 voter votes for c_2, the notation is $[\mathbf{e}_1]_5 = \mathbf{e}_2$. $\square$

An election outcome is determined by computing what fraction of voters from the profile $\mathbf{p} \in Si(3!)$ cast each vector ballot. The resulting sum, the election tally, is a normalized election vector in $Si(3)$. Thus the election mapping

$$f : Si(6) \to Si(3) \tag{2.2.3}$$

is defined by

$$f(\mathbf{p}, \mathbf{e}_1) = \sum_{j=1}^{6} p_j [\mathbf{e}_1]_j \qquad (2.2.4)$$

Aiding the analysis are the "linear" properties of f and the unanimity profiles where

$$f(\mathbf{E}_j, \mathbf{e}_1) = [\mathbf{e}_1]_j, \quad j = 1, \dots, 6 \qquad (2.2.5)$$

As Eq. 2.2.4 is a linear equation, the election mapping linearly transforms a sum of profiles into a sum of election outcomes. Using the linear representation of a profile (Eq. 2.2.2), the separation property of linear equations (Eq. 1.4.4), and Eq. 2.2.5, we recapture Eq. 2.2.4.

$$f(\mathbf{p}, \mathbf{e}_1) = f(\sum_{j=1}^{6} p_j \mathbf{E}_j, \mathbf{e}_1) = \sum_{j=1}^{6} p_j f(\mathbf{E}_j, \mathbf{e}_1) = \sum_{j=1}^{6} p_j [\mathbf{e}_1]_j \qquad (2.2.6)$$

Example 2.2.3. The plurality election outcomes for each of the above profiles are given next.

- For the beverage example from the fable,

$$f(\mathbf{p}_b, \mathbf{e}_1) = \frac{6}{15}[\mathbf{e}_1]_2 + \frac{4}{15}[\mathbf{e}_1]_4 + \frac{5}{15}[\mathbf{e}_1]_5$$
$$= \frac{6}{15}\mathbf{e}_1 + \frac{4}{15}\mathbf{e}_3 + \frac{5}{15}\mathbf{e}_2 = (\frac{6}{15}, \frac{5}{15}, \frac{4}{15})$$

This normalized election vector is in the ranking region for $c_1 \succ c_2 \succ c_3$.
- For the profile $\mathbf{p}_m$ from the departmental meeting, the outcome is

$$f(\mathbf{p}_m, \mathbf{e}_1) = \frac{1}{3}[\mathbf{e}_1]_1 + \frac{1}{3}[\mathbf{e}_1]_3 + \frac{1}{3}[\mathbf{e}_1]_5 = (\frac{1}{3}, \frac{1}{3}, \frac{1}{3})$$

which is in the ranking region $\mathcal{I}$ representing $c_1 \sim c_2 \sim c_3$.
- The ranking for the first Dean's Council subcommittee is $f(\mathbf{p}_{DC(1)}, \mathbf{e}_1) = (\frac{4}{13}, \frac{6}{13}, \frac{3}{13})$ or $c_2 \succ c_1 \succ c_3$.
- The outcome for the second subcommittee is $f(\mathbf{p}_{DC(2)}, \mathbf{e}_1) = (\frac{4}{13}, \frac{3}{13}, \frac{6}{13})$ or $c_3 \succ c_1 \succ c_2$.
- For the full committee, the outcome is $f(\mathbf{p}_{DC}, \mathbf{e}_1) = (\frac{8}{26}, \frac{9}{26}, \frac{9}{26})$ or $c_2 \sim c_3 \succ c_1$. Notice that although c_1 (Ann) is one of the two top-ranked candidates for each subcommittee, she is bottom-ranked in the committee of the whole. □

2.2.2 The Geometry of Election Outcomes

While a normalized profile is a rational point from $Si(6)$, most $Si(6)$ points have a component with an irrational value. These points cannot be identified with integer profiles, but they can, as indicated in the exercises, be identified with limits of integer profiles and/or with profiles from a weighted voting system. For instance, recall from the pope selection discussion (Sect. 1.3) that a *weighted* voting system is where some voters are "more equal than others."

More specifically, assign the ith voter a weight, δ_i, and count this voter's ballot as though δ_i voters voted in this manner. In a law firm, for instance, a partner's ownership share may determine her δ weight. There is no restriction on the value of δ_i; it could be an integer, say $\delta_i = 2$, a fraction, such as $\delta_i = \frac{3}{8}$, or even be an irrational value such as $\sqrt{2}$. The modification of Eq. 2.2.6 to include weighted voting is immediate.

Among the many situations where weighted voting is appropriate, consider a group consisting of members with diverse talents. When faced with a particular decision, maybe the better informed should have a greater say in the outcome. A way to do so is to allow each person to distribute some of his or her voting power to other decision makers. In this iteration, at the end of each round each voter redistributes some of his changed level of influence. (See, for example, [De].) In the limit, the voting power of certain agents can be an irrational number.

So, by defining an election as a mapping from *all points* in $Si(6)$, rather than just the rational ones, we can model and analyze a much richer class of problems. *This assumption holds unless specifically stated otherwise!*

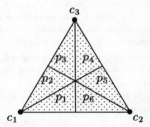

Fig. 2.2.2. The plurality election outcomes

It remains to understand the normalized election outcomes. The answer is immediate now that elections are identified with a linear mapping. Here, the geometric representation uses the discussion of Sect. 1.4. The domain, or space of normalized profiles $Si(6)$, is the convex hull defined by the vertices $\{\mathbf{E}_j\}$. Therefore, as argued in Sect. 1.4, the normalized election outcomes is the convex hull defined by $\{f(\mathbf{E}_j, \mathbf{e}_1)\}_{j=1}^6$. Consequently, any election outcome can be represented by $\sum_{j=1}^6 \lambda_j f(\mathbf{E}_j, \mathbf{e}_1)$ for some choice of $\lambda_1, \ldots, \lambda_6$ where $\lambda_j \geq 0$ and $\sum_{j=1}^6 \lambda_j = 1$. There is no mystery here; by comparing this expression with Eq. 2.2.4, it follows immediately that $\lambda_j = p_j$ for $j = 1, \ldots, 6$.

The election outcomes of the unanimity profiles are the vertices of the representation triangle (Eq. 2.2.5), so, as indicated in Fig. 2.2.2, the space of normalized election outcomes is the full simplex $Si(3)$. Namely, any point in the *convex hull* defined by $\{f(\mathbf{E}_j, \mathbf{e}_1) = [\mathbf{e}_1]_j\}_{j=1}^3$, is the election outcome for some choice of $\mathbf{p} \in Si(6)$.

2.2.3 Exercises

1. Show that $f(\mathbf{p}, \mathbf{e}_1) = (p_1 + p_2, p_5 + p_6, p_3 + p_4)$. Using Fig. 2.2.2, show that each candidate's tally is given by adding the profile entries in the ranking regions sharing the vertex identified with the candidate. Use this geometric approach to tally the elections for the profiles of Fig. 2.2.1.

2. The definition of the election mapping asserts that the election outcome is a *normalized* election tally. Justify this comment. In other words, prove that because $\mathbf{p} \in Si(6)$, the election outcome $f(\mathbf{p}, \mathbf{e}_1)$ satisfies the two required conditions for a point to be in $Si(3)$.

3. Assign three voters the weights $\delta_1 = \frac{\pi}{2} = \frac{3.14159\ldots}{2}$, $\delta_2 = 1$, $\delta_3 = 0.500$.
a. If the voters are of the respective types one, three, five, find the weighted election outcome.
b. Express the profile of part a as a normalized profile in $Si(6)$.
c. Show for these weights that whatever voter-one wants, voter-one gets. Namely, *voter-one is a dictator*. Show that if voter-one does not vote, then voter-two becomes a dictator.
d. To extend a voting vector from strict preferences to all preferences, average the number of votes cast over all ways indifference can be broken. In this manner, a voter with ranking $c_1 \sim c_3 \succ c_2$ would cast the ballot $(\frac{1}{2}, 0, \frac{1}{2}) = \frac{1}{2}([\mathbf{e}_1]_2 + [\mathbf{e}_1]_3)$. Show that the above weights define a *sequential dictatorship*. Namely, voter-one always gets his way – but when he is indifferent between two candidates, voter-two's preferences dominate. Voter-three's views are manifested only when the first two voters are indifferent.

4. An important theme from voting theory is to analyze what occurs with large numbers of voters. In this spirit find a sequence of normalized profiles (where the coordinates have rational values) so that the election ranking always is $c_1 \succ c_2 \succ c_3$ but the normalized tallies approach the point from Prob. 8, Sect. 2.1. (So, the limit ranking is $c_1 \sim c_2 \succ c_3$.) Find one sequence where the normalized profiles approach a specific normalized profile, and then find another sequence which does not approach a single normalized profile.

5. For the three threshold methods from the Exercises of Sect. 2.1, let $\delta_2 = \frac{1}{2}$, $\gamma_2 = \frac{3}{5}$, $\epsilon = 0.21$.
a. Find a profile $\mathbf{p}_1$ so that c_1 is top-ranked with the Universal but not with the Distinct or Quasi transitive threshold methods.
b. Find a profile $\mathbf{p}_2$ so that c_2 is top-ranked with the Distinct, but not with the Universal or Quasi-transitive threshold methods.
c. Can a profile be found where c_3 is top-ranked with the Quasi-transitive threshold method but not with the other two?
   Give a geometric one for tallying the plurality vote in terms of the entries near the vertex.

6. How many components are there for a four-candidate profile? Find both the normalized profile and the normalized plurality election outcome for the preferences where six voters have $c_1 \succ c_3 \succ c_2 \succ c_4$, four have $c_3 \succ c_1 \succ c_4 \succ c_2$, and two have $c_4 \succ c_1 \succ c_3 \succ c_2$. (In doing so, remember that you can define the types in any order you wish.)

CHAPTER III

THE PROBLEM WITH CONDORCET

The beverage brouhaha, which initiated the season of dissent for the hypothetical department of the fable, started with the winer's discovery that the department's plurality ranking conflicts with their rankings of pairs of beverages. The radical disagreement raises interesting theoretical questions. How does a majority vote ranking of a pair relate to its relative ranking within a plurality outcome? Can anything go wrong with pairwise rankings?

In this chapter geometric techniques are developed to analyze voting and discover sources of election paradoxes. In doing so, coordinate representations and profile decompositions for three-candidate profiles are introduced so we can "see" which profiles define which outcomes. Among the surprises uncovered by this geometry is that certain problems arise because the pairwise vote tends to carefully respect the wishes of phantom voters! Then, Arrow's Theorem is introduced and extended. This striking conclusion appears to claim that we cannot do what we thought we could. I explain this later, but, as an enticement, expect the (nonexistent) phantom voters to cause problems.

3.1 Why Can't an Organization Be More Like a Person?

A natural way to rank candidates is with pairwise competitions. After all, by comparing the merits of a candidate directly with those of her competitor, we avoid distracting side issues. This kind of reasoning supports the adoption of agendas and other pairwise procedures. After embracing the value of pairwise comparisons, we should identify the profiles which escape the difficulties of Sect. 1.1-2. Namely, for which profiles does one candidate win with any reasonable pairwise procedure?

Definition 3.1. Candidate c_k is a *Condorcet winner* if she wins all pairwise majority vote elections against all other candidates. Candidate c_j is a *Condorcet loser* if she loses all pairwise elections. □

In the beverage example, wine and milk are, respectively, the Condorcet winner and loser. There is, of course, at most one Condorcet winner and/or loser.

It is easy to embrace the idea of a Condorcet winner; it comes with the comfort of using the familiar pairwise, majority vote elections. This concept captures a sense of rugged individualism – raising images of a Western movie with a shootout at the "OK Corral" – because c_k reigns as the Condorcet winner only if she can beat all comers. All this electoral strength ensures her victory with any reasonable procedure based on pairwise rankings. (Namely, exclude perverse approaches that ignore candidates or reward the loser, rather than the winner, of a contest.) She wins, for instance, with any agenda. For these reasons, it is widely accepted that a Condorcet winner always should be selected.

Bucking this nearly universal acceptance, I find the Condorcet winner to be a lousy concept full of dangers. My "nay-saying" is based on its many serious problems that emerge from the geometry of voting. As a first flaw, a Condorcet winner and/or loser need not exist. Condorcet demonstrated this limitation with his *Condorcet profile* p_m illustrated by the departmental meeting of the fable. With p_m, each alternative loses to a candidate (while beating another) denying a Condorcet winner. So, this existence complication is not due to a lack of pairwise winners; there are too many of them. A "Condorcet winner," then, is a "sometimes" concept – sometimes it is useful; sometimes it is not. This in itself suggests that the Condorcet winner should be critically re-examined.

The Money Pump. The Condorcet cycle $c_1 \succ c_2$, $c_2 \succ c_3$, $c_3 \succ c_1$ created by $p_m = (\frac{1}{3}, 0, \frac{1}{3}, 0, \frac{1}{3}, 0, \frac{1}{3})$ is particularly bothersome because it violates intuition and expectations about rational behavior. Some of us, after all, claim to be "rational individuals" who affiliate only with rational behaving groups. A Turing test of this claim means it is impossible to decide whether a given set of outcomes are the decisions of a rational individual or the group.

First, we need a description of rational behavior. Standard definitions require the preference rankings to be as orderly as points on a line. If three points satisfy the inequalities $p_1 \leq p_2$ and $p_2 \leq p_3$, then $p_1 \leq p_3$. Similar predictable behavior, *transitivity*, is expected of personal and group preferences; we expect a person with preferences $c_1 \succ c_2$ and $c_2 \succ c_3$ to have the ranking $c_1 \succ c_3$.[1]

So, if Susie prefers strawberries to apple pie, and apple pie to raspberries, is she being irrational if she prefers raspberries to strawberries? Maybe; but maybe not. Reasonable scenarios (Prob. 2) color such nontransitive actions as sophisticated; well, maybe pseudosophisticated.

Transitivity may, or may not, adequately model rational behavior, but it is a reasonable starting assumption. After all, without rational voters, we must expect chaotic election outcomes! When garbage is fed into a procedure (i.e., imposing no structure on voters' preferences) we should expect garbage to come out (cycles and paradoxes). But, while weird outcomes are anticipated with irrational voters, we must be concerned with a method that performs poorly with rational voters. Thus, for there to be any hope of understanding election procedures, a central, critical assumption is that voters have transitive preferences; this avoids the "garbage in, garbage out" phenomenon.

A standard way to justify this assumption is to invoke the "Dutch Book" or "money pump" which argues that anyone with intransitive rankings quickly will

---

[1] Not all binary relationships are transitive. For instance, define the binary relationship $s_1 \mathcal{L} s_2$ to mean that s_1 loves s_2. Now, it may be that "John $\mathcal{L}$ Katri", and "Katri $\mathcal{L}$ Erik," but it need not be true that "John $\mathcal{L}$ Erik."

exchange them for transitive preferences. To see why, suppose cyclic Susie *does* prefer raspberries to strawberries. When offered a choice between strawberries and raspberries, she will, of course, choose raspberries. Now, along comes Mike. For a small fee, Mike will arrange for Susie to choose between raspberries and apple pie. Offered this preferred choice, presumably she would pay. Then, clever Mike would arrange another deal for "soon to be poor" Susie! Again for a small fee, she could choose between apple pie and strawberries.

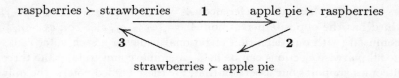

The money pump now is in full operation. Should Susie pay and select strawberries, Mike would dangle another opportunity that can't be refused; she can, for a small fee, choose between strawberries and raspberries! Susie's choices return to where they started, but she has a lighter wallet. Around the cycle Mike would go, trying to pump out all of Susie's money. However, if you know Susie like I know Susie, you know that this strategy will fail; she would instantly detect and foil Mike's devious intentions by adopting transitive preferences.

If Mike would try to pump money from Susie, why not an organization? There are plenty of opportunities[2] offered by the p_m (sincere) voting cycle. Would a group learn? More immediate is the need to understand how such an option could arise with an organization of rational voters. To poorly paraphrase the scholarly Professor Higgens of *"My Fair Lady"* fame, "why can't an organization be more like a person?" Any explanation must delve into the mysteries of how the simple aggregation of transitive opinions can destroy transitivity.[3]

3.1.1 Confused, Irrational Voters

Would you trust a surgeon, a dentist, or a lawyer who consistently makes decisions while ignoring critical available information? Of course not. But, similar deficiencies plague the pairwise vote. As I show, this method systematically ignores vital, available information. So, can we trust pairwise voting or any procedure based on it?

To understand the lost information, envision the pairwise vote as an accommodating servant carefully trained to ignore peculiarities of the guests. Conse-

---

[2]Suppose each of the three members $\{A, B, C\}$ of a condo organization has $100. For a fee, the manager, M, offers to assess some member $5; one dollar (say, in services) goes to each of the two unassessed members while the remaining $3 is the manager's fee. With the advantage to the majority, one can see how a money pump cycle would be set up. At the end of the first vote where B, C voted against A, we have $A - \$95$, $B - \$101$, $C - \$101$, $M - \$3$; at the end of the second vote A, C vote down B to obtain $A - \$96$, $B - \$96$, $C - \$102$, $M - \$6$; and so forth.

[3]This conflict between individual/group behavior is central to statistics and the social sciences. The essence of the arguments developed here extends to other aggregation processes.

quently, this servant - the pairwise vote - serves the confused, irrational, cyclic voter with the same respect as the more staid, transitive individual who has painfully learned the lessons of the money pump. Of course, by being unable to distinguish whether a guest is transitive or intransitive, the servant cannot coordinate or anticipate requests.

To illustrate, suppose three voters consider proposal A where two are in favor and one is against. No problem; the only fair outcome is the $2:1$ vote in favor of A. This is true whatever the choice of A; even if we are dealing with confused, cyclic voters where two have the preferences $A = \{c_1 \succ c_2, c_2 \succ c_3, c_3 \succ c_1\}$, while the third has the opposite persuasion $A^c = \{c_2 \succ c_1, c_1 \succ c_3, c_3 \succ c_2\}$. Although confused (with our definition of rational behavior), each voter ranks each pair, so all pairwise elections can be held. A simple count to tally the three pairwise outcomes supports our assertion that, for these baffled voters, the only fair conclusion is a $2:1$ vote favoring A. This is not surprising; when dealing with confused voters, expect confused outcomes.

The Condorcet profile of three transitive voters, $c_1 \succ c_2 \succ c_3, c_2 \succ c_3 \succ c_1, c_3 \succ c_1 \succ c_2$, supports the same pairwise election outcomes. This is a surprise; these are not confused voters. However, with a little thought, the mystery vanishes; the outcome is exactly as it should be. After all, by combining anonymity with the voters' pairwise rankings, *it is impossible for the procedure to distinguish between the Condorcet profile of transitive voters and the confused voter profile.* This is illustrated in the following table where the pairwise rankings from Condorcet's profile are reassembled into the confused voter profile. (The kth row lists the pairwise ranking of the kth transitive voter and subscript j indicates rankings for the jth cyclic voter, $j, k = 1, 2, 3$.)

$$(3.1.1) \quad \begin{array}{ccc} (c_1 \succ c_2)_1 & (c_2 \succ c_3)_2 & (c_1 \succ c_3)_3 \\ (c_2 \succ c_1)_3 & (c_2 \succ c_3)_1 & (c_3 \succ c_1)_2 \\ (c_1 \succ c_2)_2 & (c_3 \succ c_2)_3 & (c_3 \succ c_1)_1 \end{array}$$

By being unable to determine whether the voters are rational or confused, the only "fair" outcome is the cycle.

Thus the critical flaw of the pairwise vote is an inability to distinguish between transitive or intransitive preferences; consequently the *pairwise vote loses the critical assumption of transitive voters!*[4] But, without transitivity, we have – unintentionally but effectively – returned to a "garbage in, garbage out" environment. No wonder we encounter cycles and other pairwise voting problems! They manifest this enormous loss of critical information. Indeed, as indicated throughout this chapter, when a profile causes cycles or other disturbing problems, there is an associated profile involving confused voters where the outcome now is "reasonable." Namely, the difficulties of pairwise voting can be attributed to its emasculation of transitivity; instead of honoring rational opinions, the procedure caters to phantom confused voters.

---

[4] As Diana Richards and I noted, a tacit assumption in the literature is the transitivity of strategic actions. As the procedure can't detect rationality, the space of strategic actions is much richer than commonly believed.

So, contrary to what we expect, procedures based on pairwise rankings, such as the Condorcet winner, are *not* based on the rationality of voters. Yes, this condition is carefully imposed, but the *procedure* surreptitiously drops it! How can we trust outcomes from such procedures? On the other hand, this informational gap is not suffered by methods such as the BC. The BC *requires* voters to specify a transitive ranking, so this more discerning servant cannot accommodate confused voters – the respect of transitivity is built into the procedure. As such, (Chap. 4) we must anticipate the BC and related methods to possess distinct advantages over pairwise voting.

3.1.2 Information Lost from Pairwise Majority Voting

Asserting that information is lost is one matter; characterizing it is another. To do this with geometry, start with the profile representation of p_b (the beverage example) by placing p_j in the ranking region $\mathcal{R}(j)$, $j = 1, \ldots, 6$, of the representation triangle in Fig. 3.1.1. Voter types with the $c_1 \succ c_2$ relative ranking are to the left of the $c_1 \sim c_2$ indifference line, while those with the $c_2 \succ c_1$ relative ranking are to the right. Thus, the majority vote tallies for c_1 and c_2 are, respectively, the sum of the numbers listed to the left and to the right of the $c_1 \sim c_2$ line. The tally $\left(\frac{2}{5}, \frac{3}{5}\right)$ defining the ranking $c_2 \succ c_1$, is listed below the c_1, c_2 edge of the simplex.

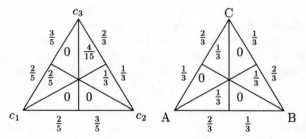

Fig. 3.1.1. Pairwise votes as projections

Geometrically, then, the pairwise vote is a projection; e.g., the $\{c_j, c_k\}$ majority vote is obtained by projecting the simplex entries to the c_j, c_k edge and summing the projected values. In this manner, the $\{c_2, c_3\}$ and $\{c_1, c_3\}$ majority vote outcomes are as listed next to the appropriate edge in the figure. To understand the loss of transitivity, notice that the projection preserves only the relative ranking of the two alternatives. For instance, in the beverage comparison of $\{c_1, c_2\}$, only one voter type (type-two) has the ranking $c_1 \succ c_2$. However, we know that not only do these voters prefer $c_1 \succ c_2$ (milk $\succ$ beer), they want milk so intensely that should c_3 (wine) be available, c_3 is used to separate c_1 and c_2 as indicated by the $c_1 \succ c_3 \succ c_2$ ranking. Similarly, the intensity of the type-five voters' $c_2 \succ c_1$ ranking becomes apparent only when c_3 is available to separate c_1, c_2 as manifested by $c_1 \succ c_3 \succ c_2$. Compare these situations with the type four-voters. Here, the availability of wine does not delineate the $\{c_1, c_2\}$

ranking; the pair remains unseparated in the full ranking of $c_3 \succ (c_2 \succ c_1)$.

So, with *another available alternative*, the two types of information concern

1.   The $c_i \succ c_j$ relative ranking
2.   The intensity of $c_i \succ c_j$ *relative to the third available alternative*

Strong intensity is where the ranking of the pair is separated by the third alternative. *Weak intensity* is where the pair remains intact; the undivided pair is compared with the third alternative. For $n > 3$ candidates, the $c_1 \succ c_2$ intensity levels depend on the number of candidates separating c_1 and c_2.[5]

Weak and strong intensity involve objective, pragmatic criteria. Rather than juggling voters' subjective comments, where one voter's "like, awesome!" might equate with another voter's "well, somewhat," this intensity measure is revealed by whether other alternatives are used to separate a pair. Of great importance, *the intensity of pairwise comparisons is a minimal way to signal that the voters have transitive rankings.* After all, strong intensity requires transitivity; all binary rankings of a cyclic voter are weak.

Observe my emphasis on whether another alternative is available. In the beverage example, if the only choice is between milk (c_1) and beer (c_2), there is no debate; the voters prefer $c_2 \succ c_1$. (With only two alternatives, the pairwise rankings are transitive.) When wine (c_3) is a choice, as indicated above, the intensity of the pairwise comparisons is an important informational variable – if only to indicate that voters have transitive rankings. With three alternatives where the pairwise rankings are intended to select the "best choice," the $\{c_1, c_2\}$ ranking must, somehow, reflect the availability of c_3. But, for intensity to be a pragmatic measure, the third alternative must be an honest option. The intensity of my ranking *Crime and Punishment* $\succ$ *War and Peace* is not reflected by comparing them to the non-existent *The Algebraic Closing Lemma*, H. Poinchoff (1976).

Fourth-Graders.   To argue that intensity comparisons are natural let me relate what once happened during a lecture. As part of the Pittsburgh Public School System's celebration of the annual national *Mathematics Awareness Week,* I was invited to discuss "recent developments in mathematics" to several school classes. It was enjoyable, but a sense of trepidation set in when I discovered that my schedule included a talk to a fourth-grade class at the East Hill School. *What does one say to fourth-graders!*

Searching for a way to survive my allotted forty minutes, I decided to introduce voting paradoxes in terms of three popular (for the trendy nine year old) TV shows denoted here by A, B, C. One problem was to determine the show a hypothetical group of children should watch when

• Five children like A better than B better than C.
• Five children like B better than C better than A.
• Five children like C better than A better than B.

---

[5] "Intensity" is closely related to "conditional probability" where the likelihood of events A and B can change when the comparison is subject to event C occurring.

Upon seeing the data (the Condorcet profile $\mathbf{p}_m$), the students immediately argued that *no* show was preferred to any other! They pointed out that each show is in first-, second-, and last-place the same number of times, so the only fair ranking is $A \sim B \sim C$. When I tried to generate controversy by computing the pairwise ranking $A \succ B$ by the vote of $10 : 5$, these fourth-graders beat me to my punch line by instantly arguing that, sure, but it also is true that $B \succ C$ and $C \succ A$ by the same vote. Not only did they instantly see the symmetry of the profile (Prob. 3), but these nine year olds seized upon and emphasized the subtle difference between a pairwise vote when only two alternatives are available and when there is a viable third choice.

With only two alternatives, say A, B, there is no debate – the fourth-graders and the rest of us agree that the hypothetical group overwhelmingly prefers $A \succ B$ with a $10 : 5$ vote. Once C becomes a viable third alternative, however, intensity information must be invoked to let us know we are dealing with transitive rather than confused voters. In some sense, when this information is used, we should end up with the pairwise ranking $A \sim B$ *given that C is available.* The pairwise vote cycle, then, is just an artifact of the lost, vital data. This loss is further supported by the fact that all methods requiring the transitivity of the rankings, such as BC or the plurality vote, support the completely tied ranking $\mathcal{I}$.

(The intensity level of the binary ranking $B \succ A$ is strong because the voters use C to separate the pair into the ranking $B \succ C \succ A$. On the other hand, the two voter types with the pairwise ranking $A \succ B$ exhibit a weak intensity because the pair is compared as a unit with the third alternative C; C is either placed after the pair (for the type-one ranking of $(A \succ B) \succ C$), or before it (for the type-three ranking of $C \succ (A \succ B)$).)

This need to distinguish between the ranking of a pair in isolation and when accompanied by another alternative was explained to me by an incredibly short boy from that fourth-grade classroom. Because I remained "puzzled" by my Condorcet cycle example, he took pity on me by carefully offering, "Let me explain. Nobody is better; they are all the same. It is like the rock and the scissors and the paper. The rock can dull the scissors and the scissors can cut the paper and the paper can cover the rock, so nothing is better than the others." He is correct, of course.

3.1.3 Reduced Profiles

Maybe we should learn from these fourth-graders. As they correctly observe, no alternative is favored with a Condorcet profile. Yet this profile, which should be neutral in determining the outcome, is readily identified by the pairwise vote as representing irrational voters (Eq. 3.1.1) – this is where transitivity is lost. Common sense suggests dropping those portions of $\mathbf{p}$ that should not affect the outcome but can spawn problems.

To motivate, suppose a two-candidate vote is 50 for Monica and 40 for Cindy. One way to justify Monica's victory is to observe that her first 40 voters cancel out the opposing 40 Cindy voters; the outcome is determined by the *reduced profile* assigning 10 votes to Monica. "Cancelling" is part of our culture where a husband and wife, with opposing views, justify their failure to vote by explaining how their votes would cancel – the outcome would remain the same. This cancelling argument even attains a sense of formality in the protocol bound US Senate where, when faced with obligations outside of Washington during an important vote, Senators with opposite views may formally agree for neither to return to vote.

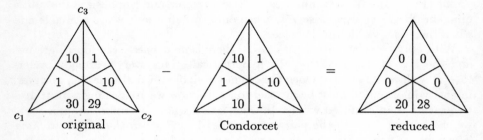

Fig. 3.1.2. Cancelling irrational behavior

So, a natural three-candidate cancellation is to drop from a profile all Condorcet triplets. To illustrate, while the outcome for the integer profile $\mathbf{p} = (30, 1, 10, 1, 10, 29)$ is not apparent, hidden in $\mathbf{p}$ are two Condorcet triplets. The $(10, 0, 10, 0, 10, 0)$ portion, corresponds to a 30 voter Condorcet triplet $c_1 \succ c_2 \succ c_3$, $c_2 \succ c_3 \succ c_1$, $c_3 \succ c_1 \succ c_2$ while the $(0, 1, 0, 1, 0, 1)$ part generates the three-voter triplet $c_1 \succ c_3 \succ c_2$, $c_3 \succ c_2 \succ c_1$, $c_2 \succ c_1 \succ c_3$. By removing this $(10, 1, 10, 1, 10, 1)$ Condorcet portion of $\mathbf{p}$, which should be a natural cancellation, we have the *reduced profile* $(20, 0, 0, 0, 0, 28)$. Representing this cancellation on representation triangles (Fig. 3.1.2), the reduced profile – the portion that should decide the outcome – indicates a two-candidate contest with a natural group ranking $c_2 \succ c_1 \succ c_3$. This conclusion makes sense; the Condorcet portion in the middle triangle is where, as the fourth-graders effectively argued, no candidate should be favored as all are ranked equally.[6]

This cancellation provides a powerful, easily used tool to analyze the consequences of ignoring transitivity. As transitivity is compromised by the Condorcet portions of $\mathbf{p}$, just examine how the presumably neutral Condorcet portion of a profile alters the conclusion. Changes, of course, must be attributed to the imbecilic sense of fairness the pairwise vote extends to the nonexistent confused voters; these changes identify the costs of losing transitivity.

To illustrate with the triangles of Fig. 3.1.2, the reduced profile ranking is $c_2 \succ c_1 \succ c_3$ for all procedures such as Condorcet's approach, agendas, runoffs, or positional methods (where points are assigned to a voter's first, second and third ranked candidates). Contradicting this overwhelming evidence is the

---

[6] For readers familiar with group theory, notice that the Condorcet profiles are orbits of a Z_3 action and that the reduced profile involves a natural quotient. For other algebraic structures, consider Prob. 11 from an algebraic perspective.

crowning of c_1 as the Condorcet winner for the original profile. The change is
due to the supposedly neutral Condorcet portion; this portion of the profile in
the middle triangle demonstrates a consequence of lost transitivity. Namely, the
phantom "irrational voters" have struck again!

As this example demonstrates, the Condorcet winner is subject to the troubling consequences of the pairwise vote's inability to honor transitivity. Condorcet was a good mathematician, so I have no doubt that had he recognized
this serious flaw he would have immediately abandoned his approach. To add
history, Condorcet used the Fig. 3.1.2 profile to try to discredit Borda's method.
(See [MH]; the profiles of Prob. 9 also are from Condorcet's work.) By not
understanding the perils of pairwise voting, Condorcet could only consider the
original profile where his Condorcet winner was not top-ranked by any positional
method. But, as we now know, the flaw resides in Condorcet's approach – not in
the positional methods. Even today examples of this type are used as arguments
against the BC. However, the Condorcet winner cannot be used as a standard
when, de facto, it ignores transitivity by catering to nonexistent confused voters!

Throughout this chapter I show how *the loss of transitivity from the Condorcet
portion of a profile explains most pairwise voting problems.* This assertion is true
whether the procedure is an agenda, a Condorcet winner, a Copeland winner
[SM, MS], or anything else. Support is in Sect. 3.3 where it is established that
the reduced profile never admits cycles; the outcomes always are transitive. As
shown in Prob. 9, the ranking of the original and reduced profiles are the same
with a positional procedure; they correctly cancel the Condorcet part. Indeed,
this cancelling holds for any procedure serving transitive voters and satisfing a
couple of other natural, agreeable properties.

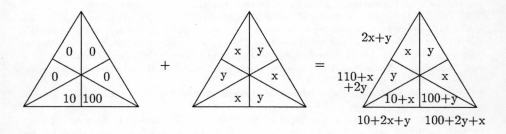

Fig. 3.1.3. Creating problem profiles

These comments shed important light on the Chap. 1 mystery where the
outcome can change with the procedure. The *loss of transitivity explains why
pairwise outcomes can differ from methods that can be used only with transitive
voters.* In fact, it now is easy to design illustrating examples. Start with a
reduced profile, say the extreme $(10, 0, 0, 0, 0, 100)$ exhibited in Fig. 3.1.3, with a
desired outcome, and add a Condorcet portion (x, y, x, y, x, y) as exhibited by the
middle triangle. Whatever the choice of x and y, the positional rankings remain
the same. On the other hand, as these x, y values introduce an intransitive

element to the pairwise vote, they can alter the pairwise rankings needed for agendas and so forth. Indeed, by using the far right triangle, x and y values can be chosen to generate conflict between pairwise rankings and other procedures. For instance, c_1 is the Condorcet winner with the inequalities $10 + 2x + y > 100 + 2y + x$, $110 + x + 2y > 2x + y$, or $110 + y > x > 90 + y$; e.g., if $x = 95$, $y = 0$. Cycles can be generated by solving the appropriate inequalities.

The large literature characterizing procedures that always select a Condorcet winner now has another important property; the method cannot honor transitivity. In fact, this answers the question, *"Why can't an organization be more like a person?"* It can. But, if an organization desires rational outcomes, it must use procedures that respect the rational beliefs of its members.

3.1.4 Exercises

1. The motivation for a Condorcet winner is that she would win with any reasonable procedure. To complete the proof, show that for any rankings of pairs where c_1 is not a Condorcet winner, a procedure (that people would accept) can be created where c_1 is not be elected. For $n = 3$, show that if there is a Condorcet winner, she wins no matter which of the three agendas are used. Characterize all pairwise procedures that always select a Condorcet winner when one exists. Show there are profiles where the agenda winner is not a Condorcet winner.

2. Suppose Susie evaluates raspberries, strawberries, and apple pie according to calories, color, and taste. Show it is possible to find transitive rankings for each criterion so that when Susie aggregates these aspects, a cycle emerges. Namely, show that a person who makes decisions by aggregating over several criteria (a connoisseur or one of those wavering faculty members who never can make up his mind) can exhibit cyclic preferences.

3. a. For the four profiles represented in Fig. 2.2.1, use the geometric method of projecting to compute all pairwise elections, and use the geometric method (Prob.1, Sect. 2.2) to compute the plurality outcomes. Mark the ranking regions used in the c_1 tallies for the pairwise outcomes and for the plurality outcome. From the difference, explain the beverage example.
b. In Fig. 2.2.1b, notice how the resulting cycle manifests the symmetry of the numbers for the profile in the representation triangle. To see this symmetry, compute the number of entries to the left and to the right of the vertical dividing line. Next, rotate this triangle so a different edge is horizontal. What is the relative arrangement of entries for the profile relative to the new vertical line. There is only one more rotation; what is found? Relate this symmetry with the fourth-graders' argument.
c. Using the insight from b, find a related but different symmetry profile that exhibits a similar behavior.
d. In part a, the plurality election for the Condorcet profile is computed. Because the tally for each candidate depends only on the entries in the two ranking regions, this $\frac{1}{3}$ value can be split in any desired way between the two regions without effecting the plurality outcome. But, this does change the pairwise outcomes. Find all possible pairwise election outcomes.

4. a. Problem 4, Sect. 1.1, shows how to create a Condorcet profile for any number of candidates. For instance, for $n = 4$, this would be $c_1 \succ c_2 \succ c_3 \succ c_4, c_2 \succ c_3 \succ c_4 \succ c_1, c_3 \succ c_4 \succ c_1 \succ c_2, c_4 \succ c_1 \succ c_2 \succ c_3$. Show that the pairwise outcomes for this Condorcet profile admit the cycle $c_1 \succ c_2, c_2 \succ c_3, c_3 \succ c_4, c_4 \succ c_1$. Show how to rearrange the pairwise rankings in the Condorcet profile to create a confused voter profile where four-voters are of one type and the last is of the remaining type. Generalize to all n.
b. For the more adventurous, construct a physical model of the representation tetrahedron (an equilateral tetrahedron), and identify each vertex with a candidate. In this tetrahedron, plot a four-candidate Condorcet profile, and characterize the positions of the entries when the tetrahedron is placed on a table. Rotate the tetrahedron so that a different face is horizontal,

and note the positions of the entries for the profile. In this way, show how to construct several other Condorcet profiles. (The same geometry holds for all n, but, because the physical rotations must be in a four or higher dimensional space, it becomes a bit difficult to perform.)

5. a. Find all rankings where $c_1 \succ c_2$. From this list, find all rankings where $c_1 \succ c_2$ is weak. Find all rankings where $c_1 \succ c_2, c_3 \succ c_2$. Find all rankings of this type where $c_1 \succ c_2$ has weak intensity. Notice the minimal amount of information about intensity required to ensure transitivity.

b. For $n \geq 3$ candidates, say that $c_1 \succ c_2$ has a k-level intensity if in the full transitive ranking, k candidates separate c_1 and c_2. For $n = 3$, what is the k-level intensity for "strong intensity" and for "weak intensity?" For $n = 5$, give a preference ranking where $c_1 \succ c_2$ has a three-level intensity; give one where this ranking is a one-level intensity. For any n, what are all admissible values of k?

c. We wouldn't expect a sophisticated connoisseur to fall into a trap of cyclic preferences. (See Prob. 2.) Instead, by incorporating the intensity of pairwise comparisons over the various traits, we would expect a well defined ordering to emerge. Similarly, the problem with a pairwise election is that it only uses voters' rankings of a pair of candidates; it ignores all intensity information. Construct a pairwise procedure that uses the intensity information. A test of your procedure is whether it leads to tie votes of all pairs for the Condorcet profile. (For instance, how many "weak" preferences should equal a "strong" preference.)

6. a. Plot the integer profile $(0, 4, 0, 3, 0, 3)$ in a representation triangle, and use the projection approach to show that it defines a pairwise cycle. Find a profile involving confused voters that leads to the same outcome.

b. For this profile, compute the $< c_1, c_2, c_3 >$ agenda outcomes. Use an associated confused voter profile to justify this outcome. (Suggestion: A confused voter tends to view each pair as a separate entity.)

c. Find the reduced profile and use it to determine a "natural ranking."

7. a. For the three voter profile $c_1 \succ c_2 \succ c_3 \succ c_4, c_2 \succ c_3 \succ c_4 \succ c_1, c_3 \succ c_4 \succ c_1 \succ c_2$, it is easy to argue that c_3 should not be the group's top-ranked candidate (e.g., everyone prefers her to c_4). Find a reasonable group ranking for this profile along with a justification. Compute the outcome for each stage of the $< c_2, c_3, c_1, c_4 >$ agenda. After comparing your result with part a, explain what happened. Create a three-voter, five-candidate example and an agenda where *everyone* prefers the same two other candidates to the winning candidate.

b. Create an associated profile, allowing confused voters, that would justify the above election outcomes.

8. Show how the construction of the cube in Prob. 3, Sect. 2.1, represents all possible choices of voters – including confused voters, while the representation triangle only represents the rational voters. How does the representation triangle fit into the cube?

9. a. Plot the integer profiles $\mathbf{p}_1 = (23, 0, 10, 8, 17, 2)$, $\mathbf{p}_2 = (5, 18, 5, 13, 16, 3)$, and $\mathbf{p}_3 = (9, 3, 4, 4, 6, 4)$ on representation triangles. Then, find the Condorcet and the reduced portion for each. Find the pairwise rankings (and the Condorcet winner, if one exits), and the plurality, antiplurality, and BC rankings for the reduced portion of each profile. Next find the pairwise rankings for the original profiles. Explain any differences in outcomes.

b. A positional method is where w_j points are assigned to a voter's jth ranked candidate where $w_1 \geq w_2 \geq w_3$ and $w_1 > w_3$. Using the Condorcet portion of Fig. 3.1.3, show that a positional method always has a complete tie with the Condorcet portion of a profile. In this manner, show that a positional election outcome always is determined by the reduced profile.

c. Using part b and the approach indicated in Fig. 3.1.3, create an example where *all positional methods* have the election outcome $c_3 \succ c_2 \succ c_1$ even though c_2 is the Condorcet winner.

d. Let $cp(\mathbf{p})$ be the portion of all voters in $\mathbf{p}$ creating the Condorcet portion. Compute $cp(\mathbf{p})$, for $\mathbf{p}_j, j = 1, 2, 3$, the profiles of Figs. 3.1.2, 3.1.3, and part c, find the percentage of all voters that define the Condorcet portion of a profile. Use part c and the profiles from the two figures to find a statement about the cp value which ensures that the Condorcet winner differs from the positional procedure winner.

e. Use cp to prove that the Condorcet part of a profile can affect the outcome with the threshold methods introduced in Sect. 2.1.

f. Suppose $\mathbf{p}$ has no reduced portion; it only has a Condorcet portion. Show that the sum of points received by each candidate in the two pairwise elections is the same.

10. a. Show that a profile is a reduced profile if and only if there are no voters of a type with an odd subscript and no voters of a type with an even subscript.

b. Show that the sum of two Condorcet portions of a profile is a Condorcet portion. Show that the sum of two reduced portions of a profile can have a Condorcet portion. Using part a, find a condition so that the sum of two reduced profiles is a reduced profile.

11. a. This exercise hints at what can happen with more candidates. Using the approach described in Prob. 4, Sect. 1.1. create a four-candidate Condorcet profile. Explain why the outcome for this profile should be a complete tie. What is the positional election outcome of this profile? Why? Find the tallies for the resulting pairwise cycle. What would be the tally for each pair in a cycle for a n-candidate Condorcet profile?

b. There are four sets of three candidates; for each set compute the plurality and BC outcomes. Compare the conclusion with part a and find an explanation (if you can).

c. Start with the profile where 20 voter have the ranking $c_1 \succ c_2 \succ c_3 \succ c_4$ and 10 have $c_2 \succ c_1 \succ c_3 \succ c_4$. Find the plurality and BC outcome for the four-candidate set and the four three-candidate sets. Now, add a Condorcet portion to this profile so that c_2 is the Condorcet winner. (For $n = 3$ candidates, there are two choices for Condorcet profiles; for $n = 4$ there are six. In general, there are $(n-1)!$ choices.) What happens to the three-candidate elections? Can you add a Condorcet portion to the original profile so that c_4 is the winner in some set?

3.2 Geometry of Pairwise Voting

To appreciate the difficulties caused by pairwise voting ignoring transitivity, I use geometry and some "m equations in n unknowns" algebra. Incidentally, the geometry explains the obsession of pairwise voting to reward the phantom confused voters.

Using the earlier (Sect. 3.1) "projection and summation" description, a pairwise vote converts a profile from $Si(6)$ into a value in $[-1, 1]$. Thus the $\{c_1, c_2\}$ majority vote mapping $f_{\{c_1,c_2\}} : Si(6) \to [-1, 1]$ is

$$(3.2.1) \qquad f_{\{c_1,c_2\}}(\mathbf{p}) = \sum_{j=1}^{3} p_j - \sum_{j=4}^{6} p_j.$$

If $f_{\{c_1,c_2\}}(\mathbf{p}) > 0$, the first summation is larger, so more voters are to the left of the $c_1 \sim c_2$ line than to the right; c_1 beats c_2. Similarly, if $f_{\{c_1,c_2\}}(\mathbf{p}) < 0$, then c_2 beats c_1. The last possibility, $f_{\{c_1,c_2\}}(\mathbf{p}) = 0$, is the tie ranking $c_1 \sim c_2$.

Similar equations hold for the other two pairs. By using the profile to determine who would vote for whom, we have

$$f_{\{c_2,c_3\}}(\mathbf{p}) = p_1 + p_5 + p_6 - \sum_{j=2}^{4} p_j,$$

$$(3.2.2) \qquad f_{\{c_3,c_1\}}(\mathbf{p}) = \sum_{j=3}^{5} p_j - (p_1 + p_2 + p_6),$$

where a positive value $f_{\{c_i,c_j\}}(\mathbf{p})$ value corresponds to the majority ranking $c_i \succ c_j$.

To develop techniques and intuition, start with the simpler problem of comparing $x = f_{\{c_1,c_2\}}(\mathbf{p})$ and $z = f_{\{c_3,c_1\}}(\mathbf{p})$. The potential values are $-1 \le x \le 1$, $-1 \le z \le 1$; so (x,z) is a point in the square $[-1,1] \times [-1,1]$ depicted in Fig. 3.2.1b. We want to find the image subset; i.e., those (x,z) points that are election outcomes.

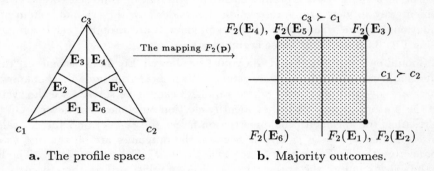

a. The profile space   **b.** Majority outcomes.

Fig. 3.2.1. The unanimity profile representation of majority vote outcomes

To review why $[-1,1] \times [-1,1]$ is a square, observe that a x value, imposes no a priori reason to restrict the accompanying z value; it might be any $[-1,1]$ value. For each x, then, the potential (x,z) combinations are represented by attaching a vertical line interval, $[-1,1]$, of potential z values to the x point. By varying the value of $x \in [-1,1]$, the vertical line intervals sweep out the square.

The equations for the two pairs define the mapping

$$(3.2.3) \qquad F_2 = (f_{\{c_1,c_2\}}, f_{\{c_3,c_1\}}) : Si(6) \to [-1,1] \times [-1,1].$$

A majority vote outcome is based on three equations (the two in Eq. 3.2.3 and the profile constraint $\sum_{j=1}^{6} p_j = 1$ from $\mathbf{p} \in Si(6)$) in six variables, so the algebraic techniques of Sect. 1.4 apply. It seems difficult to characterize all possible election outcomes, the image of F_2, but it is not. Remember, F_2 is linear and $Si(6)$ is the convex hull defined by the vertices $\{\mathbf{E}_j\}_{j=1}^{6}$ of unanimity profiles. So, according to the convexity property of Sect. 1.4, the set of election outcomes is the convex hull with vertices $\{F_2(\mathbf{E}_j)\}_{j=1}^{6}$.

It is easy to compute an unanimity outcome $F_2(\mathbf{E}_j)$ because one candidate from each pair receives all of the vote. Namely the unanimity election points are of the form $(\pm 1, \pm 1)$, so they are vertices of the square in Fig. 3.2.1. For example, $\mathbf{E}_3$ requires all voters to believe $c_3 \succ c_1 \succ c_2$, so c_1 wins all of the votes in the $\{c_1,c_2\}$ election while c_3 receives all votes in the $\{c_3,c_1\}$ election. Thus, $F_2(\mathbf{E}_3) = (1,1)$. The remaining unanimity vertices are indicated in the figure; the shaded area – the full square – is the convex hull defining the F_2 image set of election outcomes. As the image set is the full square, all $[-1,1]^2$ points are outcomes for some election; anything can happen.

Notice how easily elections can be understood just by computing the unanimity outcomes! This approach is further illustrated with the following profile restrictions.

Example 3.2.1. A way to eliminate paradoxes is to impose profile restrictions. The idea is that by restricting which voter types are admitted, "good" election relationships might emerge.[7] Actually, we already have done this; requiring transitive preferences is a profile restriction eliminating confused voters. A convenient way to view profile restriction is consider how the original system of m equations change when some of the n unknowns are dropped. (I recommend using Fig. 3.2.1 to follow these arguments.)

a. Should only type-three and -six voters be allowed, Eq. 3.2.3 becomes a "three equation, two unknown (p_3, p_6) system." With more equations than unknowns, there are $q_{1,2}$ and $q_{3,1}$ values where Eq. 3.2.3 cannot be solved (See the system on the bottom of page 24.); they identify election outcomes that never occur. In particular, the specified profile restriction forces the $\{c_1, c_2\}$ and $\{c_3, c_1\}$ tallies to agree; i.e., $q_{1,2} = q_{3,1}$. This is because the outcomes are on the line $y = x$ connecting the $F_2(\mathbf{E}_6)$ vertex $(-1, -1)$ with the $F_2(\mathbf{E}_3)$ vertex $(1, 1)$. (The line is the convex hull of the two vertices.) Election relationships, then, occur when the image is a proper subset of the full square; not everything can happen. But, what an expensive relationship; it is valid only for profiles, $(0, 0, p_3, 0, 0, 1 - p_3)$, constrained to live on a one-dimensional edge of $Si(6)$. Namely, this restriction allows us to say a lot about very little.

b. As many art collections readily prove, with care, it is possible to spend vast sums of money to achieve mediocrity. Similarly, it is possible to incur the high cost of a profile restriction without obtaining any benefits. This happens by excluding all type-one and -five voters. (The admissible profiles are on the $Si(6)$ surface defined by the unanimity vertices $\{\mathbf{E}_2, \mathbf{E}_3, \mathbf{E}_4, \mathbf{E}_6\}$; Eq. 3.2.3 becomes a system of three equations in four unknowns.) The restriction admits no election relationships because the images of the four remaining unanimity profiles $(\{\mathbf{E}_2, \mathbf{E}_3, \mathbf{E}_4, \mathbf{E}_6\})$ are the four vertices of the square. As the image is everything, anything can happen.

c. Instead of the useless part b restriction, just exclude type-three voters. (So Eq. 3.2.3 becomes a system of three equations in five unknowns; the profiles are in a four-dimensional boundary surface of $Si(6)$.) Accompanying the expulsion of the type-three voters is the $(1, 1)$ vertex of the square. As the convex hull of the remaining three vertices – a triangle – is a *proper* subset of the square, we have election relationships; not everything can happen! Notice from parts b and c that it is not the size of your profile restriction that matters, but how you use it. □

All Three Pairs of Candidates. The real issue is to compare the outcomes of all three pairs of candidates, so let's do it. Because $f_{\{c_i, c_j\}}(\mathbf{p}) \in [-1, 1]$, the

---

[7]Conclusions based on these restrictions are valid only should the voters carefully select preferences in the specified manner.

three-pair outcome is a point in $[-1,1] \times [-1,1] \times [-1,1] = [-1,1]^3$. To describe $[-1,1]^3$, recall that $[-1,1] \times [-1,1]$ is a square where each point identifies an outcome for two pairwise rankings. Until there is reason to restrict the third outcome, we must admit the possibility that it can be any $[-1,1]$ value. Thus, attach to each point in the square an interval $[-1,1]$ in an orthogonal direction. By varying the point in the square, the line traces out a cube; i.e., $[-1,1]^3$ is a three-dimensional cube. So, the mapping for the three pairwise elections,

$$F_3 = (f_{\{c_1,c_2\}}, f_{\{c_2,c_3\}}, f_{\{c_3,c_1\}}) : Si(6) \to [-1,1]^3,$$

converts profiles into cube points. To understand these elections, we need to characterize the F_3 image.

Start with the ranking regions of the cube. A point in the positive orthant (i.e., a point (x,y,z) where all components are positive) defines the cycle $c_1 \succ c_2, c_2 \succ c_3, c_3 \succ c_1$. Without imagination, this is called a *positive cycle*. Similarly, a point in the negative orthant defines the reversed, or *negative cycle* $c_2 \succ c_1, c_1 \succ c_3, c_3 \succ c_2$. With the exception of $(0,0,0)$, a boundary point of these two orthants (on a coordinate axis or plane) represents a quasi-transitive ranking. (See Prob. 5, Sect. 2.1.) All remaining cube points define transitive rankings. (With $n \geq 3$ candidates, there are $\binom{n}{2} = \frac{n(n-1)}{2}$ pairs, so the pairwise comparisons defines a cube in a $\binom{n}{2}$ dimensional space. The analysis of the corresponding mapping, $F_n : Si(n!) \to [-1,1]^{\binom{n}{2}}$, is similar to that developed for $n = 3$. Differences are caused by the higher dimensional geometry which admits all sorts of other possibilities; e.g., there are ranking regions corresponding to all imaginable pathologies associated with binary relationships.)

The F_3 image is used so often that it is worth creating a physical model. (Cut up a cubic rubber eraser as indicated or see page 100.) To find all possible election outcomes, first plot the unanimity outcomes $\{F_3(\mathbf{E}_j)\}_{j=1}^6$; the F_3 image set is the associated convex hull. Using the earlier F_2 argument about unanimous votes, it follows that $F_3(\mathbf{E}_j)$ has the form $(\pm 1, \pm 1, \pm 1)$; it is a vertex of the cube $[-1,1]^3$. Again, the assignment of $F_3(\mathbf{E}_j)$ to a vertex is determined by the three pairwise rankings defined by $\mathbf{E}_j$. Therefore, six vertices of the cube are marked and identified with different unanimity profiles.

As the cube has more vertices (eight) than $Si(6)$ has unanimity profiles (six), two vertices are not assigned anything. They are, of course, the cyclic vertices $(1,1,1)$ and $(-1,-1,-1)$; each vertex is the "unanimity" outcome for a "confused voter." The convex hull of the remaining six vertices, depicted in Fig. 3.2.3, is the F_3 image set; call this set of all possible pairwise election outcomes the *representation cube*. So, with a cube, or rubber eraser, discard the vertices $(1,1,1), -(1,1,1)$ and other points that are not assigned a rational outcome by slicing through the vertices with odd indices, $\{F_3(\mathbf{E}_j)\}_{j=1,3,5}$, and put aside (but do not discard) the resulting corner piece. (The scar from this operation is the lightly shaded region in the figure which passes through the center of each of the three faces of the original cube.) Next, slice through the even vertices, $\{F_3(\mathbf{E}_j)\}_{j=2,4,6}$ (indicated by the dashed, hidden lines), and put away that corner. (According to standard equations for volumes of tetrahedron, the slicing process eliminates $\frac{1}{3}$ of the original volume of the cube.) All remaining points are election outcomes for some $\mathbf{p} \in Si(6)$; this is the *representation cube*.

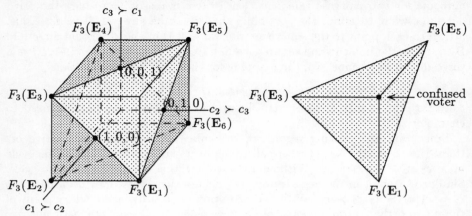

Fig. 3.2.2. The representation cube for the three pairs of candidates

A way to view this construction is that we impose the profile restriction of excluding confused voters. Thus, the development of the representation cube mimics the geometric construction of profile restrictions in Example 3.2.1. If for some reason confused voters are admitted, the F_3 image would be the full cube. But note, even after discarding large regions of $[-1, 1]^3$ to eliminate confused voters, the outcome is not sufficiently discriminatory to make F_3 transitive. For instance, the lightly shaded area passes through the points $(1, 0, 0), (0, 1, 0)$, and $(0, 0, 1)$, so the representation cube includes points in the cycle generating positive orthant. Similarly, the triangular hidden line region passes through the negative orthant. The convex geometry forces the representation cube to meet all 27 ranking regions, so, with respect to admissible pairwise election rankings, "anything can happen!"[8]

3.2.1 The Geometry of Cycles

Ideally, we want to compare profiles with their associated election outcomes. This goal can be attained through geometry,

Rectangular coordinates describe a point in terms of its distances in the three coordinate directions. For instance, $(1, 0, 0)$, defining the rankings $c_1 \succ c_2, c_1 \sim c_3, c_2 \sim c_3$, is the farthest point on the $c_1 \succ c_2$ axis; it is on the edge of the

---

[8] There are three rankings for each pair – one is a tie vote and the other two has one candidate winning – so there are $3^3 = 27$ potential rankings. With n candidates, there are $3^{\binom{n}{2}}$ ranking regions for the majority vote comparisons, and all can occur! For $n = 3$, as each cycle generating regions is a tetrahedron with volume $\frac{1}{6}$, the cyclic regions constitute only $\frac{1}{16}$ of the total volume of the image set.

representation cube midway between $F_3(\mathbf{E}_3)$ and $F_3(\mathbf{E}_1)$. By linearity,

$$(1,0,0) = \frac{1}{2}(F_3(\mathbf{E}_1) + F_3(\mathbf{E}_3)) = F_3(\frac{\mathbf{E}_1 + \mathbf{E}_3}{2}),$$

so this election outcome occurs iff the profile evenly splits the voters between types-one and three. This makes sense; half the voters have the rankings $c_1 \succ c_2, c_2 \succ c_3, c_1 \succ c_3$ while the other half have $c_1 \succ c_2, c_3 \succ c_2, c_3 \succ c_1$, so they agree on the $c_1 \succ c_2$ outcome but they are indecisive over the other two pairs. Likewise, the outcomes $(0,1,0)$ and $(0,0,1)$ occur, respectively, with the profiles $\frac{\mathbf{E}_1+\mathbf{E}_5}{2}$ and $\frac{\mathbf{E}_3+\mathbf{E}_5}{2}$.

Similarly, a point is in the triangular lightly shaded region T_1 (one of the new faces obtained by the cutting process on the plane $x + y + z = 1$ guided by the odd vertices $F_3(\mathbf{E}_1)$, $F_3(\mathbf{E}_3)$, $F_3(\mathbf{E}_5)$) if and only if all voters are of types-one, three, and five. By linearity, $(x, y, z) \in T_1$ is expressed as

$$x(1,0,0) + y(0,1,0) + z(0,0,1)$$
$$= xF_3(\frac{\mathbf{E}_1 + \mathbf{E}_3}{2}) + yF_3(\frac{\mathbf{E}_1 + \mathbf{E}_5}{2}) + zF_3(\frac{\mathbf{E}_3 + \mathbf{E}_5}{2})$$

(3.2.4)
$$= F_3(\frac{x + y}{2}\mathbf{E}_1 + \frac{x + z}{2}\mathbf{E}_3 + \frac{y + z}{2}\mathbf{E}_5),$$

so the unique supporting profile, $(\frac{x+y}{2}, 0, \frac{x+z}{2}, 0, \frac{y+z}{2}, 0)$, involves only odd voter types. Likewise, a point (x, y, z) on the hidden, opposing triangular surface T_2 (the part of the plane $x + y + z = -1$ denoted by the dashed lines in Fig. 3.2.2), is uniquely supported by profiles with even voter types $(0, -\frac{x+y}{2}, 0, -\frac{y+x}{2}, 0, -\frac{x+z}{2})$. So, at least in the special settings of T_1, T_2, each election outcome is uniquely identified with a profile.

These special cases are interesting because they define the regions of troublesome pairwise outcomes. For instance, the positive orthant corresponds to the positive cycles, and the representation cube boundary in this orthant is the portion of T_1 where all components of $(x, y, z) \in T_1$ are positive. This triangular portion, then, identifies the extreme *positive cycles*. From the geometry, a profile for such a cycle involves only odd voter types. Because $(\frac{1}{3}, \frac{1}{3}, \frac{1}{3}) \in T_1$ is farthest from any transitive ranking, it is the "most" positive cyclic election outcome. In particular, $(\frac{1}{3}, \frac{1}{3}, \frac{1}{3})$ arises iff the profile is the Condorcet profile $\mathbf{p}_m = (\frac{1}{3}, 0, \frac{1}{3}, 0, \frac{1}{3}, 0)$ from the departmental meeting. Similar comments apply to the portion of T_2 that meets the negative orthant and the election outcome $(-\frac{1}{3}, -\frac{1}{3}, -\frac{1}{3})$ with its unique, even-voter profile $\mathbf{p}_m^r = (0, \frac{1}{3}, 0, \frac{1}{3}, 0, \frac{1}{3})$.

This geometry allows us to answer natural questions about pairwise elections. For instance, can we be assured that no cycles occur if c_1 overwhelmingly beats c_2? (No.) How extreme can the pairwise victory margins be while admitting a cycle? How large are profile sets supporting certain outcomes? The following sample of answers has assertions that different $\mathbf{q}$ choices are supported by profile sets with different dimensions; these statements come from a "m equations in n unknowns define a $n - m$ dimensional space of solutions" argument. (For instance, $2x + y = 6$ has the one dimensional solution $y = 6 - 2x$ obtained by varying the x value.) In reading this theorem, each $\mathbf{q}$ should be located in Figs. 3.2.2, 3.2.3, or on a constructed version of a representation cube.

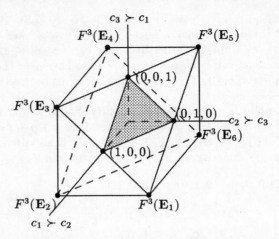

Fig. 3.2.3. Can cycles (the shaded region) be avoided?

Theorem 3.2.1. a. *For each pair of candidates, choose any of the three possible rankings. There are profiles that simultaneously support all rankings.*

b. If $\mathbf{q}$ is an interior point of the representation cube, it is supported by a two-dimensional linear subspace of profiles in $Si(6)$. If $\mathbf{q}$ is on a surface of the representation cube, it is supported by a unique profile.

c. For any small $\epsilon > 0$ value, there are profiles where a cycle occurs even though c_1 beats c_2 with more than $1 - \epsilon$ of the total vote. On the other hand, it is impossible to have a cycle where each candidate beats another candidate with more than two-thirds of the vote.

Compare c with the Pope selection (Sect. 1.3); requiring the winner to receive one more than two-thirds of the vote eliminates all dangers of a cycle where another candidate receives more votes. For $n \geq 2$ candidates, replace $\frac{2}{3}$ with $\frac{n-1}{n}$.

Idea of the Proof. The first part of c follows by choosing $(1 - \frac{\epsilon}{2}, \frac{\epsilon}{4}, \frac{\epsilon}{4})$ from the cyclic region of T_1. This point is in the positive orthant of the representation cube, so the conclusion follows. (To find a supporting profile, use Eq. 3.2.4.) The second part of c follows by using the "most cyclic" point $(\frac{1}{3}, \frac{1}{3}, \frac{1}{3})$. For example, $x = \frac{1}{3}$ means that c_1 beats c_2 with two-thirds of the vote.

The proof for the assertion about $\mathbf{q} \in T_1$ is given above. For the remaining assertions, suppose a profile is in the two-dimensional boundary of the representation cube where $x = 1$. From the geometry, this result requires *all* voters to prefer $c_1 \succ c_2$; consequently, there are no voters of types four, five or six. A supporting profile, then, is in the two-dimensional boundary surface of $Si(6)$ defined by $\{E_1, E_2, E_3\}$. The remaining conclusions follow with similar arguments. $\square$

3.2.2 Cyclic Profile Coordinates

A standard trick in geometry is to invent convenient coordinate systems to simplify the properties being studied. For instance, Cartesian coordinates[9] are used to analyze rectangular objects while spherical coordinates are employed to position points on spheres. Similarly, I introduce "profile coordinates" so we can "see" which profiles define which pairwise election outcomes. This is done by dividing the voter types into natural groupings, and then determining the election outcomes for each subgroup. The $\mathbf{q}$ outcome combines the election outcomes for the two subgroups by using the proportion of all voters in each subgroup.

Remember "counting off" to choose teams in those school gym courses? Similarly, divide the voter types into the "odds" and "evens" as identified by their subscripts. The "odds," then, are the voters of types $\{1, 3, 5\}$ while the "evens" are of types $\{2, 4, 6\}$. Recall, the outcome of a profile that consists only of odd voters is in T_1. Similarly, with only even voters in a profile, the outcome is in T_2. These outcomes are

$$F_3((p_1, 0, p_3, 0, p_5, 0)) = (p_1 + p_3 - p_5, p_1 + p_5 - p_3, p_3 + p_5 - p_1)$$

(3.2.5)

$$F_3((0, p_2, 0, p_4, 0, p_6)) = -(p_4 + p_6 - p_2, p_2 + p_4 - p_6, p_2 + p_6 - p_4).$$

While Eq. 3.2.5 specifies the precise election values, the geometry is more useful. For example, an outcome $\alpha \in T_1$ close to $F_3(E_1)$ clearly requires type-one voters to dominate the odd group.

To describe $F_3(\mathbf{p})$ for $\mathbf{p} = (p_1, \ldots, p_6)$, suppose only the odd voters vote. To resolve the problem that $(p_1, 0, p_3, 0, p_5, 0)$ is not a profile when $p_1 + p_3 + p_5 = d < 1$, use the profile $\frac{1}{d}(p_1, 0, p_3, 0, p_5, 0)$. This motivates the definition of the *cyclic group coordinate representation of a profile*, (α, β, d).

$$d = p_1 + p_3 + p_5$$

$$a_i = \frac{p_i}{d}, \; i = 1, 3, 5, \quad \alpha = (a_1 + a_3 - a_5, a_1 + a_5 - a_3, a_3 + a_5 - a_1) \in T_1$$

(3.2.6)

$$b_j = \frac{p_j}{1-d}, \; j = 2, 4, 6, \quad \beta = -(b_4 + b_6 - b_2, b_2 + b_4 - b_6, b_2 + b_6 - b_4) \in T_2.$$

By definition, $\mathbf{p} = d(a_1, 0, a_3, 0, a_5, 0) + (1-d)(0, b_2, 0, b_4, 0, b_6)$, so by the linearity of F_3 it follows that

(3.2.7)
$$F_3(\mathbf{p}) = d\alpha + (1-d)\beta.$$

---

[9]These coordinates are attributed to R. Des Cartes (1595-1650). As true with most discoveries, other philosophers, such as I. M. Des Horst, experimented with related concepts. While I have not found reliable publication dates for Des Horst's weighty contributions, I doubt that Des Horst came before Des Cartes.

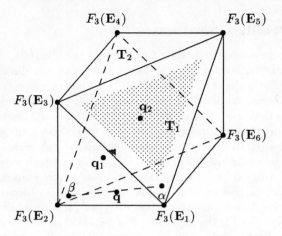

Fig. 3.2.4. The $\alpha - \beta$ line at the bottom of the figure represents a profile. For Example 3.2.2, the light shaded area is the α cone for $\mathbf{q}_2 = (.1, .1.1)$; the small dark region is the profile cone for $\mathbf{q}_1 = (.9, 0, 0)$.

Stated in words, α is the odd's outcome, β is the even's, d measures the relative strength of one subgroup over the other, and the election is a weighted sum of α, β as determined by d. Geometrically, plot $\alpha \in T_1$, $\beta \in T_2$, and then find the point on the line segment joining α and β that is d of the distance from β to α. Thus, *the line segment and the designated point represent the profile.* Notice how the designated point does double duty; it also designates the election outcome $F_3(\mathbf{p}) = \mathbf{q}$. (See the bottom portion of Fig. 3.2.4.) A virtue of the cyclic coordinates, then, is that a profile and its outcome are jointly represented. Justification for calling (α, β, d) a *coordinate representation* of $\mathbf{p}$ follows.

Proposition 3.2.2. *There is a smooth, one to one mapping from the profiles* $\mathbf{p} \in Si(6)$ *onto the set of points* (α, β, d) *where* $\alpha \in T_1, \beta \in T_2, d \in [0, 1]$.

This technical statement is a "Robert also can be called Bob" assertion; it means that each profile can be called by its $\mathbf{p}$ or its (α, β, d) name, and that each name uniquely identifies the other name. The "name changes," or the analytic relationships between the two profile representations are given by Eq. 3.2.5 and the equations following Eq. 3.2.4. Even though the α and β values translate immediately into a_i, b_j values, the geometric positioning of α, β (the line segment) and the designated point (the value of d) are more suggestive of the properties of $\mathbf{p}$. For instance, an α near $F(\mathbf{E}_1)$ (as in Fig. 3.2.4) requires most odd voters to be type-one and a large d value (where the designated point is close to the T_1 surface) requires more odd than even voters. Similarly, if β is on a T_2 edge, then there are no voters of a particular even type. Thus, the geometric positions of α and β determine which voter types dominate in the profile while the proximity of the designated point to T_1 or T_2 indicates the proportion of odd and even voters. Also, the $Si(6)$ boundaries are identified with points on the edges of T_1, T_2 and/or where the d values are 0 and 1. For instance, the edge of the representation cube connecting $F_3(\mathbf{E}_1)$ with $F_3(\mathbf{E}_2)$ corresponds to the one-dimensional $Si(6)$ edge of normalized profiles of the form $(p, 1-p, 0, 0, 0, 0)$, $p \in [0, 1]$.

3.2.3 Power of Cyclic Coordinates

The power of cyclic group coordinates can be exhibited by extending Theorem 3.2.1 and by describing all profiles defining cycles. As a starting point, observe that Theorem 3.2.1 offers only crude descriptions about profile sets. It asserts, for instance, that $\mathbf{q}$ in the interior of the representation cube is supported by a two-dimensional set of profiles in $Si(6)$. But, *which* two-dimensional set; *what kinds* of profiles are involved? These more important issues are answered immediately with the (α, β, d) profile representation.

The approach is simple; because *any line segment* passing through $\mathbf{q}$ defines a profile where $F_3(\mathbf{p}) = \mathbf{q}$, the *cone of all such line segments* defines the supporting profile set. To see how to construct the cone, think of the profile line segment as a pencil. Grab the pencil at $\mathbf{q}$ and wiggle it. All ways this pencil can be moved with the ends in T_1 and T_2 identify all profiles supporting the $\mathbf{q}$ election outcome. The set of admissible positions for $\alpha \in T_1$ is $\mathbf{q}$'s α-cone; the β-cone is similarly described. Again, for each profile (each line), the position of α and β determines which voter types dominate while the proximity of $\mathbf{q}$ to T_1 or T_2 explains the proportion of odd and even voters.

This geometry makes it easy to "see" the trade-offs to realize a specified $\mathbf{q}$. For instance, by moving one endpoint, say α, the pivoting role of $\mathbf{q}$ forces the other endpoint, β, to move in an opposite direction. (Try it with a pencil.) Extreme changes occur with large or small d value because the line is held near an end (with the pencil, near the eraser or point); even the slightest change in the short end induces a major change on the other side. For instance, to keep the $\mathbf{q}$ outcome with d near unity, a small change in the distribution of the even voters must be compensated by a major redistribution of odd voters. Other extremes arise when, say, the β end is on the boundary of T_2. Indeed, by wiggling the line to find the extreme α and β vertices, the α- and β-cones are traced out.

For $\mathbf{q}$, an α choice uniquely determines the β, d values. The two degrees of freedom in selecting α depict the two-dimensional surface of profiles ensured by Theorem 3.2.1. Not only does each line segment illustrate which voter types are required, but *the size of the α and β-cones indicate the relative size of the set of supporting profiles.* Clearly, if $\mathbf{q}$ can brag about a larger α- and β-cone than $\mathbf{q}_1$, then $\mathbf{q}$ has a larger supporting set of profiles.

To more accurately assess the size of a profile set, use the smaller of the α or β-cones. To see why, suppose only three of 10,000 voters belong to the evens. With $d = \frac{9,997}{10,000}$, $\mathbf{q}$ is so close to T_1 that the distribution of even voters is of little interest; it is the distribution of the odd voters that matters. Stated in geometric terms using the $\mathbf{q}$ pivoting action, if $d \geq \frac{1}{2}$ a small α change creates a huge β change, so the smaller α-cone better indicates the size of the profile set. Similarly, if $d \leq \frac{1}{2}$, the β-cone is the better choice.

Example 3.2.2. a. The integer profile $(5, 3, 7, 2, 1, 1)$ has the normalized profile $(\frac{1}{4}, \frac{3}{20}, \frac{7}{20}, \frac{1}{10}, \frac{1}{20}, \frac{1}{10}) \in Si(6)$ and, according to Eq. 3.2.6, the cyclic coordinate representation $(\alpha = (\frac{11}{13}, \frac{-1}{13}, \frac{3}{13}), \beta = -(\frac{1}{7}, \frac{3}{7}, \frac{3}{7}), d = \frac{13}{20})$.

To design a profile that "nearly" defines a cycle, but the actual outcome is the transitive $c_1 \succ c_2$, $c_2 \succ c_3$, $c_1 \succ c_3$ (or, $x > 0, y > 0, z < 0$), choose α in the cyclic region near the $F_3(\mathbf{E}_1) - F_3(\mathbf{E}_3)$ edge, β in the negative cyclic region near the $F_3(\mathbf{E}_2) - F_3(\mathbf{E}_6)$ edge, and d near $\frac{1}{2}$. One such profile is $(\alpha = (\frac{5}{10}, \frac{4}{10}, \frac{1}{10}), \beta = -(\frac{5}{10}, \frac{1}{10}, \frac{4}{10}), d = \frac{6}{10})$. By use of Eqs. 3.2.4 - 6, this corresponds to $a = (0.45, 0, 0.3, 0, 0.25, 0), b = (0, 0.25, 0, 0.3, 0, 0.45)$ which defines $(0.27, 0.1, 0.18, 0.12, 0.15, 0.18) \in Si(6)$. Alternatively, choose $\mathbf{q}$ to satisfy the specified condition and then find the coordinate representation of any line segment passing through $\mathbf{q}$. There are, of course, a cone of examples. The main point is that *with the cyclic coordinate system, constructing profiles to illustrate specified outcomes becomes a simple exercise.*

b. To illustrate how to use cyclic coordinates to compare the profile sets supporting different election outcomes, consider $\mathbf{q}_1 = (0.9, 0, 0)$ and $\mathbf{q}_2 = (0.1, 0.1, 0.1)$. Theorem 3.2.1 ensures that both $\mathbf{q}_j$ outcomes are supported by a two-dimensional set of profiles, but, which is larger? The answer, illustrated in Fig. 3.2.4, comes from comparing the α-cones of each $\mathbf{q}_j$.

The pivot point $\mathbf{q}_1$ is so close to the front surface of the representation cube that it severely restricts the wiggling of profile lines; i.e., it restricts the size of the $\mathbf{q}_1$ profile cone. Think of this in terms of using a small child's teeter-totter where the low pivot point quickly acquaints you with your knees. Similarly with $\mathbf{q}_1$, even when β is on a T_2 edge, the restrictive pivot action of $\mathbf{q}_1$ keeps α close to the same T_1 edge. Again, on a teeter-totter, the maximum height of an end is determined by the pivot point when the other end is on the "boundary" – the ground. Similarly, the line going through the T_2 corner $(1, -1, -1)$ and $\mathbf{q}_1$ is $(1 - t)(1, -1, -1) + t(0.9, 0, 0) = (1 - 0.1t, -1 + t, -1 + t)$, so it reaches T_1 (the $x + y + z = 1$ plane) where $t = \frac{2}{1.9}$. Thus $\alpha = (0.895, 0.053, 0.053)$. By considering the other extreme $\beta \in T_2$ locations, the α-cone is the triangle defined by the vertices $(0.895, 0.053, 0.053), (1, -0.053, 0.053), (1, 0.053, -0.053)$. This cone of profiles is so small that its size is exaggerated in Fig. 3.2.4.

Compare $\mathbf{q}_1$'s fate with that of $\mathbf{q}_2$. As the election outcome (and pivot point) $\mathbf{q}_2$ is sufficiently far from the T_1 or T_2 edges, $\mathbf{q}_2$ allows considerable of the wiggling of profile lines. In other words, the more central $\mathbf{q}_2$ location permits wider swings in the admissible profile line segments. Consequently, we must (accurately) expect $\mathbf{q}_2$ to be supported by a larger profile set than $\mathbf{q}_1$. Again, the α-cone is found by drawing the three lines from the T_2 vertices through $\mathbf{q}_2$; namely, the α-cone is the triangle with three vertices obtained by permuting the values $-0.4, 0.7, 0.7$. (Thus, for example, if an odd voter-type has less than $\frac{1-0.4}{2} = 0.3$ of all the odd voters, then α is not in this triangle and $\mathbf{q}_2$ is not an admissible outcome.) This much larger triangle, reflecting the larger numbers of profiles, is the lightly shaded region of Fig. 3.2.4.

To underscore the care needed to compare α-cones, observe that the profile cone for $\mathbf{q}_3 = -(0.1, 0.1, 0.1)$ just reverses the roles of the odd and even voter types for $\mathbf{q}_2$, so both outcomes have the same size sets of supporting profiles. However, the $\mathbf{q}_3$ α-cone is all of T_1, and its β-cone is mirrors the $\mathbf{q}_2$ α-cone of T_1. This is because $-(0.1, 0.1, 0.1)$ is closer to T_2 than to T_1 ($d < \frac{1}{2}$), so the pivot action of $\mathbf{q}$ is more sensitive to small changes of the T_2 endpoint. Thus, the smaller cone in the closer region, T_2, is the better indicator of the size of the profile set.[10]

c. With cyclic coordinates, it is easy to determine relationships between profiles and election outcomes. For instance, choose any two points $\alpha \in T_1, \beta \in T_2$. Unless these points satisfy $\beta = -\alpha$ (which is a necessary and sufficient condition for the connecting line segment to pass through the origin), some portion of the connecting line misses the positive and the negative orthants. Consequently, *for any $\beta \neq -\alpha$, there is an open interval of d values where the election outcomes of the (α, β, d) profiles are transitive.* This statement illustrates the importance of the variable d. □

This profile coordinate system, then, makes it geometrically clear wha. profiles and how many of them support different outcomes. This tool is exploited in Sect. 3.3 to understand Black's profile restrictions that prevent cycles. But first, let's examine what this geometry tells us about the phantom voters.

3.2.4 The Return of Confused Voters

To understand how and why the phantom confused voters strongly influence pairwise voting, start with the "fairness" notion that an outcome should reflect the type of voters who dominate a profile. For instance, should almost all voters believe $c_1 \succ c_3 \succ c_2$, then this should be the conclusion. With the exception of the cyclic regions, this fairness is supported by the geometry of pairwise voting; the $\mathbf{q}$ ranking is that of the nearest vertex in the representation cube. Moreover, by computing the profile cones, we find that if $\mathbf{q}$ is close to a particular vertex, voters of that type dominate in the supporting profiles.

Remember, the pairwise vote cannot distinguish between rational or confused preferences. So, to analyze the role of the confused voter, bring these voters back by dropping the "transitive voter" profile restriction. Namely, consider what happens when the excised vertices are glued back on. The fairness criterion mandates that the $\mathbf{q}$ outcome should reflect the voter type of the nearest vertex. So, with a $\mathbf{q} \in T_1$ outcome and with the return of the positive confused voter, there are the four, rather than three possibilities indicated in Fig. 3.2.5a. Observe that *the cyclic rankings are closer to the confused voter vertex than any other!* This geometry, then, supports the assertion that, from the nondiscriminating perspective of the pairwise vote, cycles are fair, logical conclusions. We know that the confused voters have been excluded, but the pairwise vote does not.

---

[10] These cones are useful indicators, but they do not provide accurate values.

Without this knowledge and exhibiting a sense of fairness, the cycle is the only possible outcome.

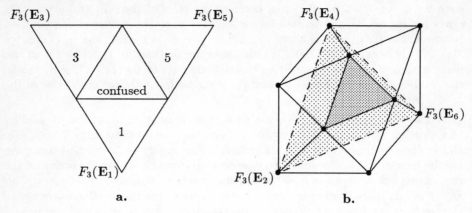

Fig. 3.2.5. The impact of confused voters.

The geometry of fairness extends. In the full cube, the points in a cyclic region are closest to a confused voter vertex. Again, because these pairwise voting cycles merely reflect the procedure's tendency to be "fair" (so the outcome reflects the type of the nearest vertex), the cyclic outcome is as it should be.

In Sect. 3.1.1, the Condorcet triplet was torn into pairwise components and reconstituted into a confused voter profile. This reconstruction is easy to do with cyclic coordinates. For instance, not only can $\mathbf{q} = (\frac{1}{3}, \frac{1}{3}, \frac{1}{3})$ be represented by the odd voters, but, because it is on the line connecting the confused voters, it admits the representation $\mathbf{q} = \frac{2}{3}(1, 1, 1) + \frac{1}{3}(-1, -1, -1)$. This second representation is a geometric description of Eq. 3.1.1. More generally, instead of restricting the α endpoint of a line to T_1, let α be anywhere in the solid segment cut from the cube to make the representation cube. (This piece is to the right in Fig. 3.2.2.) Because any point in this region can be uniquely expressed as a combination of odd and positive confused voters, it is clear that almost all $\mathbf{q}$ admit supporting profiles with a confused voter component! To indicate the powerful presence of this loss of transitivity, the shaded region of Fig. 3.2.5b indicates the surprisingly large set of pairwise outcomes that can be explained solely in terms of a positive cyclic voter (with no odd voters involved). (This region is the convex hull defined by even voters and positive confused voters. The figure is the portion of this hull in the representation cube.)

Reduced Profiles. This geometry can be used to represent the reduced profiles. (See Sect. 3.1.3.) As we know (Prob. 10, Sect. 3.1), such a profile requires both α and β have a zero component; e.g., both α and β are on T_j boundaries. It is easy (Prob. 6c) to show that the reduced profile, (α_r, β_r, d_r) is obtained from (α, β, d) is the following manner. First, α_r is where the line from $(\frac{1}{3}, \frac{1}{3}, \frac{1}{3})$ through α

meets the T_1 boundary (see Fig. 3.2.6a), and β_r is where the line from $-(\frac{1}{3}, \frac{1}{3}, \frac{1}{3})$ through β meets the T_2 boundary. A simple way to find d_r is to convert (α, β, d) into an integer profile. For the reader who craves formulas, let me hint how to derive one by using Fig. 3.1.2. Had this profile had been expressed in fractional form, the computations for type-one voters would be $\frac{20}{48} + \frac{10}{33} = \frac{20+10}{48+33} = \frac{30}{81}$. Although generations of fifth-grade teachers have come close to mortgaging their sanity to convince students that this is the wrong way to add fractions, this approach is used for certain probability problems. Namely, the conversion of d to d_r duplicates standard equations from probability.

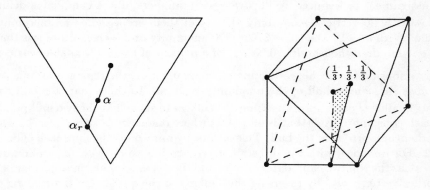

Fig. 3.2.6. Finding reduced profiles

It is important to understand how the Condorcet portion of a profile distorts the the reduced profile. Again, this comes from the geometry. Let the *confused voter line* be the segment connecting $\pm(\frac{1}{3}, \frac{1}{3}, \frac{1}{3})$; it is the set of points defining the Condorcet portion of a profile. The reduced profile is given by a distinguished point on a line segment connecting T_1 and T_2 boundary points. The profile set associated with this reduced profile is represented by the triangle defined by the vertices $\pm(\frac{1}{3}, \frac{1}{3}, \frac{1}{3})$ and the distinguished point. (See Fig. 3.2.6b.) Any point in this triangle is the outcome when the reduced profile is joined with some combination of confused voters. A little experimentation uncovers surprising facts. For instance, there are many reduced profiles where, by varying the strengths and choices for the Condorcet portion of a profile, the new profile travels through as many as seven different ranking regions! This, again, underscores the dangers associated with the pairwise vote's inability to honor transitivity. Instead of respecting the preferences of the actual voters, pairwise voting allocates considerable influence to the phantom confused voters.

More Candidates; Many More Problems. The troubles, problems, concerns, and analysis extend to $n \geq 4$ candidates, except that much more goes wrong! (The reader willing to accept this assertion might move on to the exercises.) An election for a pair of candidates defines a value in $[-1, 1]$, so the geometry requires as many different directions as there are pairs of candidates. With $n = 4$, for instance, the $\binom{4}{2} = 6$ pairs decrees a six-dimensional geometry, while a ten-candidate analysis properly belongs in a $\binom{10}{2} = 45$ dimensional space. For n candidates, the geometry is in a cube in $R^{\binom{n}{2}}$.

While we cannot envision these higher dimensional spaces, the tools of Sect. 1.4 help us extract properties. As above, start with the cube defined by the $\binom{n}{2} = \frac{n(n-1)}{2}$ line segments $[-1, 1]$, and find the unanimity profiles. This cube has $2^{\binom{n}{2}}$ vertices but only $n!$ unanimity vertices, so most vertices miss out on the assignment procedure. To illustrate with numbers, $n = 4$ candidates define $2^{\binom{4}{2}} = 2^6 = 96$ vertices where only $4! = 24$ of them are assigned an unanimity profile. With $n = 10$, the $10! = 3,628,800$ unanimity profiles constitute less than *one one-hundred thousandth (0.00001) of a percent* of the 2^{45} available vertices!

By imposing the profile restriction of rational voters, the representation cube becomes the convex hull of the unanimity vertices. To show that this hull has points in all $2^{\binom{n}{2}}$ orthants of the square, it suffices to show that the two unit points on each coordinate axis (that is all points where one entry is either 1 or -1 and all others are zero) is in the hull. This is done by mimicking the approach of Sect. 3.2.1. For instance, with the direction corresponding to $c_1 \succ c_2$, one unanimity vertex has the top two candidates $c_1 \succ c_2$ and the rest are ranked in some manner. Another vertex starts by reversing the ranking of this profile (so the ranking of the bottom two candidates is $c_2 \succ c_1$) and then reversing the bottom pair. (A $n = 5$ example is $(c_1 \succ c_2) \succ c_3 \succ c_4 \succ c_5$ and $c_5 \succ c_4 \succ c_3 \succ (c_1 \succ c_2)$.) As these profiles agree on the $c_1 \succ c_2$ ranking, but disagree on all other pairs, their average is the unit point on the $c_1 \succ c_2$ coordinate axis. This same argument holds for all c_i, c_j pairs.

Because the two unit points on each axis are in the representation cube, the hull of these points cuts across all regions. As a result, *for $n \geq 4$, choose a ranking for each of the $\binom{n}{2}$ pairs; there is a profile supporting these rankings.* In fact, by playing with the geometry (and mimicking what the T_1 and T_2 analysis), it is not difficult to specify the admissible coordinate values for the **q** points.

From this description, it is clear that the portion of the representation cube allocated to transitive outcomes, or even outcomes with a Condorcet winner, quickly dwindles to insignificance with increasing n values. Similarly, it is not difficult to show that the same fate holds for the size of the set of profiles supporting "rational" outcomes. (This is done by using the linearity of the f_{c_i, c_j} mappings and the shrinking size of the image set with "rational" outcomes.) Again, the problems are caused by the inability of the pairwise vote to distinguish between rational and the increasing variety of new kinds of baffled voters (represented by the $2^{\binom{n}{2}} - n!$ vertices not assigned an unanimity profile.) A theory parallel to the discussion of three-candidate confused voters, with reduced profiles, etc., can be developed. Clearly, there are serious problems! Pairwise voting is a mess!

3.2.5 Exercises

1. In Example 3.2.1, find all profile restrictions where only one voter type is excluded, but election relationships emerge. Do the same for restrictions proscribing two voter types. Is it possible to choose a profile restriction prohibiting three voter types so that no election relationships emerge? Why or why not.

2. Find all profiles where $F_2(\mathbf{p}) = (\frac{1}{2}, \frac{1}{3})$. Find all profiles where $F_3(\mathbf{p}) = (\frac{1}{2}, 0, \frac{1}{3})$. Convert the profile $(\alpha = (.2, .3, .5), \beta = -(.6, .3, .1), d = \frac{2}{3})$ into the corresponding $\mathbf{p} \in Si(6)$.

3. Using the same kind of geometric argument showing that $([-1, 1] \times [-1, 1]) \times [-1, 1]$ is a cube, describe geometrically $Si(3) \times [-1, 1]$–the product of the representation triangle with a line segment.

4. Using Fig. 3.2.3, find the maximum victory margins for $c_1 \succ c_2, c_2 \succ c_3$ that still allow the outcome $c_3 \succ c_1$.

5. Find the cone of profiles for $\mathbf{q} = (.8, .1, 0)$. Compare it with the cone for $(0, 0, 0)$. Describe the one-dimensional set of profiles supporting $(\frac{1}{2}, -\frac{2}{3}, 1)$.

6. a. Find a profile of confused voters leading to the same outcome as $\frac{1}{2}(F_3(\mathbf{E}_3) + F_3(\mathbf{E}_6))$. The profile where four voters are of type-two, three of type-four, three of type-six defines a cycle. Find a corresponding set of confused voters leading to the same outcome. Characterize all profiles where the profile cone for the outcome has no profile involving a confused voter.
b. Show that it is possible for $\mathbf{q}$ to have a supporting reduced profile and a supporting profile involving confused voters. Show, however, that the pairwise rankings from a reduced profile cannot be redistributed to create a profile with a confused voter.
c. Provide a geometric argument showing how to find (α_r, β_r, d_r) from (α, β, d).
d. Use the representation cube geometry and a reduced profile to show that by adding appropriate Condorcet portions, the new outcome can enter up to seven different ranking regions.

7. a. Find and plot the cyclic coordinate representation for the profiles of Fig. 3.2.2 and of Prob. 9, Sect. 3.2. Geometrically find the associated reduced profiles.
b. For the $\mathbf{q}$ values of part a, find the α-cones.
c. By use of the α- and β-cones (or by wiggling a pencil), find $\mathbf{q}$ choices which are not supported by a reduced profile. Use your examples to derive a simple geometric way to characterize these $\mathbf{q}$ choices in the representation cube.

8. For $n = 4$ candidates, there are $\binom{4}{2} = 6$ coordinate axes. Thus, there are twelve vectors with either ± 1 for one coordinate and zeros for all others. Find a supporting profile for each such vector.
b. Using the profiles of part a, find a profile supporting $c_1 \succ c_2, c_2 \succ c_3, c_3 \succ c_4, c_4 \succ c_3$. Find another profile supporting the rankings $c_1 \succ c_2, c_2 \succ c_3, c_3 \succ c_1, c_4 \succ c_j, j = 1, 2, 3$.

3.3 Black's Single-Peakedness

Cyclic coordinates make it easy to characterize *all possible profiles that avoid cycles*. As indicated by Fig. 3.3.1, these restrictions are where the (α, β, d) profiles keep the election point out of the positive and negative orthants of the figure.

A trivial way to avoid positive cycles (the positive orthant) is to restrict α to a T_1 edge. For example, if α is on the $F_3(\mathbf{E}_1)$ - $F_3(\mathbf{E}_3)$ edge, then for any β, the connecting profile line misses the positive orthant. (See Fig. 3.3.1.) The worse case scenario requires $\alpha = (1, 0, 0)$ and $\beta = -\alpha = (-1, 0, 0)$ where the profile line is on the quasi- transitive x-axis. In other words, *the geometry of the representation cube proves that if α is on a T_1 edge, then (α, β, d) has no positive cycles.*

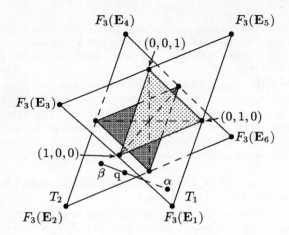

Fig. 3.3.1. The shaded areas represent the two cyclic regions.

While this α restriction avoids positive cycles, there are β choices where the connecting line segment passes through the negative cyclic region. Using the philosophy that what is good for the odds is good for the evens, all cycles can be avoided by further restricting β to a T_2 edge. But the T_1, T_2 edges correspond to profiles without voters of certain types. Because this edge condition characterizes a reduced profile (Prob. 10, Sect. 3.1), we have proved the following.

Theorem 3.3.1. *If a profile has no voters of at least one odd and one even voter types, the pairwise majority votes do not define a cycle. In particular, a reduced profile never admits a cycle.*

3.3.1 Black's Condition

Important special cases of Theorem 3.3.1 – situations which specify the even and odd voter types to be excluded – are the Black *single-peakedness* conditions. This condition *requires the excluded voter types to have the same candidate bottom-ranked*. Using the representation triangle, Black's condition requires the excluded even and odd voter types to be in adjacent ranking regions sharing an edge of the representation triangle. For example, the adjacent regions $\mathcal{R}(1), \mathcal{R}(6)$ share the bottom edge of the representation triangle, so Black's condition holds by excluding voters of types $\{1, 6\}$. As these *excluded* rankings are the only ones with c_3 bottom-ranked, she never is bottom-ranked with the *admitted* voter types. The other two choices of excluded types with Black's condition are $\{2, 3\}$ and $\{4, 5\}$.

The name *single peakedness* derives from a delightfully simple property exhibited by the graphs of each voter's cardinal rankings of the candidates. There is a way to place the candidates along the line (put the candidate who never is bottom-ranked in the middle) so that the graphs of the voter's cardinal rankings have a single peak. This is illustrated in Fig. 3.3.2 where the solid lines are graphs of admitted voter types and the dashed line with two peaks (on each end) is the graph of an excluded voter type.

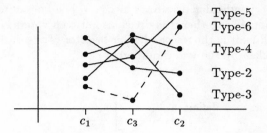

Fig. 3.3.2. Single peakedness where c_3 never is bottom- ranked

Corollary 3.3.2. *If a profile satisfy Black's single peakedness condition, then a pairwise cycle does not occur.*

Spatial Voting. When an election campaign centers about a single issue, say, foreign aid for the proposed state of Superior, single peakedness is a natural condition. To see why, let each candidate's position (specifying the amount of aid) be denoted by a point on the line as indicated the labeled bullet in Fig. 3.3.3. The voter's *ideal point* – the point characterizing the voter's stand on this issue – is denoted by a labeled dagger.

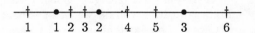

Fig. 3.3.3. A single issue and single-peakedness

Presumably, the closer a candidate's position is to a voter's ideal point, the better he likes her. This *Euclidean distance preference ranking* defines each voter's ranking of the three candidates where "closer is better." It now follows that the rankings are single-peaked as no voter has the middle positioned candidate, c_2, bottom-ranked. Thus, the combination of a single issue and Euclidean preferences ensures single-peakedness.

This makes sense; "single-peakedness" captures the essence of preferences coming from a single-dimensional space. With a one-dimensional situation, we should not be overly surprised when the homogeneity of the voters prohibits cycles. The situation changes dramatically, however, with two or more issues; say, aid to the state of Superior and reducing the deficit. To illustrate the wealth of new possibilities, start with two candidates and a single issue, say, aid to Superior. A candidate's position on this issue is defined by a point on the x-axis. With Euclidean preferences, indifference between these candidates corresponds to the perpendicular bisector; this is the vertical line passing through the x axis in Fig. 3.3.4. So, voters with ideal points to the left of this line vote for c_1; voters with ideal points to the right vote for c_2. The second issue (deficit) is modeled by the points on the y-axis; the dividing line determining who votes for whom is, again, the perpendicular bisector which now is a horizontal line. When both issues are considered together, the divisions between voters is given in the figure by the slanted line; it is the perpendicular bisector of the dashed line connecting the positions taken by the two candidates.

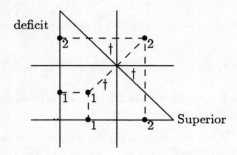

Fig. 3.3.4. Two issues and two candidates allow for cycles

The three lines intersect in a point, and they define six regions. These regions depict the differing ways a voter can rank the candidates depending on the mix of issues. Observe how this geometry closely resembles the division of the ranking regions in the representation triangle. Consequently, even though this construction only admits transitive voters, we must expect the bizarre attention the pairwise vote pays to non-existent confused voters to introduce serious problems for spatial voting. This is the case; the following is a sample.

Theorem 3.3.3. *With $k \geq 2$ issues, there are $2^k - 1$ subsets of issues. Suppose the candidates' positions differ on all issues. For each of the $2^k - 1$ subsets of issues, choose a ranking for the candidates. There exist examples of ideal points for the voters so that the sincere outcome for the j set of issues is the selected ranking.*

Outline of proof. Equations similar to those for F_{c_j, c_k} designate the number of voters needed in each region. The assumption on the voters' preferences ensures the independence of the equations. The conclusion now follows from an "m equation and n unknown" argument. See [S17] for more details. $\square$

This theorem is amply illustrated in Fig. 3.3.4 where c_1 wins with either single issue, but c_2 wins when both issues are on the floor. Again, by mimicking Eq. 3.1.1, the source of the problem is apparent; there is an associated confused voter profile which defines the same outcome. The problem, then, is by not admitting the intensity of preferences, the procedure is incapable of knowing that only rational voters are admitted.

Extensions of Black's Conditions. By experimenting with the geometry of Fig. 3.3.1, it becomes easy to extend Theorem 3.3.1 (and Black's condition). An immediate extension is indicated in the figure where α is in in a T_1 region favoring $c_1 \succ c_2 \succ c_3$ (so type-one voters dominate the odds) and β is in either the type-two or six region of T_2. The first pairing corresponds to where the dominant types for the odd and the even voters have the same candidate top-ranked, while the second ($\alpha - \beta$ pairing corresponds to where dominant types for the odd and the even voters have the same candidate bottom-ranked.

All sorts of other extensions are possible. For instance, as long as α is not in the cyclic region of T_1, we can determine all admissible β positions which do not allow a cycle. Also, for any α and β, the d values avoiding a cycle can be determined. But rather than indulging in this mathematical exercise, notice what these constructions tell us about the impact of the Condorcet portion of a profile. Namely, the stronger the Condorcet influence on a profile (as manifested by α or *beta* being more in the interior of T_j), the more difficult it is to establish conditions where the outcome is transitive. This makes sense; it asserts that the larger the portion of the profile that the pairwise vote treats as coming from irrational preferences, the more difficult it is to avoid cycles and other problems.

3.3.2 Condorcet Winners and Losers

These profile coordinates can be used to determine new properties of the Condorcet winner; related results hold for a Condorcet loser. While many of the Condorcet problems can be attributed to the destructive tendency of the pairwise vote to lose the transitivity assumption, other problems arise with the loss of intensity information. Indeed, all of the problems described in this section hold even with reduced profiles, so, here, no blame can be placed on the maligned confused voters.

Because the pairwise vote ignores intensity, it is reasonable to worry whether a Condorcet winner is an appropriate solution concept. Is a Condorcet winner always the overwhelming favorite of the voters, or can she be a compromise candidate? When do the profiles support a Condorcet winner, and when do they suggest that someone else is the appropriate choice?

To simplify the discussion, let c_1 be the Condorcet winner. This suggests dividing the voters into the "Yes" group consisting of voter types with c_1 top-ranked, and the "No" group where c_1 is not top-ranked. The division defines a new coordinate representation where the "Yes" group's outcome is a point α along the $F_3(\mathbf{E}_1)$–$F_3(\mathbf{E}_2)$ edge, $\mathcal{E}_1$, of the representation cube while the "No" group's outcome is a point in the tetrahedron (or polytope) P_2 with vertices $\{F_3(\mathbf{E}_j)\}_{j=3}^6$. The *group strength* variable, d, is the distance from β to α, so it is the fraction of all voters with c_1 top-ranked while $1 - d$ is the fraction that just says No. The geometry is depicted in Fig. 3.3.5 where the shaded region are the outcomes where c_1 is the Condorcet winner. (This shaded region is where $x > 0$ ($c_1 \succ c_2$) and $z < 0$ ($c_1 \succ c_3$).)

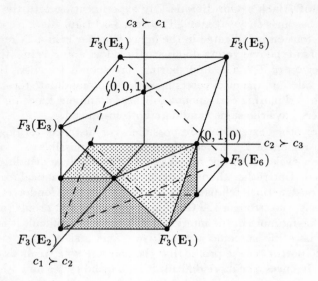

Fig. 3.3.5. The outcome space where c_1 is a Condorcet winner

Analytically, the c_1-*Condorcet group representation* is defined as

$$p_1 + p_2 = d; \quad a_i = \frac{p_i}{d}, \, i = 1, 2, \quad \alpha = (1, -1, a_1 - a_2) \in E_1$$

$$b_j = \frac{p_j}{1 - d}, \, j = 3, \ldots, 6, \, \beta = \left(b_3 - \sum_{j=4}^{6} b_j, b_5 + b_6 - b_3 - b_4, \sum_{j=3}^{5} b_j - b_6\right) \in P_2$$

(3.3.1)
$$F_3(\mathbf{p}) = d\alpha + (1 - d)\beta.$$

While the exact values are useful for computations, the geometry better indicates the divisions within the profile.

Use of c_1-Condorcet Coordinates. As true with cyclic group coordinates, Eq. 3.3.3 defines a smooth, invertible identification with $Si(6)$ profiles. This means that a profile can be described with a line segment where the designated point denotes both the d value and the election outcome. A profile defining the c_1-Condorcet outcome $\mathbf{q}$ is a line passing through $\mathbf{q}$ with one end on the edge $\mathcal{E}_1$ and the other in the convex hull P_2. The α point defines the relative split between the type-one and two voters, while β does the same for the four voter types who are not enamoured by c_1. As the designated outcome $\mathbf{q}$ plays a pivoting role for all line segments, we can see how changes in α affect the corresponding value of β; the d value describes the proportion of the "Yes" group among all voters. Boundary profiles correspond to where α, β or d reach boundary values for their respective ranges. The two-dimensional set of profiles corresponding to a given $\mathbf{q}$ can be characterized by the single degree of freedom available to choose $\alpha \in \mathcal{E}_1$

and the freedom to choose d. The cone of line segments (which is on a plane because $\mathcal{E}_1$ is a line) defined in this manner represents $\mathbf{q}$'s profile set.

Armed with this geometric tool, we can analyze all profiles where c_1 is the Condorcet winner. To start, if $d = 1$, then $F_3(\mathbf{p}) = \alpha$ is along $\mathcal{E}_1$, so c_1 is the Condorcet winner. Indeed, as long as $d > \frac{1}{2}$, the geometry ensures that $\mathbf{q}$ is in the c_1-Condorcet region. These profiles reflect the reasonable expectation that a Condorcet winner is top-ranked by most voters. Indeed, the other extreme value is $d = 0$ where nobody has c_1 top-ranked; here c_1 is not a Condorcet winner because $F_3(\mathbf{p}) = \beta \in P_2$, and P_2, the convex hull of the unanimity outcomes $\{F_3(\mathbf{E}_j)\}_{j=3}^6$, misses the c_1 Condorcet region. So, *if c_1 is the Condorcet winner, she is top-ranked by at least one voter.*

How about the converse; if the voters view c_1 as being mediocre because only one of them has her top-ranked, could she be the Condorcet winner? She could! The geometric reason is that the midpoint of the line connecting $F_3(\mathbf{E}_3)$ with $F_3(\mathbf{E}_6)$ is a boundary point of the c_1-Condorcet region. Consequently, if β is this boundary point, any small positive d value allows the $\alpha \in \mathcal{E}_1$ value to force the election outcome into the c_1-Condorcet region. (See Fig. 3.3.5.) The geometry even dictates which profiles permit mediocre c_1 to be the Condorcet winner. If d has a small value, then for $\mathbf{q}$ to be in the c_1-Condorcet region, β must be near the origin of the representation cube. But, β near the origin requires most "No" voters to be evenly divided between type-3 ($c_3 \succ c_1 \succ c_2$) and type-6 ($c_2 \succ c_1 \succ c_3$). This nearly even split over the excellence of c_2 and c_3 suggests that one of them would be selected, but mediocre c_1 wins by Condorcet's standards. Thus a Condorcet winner might be viewed by most voters as representing mediocrity rather than excellence.

The geometry even offers explanations for this outcome. For instance, in its ignorance of the intensity information, the pairwise vote cannot distinguish between the specified $\frac{1}{2}(\mathbf{E}_3 + \mathbf{E}_6)$ and the profile $\frac{1}{2}(\mathbf{E}_1 + \mathbf{E}_4)$ where c_1 is top-ranked by half of the voters and bottom-ranked by the other half. For the second profile, by being top-ranked by half the voters, it is arguable that c_1 *does* manifest excellence. (The tie vote is decided in favor of c_1 with one voter having c_1 top-ranked.) To see the confusion that can occur when intensity information is ignored, the subscripts show how to reassign the binary rankings from $\frac{1}{2}(\mathbf{E}_3+\mathbf{E}_6)$ to create $\frac{1}{2}(\mathbf{E}_1 + \mathbf{E}_4)$.

3	$(c_1 \succ c_2)_1$	$(c_3 \succ c_1)_4$	$(c_3 \succ c_2)_4$
6	$(c_2 \succ c_1)_4$	$(c_1 \succ c_3)_1$	$(c_2 \succ c_3)_1$

In other words, the pairwise vote cannot distinguish between the actual profile (where c_1 is a questionable winner) from a radically different profile where the selection of c_1 is justified. Being unable to distinguish among preferences is a sad thing for a procedure to lose.

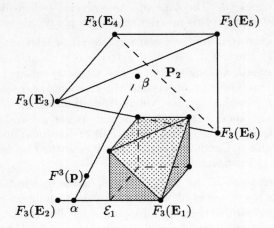

Fig. 3.3.6. The space where c_1 is a Condorcet winner
and c_3 is a Condorcet loser

Can it be worse? Can an inferior candidate be a Condorcet winner? Fortunately, no. The larger the fraction of voters with c_1 bottom-ranked, the closer β is to the $F_3(\mathbf{E}_4)$–$F_3(\mathbf{E}_5)$ edge. So, from the geometry, c_1 is the Condorcet winner only if more voters have her top- ranked than bottom-ranked. On the other hand, this difference between the c_1 lovers and haters can be as large or small (but positive) as desired while still admitting c_1 as the Condorcet winner.

If mediocre c_1 is the Condorcet winner, what happens to the other candidates? Could a candidate who is sufficiently popular to be top-ranked by almost half of the voters be stigmatized with a "Condorcet loser" label? Yes. The shaded region of Fig. 3.3.6 is where c_1 and c_3 are, respectively, the Condorcet winner and loser (so $x > 0, z < 0, y > 0$). For a small $\epsilon > 0$ value, $\mathbf{q} = (\epsilon, \epsilon, -\epsilon)$ is close to the origin while living in this c_1-winner – c_3-loser region. To find a supporting profile, take a line where the P_2 endpoint is near the midpoint of the $F_3(\mathbf{E}_3)$ – $F_3(\mathbf{E}_6)$ connecting line. Small ϵ values represent where the fraction of voters with c_3 top-ranked is nearly $\frac{1}{2}$. On the other hand, because d has a small value, very few voters are impressed by c_1. Thus, even though almost all voters view the Condorcet winner as mediocre (middle-ranked), it could be that nearly half of them find excellence (top-ranked) in the Condorcet loser!

The Boundary of the c_1-Condorcet Region. As the geometry tells us, the profiles which raise doubts about the validity of choosing c_1 correspond to $\mathbf{q}$ values near the boundary of the c_1-Condorcet region. The reason is clear; the boundary is where slight changes can alter an outcome. In particular, this is where knowledge about the intensity of the pairwise comparisons could significantly influence the selection. Therefore, to understand other strengths and weaknesses of the Condorcet winner, examine $\mathbf{q}$ outcomes near the boundary.

There is no problem with $\mathbf{q} \in \mathcal{E}_1$; all supporting profiles demonstrate the unanimous acceptance of c_1. Similarly, the boundary point $(0, 1, -1)$ occurs only when the voters are split between $c_1 \succ c_2 \succ c_3$ and $c_2 \succ c_1 \succ c_3$, so this represents a de facto two person race between c_1 and c_2 where the Condorcet region selects the "majority" winner. (Both $\{c_1, c_2\}$ comparisons are weak, so it is easy to justify the Condorcet winner.)

A remaining boundary point is $(0, 1, 0)$ on the y axis. To analyze a $\mathbf{q}$ near this point, suppose 5000 voters have the ranking $c_1 \succ c_2 \succ c_3$ while the other 5000 have the preferences $c_2 \succ c_3 \succ c_1$. Here, c_3 should be bottom-ranked because nobody ranks her above the middle; similarly, c_1 should be middle-ranked with her split between extreme rankings. On the other hand, everyone ranks c_2 at least in the middle, while half of the voters have her at top. The outcome should be $c_2 \succ c_1 \succ c_3$ even if, say, another hundred voters of any type arrive. However, just one more voter liking c_1 will tilt the balance to crown her the Condorcet winner! This situation, perhaps more than any other, demonstrates how the informational limitations of the pairwise vote further compromises the integrity of the Condorcet solution concept.

It easy to construct confused voter explanations, but I am more concerned over the failure of the pairwise vote to recognize that c_1 is only weakly preferred over c_2 by half of the voters while the other half strongly prefer c_2 to c_1. This indifference explains the disturbing Condorcet result. More generally, transitivity of preferences, and the implicitly defined intensity of pairwise preferences, must be reflected in the outcome, but this never can happen with pairwise voting! By reviewing all of its problems, it becomes clear that we should seriously question the wisdom of using the Condorcet winner or any other procedure based on pairwise rankings.

3.3.3 A Condorcet Improvement

Rather than ending by criticizing the Condorcet winner, we could try to correct its problems. First, we need to overcome the problem that a Condorcet winner is not always defined. This can be remedied by dividing the cyclic outcomes among the three candidates where the better a candidate does in the majority vote tallies, the stronger the argument for choosing her. Conversely, the tie outcome $(\frac{1}{3}, \frac{1}{3}, \frac{1}{3})$ should be on the boundary of each candidate's region. Second, reassign the outcome for those $\mathbf{q}$ values where the selection of the Condorcet winner is indefensible; e.g., for $\mathbf{q}$ near $(0, 1, 0)$, c_2 rather than c_1 should be declared the winner. Finally, to avoid those fable problems where subcommittees have one conclusion, but the full group has a different outcome, the set of election outcomes associated with a particular candidate must be convex. (See Sect. 5.1.) These minimal conditions divide the representation cube into regions $C(c_j)$ where if $\mathbf{q} \in C(c_j)$, then c_j is selected.

Definition 3.3.1. The sets $\{C(c_j)\}_{j=1}^{3}$ define a *Condorcet Improvements* if they are pairwise disjoint and satisfy the following.

1. If all voters in $\mathbf{p}$ have c_j top-ranked, then $F_3(\mathbf{p}) \in C(c_j)$.
2. Each set $C(c_j)$ is convex with $(\frac{1}{3}, \frac{1}{3}, \frac{1}{3})$ and $(0, 0, 0)$ as boundary points.

3. If no voter in $\mathbf{p}$ has c_i or c_j bottom-ranked each candidate top-ranked by half of the voters, then $F_3(\mathbf{p})$ is a boundary point of $C(c_j)$ and $C(c_i)$.

4. The set of $\mathbf{q}$ values not in $\cup_{j=1}^3 C(c_j)$ has zero three-dimensional volume.□

The first condition asserts that when all voters have c_1 top-ranked, she should be selected; this outcome must be in $C(c_j)$. As already indicated, the second condition avoids the Dean selection problems of the fable. Clearly the two specified points cannot be assigned to any one candidate, so they should be boundary points of each $C(c_j)$. The third condition essentially asserts that if an election is a de facto two person race, then it should be decided by a majority vote. The fourth condition requires decisiveness; it relegates those situations where an outcome is not defined to a lower dimensional set of profiles. Even though these four conditions are minimal, they define a procedure.

Theorem 3.3.5. *If the sets* $\{C(c_j)\}_{j=1}^3$ *are Condorcet Improvements, they are uniquely defined by the three planes*

$$(3.3.2) \qquad 2x = y + z, \quad 2y = x + z, \quad 2z = x + y$$

identified, respectively, with $\{c_1, c_2\}, \{c_2, c_3\}, \{c_3, c_1\}$. *For each* $\{c_i, c_j\}$, *the associated plane divides the representation cube into two parts; points on the side with the* $c_i \succ c_j$ *axis are assigned this ranking. The intersection of these planes define six symmetric, open regions of election outcomes; each open region corresponds to a transitive ranking;* $C(c_j)$ *is the union of the two regions (and their common boundary) where* c_j *is top-ranked.*

So, with the exception of ties (outcomes on the three planes), there is a unique Condorcet Improvement. A surprising fact (Chap. 4) is that these natural corrections of the Condorcet faults define the BC! The following example illustrates how to use Eq. 3.3.2.

Example 3.3.1. a. The point $\mathbf{q} = (0.1, 0.1, -0.1)$ is in the c_1-Condorcet region. To find its CI (Condorcet Improvement) ranking, start with the first equation of Eq. 3.3.2. As $2x - (y + z) = 0.2 - (0.1 - 0.1) > 0$, the CI ranking is $c_1 \succ c_2$. Similarly, as $2y - (x + z) = 0.2 - (0.1 - 0.1) > 0$ and $2z - (x + y) = -0.2 - (0.1 + 0.1) < 0$, the remaining CI rankings are $c_2 \succ c_3$, $c_1 \succ c_3$. Here, the Condorcet and CI rankings agree.

For $\mathbf{q}_1 = (0.1, 0.31, -0.1)$, the Condorcet ranking is the same as above. However, because $2x - (y + z) = 0.2 - (0.31 - 0.1) < 0$, $2y - (z + x) = 0.62 - (-0.1 + 0.1) > 0$, $2z - (x + y) = -0.1 - (0.1 + 0.31) < 0$, the CI rankings are $c_2 \succ c_1$, $c_2 \succ c_3$, $c_1 \succ c_3$.

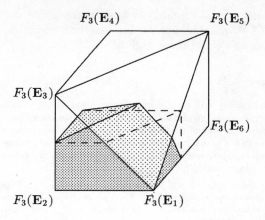

$F_3(\mathbf{E}_4)$ $F_3(\mathbf{E}_5)$

$F_3(\mathbf{E}_3)$

$F_3(\mathbf{E}_6)$

$F_3(\mathbf{E}_2)$ $F_3(\mathbf{E}_1)$

Fig. 3.3.7. The region where c_1 is a Condorcet Improved winner

With simple algebra, the portions of the c_1-Condorcet region that are reassigned
to other candidates are easy to compute. For instance, the wedge bordering
the y axis defined by the four vertices $(0,0,0)$, $(0,1,0)$, $(0,1,-1)$, $(\frac{1}{3},1,-\frac{1}{3})$ is
reassigned to c_2 as it should be. Likewise, a wedge from the c_1- Condorcet region
about the negative y axis defined by the vertices $(0,0,0)$, $(0,-1,0)$, $(0,-1,-1)$,
$(-\frac{1}{3},-1,-\frac{1}{3})$ is appropriately reassigned to c_3. Similar regions are added to
$C(c_1)$ around the positive x and negative z axes. Figure 3.3.7, which indicates
where c_1 is top-ranked, should be compared with the one showing where c_1 is
the Condorcet winner (the dashed lines in the figure).□

To see how the CI handles those indefensible situations where the Condorcet
winner is not the voters' top choice, suppose the voters are divided between type-
one $(c_1 \succ c_2 \succ c_3)$ and type-five $(c_2 \succ c_3 \succ c_1)$. As already argued, even with
slightly more type-one than type-five voters, c_2 should be treated as the voters'
top choice. The problem is to determine an appropriate threshold dividing the
selection of c_1 over c_2. According to the CI, if c_1 receives one more than $\frac{2}{3}$ of
the vote, the type-one voters' rankings need to be honored. (Compare this value
with the Pope selection procedure.)

Proof. The boundary separating $C(c_i)$ and $C(c_j)$ must be a plane. If not,
then two points on the boundary can be found where the connecting line is in
one of the regions. If this line is in $C(c_i)$, then it cannot be in $C(c_j)$; this means
that $C(c_j)$ is not be convex which violates the assumption.

A plane is defined by three points, so the boundary conditions completely
specify the plane dividing $C(c_i)$ and $C(c_j)$. With a specific example of $C(c_1)$
and $C(c_2)$, the plane is $ax + by + cz = e$. Because the origin is on the plane (it
is a boundary point for each region), $e = 0$. Because $(\frac{1}{3},\frac{1}{3},\frac{1}{3})$ is on the plane,
$a + b + c = 0$. Finally, the point $(0,1,-1)$ is the election point where the voters
are evenly split between $c_1 \succ c_2 \succ c_3$ and $c_2 \succ c_1 \succ c_3$, so it is a point on the
plane. Thus, $b = c$. This means that coefficients must satisfy $a = -2b = -2c$.
By choosing $b = 1$, the conclusion follows.

The first condition for a CI uniquely defines which plane and which side of this plane is assigned to a ranking $c_i \succ c_j$. The last condition precludes the possibility of choosing subsets of these regions. $\square$

3.3.4 Exercises

1. For single issue spatial voting with an odd number of voters, suppose we know each voter's ideal point. Furthermore, suppose candidate c_1 is the first to announce her position on these issues. Determine a position for her so she wins any pairwise contest independent of what the other candidates declare. (This is the "median voter" theorem.) With two issues, suppose the odd number of voters' ideal points are known (and not on a line), candidates c_2 and c_3 have declared their positions. Find a stand for c_1 to ensure she wins.

2. For two issues, let the three voters' ideal points be $(0,0)$, $(4,0)$, $(2,3)$. Suppose the declared positions of c_1, c_3 are, respectively, $(0,1)$, $(4,1)$. Find all positions for c_2 so that the voters' preferences are single peaked and she is never bottom-ranked. (Hint: This happens if c_2's position is on the line connecting $(0,1)$ with $(4,1)$. Now, move c_2 so that the figure similar to Fig. 3.3.4 keeps the voters' ideal points in the same ranking regions.) Use this to generalize the statement about single peakedness over a single issue to certain two-dimensional configurations. Now, find positions for c_2 so that a cycle occurs.

3. With two candidates and two issues, a, b, find positioning of three ideal points so that on issue a, c_1 wins, on issue b, c_2 wins, and on both issues, c_1 wins. With two candidates and three issues, a, b, c, find a positioning of the three voters' ideal points so that c_1 wins whenever a single issue or any two issues are considered, but c_2 wins when all three issues are considered. Create another example where c_1 wins whenever one or three issues are considered, but c_2 wins whenever two issues are considered.

4. a. If $\alpha = (0.8, 0.3, -0.1)$, find all β for which the profile line misses the cycle generating regions.
b. Suppose all we know is that α is defined by where 80% of the odd voters are type-three and no more than 10% are of type-one. Find the restrictions on β so that all α-β lines miss the cycle generating regions.
c. Following the discussion of spatial voting are some comments about the extension of Black's conditions. In this discussion, there is a comment that if voters of a certain type dominate the odds and if voters of another certain type dominate the evens, then no cycles occur. Make this precise by determining how many voters of a type it takes to have this dominate role.
d. For $\alpha = (0.3, 0.4, 0.3)$ and $\beta = -(0.25, 0.35, 0.4)$, find all d values which avoid a cycle.
e. Find two profiles which satisfy Black's condition, but where the sum of the profiles defines a cycle.

5. The outcome $\mathbf{q} = (0.1, 0.9, -0.1)$ crowns c_1 as the Condorcet winner. Using c_1-Condorcet coordinates, find the cone of supporting profiles. This profile set is two-dimensional, so indicate where both dimensions are captured in this cone. Are there profiles where it seems inappropriate to choose c_1 as the winner? Now compare the above with the cone of profiles supporting $(.1, 0, -.1)$. Which set appears to be larger? Why?

6. a. Find the CI rankings for $\mathbf{q}_1 = (0.2, -0.1, 0.3)$, $\mathbf{q}_2 = (-0.1, 0.4, 0.3)$, $\mathbf{q}_3 = (0.9, -0.75, 0.2)$.
b. The CI defines a ranking for each pair, but cycles are not admitted. As such, the CI must distinguish between weak and strong binary preferences. Show that the CI can be described as assigning a certain number of points to a voter's preferred candidate with strong intensity, and another number of points if the comparison is weak. Find these points. (Hint: Start with profiles, such as the Condorcet triplet, that give tied outcomes on the boundary between two outcomes.)

7. a. Show that c_3 wins with the agenda $< c_1, c_2, c_3 >$ if she is a Condorcet winner or if there is a cycle. Next, show that either of the other two candidates wins only by being a

Condorcet winner. Use the representation cube to estimate the portion of profiles that crown c_1 the agenda winner. Compare this with the portion of all profiles where c_3 wins. (This shows that with any "neutral" probability distribution over the profiles, the candidate last listed in an agenda has the best chance of winning.)

b. By use of profile coordinates, find the vertices of the convex set of profiles where c_1 is the Condorcet winner, c_3 is the Condorcet loser, but c_1 is *not* top-ranked with the Condorcet Improvement. (If the reader knows how to compute the volume of this set, do so.)

8. Show that some of the profiles admitted by Theorem 3.3.1 define quasi-transitive rankings.

3.4 Arrow's Theorem

Maybe, by being sufficiently clever, we can avoid these voting problems. The standard pairwise rankings lose transitivity, so they need not agree with the plurality or BC rankings (Fig. 3.1.2). Maybe we can replace them with new pairwise and general methods. Surely, with creativity, we can discover procedures where the three-candidate ranking always is compatible with voters' beliefs about pairs. This seems reasonable, but K. Arrow [Ar] proved it is impossible *if we use standard assumptions.*

3.4.1 A Sen Type Theorem

Even with the many proofs of Arrow's Theorem, his mysterious conclusion continues as an intellectual magnet. Its attraction is the message that we cannot do what we always took for granted. While I extend Arrow's conclusion, my main goal is to remove the mystery by explaining why we should expect the conclusion – it is another confused voter attack! Once we know what causes the conclusion, it becomes easy to circumvent the difficulties.

Example 3.4.1. This example, which is related to Sen's Theorem [Se1,2] and introduces the basic geometry, examines "individual rights" where the relative rankings of certain alternatives are strictly within the purview of a particular agent. For instance, I, rather than society, should determine whether to wear a sport coat or my favorite torn and worn sweater when lecturing.

This seems easy; let me decide the relative ranking of $\{c_1, c_2\}$ while Lillian has full power over the relative ranking of $\{c_2, c_3\}$. (This, then, defines a pairwise procedure for each pair.) As for the remaining pair $\{c_1, c_3\}$, it is reasonable that at least when we agree, that is the ranking.

Here we encounter a surprise; these seemingly innocuous requirements are incompatible! To see the conflict, suppose we both want $c_1 \succ c_3$; by agreement, $c_1 \succ c_3$ is our joint ranking. This ranking is the shaded regions of the representation triangles of Fig. 3.4.1.

The arrow in the first triangle denotes how I can satisfy the $c_1 \succ c_3$ condition while changing my $\{c_1, c_2\}$ rankings; the arrow in the second triangle indicates how Lillian observes $c_1 \succ c_3$ while altering her $\{c_2, c_3\}$ rankings. The third triangle demonstrates the conflict; our unanimous $c_1 \succ c_3$ agreement restricts the outcome to the shaded region. However, if my ranking is $c_2 \succ c_1$, as indicated by the bullet on the bottom edge, and Lillian's ranking is $c_3 \succ c_2$, as indicated by the dagger, it follows (by intersecting the two binary triangles) that the joint ranking is $c_3 \succ c_2 \succ c_1$ – the region with a black square. As this black square is not in the mandatory shaded area, the conditions conflict. $\square$

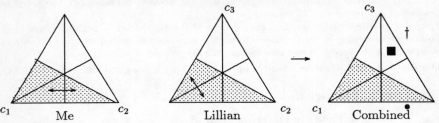

Fig. 3.4.1. A special case of Sen's Theorem

The incompatibilty of these seemingly reasonable assumptions is caused by an interesting mixture of flexibility and restrictiveness required by the geometry of the representation triangle. (See Prob. 2, Sect. 2.1.) The flexibility is manifested by the freedom to vary the relative rankings of a particular pair even when the relative rankings of the remaining pairs are fixed! But, while these relative rankings are preserved, their intensity changes. This suggests resolving the conflict by incorporating intensity information.

The restrictive nature of the geometry is indicated with the third triangle. Here, two carefully chosen pairwise rankings dictate the ranking of the last pair; this forces the contradictory $c_3 \succ c_1$ ranking in the example. To see what else can happen, let $\mathbf{p}_1$ be the above profile. Let $\mathbf{p}_2$ be where Lillian changes to $c_1 \succ c_2 \succ c_3$. No conflict occurs with $\mathbf{p}_2$ because when we choose rankings for the pairs assigned to each of us, the outcomes can be either $c_2 \succ c_1 \succ c_3$ or $c_2 \succ c_3 \succ c_1$; the first is selected according to our unanimity requirement. Now, suppose I, too, change the ranking of my assigned pair (as allowed by the arrow) to define $\mathbf{p}_3$. Our individual binary choices force the outcome to be $c_1 \succ c_2 \succ c_3$ which conflicts with the unanimity clause. Thus the $\mathbf{p}_1 \to \mathbf{p}_2 \to \mathbf{p}_3$ profile change converts one conflicting setting to the other.

It is this geometric mixture permitting flexibility in inputs while imposing restrictiveness of conclusions – this algebraic sense of too many unknowns (voters' preferences) and too many equations (the three pairs) – that explains Arrow's Theorem and most other social choice "impossibility" conclusions. After the three-candidate case is explained, the $n \geq 3$ setting is described. But first, basic assumptions need to be introduced.

3.4.2 Universal Domain and IIA

A procedure needs to permit *each voter to strictly rank the candidates in any desired manner.* No "Big Brother" is permitted in the voting booth to force voters to vote in a particular manner. This is the *universal domain* condition.

The next requirement is the goal to eliminate paradoxes; we seek a procedure where its three-candidate ranking always agrees with the ranking of the pairs. As illustrated in the example, this may be difficult; after all, the compatibility condition fails even if each individual chooses the ranking of a particular pair while unanimity decides the ranking of the last pair. On the other hand, it is easy to construct examples by mimicking how election rankings are (mistakenly) used. Namely, for any procedure that ranks the candidates, assert that the ranking of a pair is its relative rankings from the full election ordering. Unfortunately, this decision by assertion does not resolve the paradox, it is a feeble attempt to camouflage it. To see why such an imposed pairwise ranking may lack credibility, consider the plurality ranking $c_1 \succ c_3 \succ c_2$ coming from the profile where 9,999,999 people have the preference $c_1 \succ c_2 \succ c_3$ and only c_3 has $c_3 \succ c_2 \succ c_1$. The imposed pairwise ranking $c_3 \succ c_1$ is nonsense; almost all voters prefer $c_1 \succ c_3$.

This issue can be resolved. For instance, Prob. 6, Sect. 3.3 shows that the CI ranks pairs according to intensity information and it leads to transitive rankings of the candidates. As shown in Chap. 4, the compatibility concern is completely resolved by using the BC. But, can this "CI – BC" success story be duplicated by using only the relative rankings of pairs? Namely, can we design a procedure, where the rankings of the triplet and the pairs always agree when intensity information is ignored? (We cannot.) This goal is made precise with *Independence of Irrelevant Alternatives* (IIA). IIA *requires the relative ranking of a pair of candidates to be determined strictly by the voters' relative rankings of the same pair.* Thus, information about the remaining candidates, even intensity, is not admissible.

To see that IIA clearly captures what we want, consider the woes of a prize committee which selected Poinchoff as the winner by virtue of their ranking Poinchoff $\succ$ Poincaré $\succ$ Birkhoff. After reporting their decision, suppose the committee explains to the overly vocal Birkhoff supporters that, "Well, yes, we do find that Birkhoff is better than Poinchoff. But, well, Poincaré also was a candidate, so we decided that Poinchoff is top-ranked. Of course, had Poincaré withdrawn, we definitely would have chosen Birkhoff over Poinchoff!" I wouldn't want to speculate about the committee's popularity quotient after such a report. This is precisely the type of problem IIA tries to avoid; the relative ranking of two candidates should be determined by their relative merits. (Sound familiar? See Sect. 3.1.) Conversely, if a procedure fails to satisfy IIA, then, unless a committee recognizes the critical importance of the intensity of binary rankings (with its signal of rational voters), we must anticipate embarrassing reports that are difficult to defend.[11]

3.4.3 Involvement and Voter Responsiveness

Next, eliminate those procedures that ignore candidates. For instance, there is no suspense or use for a procedure that has only the one outcome $c_1 \succ c_2 \succ c_3$, independent of what the voters believe. Similarly, a procedure with only the two

---

[11] Examples abound in professional and academic circles and anywhere else where committee members are afflicted with a driving need to pontificate upon their decisions.

outcomes $c_1 \succ c_2 \succ c_3$ and $c_2 \succ c_1 \succ c_3$ does not involve c_3; the real decision is between c_1 and c_2 with c_3 always relegated to last place.

We need a condition to ensure that all candidates are, in some manner, involved. All three candidates appear in any two pairs of candidates, say $\{c_2, c_3\}$ and $\{c_1, c_3\}$. So, the weakest condition, *"Involvement,"* is that *for at least each of two pairs of candidates $\{c_i, c_j\}$ there is profile providing the relative ranking $c_i \succ c_j$ and another profile leading to the relative ranking $c_j \succ c_i$.*

Any procedure which even minimally involves all three candidates satisfies involvement. A special case, for instance, is *Arrow's unanimity condition* where, if all voters have the same ranking, then that is the group outcome. After all, *unanimity* forces *all* strict rankings to be admissible group outcomes, so, for each pair $\{c_i, c_j\}$, one unanimity profile has the ranking $c_i \succ c_j$ and another has $c_j \succ c_i$. Indeed, "involvement" is sufficiently flexible to admit procedures which even prohibit rankings. To illustrate, suppose for reasons of cost or prejudice, it is impossible to accept an outcome with c_2 top-ranked. The method might, instead, honor unanimity *except* in the two proscribed situations. It is easy to check that the four remaining outcomes suffice to satisfy involvement.

Involvement only depends upon what outcomes are admitted – it ignores how the outcomes are related to voters' preferences. Consequently, this condition is satisfied even for an "Ivan the Terrible" procedure where, when the voters are unanimous, the group outcome is the reverse of what they want. In fact, involvement is so inclusive that it even admits a procedure with just the two outcomes $c_1 \succ c_2 \succ c_3$ and $c_3 \succ c_2 \succ c_1$. This is because for each pair $\{c_i, c_j\}$, $c_i \succ c_j$ is the relative ranking of one outcome and $c_j \succ c_i$ is the ranking for the other. So, by replacing Arrow's "unanimity" with "involvement," we admit a much richer set of procedures.

Finally, we do not want procedures where the outcome always depend upon the rankings of a particular voter; dictators need not apply! Thus, *"Voter Responsiveness,"* requires that *the outcomes of the procedure cannot always agree with those of another procedure which depends on the rankings of a single voter.* Actually, examples where voter responsiveness[12] fails are easy to find in the corporate world where the number of votes a voter can cast equals her stock holdings. A voter with a sufficient number of stocks is a de facto dictator; the beliefs of the other voters are amusing footnotes with no bearing on decisions. Thus, voter responsiveness eliminates explicit or implicitly defined dictators where the wishes of one voter, the dictator, always are granted. As another example, voter responsiveness rules out an anti-dictator where the group ranking always reverses a voter's ranking. As such, it rules out situations where to spite a sufficiently annoying voter the choice is always the opposite of what he wants.

---

[12] If each of 60 voters has t votes and I have 120 votes, then as long as $t \in [0, 2)$, I am the de facto dictator. Letting $t \to 0$, defines the usual dictator. Mathematically, this means that these procedures belong to the same homotopy class.

3.4.4 Arrow's Theorem

We want to find all procedures satisfying these four conditions. While the requirements are basic and seemingly innocuous, they are not compatible; no such procedure exists. The reason for the conflict is closely related to that described in Example 3.4.1.

Theorem 3.4.1. *No procedure exists which has strict rankings of three candidates as outcomes and which satisfies universality of domain, IIA, involvement, and voter responsiveness.*

A procedure yielding strict rankings of the three candidates which satisfies universality of domain, IIA, and involvement is a dictatorship or an antidictatorship.

A special case of Theorem 3.4.1 is Arrow's famous conclusion.

Arrow's Theorem. *The only procedure that always gives strict rankings of the three candidates and satisfies universality of domain, IIA, and unanimity is a dictatorship.*

Attention is restricted to strict rankings only for simplicity. Other formulations of Arrow's Theorem use choice procedures where the goal is to select a candidate rather than a ranking of the candidates. Outlines how to extend Arrow's Theorem and Theorem 3.4.1 to choice procedures, for group rankings with a tie (or indifference) between certain candidates are in the exercises. The key always is IIA.

The next statement (a corollary of the proof of Theorem 3.4.1) asserts that (without intensity) it is impossible to design pairwise procedures where the outcomes transitively rank all three candidates. This statement, therefore, subsumes Example 3.4.1.

Corollary 3.2.2. *Suppose for each pair of candidates a procedure F_{c_i,c_j} is used to find a strict ranking for $\{c_i, c_j\}$ where only the voters' rankings of these two candidates is used. Suppose at least two of these pairwise procedures are non-constant. Furthermore, assume that at least one procedure satisfies the voter responsiveness requirement. With no restrictions on profiles, there are profiles so that the pairwise rankings define a cycle.*

3.4.5 A Dictatorship or an Informational Problem?

Rather than endorsing dictatorships, these assertions just prove that we can not always get what we want. They claim that, for any procedure, a profile can be found so that the ranking of some pair fails to agree with how the procedure ranks all three candidates. With the fable and our discussion of pairwise voting, this is a familiar theme.

Instead of the Draconian conclusions often associated with Arrow's Theorem, let me offer a benign interpretation. I introduced IIA to determine whether procedures can use only the restricted information about the voters' relative

ranking of each pair. From Arrow's Theorem and Theorem 3.4.1 the answer is
no. Adopting an informational perspective, then, *these theorems just state that
procedures for three or more candidates require more information than just the
relative rankings of pairs.*[13]

With reflection, this is not a surprising conclusion. In Sect. 3.1 we showed
that by ignoring intensity information, the procedure cannot distinguish between
rational or confused voters. As IIA returns us to a "garbage in, garbage out"
environment, why should we expect well-behaved, transitive outcomes? Stated
in another way, because IIA vitiates the assumption of transitive voters, Arrow's
Theorem can be viewed as a quest to determine whether a procedure can serve
both transitive and confused voters while always providing transitive outcomes.
When posed in this fashion, the answer is obvious; of course not! The true
message, then, is that if rational outcomes and the rational voter assumption
are important, then we need to incorporate information about the intensity of
pairwise rankings.[14]

An explanation of these important theorems involves nothing more difficult
than elementary algebra where we learn to expect solutions for m equations in
n unknowns, $n \geq m$. To make explain, IIA is used to define $m = 3$ equations.
"Involvement" guarantees that at least two of them are non-constant; there are
at least $m \geq 2$ equations to be "solved." The "unknowns" are the voters' A
preferences. "Universal domain" and "voter responsiveness" (which require at
least two voters to be involved) ensure that the number of variables satisfies
the relationship $n \geq m$. The rank condition, which ensures that at least two
equations are independent, remains to be verified; this argument is related to
the geometric arguments used in Fig. 3.4.1.

IIA and Three Pairwise Procedures. To make precise the central ideas,
Theorem 3.4.1 is proved first for $n = 2$ voters. Each voter's ranking of the three
candidates is a strict ranking from $Si(3)$, so, according to the universality of
domain condition, we search for a mapping

$$(3.4.1) \qquad\qquad F : Si(3) \times Si(3) \to Si(3)$$

This equation is represented by Fig. 3.4.1 where the jth term of the product
$Si(3) \times Si(3)$ represents the jth voter's ranking of the three candidates, $j = 1, 2$.

Assume the theorem is false; we have such a mapping F. Function F combined with IIA implicitly defines the three functions $(F_{c_1,c_2}, F_{c_2,c_3}, F_{c_3,c_1})$ where
$F_{c_i,c_j}(\mathbf{p})$ is the $\{c_i, c_j\}$ relative ranking obtained from $F(\mathbf{p})$. For instance, if
$F(\mathbf{p}) = c_2 \succ c_1 \succ c_3$, then $F_{c_1,c_2}(\mathbf{p}) = c_2 \succ c_1$, $F_{c_2,c_3}(\mathbf{p}) = c_2 \succ c_3$, and
$F_{c_3,c_1}(\mathbf{p}) = c_1 \succ c_3$. Namely, *the F_{c_i,c_j} functions are the imposed rankings of
the pairs as determined by the F outcome*; if F exists, so do these functions.

---

[13] This assertion, of course, applies to all aggregation procedures even those from, say,
economics or statistics.

[14] We can use less than the pairwise rankings *and* their intensity levels, but, to avoid stilted
methods, this is close to being a minimal requirement.

Moreover, because F defines transitive rankings, the pairwise rankings obtained by the F_{c_i,c_j} functions never admit cycles.

Instead of using rankings, let $F_{c_i,c_j} = 1$ if $c_i \succ c_j$, and $F_{c_i,c_j} = -1$ if $c_j \succ c_i$. With this convention, the outcome for the above profile is

$$F^*(\mathbf{p}) = (F_{c_1,c_2}(\mathbf{p}), F_{c_2,c_3}(\mathbf{p}), F_{c_3,c_1}(\mathbf{p})) = (-1, 1, -1);$$

thus, the image of $F^*(\mathbf{p})$ is a vertex of the cube $[-1,1]^3$. The theorem follows if one of the cyclic vertices, $(1,1,1)$ or $-(1,1,1)$, is in the F^* image set. In other words, the theorem is proved by "solving" either $F^*(\mathbf{p}) = (1,1,1)$ or $F^*(\mathbf{p}) = (-1,-1,-1)$.

Now that we have the three F_{c_i,c_j} functions, we need to determine the relevant variables. An important aspect of IIA is that the $F_{c_i,c_j}(\mathbf{p})$ outcome depends on each voter's relative ranking of the pair. Thus, $F_{c_1,c_2}(\mathbf{p})$ uses only whether each voter's relative ranking is $c_1 \succ c_2$ or $c_2 \succ c_1$; e.g., $F_{c_1,c_2}(\mathbf{E}_1, \mathbf{E}_6) = F_{c_1,c_2}(\mathbf{E}_2, \mathbf{E}_4)$ because there is no change in each voter's $\{c_1, c_2\}$ ranking. (The first profile is indicated by the bullets in Fig. 3.4.2; the second profile is represented by daggers.)

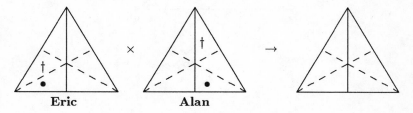

Fig. 3.4.2. Geometry of IIA for $\{c_1, c_2\}$

Thanks to IIA, the mapping F_{c_1,c_2} has a geometrical representation similar to the pairwise vote for $\{c_1, c_2\}$ (see Fig. 3.1.1); as we only care about which side of the $c_1 \sim c_2$ line contains each voter's preference, the mapping can be expressed as in Fig. 3.4.2. A similar geometric representation holds for each F_{c_i,c_j} mapping as determined by the $c_i \sim c_j$ line.

3.4.6 Elementary Algebra

by comparing Fig. 3.4.2 with the description of the pairwise vote, we find that Arrow's Theorem seeks to determine whether we can invent pairwise voting procedures F_{c_i,c_j} using the same restrictive information available to the pairwise majority vote, but where the outcomes now are transitive. The answer is no. Moreover, this relationship between the pairwise majority vote and the design of the F_{c_i,c_j} functions suggests that intuition for the proof of Theorem 3.4.2 can be derived by better understanding how the two approaches are related. Recall, the pairwise vote defines the three equations in six unknowns

$$x_1 + x_2 + x_3 - x_4 - x_5 - x_6 = q_{1,2}$$
$$x_1 - x_2 - x_3 - x_4 + x_5 + x_6 = q_{2,3}$$
$$(3.4.2) \qquad -x_1 - x_2 + x_3 + x_4 + x_5 - x_6 = q_{3,1}.$$

One way to prove that cycles exist is to show that there are solutions satisfying $\sum_{j=1}^{6} x_j = 1$ where all $q_{i,j}$ values have the same sign. Algebra tell us that this is true if the system of four equations in six unknowns has rank four. A simple computation proves that it does, so solutions exist for any $q_{i,j}$ values; in particular, by choosing the $q_{i,j}$ values with the same sign, cycles occur.

Compare the pairwise voting problem with our goal of solving the three equations $F^*(\mathbf{p}) = \pm(1, 1, 1)$. Again, we are done if this system of equations has an appropriate "rank." However, by not knowing the definition of F, standard computational approaches cannot be used with F^*. Instead, an alternative, geometric approach is created to analyze the rank of a system based on its properties.

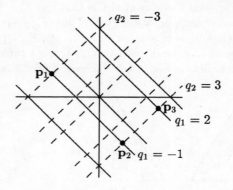

Fig. 3.4.3. Level set solution for an algebraic system

To demonstrate the ideas with a simple system, the level sets of

$$(3.4.3) \qquad\qquad x + y = q_1, \; x - y = q_2,$$

are given in Fig. 3.4.3. (The downward sloping lines are the level sets for $x + y$; the upward sloping dashed lines are level sets for $x - y$.) The crossing of the level sets corresponds to the independence of these equations; they satisfy the rank condition. Namely, Eq. 3.4.3 can be solved for any (q_1, q_2) choice. Because each downward sloping line defines all (x, y) values leading to a particular q_1, use the q_1 value as an identifying name of the line. Similarly, a q_2 value identifies a particular upward sloping line.

Finding the $(q_1, q_2) = (2, 3)$ solution is easy, but try to solve it with the geometry of level sets. Think of this as finding a restaurant near the corner of Main Street and Chicago Avenue. Chicago runs north-south, so from a starting position $\mathbf{p}_1$ drive east along a street until you find Chicago Avenue at $\mathbf{p}_2$. The rest is easy; drive south on Chicago until you find Main at $\mathbf{p}_3$. Similarly, for the algebra problem, start at, say $\mathbf{p}_1 = (-2, 1)$ which is at the corner $(q_1, q_2) = (-1, -3)$. To solve the problem an equation at a time, move from $\mathbf{p}_1$ along the $q_1 = -1$ street; i.e., move from $\mathbf{p}_1$ along the $q_1 = -1$ downward slanting level set until reaching the dashed line set $x - y = 3$ (at $\mathbf{p}_2 = (1, -2)$). (This is equivalent to driving east on a street until Chicago Avenue.)

Point $\mathbf{p}_2$ solves the $x - y = 3$ equation. To solve the second equation, move from $\mathbf{p}_2$ along the street $x - y = 3$. (Namely, stay on Chicago until Main.) By staying on this dashed line, the solution for the first equation remains intact while we search for the solution for the second equation; this is at the downward sloping level set of $x + y = 2$. The solution is $\mathbf{p}_3 = (2.5, -0.5)$. The full rank of these equations ensures that this $\mathbf{p}_1 \to \mathbf{p}_2 \to \mathbf{p}_3$ adjustment process works.

Cycle Construction. To use $\mathbf{p}_1 \to \mathbf{p}_2 \to \mathbf{p}_3$ to construct a pairwise cycle (for Eqs. 3.4.2), start with an arbitrary profile $\mathbf{p}_1$; $q_{1,2}$ has some value, so assume it is positive. To create the cycle, change the profile so that $q_{2,3}, q_{3,1}$ also are positive. So, move from $\mathbf{p}_1$ on the level set of the first equation (so $q_{1,2}$ remains fixed) while changing the value of $q_{2,3}$ until it becomes positive at $\mathbf{p}_2$. The final stage is move from $\mathbf{p}_2$ by staying on the level sets of the first two equations while changing the $q_{3,1}$ value until it becomes positive at profile $\mathbf{p}_3$. The success of this $\mathbf{p}_1 \to \mathbf{p}_2 \to \mathbf{p}_3$ construction, which creates a positive cycle, is guaranteed by the rank conditions.

Not only does the rank condition allow this $\mathbf{p}_1 \to \mathbf{p}_2 \to \mathbf{p}_3$ approach, but, with added conditions, this $\mathbf{p}_1 \to \mathbf{p}_2 \to \mathbf{p}_3$ process is a geometric way to determine the "rank." This technique, used in Example 3.4.1, is how I prove Theorem 3.4.1. Namely, in the approach developed here, the proof of Arrow's Theorem is converted into a discrete version of the standard algebra conclusion about "m equations and n unknowns."

Who Can Do What? In solving a system of equations, the first step is to determine which variables change the values of which equations. For instance, with $x + y = 6$, $y - z = 7$, z is not an interesting variable for the first equation. Similarly, we need to understand which variables change the F_{c_i, c_j} values.

As involvement requires F to have at least two outcomes, there exist profiles $\mathbf{p}, \mathbf{p}'$ where $F(\mathbf{p}) \neq F(\mathbf{p}')$. The two F rankings differ iff the relative ranking of some pair changes iff for some pair $\{c_i, c_j\}$ we have that $F_{c_i, c_j}(\mathbf{p}) \neq F_{c_i, c_j}(\mathbf{p}')$. If $\mathbf{p}_{c_i, c_j}$ denotes each voter's relative $\{c_i, c_j\}$ rankings of $\mathbf{p}$, then IIA requires that

$$(3.4.4) \qquad F_{c_i, c_j}(\mathbf{p}_{c_i, c_j}) \neq F_{c_i, c_j}(\mathbf{p}'_{c_i, c_j}).$$

According to Eq. 3.4.4, $\mathbf{p}_{c_i, c_j} \neq \mathbf{p}'_{c_i, c_j}$, so, at least one voter, Eric or Alan, changed his relative ranking of $\{c_i, c_j\}$. If only one of them switched $\{c_i, c_j\}$ rankings, then we have identified a situation where a single voter changing his $\{c_i, c_j\}$ ranking forces changes in the F_{c_i, c_j} ranking.

A second possibility is that both Eric's and Alan's relative $\{c_i, c_j\}$ rankings differ in the profiles $\mathbf{p}_{c_i, c_j}$ and $\mathbf{p}'_{c_i, c_j}$. So, let $\mathbf{p}''_{c_i, c_j}$ represent the change of $\mathbf{p}_{c_i, c_j}$ defined when only Eric changes his $\{c_i, c_j\}$ ranking. Thus, the change in profiles

$$(3.4.5) \qquad \mathbf{p}_{c_i, c_j} \to \mathbf{p}''_{c_i, c_j} \to \mathbf{p}'_{c_i, c_j}$$

is a stepwise process where first Eric changes his pairwise preference, and then Alan does. Clearly, at least two of the $F_{c_i, c_j}(\mathbf{p}), F_{c_i, c_j}(\mathbf{p}), F_{c_i, c_j}(\mathbf{p})$ outcomes differ, so *there always exists a situation where when a single voter changes his* $\{c_i, c_j\}$ *ranking, the* F_{c_i,c_j} *ranking changes.*

Involvement ensures there are at least two pairs $\{c_i, c_j\}$ where F_{c_i,c_j} changes rankings with changes in profiles. The above argument shows that there is a situation where a F_{c_i,c_j} change is caused by one voter varying his relative ranking. For our purposes, the worst possibility is if, for all situations and all pairs, it is the same voter – say, Eric – who changes his ranking. Namely, the only way F can change is according to Eric's wishes which, of course, violates "voter responsiveness." (A word of warning: This does not mean that every voter can influence the relative ranking of every pair. Instead, it could be that Eric *always* determines the $\{c_1, c_2\}$ and $\{c_1, c_3\}$ relative rankings, and sometimes he determines the $\{c_2, c_3\}$ relative rankings. Nevertheless, to satisfy voter responsiveness, there always exists at least one situation where, if Eric has a particular $\{c_2, c_3\}$ relative ranking, then Alan's preferences determine the F_{c_2,c_3} outcome.)

Voter responsiveness requires that each voter influences the outcome of a different pair of candidates; say, Eric is assigned $\{c_1, c_2\}$ while Alan is assigned $\{c_2, c_3\}$. Of course, it may be that Eric can influence the F_{c_1,c_2} ranking only when Alan has a particular $\{c_1, c_2\}$ ranking.[15] Similarly, for Alan to influence the F_{c_2,c_3} ranking, Eric might need to have a particular $\{c_2, c_3\}$ ranking. These requirements identify portions of the F_{c_i,c_j} level sets.

3.4.7 The F_{c_i,c_j} Level Sets

The rank conditions involve a $\mathbf{p}_1 \to \mathbf{p}_2 \to \mathbf{p}_3$ adjustment argument. First assign Eric the $\{c_2, c_3\}$ ranking so that Alan can change the F_{c_2,c_3} outcome. If it is $c_2 \succ c_3$, then by varying between type-one and six, Eric keeps the same $\{c_1, c_3\}$ and $\{c_2, c_3\}$ relative rankings, while changing his $\{c_1, c_2\}$ ranking. Alternatively, if Eric must have a $c_3 \succ c_2$ ranking, then he varies between type-three and four. Eric's choices are indicated by arrows in Fig. 3.4.4. Observe the strong similarity with Fig. 3.4.1.

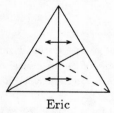   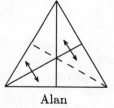

Eric   Alan

Fig. 3.4.4. Changing level sets keeping $\{c_1, c_3\}$ fixed

Similarly, Alan might need a particular $\{c_1, c_2\}$ ranking before Eric can change the F_{c_1,c_2} ranking. Whatever the assignment, Alan's possible voter types can be

---

[15] In Example 3.4.1, Lillian and I altered rankings of our assigned pairs independent of what the other person believed about that pair. To avoid the same impossibility difficulty, a procedure may constrain Eric's influence in terms of Alan's choices.

chosen so that his $\{c_1, c_3\}$ relative ranking remains fixed, his $\{c_1, c_2\}$ relative ranking is as assigned, and his $\{c_2, c_3\}$ relative ranking varies. Thus, the assignment for the voters is as given in Fig. 3.4.4. Observe that while Eric's and Alan's permitted moves keep invariant the binary rankings of two pairs, their *intensity level* changes. This is where IIA ignores intensity information.

To prove the theorem, choose a profile where Eric and Alan have the appropriate rankings so the other person can change the outcome of his assigned pair. Choosing the profile satisfying this condition so that it also is in a region with arrows, we have the starting profile $\mathbf{p}_1$ and a value for $F_{c_3,c_1}(\mathbf{p}_1)$. (Remember, this value is 1 or -1.) Now, as Eric varies his ranking between the two admissible voter types, both Alan's and Eric's $\{c_2, c_3\}$ and the $\{c_3, c_1\}$ rankings remain fixed, (so there is no change in F_{c_2,c_3} and F_{c_3,c_1}), but the F_{c_1,c_2} value changes. Choose Eric's ranking to define a profile $\mathbf{p}_2$ where

$$F_{c_3,c_1}(\mathbf{p}_1) = F_{c_1,c_2}(\mathbf{p}_2).$$

As Eric did not change $\{c_2, c_3\}$ or $\{c_3, c_1\}$ rankings, the profile change $\mathbf{p}_1 \to \mathbf{p}_2$ is on the level sets of F_{c_2,c_3} and F_{c_3,c_1}. (We found Chicago Avenue!)

Next, change $\mathbf{p}_2$ by varying Alan's $\{c_2, c_3\}$ rankings between the two indicated voter types. This, of course, changes the F_{c_2,c_3} value without affecting the value of the other two functions. (The change is on level sets of the other two functions because the relative ranking of $\{c_1, c_2\}$ and $\{c_1, c_3\}$ remain fixed.) Thus, $\mathbf{p}_2$ can be changed to $\mathbf{p}_3$ where

$$F_{c_1,c_2}(\mathbf{p}_3) = F_{c_2,c_3}(\mathbf{p}_3) = F_{c_3,c_1}(\mathbf{p}_3).$$

Thus $\mathbf{p}_3$ defines a cycle for F^*; as a cycle cannot be defined from a transitive ranking, the assumed F does not exist.

To extend the proof to $n \geq 2$ voters, just mimic the Eq. 3.4.5 argument. Using involvement, there are profiles whereby $F_{c_i,c_j}(\mathbf{p}) \neq F_{c_i,c_j}(\mathbf{p}')$. Convert profile $\mathbf{p}_{c_i,c_j}$ into $\mathbf{p}'_{c_i,c_j}$ into steps where one voter at a time changes these pairwise rankings. In this manner, a F_{c_i,c_j} change can be identified with a situation where one voter changed his rankings and all other voters have specified rankings of this pair. Thus, we can identify situations where when Fred changes, say, $\{c_1, c_2\}$ relative rankings, then F_{c_1,c_2} changes value, and there exist situations when Adrian changes, say, $\{c_2, c_3\}$ rankings, the F_{c_2,c_3} value changes. Using the profile $\mathbf{p}_1 \to \mathbf{p}_2 \to \mathbf{p}_3$ argument, only Fred and Adrian change rankings; all other voters remain fixed at the specific required rankings.

Dictator or Anti-Dictator. As IIA makes it impossible for the procedure to determine whether it is dealing with a rational or a confused voter, the procedure must serve the needs of either kind obediently. (See Sect. 3.1.) This makes the transitivity of outcomes a victim. Alternatively, a procedure with transitive outcomes satisfying involvement, universality of domain, and IIA, must depend upon the rankings of a particular voter. But, this conclusion should be expected. After all, if only one-dimensional information is admitted, the resulting procedure should be single-dimensional in nature – it should depend upon the preferences of a single voter. The rationality of this single voter should manifest itself in the relationship between the outcome of the procedure and the voter's ranking. As asserted, this defined a dictatorship or an anti-dictatorship.

The "level set" proof of Theorem 3.4.1 exploits the flexibility of movement in a profile while fixing two relative rankings. To prove this dictator assertion, the restrictiveness feature, where the relative ranking of a pair is uniquely determined by the relative rankings of the other pairs, is used. (See Example 3.4.1.)

Involvement requires the rankings of at least two F_{c_i, c_j} functions to vary. Assume they are F_{c_1, c_2} and F_{c_2, c_3} and that the F_{c_i, c_j} ranking of each pair agrees with the voter's relative ranking. Thus, if $\mathbf{p} = c_1 \succ c_2 \succ c_3$, then $F_{c_1, c_2}(\mathbf{p}) = c_1 \succ c_2$, $F_{c_2, c_3}(\mathbf{p}) = c_2 \succ c_3$. In turn, because F provides a transitive ranking, we have that $F_{c_3, c_1}(\mathbf{p}) = c_1 \succ c_3$. Similarly, if the voter has the reversed ranking of $c_3 \succ c_2 \succ c_1$, the transitivity of F forces $F_{c_3, c_1}(c_3 \succ c_1) = c_3 \succ c_1$. In other words, if two of the three F_{c_i, c_j} functions agree with the voter's relative ranking of the pair, then so must the third. This is a dictatorship. A similar argument shows that if two of the F_{c_i, c_j} functions reverse the voter's relative ranking, then so must the third. This defines an anti-dictatorship.

The remaining possibility is if one function, say F_{c_1, c_2}, agrees with the voter's relative ranking, and another function, say F_{c_2, c_3}, reverses this ranking. Now, if F_{c_3, c_1} reverses or retains the voter's ranking of the pair, then at least two of the F_{c_i, c_j} functions have the same effect on the ranking. This creates a contradiction because it requires the third to be of the same type. Therefore, F_{c_3, c_1} must be a constant mapping. Without loss of generality, assume $F_{c_3, c_1}(\mathbf{p}) = c_1 \succ c_3$.

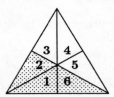

Fig. 3.4.5. Impossibility of F_{c_3, c_1} being constant

This assumption requires a F outcome to be in a $\{1, 2, 6\}$ ranking region. (See the shaded region of Fig. 3.4.5.) The contradiction (which mimics Example 3.4.1) is obtained by finding a $\mathbf{p}$ where $F(\mathbf{p})$ is a prohibited type-four ranking. This requires $F_{c_1, c_2} = c_2 \succ c_1$, so the voter's relative ranking of this pair is $c_2 \succ c_1$. To have $F_{c_2, c_3} = c_3 \succ c_2$, the reversal nature of F_{c_2, c_3} requires the voter to have the ranking $c_2 \succ c_3$. Combining this information, if the voter is either of type-three or four, we obtain the outlawed $F_{c_3, c_1} = c_3 \succ c_1$. Thus, F_{c_3, c_1} cannot be constant, and the conclusion follows. □

3.4.8 Some Existence Theorems

Proving Theorem 3.4.1 (or of Arrow's Theorem) is similar to solving m equations in n unknowns, $n \geq m$. This suggests that the negative statement of Arrow's Theorem can be avoided by reducing the number of independent equations and/or the number of unknowns. Actually, *if any condition of Theorem 3.4.1 is weakened, a possibility theorem emerges.* Consequently, Theorem 3.4.1 describes the boundary between possibility and impossibility theorems.

The only way to relax "involvement" is to admit procedures that only change the rankings of a single pair of candidates (rather than at least two). As this problem becomes single-dimension, it is trivial to design such procedures. For instance, if this pair is $\{c_1, c_2\}$, then all outcomes could vary between type-one and six; i.e., between the rankings $c_1 \succ c_2 \succ c_3$ and $c_2 \succ c_1 \succ c_3$. One such procedure satisfying the remaining requirements is the majority vote.

Relaxing the universal domain condition requires us to impose profile restrictions. Rather than providing a complete discussion,[16] examples are offered to suggest the rich selection of issues.

Example 3.4.2. "Universal domain" fails iff some candidate cannot choose a particular ranking. So, assume Alfred has no restrictions, but Gene is prohibited from choosing just one ranking; say, $c_1 \succ c_3 \succ c_2$. By proscribing only one choice for one agent, this profile restriction is as close as possible to satisfying the universal domain condition without doing so. Nevertheless, it allows a procedure to exist that satisfies the remaining assumptions.

To design this procedure, observe from Fig. 3.4.6 that keeping Gene away from $c_1 \succ c_3 \succ c_2$ leaves him with only weak $c_1 \succ c_2$ rankings. Thus Gene cannot fix the $c_1 \succ c_2$ ranking and that of another pair while varying the ranking of the third pair. Consequently the impossibility proof fails when Gene needs the $c_1 \succ c_2$ ranking for Alfred to decide the $\{c_1, c_2\}$ ranking. The procedure follows from this observation.

Let Gene be the dictator of the $\{c_1, c_3\}$ and the $\{c_2, c_3\}$ relative rankings. Indeed, go a step further; if Gene prefers $c_2 \succ c_1$, then that is the procedure's pairwise ranking. On the other hand, when Gene has the ranking $c_1 \succ c_2$, Alfred's relative ranking of this pair determines its relative ranking.

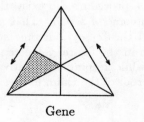 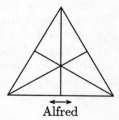

Gene   Alfred

Fig. 3.4.6. A possibility example

To see that this procedure is well defined, observe that if Gene has the relative rankings $c_3 \succ c_1$ and $c_3 \succ c_2$, or if he has $c_1 \succ c_3$ and $c_2 \succ c_3$, then the two

---

[16] The interested reader should consult [S14].

possible group outcomes are distinguished by the $\{c_1, c_2\}$ relative ranking – at times, this is Al's choice. The remaining case is where Gene has $c_3 \succ c_1$ and $c_2 \succ c_3$ rankings; here the outcome must be $c_2 \succ c_3 \succ c_1$ and the $\{c_1, c_2\}$ ranking corresponds to Gene's preference of $c_2 \succ c_1$. (It is impossible for Gene to have the rankings $c_1 \succ c_3$ and $c_3 \succ c_1$ because they would force him to have the proscribed ranking $c_1 \succ c_3 \succ c_2$.) Therefore, except where Gene has the relative ranking $c_2 \succ c_1$, the $\{c_1, c_2\}$ ranking is free to be decided. Consequently, the above procedure is well-defined.

While the procedure is defined, its quasi-dictatorial nature disqualifies it as a paradigm for emerging democracies. Instead, this procedure combines two one-dimensional methods; it specifies when each procedure is operative. The stilted nature is to be expected; whenever a choice method relies upon lower dimensional information (as required by IIA), only lower dimensional procedures emerge.

Because the above procedure can be defined with Gene's profile restriction, imagine the multitude of possible procedures if we impose more severe restrictions on him. For instance, suppose Gene is not permitted to have any ranking where $c_1 \succ c_2$; thus any ranking in the shaded region of Fig. 3.4.7 is off-limits for him. The surprising fact is that no procedure exists with this more severe restriction!

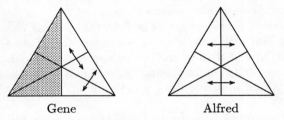

Gene   Alfred

Fig. 3.4.7. Too much of a restriction reverts to impossibility

Gene always has the $c_2 \succ c_1$ ranking, so a situation never arises where Alfred can determine an outcome; the earlier procedure becomes another vacuous campaign promise. If, contrary to the claim, a procedure did exist, then there exist situations where Gene influences the outcome of a pair. That pair must be $\{c_1, c_3\}$ and/or $\{c_2, c_3\}$. Al decides at least the $\{c_1, c_2\}$ outcome and this is done with Gene's $c_2 \succ c_1$ ranking. As shown in the figure, Gene can vary his ranking of any pair to satisfy this condition while keeping the relative ranking of the remaining pair fixed. The rest of the proof of the claim follows from the $\mathbf{p_1} \rightarrow \mathbf{p_2} \rightarrow \mathbf{p_3}$ rank argument.[17]

3.4.9 Intensity IIA

Theorem 3.4.1 asserts it is impossible to design a reasonable procedure using only the one-dimensional information about the relative ranking of pairs. In fact, the $\mathbf{p_1} \rightarrow \mathbf{p_2} \rightarrow \mathbf{p_3}$ profile change argument depends on IIA admitting

---

[17]See [S14] for more general conditions that ensure a possibility or impossibility theorem.

so little information about the profile that we cannot be sure even whether the voters have transitive preferences! This impossibility proof, however, fails when information about the "intensity of pairwise rankings" is admitted; the intensity signals that transitive preferences are used.

To see the effect of intensity information, recall that both Eric and Alan varied between a weak and a strong intensity of the two fixed binary rankings. Recall in Example 3.4.2 that if Gene is kept away from a strong binary ranking of one pair, a procedure could be constructed. Therefore, it appears that by including the information about the intensity of pairwise rankings, a wider variety of procedures could be defined. This is the case.

To add intuition, return to Fig. 3.4.4. Suppose for Alan to change the F_{c_2,c_3} value, Eric must have a *strong* binary ranking $c_2 \succ c_3$. As this restricts Eric to the single $c_2 \succ c_1 \succ c_3$ ranking, he cannot vary preferences. Similarly, if Eric is required to have a weak ranking of $c_2 \succ c_3$, then, to retain the same $\{c_1, c_3\}$ ranking (critical for the proof), Eric must have the preference $c_1 \succ c_2 \succ c_3$. This lack of movement kills the proof and the geometric rank condition. Consequently, we must expect possibility assertions when intensity information is allowed.

Definition 3.4.1. The *intensity IIA* condition is where the relative ranking of any two candidates, $\{c_i, c_j\}$, depends only on each voter's relative ranking of these candidates and the intensity of this ranking. $\square$

The main conclusion, which shows that procedures exist which are acceptable in polite groups, follows.

Theorem 3.4.3. *There exist procedures satisfying universal domain, unanimity, intensity IIA, and voter responsiveness. One such procedure is the BC or CI. Indeed, the BC is the only positional method to satisfy these conditions.*

That the CI satisfies this condition is Prob. 6, Sect. 3.3. The proof of the BC assertion must wait until the next chapter where it is shown that the BC is a CI.

Example 3.4.2 can be modified to create an procedure satisfying universal domain, involvement, voter responsiveness, and where IIA is satisfied for all but one agent; for this agent (Gene) the intensity IIA condition applies to one pair and IIA to all others. In other words, even the slightest change of the Theorem 3.4.1 assumptions changes the conclusions. The main point, however, is that a simple change in the informational requirements transforms an impossible mission into a reasonably comfortable setting. Again, the BC moves to center stage!

More Candidates. The real message of Arrow's Theorem emerges with $n = 3$; allowing more candidates does not radically change anything. The main modification is to change "involvement" so it involves more candidates. A natural condition is that for each pair of candidates $\{c_j, c_k\}$, there is a profile yielding an outcome with the relative ranking $c_j \succ c_k$ and another profile where the outcome is the reverse of this. (Weaker conditions using different terminology are in [S14].) This condition holds for any procedure admitting a strict ranking and its reversal. The other conditions remain the same, and the same negative conclusion follows.

Positive conclusions can be found by replacing IIA with an intensity version. As described in Sect. 3.1, the intensity level is determined by the number of candidates a voter uses to separate a pair. Again, once this is done, the frustrating conclusion gives way to acceptable procedures such as the BC. For more information, as well as other interpretations, see [S19].

3.4.10 Exercises

1. a. Instead of the representation triangle, in Example 3.4.1 use the representation cube to show that no conflict occurs if we admit nontransitive outcomes.
b. Show that the proof of Example 3.4.1 fails should $\{c_1, c_3\}$ ranking be determined not only by unanimity, but also by the intensity levels for this ranking. By using intensity, can a procedure be constructed?

2. If a procedure admits only the outcomes $c_1 \succ c_2 \succ c_3$, $c_2 \succ c_3 \succ c_1$, and $c_3 \succ c_1 \succ c_2$, does it satisfy involvement? Suppose a procedure only admits two rankings; $\mathcal{R}_1 = c_1 \succ c_2 \succ c_3$ and $\mathcal{R}_2$. Show that if $\mathcal{R}_2$ is the reverse of $\mathcal{R}_1$, then involvement is satisfied. Are there any other $\mathcal{R}_2$ choices which honor involvement? (Hint: use the binary intersection property of the representation triangle to prove your answer.)

3. According to Theorem 3.4.1, all positional methods violate IIA. Use Fig. 3.1.3 to design illustrating examples.

4. Theorem 3.4.1 holds even if indifference among rankings is admitted. Change the involvement condition to read that for at least two pairs, the relative ranking can be two of the three possible choice. (For instance, this is satisfied if F has the rankings $c_1 \sim c_2 \succ c_3$ and $c_1 \succ c_2 \sim c_3$ because the $\{c_1, c_2\}$ and the $\{c_2, c_3\}$ rankings change while the $\{c_1, c_3\}$ ranking remains the same.) Show that with this weaker condition, the theorem still holds. (Now, however, the dictator may get only indifference with certain strict pairwise rankings.)

5. a. When proving that F must depend upon the ranking of a single voter, one step assumed that F_{c_1,c_2} corresponds to the voter's ranking of the pair, F_{c_2,c_3} reversed it, and the last mapping was the constant $F_{c_3,c_1} = c_3 \succ c_1$. Carry out the same argument with the assumption that the constant mapping is $F_{c_3,c_1} = c_1 \succ c_3$.
b. Problem 4 extends the theorem to where the outcomes admit indifference. Suppose the only two outcomes admitted by F_{c_1,c_2} are $c_1 \succ c_2$ and $c_1 \sim c_2$. What replaces the dictator and anti-dictator?
c. Theorem 3.4.1 tries to create a procedure so that when all voters have transitive preferences, the outcome is transitive. However, IIA allows the same procedure to serve confused voters (voters without transitive preferences.) Consequently, by trying to accommodate two radically different groups, only the wishes of a single voter can be considered. If this voter is transitive, then the procedure is either a dictator or an anti-dictator. What happens if the single empowered voter is cyclic?

6. The proof of most theorems in this section used the fact that there are rankings of two pairs which uniquely determine the ranking of the third, and there are other rankings of these pairs where the ranking of the third pair is free to be determined. Describe these two situations in terms of the rankings of the first two pairs.

7. Show that IIA, involvement, and the fact that F depends upon a single voter's preferences requires $F_{c_i,c_j}(\mathbf{p}^r) = F_{c_i,c_j}^r(\mathbf{p})$ where $\mathbf{p}^r$ means that each voter's ranking of the candidates in $\mathbf{p}$ is reversed.

8. For choice functions, IIA requires that if $F(\mathbf{p}) = c_i$, and if $\mathbf{p}'$ is a profile where each voter's relative ranking of $\{c_i, c_j\}$ remains the same in both profiles, then $F(\mathbf{p}') \neq c_j$. This means, for example, that by knowing what voters are on which side of the $c_1 \sim c_2$ line, we can

determine whether the outcome is in $\{c_1, c_3\}$ or $\{c_2, c_3\}$ However, which choice is made cannot be determined just from the $\{c_1, c_2\}$ information. Thus, when choice procedures are used, IIA implicitly defines three mappings $F_{c_1,c_2}, F_{c_2,c_3}, F_{c_3,c_1}$. (Geometrically, the image of F_{c_1,c_2} is in either the union

$$\mathcal{R}(1) \cup \mathcal{R}(2) \cup \mathcal{R}(3) \cup \mathcal{R}(4),$$

or in

$$\mathcal{R}(6) \cup \mathcal{R}(5) \cup \mathcal{R}(4) \cup \mathcal{R}(3).)$$

So, if there are only two voters with fixed $\{c_1, c_3\}$ rankings, the outcome set is either from $\{c_1, c_2\}$ or $\{c_3, c_2\}$. (These sets replace the rankings $c_1 \succ c_3, c_3 \succ c_1$ from the above proof of Theorem 3.4.1.) Suppose it is the first. To prove the choice function version of Theorem 3.4.1, it suffices to show that it is possible to change the $\{c_1, c_2\}$ rankings (altering the choice between $\{c_1, c_3\}$ and $\{c_2, c_3\}$) and $\{c_2, c_3\}$ rankings (altering the outcome between $\{c_2, c_1\}$ and $\{c_3, c_1\}$) so that c_3 is the outcome. (This is when one outcome requires $\{c_3, c_1\}$ and the other has $\{c_3, c_2\}$.) This is a contradiction.

The other possibility is if the fixed $\{c_1, c_3\}$ outcome must be in $\{c_3, c_2\}$. Here, the goal is to show that c_1 can be the forced outcome from two voters. Carry out the details.

9. In Example 3.4.2, suppose the profile restriction forbids Gene from having an even ranking. Does a procedure exist? If so, characterize all of them. If not, explain why.

10. Show that the CI satisfies the conditions of Theorem 3.4.3.

11. It is asserted after Theorem 3.4.3 that a procedure can be designed even if intensity IIA condition is applied to one agent and one pair. Find such a procedure.

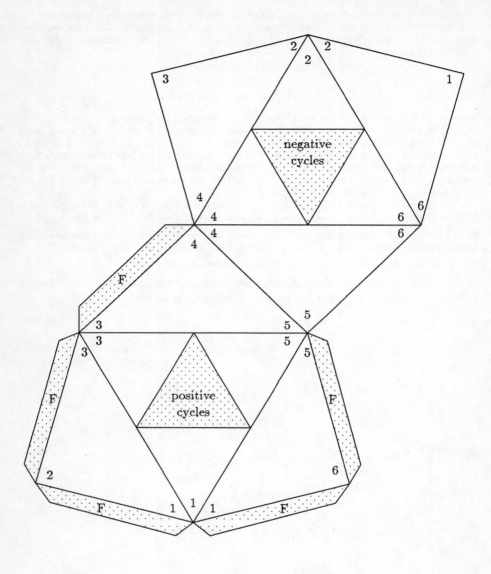

A cut out for the representation cube
suggested by Vincent Merlin

CHAPTER IV

POSITIONAL VOTING AND THE BC

As we learned in Chap. 3, problems and paradoxes must be anticipated with procedures based on pairwise rankings. The subtle reason is that these methods manage to drop the central assumption of transitivity. This suggests using methods, such as the plurality vote and the BC, which admit only rational voters. Do they have problems? Rest assured; there are plenty of them! But, with a further decomposition of profiles, it becomes easy to analyze the problems and create profile examples.

4.1 Positional Voting Methods

Mankind need not live by the plurality vote alone; there are other ways to tally ballots. To see why we should care, consider an one-voter election with, say, a type-one voter $\mathbf{p} = \mathbf{E}_1$. While the vector ballot $\mathbf{e}_1$ anoints c_1 as the unanimous winner, this outcome fails to reflect the second-ranked status of c_2. Indeed, based only on the outcome, it is equally reasonable to believe that the voter has the ranking $c_1 \succ c_3 \succ c_2$. This may, or may not matter to anyone other than c_2's father, but the missing information is important when analyzing paradoxes such as the beverage example from the fable. Here, the troublesome outcome occurs because the procedure ignores the critical information that each voter found "Wine" to be either a first or a second-ranked option. This suggests considering procedures which recognize a voter's middle-ranked candidate.

Definition 4.1.1. For $n \geq 3$ candidates, $\mathbf{W} = (w_1, w_2, \ldots, w_n) \in R^n$ is a *voting vector* if its components satisfy the inequalities

$$(4.1.1) \qquad w_i \geq w_{i+1}, \quad i = 1, \ldots, n-1, \text{ and } w_1 > w_n$$

A *positional voting method* is defined by a voting vector $\mathbf{W}^n = (w_1, w_2, \ldots, w_n)$. In tallying a ballot, w_j points are assigned to the voter's jth-ranked candidate, $j = 1, 2, \ldots, n$. The candidates are ranked according to the number of points assigned to each of them. $\square$

The first inequality of Eq. 4.1.1 prohibits rewarding a lower-ranked candidate better than a higher-ranked one. The second inequality guarantees that the tally distinguishes a voter's rankings of the candidates. For instance, there would be no suspense on election night if $(1, 1, 1)$ is used – the complete tie $\mathcal{I} = c_1 \sim c_2 \sim c_3$ is the only possible election outcome.

Example 4.1.1. a. A three-candidate *plurality vote* is defined by the voting vector

(4.1.2) $$\mathbf{W}_P^3 = \mathbf{e}_1 = (1,0,0), \quad \mathbf{W}_P^n = (1,0,\ldots,0)$$

b. The *antiplurality* procedure is where a voter is instructed to vote for all but one candidate. This is a kinder and gentler way to ask each voter to identify his bottom-ranked candidate. Thus, a natural name for

(4.1.3) $$\mathbf{W}_{AP}^3 = (1,1,0), \quad \mathbf{W}_{AP}^n = (1,1,\ldots,1,0)$$

is the *antiplurality vote*. For those who value honesty over kindness, use the equivalent voting vector $(0,0,\ldots,0,-1)$.

c. The important BC voting vector is

(4.1.4) $$\mathbf{W}_{BC}^3 = (2,1,0), \quad \mathbf{W}_{BC}^n = (n-1,n-2,\ldots,1,0)$$

It is interesting to note for three candidates that

(4.1.5)
$$\mathbf{W}_{BC}^3 = (2,1,0) = (1,0,0) + (1,1,0)$$
$$= \mathbf{W}_P^3 + \mathbf{W}_{AP}^3$$

The BC appears to split the difference between the plurality and antiplurality votes. This statement extends; for instance, the three extreme four-candidate methods are the plurality, antiplurality, and the method asking us to vote for two candidates. Again, $\mathbf{W}_{AP}^4$ is the sum of the procedure $(1,0,0,0)$, $(1,1,0,0)$, $(1,1,1,0)$. $\square$

4.1.1 The Difference a Procedure Makes

There is a practical WGAD ("Who Gives A Damn?") question. What difference does it make if an election is tallied with a plurality vote, an antiplurality vote, the BC, or something else? Won't the outcomes be essentially the same?

The answer is *No!* The fable proves that the outcomes of different procedures may appear to have nothing to do with each other! For instance, had the chair used the BC rather than the plurality vote to rank the beverages, he might have enjoyed a stress-free life. To recall, the BC tally for the beverage example with the profile $\mathbf{p}_b = (0, \frac{6}{15}, 0, \frac{4}{15}, \frac{5}{15}, 0)$ is

		Borda tally		
Voter type	p_j	Water	Beer	Wine
2	$\frac{6}{15}$	$2(\frac{6}{15})$	0	$\frac{6}{15}$
4	$\frac{4}{15}$	0	$\frac{4}{15}$	$2(\frac{4}{15})$
5	$\frac{5}{15}$	0	$2(\frac{5}{15})$	$\frac{5}{15}$
Total	1	$\frac{12}{15}$	$\frac{14}{15}$	$\frac{19}{15}$

Thus, the BC ranking of Wine $\succ$ Beer $\succ$ Water agrees with the binary majority vote comparisons while completely reversing the plurality ranking of Water $\succ$ Beer $\succ$ Wine. The message is clear; the choice of the procedure matters.

Maybe the message is clear, but there is fog surrounding the choice of a system. To improve visibility, a theory is developed for positional voting. Again, emphasis is placed on three-candidate elections.

The tally for a positional voting system has a form similar to Eq. 2.2.2. With a specified voting vector $\mathbf{W}^3 = (w_1, w_2, w_3)$, the vector ballot for a voter of type $c_2 \succ c_1 \succ c_3$ is (w_2, w_1, w_3); namely, second-ranked c_1 receives w_2 points, top-ranked c_2 gets w_1 points, and the bottom-ranked c_3 is assigned only w_3 points. As in Sect. 2.2, the vector ballot for the jth type is an appropriate permutation of $\mathbf{W}^3$; $[\mathbf{W}^3]_j$. Thus, $[\mathbf{W}^3]_4 = (w_3, w_2, w_1)$ to reflect the voter's preference of $c_3 \succ c_2 \succ c_1$. The unanimity profile outcome captures the notation

$$f(\mathbf{E}_j, \mathbf{W}^3) = [\mathbf{W}^3]_j, \quad j = 1, 2, \ldots, 6$$

An election tally just counts the proportion of all voters casting a particular vector ballot, so the election mapping for profile $\mathbf{p}$ is the linear mapping

(4.1.6) $$f(\mathbf{p}, \mathbf{W}^3) = \sum_{j=1}^{6} p_j f(\mathbf{E}_j, \mathbf{W}^3) = \sum_{j=1}^{6} p_j [\mathbf{W}^3]_j$$

Example 4.1.2. a. For the BC and $\mathbf{p}_b$, we have

$$f(\mathbf{p}_b, \mathbf{W}^3_{BC}) = p_2 [\mathbf{W}^3_{BC}]_2 + p_4 [\mathbf{W}^3_{BC}]_4 + p_5 [\mathbf{W}^3_{BC}]_5$$
$$= \frac{6}{15} [\mathbf{W}^3_{BC}]_2 + \frac{4}{15} [\mathbf{W}^3_{BC}]_4 + \frac{5}{15} [\mathbf{W}^3_{BC}]_5$$
$$= \frac{6}{15}(2, 0, 1) + \frac{4}{15}(0, 1, 2) + \frac{5}{15}(0, 2, 1)$$
$$= (\frac{12}{15}, \frac{14}{15}, \frac{19}{15})$$

b. For the antiplurality method and $\mathbf{p}_b$ we have

$$f(\mathbf{p}_b, \mathbf{W}^3_{AP}) = \frac{6}{15} [\mathbf{W}^3_{AP}]_2 + \frac{4}{15} [\mathbf{W}^3_{AP}]_4 + \frac{5}{15} [\mathbf{W}^3_{AP}]_5$$
$$= \frac{6}{15}(1, 0, 1) + \frac{4}{15}(0, 1, 1) + \frac{5}{15}(0, 1, 1)$$
$$= (\frac{6}{15}, \frac{9}{15}, \frac{15}{15})$$

As both methods rank the beverages as Wine $\succ$ Beer $\succ$ Water, the antiplurality method joins the BC in offering a beverage ranking that is consistent with the binary rankings.

c. Notice the amusing fact that the sum of the plurality and antiplurality outcome for the beverage example is the BC outcome. $((\frac{6}{15}, \frac{5}{15}, \frac{4}{15}) + (\frac{6}{15}, \frac{9}{15}, \frac{15}{15}) = (\frac{12}{15}, \frac{14}{15}, \frac{19}{15})$.) This is no coincidence; this behavior, where the BC splits the difference between these two extreme methods occurs for all profiles. Why? (Hint, review Example 4.1.1.) $\square$

4.1.2 An Equivalence Relationship for Voting Vectors

To add structure to the infinite number of different voting vectors, we appeal to
a natural equivalence relationship.

Theorem 4.1.1. *Let the n-candidate voting vectors $\mathbf{W}_1^n$ and $\mathbf{W}_2^n$ satisfy*

$$(4.1.7) \qquad\qquad \mathbf{W}_1^n = a\mathbf{W}_2^n + b(1, 1, \ldots, 1)$$

*for scalars b and $a > 0$. For any profile $\mathbf{p}$, the election ranking for $f(\mathbf{p}, \mathbf{W}_1^n)$
agrees with that for $f(\mathbf{p}, \mathbf{W}_2^n)$.*

This assertion is intuitively obvious. As the $b(1, 1, \ldots, 1)$ term adds the same
value of b to each candidate's final tally, it cannot affect the final ranking. Similarly, the multiple a changes each candidate's tally by an a multiple – the final
ranking is unchanged.

Proof. Holding a profile fixed changes the election mapping into a linear mapping
of the voting vector. From the linear separation property

$$f(\mathbf{p}, \mathbf{W}_1^n) = f(\mathbf{p}, a\mathbf{W}_2^n + b(1, 1, \ldots, 1)) = af(\mathbf{p}, \mathbf{W}_2^n) + bf(\mathbf{p}, (1, 1, \ldots, 1))$$
$$(4.1.8) \qquad = af(\mathbf{p}, \mathbf{W}_2^n) + (b, b, \ldots, b)$$

The fact that $f(\mathbf{p}, (1, 1, \ldots, 1)) = (1, 1, \ldots, 1)$ is a direct computation. □

Example 4.1.3. For $\mathbf{p} = (\frac{1}{3}, 0, \frac{1}{6}, \frac{1}{2}, 0, 0)$, the BC outcome is

$$\begin{aligned}
f(\mathbf{p}, \mathbf{W}_{BC}^3) &= \frac{1}{3}[(2, 1, 0)]_1 + \frac{1}{6}[(2, 1, 0)]_3 + \frac{1}{2}[(2, 1, 0)]_4 \\
&= \frac{1}{3}(2, 1, 0) + \frac{1}{6}(1, 0, 2) + \frac{1}{2}(0, 1, 2) \\
&= (\frac{5}{6}, \frac{5}{6}, \frac{8}{6})
\end{aligned}$$

If $a = 1$, $b = 2$ then

$$\begin{aligned}
f(\mathbf{p}, \mathbf{W}_{BC}^3 + 2(1, 1, 1)) &= f(\mathbf{p}, (4, 3, 2)) \\
&= \frac{1}{3}(4, 3, 2) + \frac{1}{6}(3, 2, 4) + \frac{1}{2}(2, 3, 4) \\
&= (2\frac{5}{6}, 2\frac{5}{6}, 2\frac{8}{6}) = (2, 2, 2) + f(\mathbf{p}, \mathbf{W}_{BC}^3)
\end{aligned}$$

Finally, if $a = 3$, $b = 0$, then

$$f(\mathbf{p}, 3(2, 1, 0)) = \frac{1}{3}(6, 3, 0) + \frac{1}{6}(3, 0, 6) + \frac{1}{2}(0, 3, 6) = 3f(\mathbf{p}, \mathbf{W}_{BC}^3). \square$$

It is left to Prob. 1 to prove that Eq. 4.1.7 defines an equivalence relationship
among the voting vectors.

Definition 4.1.2. Two n-candidate voting vectors $\mathbf{W}_1^n, \mathbf{W}_2^n$ are equivalent, $\mathbf{W}_1 \approx \mathbf{W}_2$, if there exist scalars b and $a > 0$ which satisfy Eq. 4.1.7. $\square$

Example 4.1.4. a. The earlier "antiplurality" assertion that $\mathbf{W}_{AP}^3 = (1, 1, 0)$ is equivalent to $\mathbf{W}^3 = (0, 0, -1)$, follows by choosing $a = 1$, $b = -1$

b. *A voting vector* $\mathbf{W}^3 = (w_1, w_2, w_3)$ is equivalent to the BC if and only if

$$w_1 - w_2 = w_2 - w_3;$$

that is, iff the difference between successive weights is fixed. One direction of this assertion follows by choosing $a = w_1 - w_2$ and $b = w_3$ because

$$a(2, 1, 0) = (2(w_1 - w_2), w_1 - w_2, 0) = (w_1 - w_2 + (w_2 - w_3), w_2 - w_3, 0)$$
$$= (w_1 - w_3, w_2 - w_3, 0)$$

so $a\mathbf{W}_{BC}^3 + b(1, 1, 1) = \mathbf{W}^3$. Conversely, if $\mathbf{W}^3 = a\mathbf{W}_{BC} + b(1, 1, 1)$, then $\mathbf{W}^3 = (2a + b, a + b, b)$. This means that $w_1 - w_2 = w_2 - w_3 = a$.

c. By choosing $b = -w_n$, we can assume that all n-candidate voting vectors assign zero points to a voter's bottom-ranked candidate. Hence, $\mathbf{W}^n = (w_1, \ldots, w_{n-1}, 0)$. $\square$

Exploiting the Equivalence Relationship. Following the dictate of Sect. 2.1, we must exploit the equivalence relationship of Def. 4.1.2. This particular relationship allows a single voting vector to represent a class of equivalent voting methods. Consequently, assume that all three-candidate voting vectors are in the *normalized form*

$$(4.1.9) \qquad \mathbf{w}_s = (1 - s, s, 0) \text{ for } 0 \le s \le \frac{1}{2}$$

To transform $\mathbf{W}^3 = (w_1, w_2, w_3)$ into its normalized form, start with $b = -w_3$ to define the equivalent voting vector

$$(w_1 - w_3, w_2 - w_3, 0)$$

Next, let

$$a = 1/([w_1 - w_3] + [w_2 - w_3]) = 1/(w_1 + w_2 - 2w_3)$$

The new, equivalent voting vector is of the form $\mathbf{w}_s = (1 - s, s, 0)$ where

$$(4.1.10) \qquad s = (w_2 - w_3)/(w_1 + w_2 - 2w_3)$$

For $\mathbf{W}^3 = (w_1, w_2, 0)$, the $s = \frac{w_2}{w_1 + w_2}$ value indicates the portion of the weights $w_1 + w_2$ assigned to a second-ranked candidate. The condition $s \le \frac{1}{2}$ captures the requirement that a top-ranked candidate receives at least as many points as a second-ranked candidate; i.e., $1 - s \geq s$. This s restriction follows from the above derivation and the inequality

$$w_1 - w_3 \geq w_2 - w_3$$

All three-candidate (normalized) voting vectors can be represented with *the line segment of voting vectors* $\{(1 - s, s, 0) \in R_+^3 \mid s \in [0, \frac{1}{2}]\}$ in three space as depicted in Fig. 4.1.1. Often this segment is denoted by the interval of s values $[0, \frac{1}{2}]$.

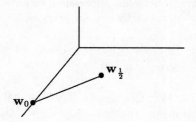

Fig. 4.1.1. The line segment of voting vectors

Example 4.1.5. The plurality voting vector $(1, 0, 0)$ already is in a normalized form where $s = 0$; thus $\mathbf{w}_0$ represents the plurality vote.

For the BC, $w_1 = 2, w_2 = 1$, and $w_3 = 0$, so, according to Eq. 4.1.10

$$s = 1/(2 + 1) = \frac{1}{3}$$

Thus, the BC normalized form is $\mathbf{w}_{\frac{1}{3}} = (\frac{2}{3}, \frac{1}{3}, 0)$. As required by Example 4.1.4b, the difference between successive components is a fixed value.

For the antiplurality vote, $w_1 = w_2 = 1, w_3 = 0$, so

$$s = 1/(1 + 1) = \frac{1}{2}$$

Therefore $\mathbf{w}_{\frac{1}{2}} = (\frac{1}{2}, \frac{1}{2}, 0)$ is the normalized antiplurality vector. $\square$

With the normalized $\mathbf{w}_s$ representation and a little imagination, it is easy to argue why any voting system is the "natural extension" of the majority vote. After all, in the pairwise vote, zero points are given to a voter's bottom-ranked candidate, and one point is divided among the remaining candidates. With two candidates, only one remains, so, by default, she receives the full point. In a three person election, however, two candidates are not bottom-ranked, so $\mathbf{w}_s$ specifies how to split this point between them. To justify a particular $\mathbf{w}_s$, just concoct a convincing argument why that s choice is the "correct one." By adequately supplementing imagination with bovine by-products, any s value can be justified.

4.1.3 The Geometry of $\mathbf{w}_s$ Outcomes

To show that the choice of a positional system matters, a geometric representation is created for the $\mathbf{w}_s$ outcomes. According to Sect. 1.4, the linear mapping transforms the convex hull $Si(6)$, defined by the unanimity profiles $\{\mathbf{E}_j\}_{j=1}^6$ into the convex hull $C\mathcal{H}(\mathbf{w}_s)$ in $Si(3)$. This hull of $\mathbf{w}_s$ election outcomes is defined by the vertices $\{f(\mathbf{E}_j, \mathbf{w}_s) = [\mathbf{w}_s]_j\}_{j=1}^6$.

Equivalently, take a voting vector $\mathbf{w}_s$ and plot the six points $\{[\mathbf{w}_s]_j\}_{j=1}^6$. A bottom-ranked candidate receives zero points, so each vector is on the $Si(3)$ boundary. Next, connect the dots with straight lines and shade in the resulting region as illustrated in Fig. 4.1.2. In this manner, the geometry associated with the plurality vote (Fig. 2.2.2) generalizes to all positional procedures.

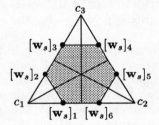

Figure 4.1.2. The convex hull $C\mathcal{H}(\mathbf{w}_s)$

Conversely, any $C\mathcal{H}(\mathbf{w}_s)$ point is a combination $\sum_{j=1}^6 p_j[\mathbf{w}_s]_j$ for some choice of $(p_1, \ldots, p_6)$, $p_j \geq 0$, $\sum_{j=1}^6 p_j = 1$. Hence, the convex weights define a profile where p_j of the voters are of type-j. Consequently, *any point in the convex set $C\mathcal{H}(\mathbf{w}_s)$ is an election outcome for some profile*, and the weights for the convex representation of this point define the associated profile.

Theorem 4.1.2. a. *For a given $\mathbf{w}_s$, let $C\mathcal{H}(\mathbf{w}_s)$ be the convex hull of $\{[\mathbf{w}_s]_j\}_{j=1}^6$. For any normalized profile $\mathbf{p}$, the normalized election outcome is in $C\mathcal{H}(\mathbf{w}_s)$. Moreover, any point in $C\mathcal{H}(\mathbf{w}_s)$ is the normalized election vector for some profile $\mathbf{p} \in Si(3!)$.*

b. *If $0 \leq s_2 < s_1 \leq \frac{1}{2}$, then*

$$(4.1.11) \qquad\qquad C\mathcal{H}(\mathbf{w}_{s_1}) \subset C\mathcal{H}(\mathbf{w}_{s_2})$$

The proof of part a follows from the discussion preceding the theorem. The proof of part b is immediate once the points are plotted on $Si(3)$. The basic fact is that if $s_2 < s_1$, then $[\mathbf{w}_{s_2}]_j$ is closer to the vertex $[\mathbf{e}_1]_j$ of the representation triangle than $[\mathbf{w}_{s_1}]_j$. This is illustrated in Fig. 4.1.3 where the full simplex $Si(3)$ is $C\mathcal{H}(\mathbf{w}_0)$, the shaded region is $C\mathcal{H}(\mathbf{w}_{\frac{1}{2}})$ and the hull defined by the lines is $C\mathcal{H}(\mathbf{w}_{\frac{1}{4}})$. In subsequent chapters, the geometric differences of these hulls explain differences in voting procedures. $\square$

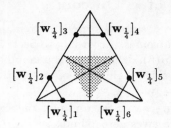

Fig. 4.1.3. A comparison of the hulls $\{\mathcal{CH}(\mathbf{w}_s)\}_{s=0,\frac{1}{4},\frac{1}{2}}$

An Optimal Solution. A candidate wants to win with the largest possible election outcome, so she tries to convert the voters to her way of thinking; e.g., she searches for an ideal profile **p** to give her the strongest possible outcome. What is this profile?

The answer is simple for the plurality vote; c_1's "best" outcome is an unanimous vote of type-one voters – the optimal profile is $\mathbf{E}_1$. This is no surprise; we should expect the optimal choice to be the unanimity profile $\mathbf{E}_1$ for all $\mathbf{w}_s$. While reasonable, it is false. For instance, with the antiplurality vote, the unanimity profile $\mathbf{E}_1$ forces c_1 into a tie with c_2! Surely, other profiles have a $\mathbf{w}_{\frac{1}{2}}$ outcome where c_1 does better! More generally, for a given $\mathbf{w}_s$, find the profile that maximizes the normalized election outcome for c_1.

Geometrically, c_1's best result is where the normalized election outcome $\mathbf{q} \in \mathcal{CH}(\mathbf{w}_s)$ is closest to the vertex $\mathbf{e}_1$. To minimize the distance from $\mathbf{e}_1$ to a point $\mathbf{q} \in \mathcal{CH}(\mathbf{w}_s)$, $\mathbf{q}$ must be on the line segment connecting $[\mathbf{w}_s]_1$ and $[\mathbf{w}_s]_2$. (See Fig. 4.1.3.)

If $s \neq 0$, then $\mathbf{e}_1$ and the points $[\mathbf{w}_s]_1, [\mathbf{w}_s]_2$ define an equilateral triangle. (The angle at $\mathbf{e}_1$ is 60° and $[\mathbf{w}_s]_1$ and $[\mathbf{w}_s]_2$ are the same distance from $\mathbf{e}_1$.) In this triangle, the $c_2 \sim c_3$ line is the perpendicular bisector of the leg connecting $[\mathbf{w}_s]_1$ and $[\mathbf{w}_s]_2$. From the geometry, the bisector $(1-s, s/2, s/2)$ is the unique $\mathcal{CH}(\mathbf{w}_s)$ point closest to $\mathbf{e}_1$. As this point is on the boundary of $\mathcal{CH}(\mathbf{w}_s)$, only voters of the indicated types (types-one and -two) are involved, and they are evenly divided. Thus the only profile supporting this outcome is $\frac{1}{2}(\mathbf{E}_1 + \mathbf{E}_2) = (\frac{1}{2}, \frac{1}{2}, 0, 0, 0, 0)$. Consequently, unless $s = 0$, *the optimal situation for c_1 requires the voters to be evenly split between types-one and two to obtain the normalized tally* $(1-s, s/2, s/2)$ with election ranking $c_1 \succ c_2 \sim c_3$. If $s = 0$, the outcome can be any split among type-one and -two voters.

4.1.4 Exercises

1. Show that Eq. 4.1.7 defines an equivalence relationship. Namely:
   1. (Reflexive) A voting vector **W** is equivalent to itself.
   2. (Symmetry) If $\mathbf{W}_1 \approx \mathbf{W}_2$, then $\mathbf{W}_2 \approx \mathbf{W}_1$.
   3. (Transitivity) If $\mathbf{W}_1 \approx \mathbf{W}_2$ and $\mathbf{W}_2 \approx \mathbf{W}_3$, then $\mathbf{W}_1 \approx \mathbf{W}_3$.

2. a. The antiplurality method $(1, 1, 0)$ is equivalent to $(0, 0, -1)$. Show that this system is equivalent to using the plurality vote with each voters *reversed ranking order* of the candidates,

and then changing the signs of the tallies. To extend this argument to a given $\mathbf{W} = (w_1, w_2, 0)$, let

$$(4.1.12) \qquad\qquad\qquad \mathbf{W}^r = (0, -w_2, -w_1)$$

be the reversed or anti-$\mathbf{W}$ voting vector. Prove that $\mathbf{W}^r$ is a voting vector, and find an equivalent form for $\mathbf{W}^r$ where zero points are assigned to a bottom-ranked candidate. Rewrite $\mathbf{W}$ and $\mathbf{W}^r$ in their normalized forms to relate their s-values. Show that the $\mathbf{W}^r$ ranking can be obtained by finding the $\mathbf{W}^r$ ranking of a profile where each voter's rankings are reversed, and then the sign of each tally is reversed.

b. Show that the BC is the unique voting system where $\mathbf{w}_s = \mathbf{w}_s^r$. This requires proving that

$$(4.1.13) \qquad\qquad\qquad \mathbf{w}_s \approx \mathbf{w}_s^r \text{ iff } s = \frac{1}{3}$$

c. Show that any point on the $Si(3)$ edge between $\mathbf{e}_1$ and $(\frac{1}{2}, \frac{1}{2}, 0)$ corresponds to a voting vector $\mathbf{w}_s$ for some s. Likewise, show that on an edge of $Si(3)$, any point between a vertex of $Si(3)$ and the $c_i \sim c_j$ point on this edge defines a voting vector $\mathbf{w}_s$ where this point is $[\mathbf{w}_s]_k$ for the appropriate ranking region $\mathcal{R}(k)$. What is this ranking region?

d. For a given voting vector $\mathbf{w}_s$, the line passing through $[\mathbf{w}_s]_1$ and $\mathcal{I}$ intersects the boundary of $Si(3)$ in $\mathcal{R}(4)$. This intersection point is $[\mathbf{w}_t]_4$ for some t. Show that $\mathbf{w}_t \approx \mathbf{w}_s^r$. (Draw the picture)

3. a. It is asserted after Theorem 4.1.1 that adding $b(1,1,1)$ does not affect the election ranking. Show that adding this term *changes the normalized election tally*. In particular, if $\mathbf{q}, \mathbf{q}_b$ represent, respectively, the normalized election outcome for $f(\mathbf{p}, \mathbf{W})$ and $f(\mathbf{p}, \mathbf{W} + b(1,1,1))$, show that $\mathbf{q}_b$ is on the line from the complete indifference point $\mathcal{I}$ passing through $\mathbf{q}$. This line is divided into two parts by $\mathbf{q}$; which part contains $\mathbf{q}_b$ if $b > 0$?

b. In the Distinct winner threshold method for $\gamma_2 = \frac{3}{5}$, candidate c_1 wins with the normalized tally of $\mathbf{q} = (\frac{8}{14}, \frac{5}{14}, \frac{1}{14})$. Find b values so that for the same profile, the outcome is a tie between c_1, c_2 if the tally had been based on the "equivalent" voting vector $(1,0,0) + b(1,1,1)$. Find values of b so that the outcome would be a three-way tie. (Thus, the equivalence assertion does not hold for the threshold methods.)

c. Re-do b with the Universal threshold method and $\delta_2 = \frac{8}{15}$.

4. a. In describing the plurality and antiplurality methods, it is suggested that the BC "splits the difference" between them. Use the normalized voting vectors to argue that $\mathbf{w}_{\frac{1}{4}} \approx (3,1,0)$ "splits the difference" between the plurality and the antiplurality methods. Then, by using different equivalent representations for the plurality and antiplurality vectors, show that any voting vector (w_1, w_2, w_3), $w_2 \neq w_1, w_3$, can be viewed as "splitting the difference" between the plurality and antiplurality methods.

b. Extend Example 4.1.4b to all $n \geq 3$; that is, show that the BC is characterized by keeping fixed the difference between successive weights.

5. a. Show that $\mathcal{CH}(\mathbf{w}_s)$ is a triangle (actually, an equilateral triangle) iff $s = 0, \frac{1}{2}$. That is, the convex hull is a triangle only for the plurality and the antiplurality methods. In particular, show that $\mathcal{CH}(\mathbf{w}_s) = Si(3)$ iff $\mathbf{w}_s$ is the plurality vote. Show that $\mathcal{CH}(\mathbf{w}_s)$ is the triangle connecting the midpoints of each leg of $Si(3)$ iff the method is the antiplurality procedure.

b. Show that the line segment connecting $[\mathbf{w}_s]_1$ and $[\mathbf{w}_s]_3$ is perpendicular to the base connecting the vertices $\mathbf{e}_1$ and $\mathbf{e}_2$ iff $s = \frac{1}{3}$. Equivalently, show that this line segment is parallel to the c_1, c_2 indifference line if and only if the procedure is the BC.

6. a. Suppose the election for each of the three threshold procedures is tallied with $\mathbf{w}_s$. Show for a given $\mathbf{w}_s$, $s \neq 0$, that there are sufficiently large values for $\epsilon_2, \gamma_2, \delta_2$ so that it is impossible to have a single winner. Find the largest $\epsilon_2, \gamma_2, \delta_2$ values in terms of s so that a single candidate can be the "winner." What about the threshold values distinguishing between a pair being designated for top-ranked and a three way tie?

b. Consider the profile $(\frac{1}{2}, \frac{1}{2}, 0, 0, 0, 0)$ and let $\gamma_2 = \frac{2}{3}$ for the Distinct winner procedure. Find s values so that this method will select the single candidate c_1.

7. Suppose $\mathbf{q}_1, \mathbf{q}_2$ are normalized election outcomes for $\mathbf{w}_s$. The maximum distance between two such vectors indicates the maximum difference in an election outcome. Find this maximum distance in terms of the s value. Find profiles associated with each outcome.

8. In weighted voting, consider the profile $(\pi, 1, 0, 2, \pi, 1)$.
a. Find the normalized version of this profile.
b. What s choices give the ranking $c_1 \sim c_2 \succ c_3$?
c. Show that the BC ranking is $c_2 \succ c_1 \succ c_3$. Show that this ranking is "robust", because, for any small change in the profile, the ranking remains the same. Show that the plurality ranking is *not* robust; an arbitrarily small change in the profile can change the ranking.

9. Some procedures assign smaller values to higher-ranked candidates. For instance, we could assign the first-place candidate one point, the second-place two points, and the third-place three points. Show how to include these methods by allowing negative a values in Eq. 4.1.7. Show that the described procedure is the BC.

4.2 What a Difference a Procedure Makes; Several Different Outcomes

Even with the same profile, different methods can generate conflicting election outcomes. Why? What causes this irritating fact? The explanation involves the extremes in philosophy where the plurality vote totally ignores a voter's second-ranked candidate while the antiplurality method accords her the same preferential treatment of a top-ranked candidate. These informational extremes are reflected geometrically by the fact that $\mathbf{w}_0$ and $\mathbf{w}_{\frac{1}{2}}$ are the endpoints of the line segment of voting vectors $\mathbf{w}_s$, $s \in [0, \frac{1}{2}]$. Another measure is the nested arrangement ensured by Theorem 4.1.2 where for $s \in (0, \frac{1}{2})$

$$\mathcal{CH}(\mathbf{w}_{\frac{1}{2}}) \subset \mathcal{CH}(\mathbf{w}_s) \subset \mathcal{CH}(\mathbf{w}_0) = Si(3).$$

The two limiting convex hulls are the shaded areas depicted in Fig. 4.2.1. The joint plurality, antiplurality outcome for a profile $\mathbf{p}$ is

$$(f(\mathbf{p}, \mathbf{w}_0), f(\mathbf{p}, \mathbf{w}_{\frac{1}{2}})) \in Si(3) \times Si(3)$$

where the notation indicates that the plurality and antiplurality outcomes are, respectively, in the left- and the right-hand simplex of Fig. 4.2.1.

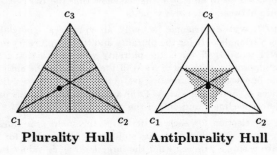

Plurality Hull   Antiplurality Hull

Fig. 4.2.1. Different hulls

A direct computation for profile $\mathbf{p}_m = (\frac{1}{3}, 0, \frac{1}{3}, 0, \frac{1}{3}, 0)$ shows that

$$(f(\mathbf{p}_m, \mathbf{w}_0), f(\mathbf{p}_m, \mathbf{w}_{\frac{1}{2}})) = ((\frac{1}{3}, \frac{1}{3}, \frac{1}{3}), (\frac{1}{3}, \frac{1}{3}, \frac{1}{3})),$$

so the normalized tally in each simplex is the barycentric point $\mathcal{I}$. Now let a type-one voter join $\mathbf{p}_m$ to create the new profile $\mathbf{p}'$. This voter breaks the tie in different ways.

The new plurality outcome moves from $\mathcal{I}$ toward $[\mathbf{w}_0]_1 = (1, 0, 0)$ to reflect the vector ballot cast by the new type-one voter. Geometrically, the tally moves from $\mathcal{I}$ along the indifference line $q_2 = q_3$ to end up in the ranking region $c_1 \succ c_2 \sim c_3$. On the other hand, this voter changes the antiplurality vote by moving the election vector from $\mathcal{I}$ toward $[\mathbf{w}_{\frac{1}{2}}]_1 = (\frac{1}{2}, \frac{1}{2}, 0)$. As the outcome moves along the indifference line $q_1 = q_2$, the new election ranking is $c_1 \sim c_2 \succ c_3$.

The exact change depends upon the number of original voters. For instance, if 15 voters define the original profile $\mathbf{p}_m$, then the 16 voters define the normalized profile $\mathbf{p}' = \frac{15}{16}\mathbf{p}_m + \frac{1}{16}\mathbf{E}_1$. The linearity of election mappings leads to

$$
\begin{aligned}
f(\mathbf{p}', \mathbf{w}_s) &= f(\frac{15}{16}\mathbf{p}_m + \frac{1}{16}\mathbf{E}_1, \mathbf{w}_s) = \frac{15}{16}f(\mathbf{p}_m, \mathbf{w}_s) + \frac{1}{16}f(\mathbf{E}_1, \mathbf{w}_s) \\
&= \frac{15}{16}(\frac{1}{3}, \frac{1}{3}, \frac{1}{3}) + \frac{1}{16}[\mathbf{w}_s]_1.
\end{aligned}
$$

This equation is a special case of the setting where if $\mathbf{p}, \mathbf{p}_1$ are, respectively, profiles of the old and new voters and t is the proportion of new to all voters, then

$$(4.2.1) \qquad f((1 - t)\mathbf{p} + t\mathbf{p}_1, \mathbf{w}_s) = (1 - t)f(\mathbf{p}, \mathbf{w}_s) + tf(\mathbf{p}_1, \mathbf{w}_s).$$

In Fig. 4.1.1, the election outcomes $f(\mathbf{p}', \mathbf{w}_0)$, $f(\mathbf{p}', \mathbf{w}_{\frac{1}{2}})$ are indicated by dots in the appropriate simplex. As dictated by Eq. 4.2.1, all other $\mathbf{w}_s, s \in (0, \frac{1}{2})$, move the outcome from $\mathcal{I}$ toward $[\mathbf{w}_s]_1 = (1 - s, s, 0)$ forcing the new ranking $c_1 \succ c_2 \succ c_3$. So, profile $\mathbf{p}'$ defines three different election outcomes depending on the geometric properties of $\mathbf{w}_s$. The choice of a procedure matters!

With imagination and by adding different mixtures of voter types to $\mathbf{p}_m$, a diverse selection of outcomes emerge. This is not overly surprising; we must expect different procedures to define different outcomes. But, how different can they be? The next theorem asserts that there are no limits.

Theorem 4.2.1. *Let voting vectors $\mathbf{w}_{s_1} \neq \mathbf{w}_{s_2}$ be given. Let β_1, β_2 be any two rankings of the three candidates – the rankings may be the same, or they may differ. There exists a profile so that when $\mathbf{w}_{s_j}$ is used to tally the ballots of the voters, the outcome is β_j; $j = 1, 2$.*

This is a shocking conclusion! While we expect different procedures to have different outcomes, this conclusion asserts that there are no restrictions on the disparity between outcomes! It admits the possibility that a minuscule change in the choice of s can cause an arbitrarily large differences in the election rankings! How can this be true? The explanation must involve the only way voting vectors disagree – by the weight assigned to a second-ranked candidate.

Example 4.2.1. a. The beverage example provides a profile where the plurality ranking is $c_1 \succ c_2 \succ c_3$, but the BC ranking is the reversed $c_3 \succ c_2 \succ c_1$.

b. Consider the voting vectors $(5, 4, 0) \approx \mathbf{w}_{\frac{4}{9}}$ and $(5, 3, 0) \approx \mathbf{w}_{\frac{3}{8}}$. According to the theorem, there is a profile where the $\mathbf{w}_{\frac{4}{9}}$ outcome is $\mathcal{I}$ while the $\mathbf{w}_{\frac{3}{8}}$ outcome is $\beta_2 = c_2 \succ c_1 \succ c_3$. Also, there is a profile where the $\mathbf{w}_{\frac{4}{9}}$ outcome is $c_2 \succ c_3 \succ c_1$ while the $\mathbf{w}_{\frac{3}{8}}$ outcome is $c_1 \sim c_2 \succ c_3$.

c. Suppose $s_1 \geq 0$, and $\frac{1}{2} \geq s_2 = s_1 + 0.0000001$. Even though the voting vectors $\mathbf{w}_{s_1}$ and $\mathbf{w}_{s_2}$ agree up to the seventh decimal place, there is a profile where the $\mathbf{w}_{s_1}$ ranking is $c_3 \succ c_2 \succ c_1$ while the $\mathbf{w}_{s_2}$ ranking is the reversed $c_1 \succ c_2 \succ c_3$. So, even almost identical procedures can have radically different outcomes!

d. The geometry shows why outcomes for a fixed profile can vary so radically. For instance, a profile consisting of types two, four, and five (as true in the beverage example) defines an election point in the hull defined by the vertices $\{[\mathbf{w}_s]_j\}_{j=2,4,5}$. For the plurality method, this hull admits any point in the representation triangle. On the other hand, for $s \geq \frac{1}{3}$ (that is, from the BC on), the outcome cannot have both c_1 and c_2 in the top two ranks. This is illustrated in Fig. 4.2.2 where the hull of outcomes for the plurality vote is the whole triangle, for the BC it is the shaded region, and for the antiplurality vote it is the heavy line. □

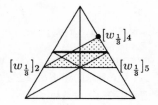

Fig. 4.2.2. Sets of outcomes for type two, four and five voters

4.2.1 How Bad It Can Get

Just imagine the mischief a young, modern Machiavelli could have once armed with this theorem. Suppose the electorate defines a profile $\mathbf{p}$ which, when tallied with the required procedure $\mathbf{w}_s$, leads to the election outcome $f(\mathbf{p}, \mathbf{w}_s) = \beta_1$. This is fine if β_1 suits Machiavelli's purposes. If not, he could campaign for an election day profile of $\mathbf{p}'$ with the desired $f(\mathbf{p}', \mathbf{w}_s) = \beta_2$. Alternatively, young Machiavelli could search for a voting vector $\mathbf{w}_{s'}$ which, with the original profile $\mathbf{p}$, delivers the desired election outcome $f(\mathbf{p}, \mathbf{w}_{s'}) = \beta_2$. By embracing "responsible government," Mr. I. M. Machiavelli could promote the "virtues" of

$\mathbf{w}_{s'}$ by starting a reform movement to replace $\mathbf{w}_s$ with $\mathbf{w}_{s'}$. [1]

This "anything can happen" assertion is disturbing. After all, Theorem 4.2.1 casts doubts about cherished democratic procedures that have painfully evolved over centuries. We might try to ignore the problem by speculating that *"Sure, maybe these assertions are true, but so what! They're probably useless because they never occur in the 'real world'!"* In other words, motivated by the outlandish Example 4.2.1.c, it's natural to conjecture that profiles supporting sufficiently dissimilar rankings β_1, β_2 must be, in some practical sense, highly restricted and nonrobust. However, unless tie votes are involved, robustness happens. Weird as it may seem, this robustness is compatible with the sensitivity exhibited by Example 4.2.1c. (Can the reader anticipate how?)

A more immediate issue motivated by Theorem 4.2.1 and Fig. 4.2.2 is to determine what else can occur. After all, if two procedures can admit two different election outcomes, then how bad can it be when three, or four, ..., or seven, or ... different procedures are applied to the same profile? To address this issue, let

$$Sup(\mathbf{p}) = \{ \text{ all election rankings of the 3 candidates that arise}$$
$$\text{from } \mathbf{p} \text{ with changes in the positional voting method}\}$$

be the set of election rankings supported by profile $\mathbf{p}$; it is important to understand the properties of $Sup(\mathbf{p})$. As an illustration, the profile $\mathbf{p}'$ from the introductory example of this section defines $Sup(\mathbf{p}') = \{c_1 \succ c_2 \sim c_3, c_1 \succ c_2 \succ c_3, c_1 \sim c_2 \succ c_3\}$. In general, how many and what kind of entries are in $Sup(\mathbf{p})$? How does $Sup(\mathbf{p})$ vary with the profile $\mathbf{p}$? For a given $\mathbf{p}$, which voting vectors yield which rankings in $Sup(\mathbf{p})$? These questions are answered next.

4.2.2 Properties of $Sup(\mathbf{p})$

of geometric Common sense suggests that if $f(\mathbf{p}, \mathbf{w}_{s_1})$ and $f(\mathbf{p}, w_{s_2})$ have radically different rankings, then the election tallies may be near $\mathcal{I}$. As a ball of radius $\rho > 0$ and center $\mathcal{I}$ intersects all ranking regions, if the only restriction on the outcomes is that they are in some ball $\mathcal{B}(\mathcal{I}, \rho)$, then any ranking can occur. This is what happens.

Theorem 4.2.2. a. *Let* $\mathbf{w}_{s_1} \neq \mathbf{w}_{s_2}$ *be given. There exists* $\rho > 0$ *so that the following is true. In* $Si(3)$, *construct the ball of radius* ρ *and center* $\mathcal{I}$, $B(\mathcal{I}, \rho)$. *(See Fig. 4.2.3.) Select any two election points* $\mathbf{q}_j$, $j = 1, 2$, *in* $B(\mathcal{I}, \rho)$. *There is a one-dimensional line of profiles,* $\mathcal{L}_{\mathbf{w}_{s_1}, \mathbf{w}_{s_2}}(\mathbf{q}_1, \mathbf{q}_2) \subset Si(6)$, *so that if* $\mathbf{p} \in \mathcal{L}_{\mathbf{w}_{s_1}, \mathbf{w}_{s_2}}(\mathbf{q}_1, \mathbf{q}_2)$, *then*

$$(4.2.2) \qquad f(\mathbf{p}, \mathbf{w}_{s_1}) = \mathbf{q}_1, \quad f(\mathbf{p}, \mathbf{w}_{s_2}) = \mathbf{q}_2.$$

---

[1] It is not difficult to find examples of "reform proposals" where it is arguable that they were motivated more by who would win than by the merits of one method over another. This appears to be the case with the debate in certain states as well as in Chicago during the 1970s and 1980s over "runoff" elections.

b. For profile $\mathbf{p} \in Si(6)$ *and* $\mathbf{w}_s$, *the election outcome* $f(\mathbf{p}, \mathbf{w}_s) \in Si(3)$ *is on the line segment connecting* $f(\mathbf{p}, \mathbf{w}_0)$ *and* $f(\mathbf{p}, \mathbf{w}_{\frac{1}{2}})$. *More precisely,*

$$(4.2.3) \qquad f(\mathbf{p}, \mathbf{w}_s) = (1 - 2s)f(\mathbf{p}, \mathbf{w}_0) + 2sf(\mathbf{p}, \mathbf{w}_{\frac{1}{2}}), \quad s \in [0, \frac{1}{2}].$$

Denote the line segment of Eq. 4.2.3, the procedure line for $\mathbf{p}$, *by* $PL(\mathbf{p})$.

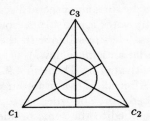

Fig. 4.2.3. The ball $\mathcal{B}(\mathcal{I}, \rho)$

The first assertion significantly improves Theorem 4.2.1 by ensuring that not only can the election rankings for the two procedures be selected in an arbitrary fashion, but, with a restriction on the ρ value, even the normalized election tally for each procedure can be randomly chosen! Moreover, the theorem ensures that the conclusion is not caused by an isolated profile; instead, a whole line of profiles, $\mathbf{p} \in \mathcal{L}_{\mathbf{w}_{s_1}, \mathbf{w}_{s_2}}(\mathbf{q}_1, \mathbf{q}_2)$, defines the same two randomly chosen election tallies!

The more important assertion, b, maintains that *the procedure line* $PL(\mathbf{p})$ *completely specifies the normalized election tally for each* $\mathbf{w}_s$. In words, once we know $f(\mathbf{p}, \mathbf{w}_0)$ and $f(\mathbf{p}, \mathbf{w}_{\frac{1}{2}})$, we know *all* outcomes $f(\mathbf{p}, \mathbf{w}_s)$! Indeed, the $\mathbf{w}_s$ outcome, $f(\mathbf{p}, \mathbf{w}_s)$, is the point on the procedure line $PL(\mathbf{p})$ that is $2s$ of the distance from $f(\mathbf{p}, \mathbf{w}_0)$ to $f(\mathbf{p}, \mathbf{w}_{\frac{1}{2}})$. So, each $f(\mathbf{p}, \mathbf{w}_s)$ outcome is uniquely determined by how $PL(\mathbf{p})$ is positioned within the representation triangle. This positioning is completely determined by its endpoints – the plurality and antiplurality election outcomes. So, *just two computations to find the* $PL(\mathbf{p})$ *endpoints determines all possible* $\mathbf{w}_s$ *election outcomes for the profile!*

Proof of b. Because $\mathbf{w}_s = (1 - s, s, 0) = (1 - 2s, 0, 0) + (s, s, 0)$ can be expressed as $\mathbf{w}_s = (1 - 2s)(1, 0, 0) + 2s(\frac{1}{2}, \frac{1}{2}, 0)$, or

$$(4.2.4) \qquad \mathbf{w}_s = (1 - 2s)\mathbf{w}_0 + 2s\mathbf{w}_{\frac{1}{2}},$$

we have that $f(\mathbf{p}, \mathbf{w}_s) = f(\mathbf{p}, (1 - 2s)\mathbf{w}_0 + 2s\mathbf{w}_{\frac{1}{2}})$. The election mapping f is linear in both variables, so the linear separation property Eq. 1.4.4 ensures that

$$f(\mathbf{p}, \mathbf{w}_s) = (1 - 2s)f(\mathbf{p}, \mathbf{w}_0) + 2sf(\mathbf{p}, \mathbf{w}_{\frac{1}{2}}). \quad \square$$

Outline of the Proof of a. To see why part a is true, notice for given $\mathbf{q}$ and $\mathbf{w}_s$ that the vector equation $f(\mathbf{p}, \mathbf{w}_s) = \mathbf{q}$ represents three linear equations (one for each $\mathbf{q}$ component) in the six unknowns $p_1, \ldots, p_6$. There is a reduction; once two $\mathbf{q}$ components are known, the third is determined from $q_1 + q_2 + q_3 = 1$. (This is the equation defining $\mathbf{q} \in Si(3)$.) Thus $f(\mathbf{p}, \mathbf{w}_s) = \mathbf{q}$ represents two independent equations in six unknowns.

We are not interested in one vector equation, but two of them. Using the above argument, the equations $f(\mathbf{p}, \mathbf{w}_{s_1}) = \mathbf{q}_1$, $f(\mathbf{p}, \mathbf{w}_{s_2}) = \mathbf{q}_2$ reduce to four equations in six unknowns. A fifth equation, $\sum_{j=1}^{6} p_j = 1$, is mandated by the constraint $\mathbf{p} \in Si(6)$. Consequently, the voting problem is equated with an algebraic problem involving five linear equations in six unknowns. Algebra tells us to expect a line of solutions expressed in terms of one of the p_j variables. (See Sect. 1.4.) The technical rank condition ensuring this conclusion is given at the end of the section.

4.2.3 The Procedure Line

Viewing Theorem 4.2.2 from the standpoint of elections, the conclusion violates intuition by asserting that there need not be any relationship between the outcomes of different procedures. Yet, when expressed as an algebraic system – five equations in six unknowns – the assertion is converted into a familiar form where the conclusion is expected.

To develop a similar explanation for the procedure line $PL(\mathbf{p})$, hold $\mathbf{p}$ fixed but vary $\mathbf{w}_s$ to convert f into a linear mapping of the *voting vectors*. As indicated by Eq. 4.2.4, the set of positional voting vectors is the convex hull defined by the vertices $\mathbf{w}_0, \mathbf{w}_{\frac{1}{2}}$. Therefore (according to Sect. 1.4) the linear election mapping picks up the line of voting vectors with vertices $\mathbf{w}_0, \mathbf{w}_{\frac{1}{2}}$, and transforms it into the procedure line defined by the vertices $f(\mathbf{p}, \mathbf{w}_0)$ and $f(\mathbf{p}, \mathbf{w}_{\frac{1}{2}})$. (See Fig. 4.2.4.)

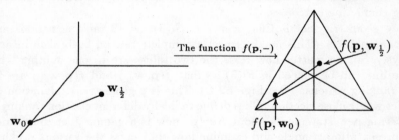

Fig. 4.2.4. The image of the line segment of voting vectors for fixed $\mathbf{p}$

More is possible. The relative lack of constraints on $f(\mathbf{p}, \mathbf{w}_0)$ and $f(\mathbf{p}, \mathbf{w}_{\frac{1}{2}})$ (Theorem 4.2.2a) combined with the fact that these two outcomes uniquely determine the procedure line $PL(\mathbf{p})$ lead to the conclusion that there are minimal restrictions on the positioning of $PL(\mathbf{p})$. The only constraint is that the endpoints are in the ball $\mathcal{B}(\mathcal{I}, \rho)$ associated with $\mathbf{w}_0$, $\mathbf{w}_{\frac{1}{2}}$. Thus, *any line segment in this ball is a procedure line* $PL(\mathbf{p})$ *for some line of profiles!* So, by choosing the line appropriately, we can find all sorts of results about $\mathbf{w}_s$ election outcomes.

What makes the procedure line a powerful tool is that $PL(\mathbf{p})$ completely determines the properties of $Sup(\mathbf{p})$. Consequently, deep results are obtained simply by drawing line segments in the representation triangle; the theorem ensures that any segment is a $PL(\mathbf{p})$ for some $\mathbf{p}$. To illustrate, draw a line segment with an endpoint on $\mathcal{I}$. Obviously, this segment enters only one ranking region. (Draw the picture.) This trivial geometry translates into the deep assertion that *if either the plurality or the antiplurality ranking is a complete tie, then, with this profile, the election ranking for all remaining positional methods agree. Indeed, if just one other $\mathbf{w}_s$ has $\mathcal{I}$ as the outcome, then the outcome for all procedures is a complete tie.*[2]

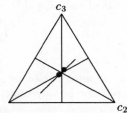

Fig. 4.2.5. Nearby points on $PL(\mathbf{p})$ with reversed rankings

To illustrate the power of the procedure line, I use it and Fig. 4.2.5 to explain the conflict between common sense and the conclusion of Example 4.2.1c. If s_1 and s_2 are close in value, Eq. 4.2.3 requires $f(\mathbf{p}, \mathbf{w}_{s_1})$ and $f(\mathbf{p}, \mathbf{w}_{s_2})$ to be near-by on the procedure line $PL(\mathbf{p})$. Thus, supporting common sense, the normalized election tallies are essentially the same. On the other hand, "essentially the same" normalized election outcomes need not be "exactly the same" ordinal rankings; the difference introduces a window of opportunity to create outcomes exhibiting conflicting outcomes.

The key geometric fact is that near $\mathcal{I} \in Si(3)$, all 13 ranking regions are close to one another. (This makes sense; a complete tie can be broken in any of 12 ways.) So, no matter how close the two tallies are to one another, the procedure line can be placed in $Si(3)$ so that $f(\mathbf{p}, \mathbf{w}_{s_1})$ and $f(\mathbf{p}, \mathbf{w}_{s_2})$ are in specified ranking regions. (See Fig. 4.2.4.) This is a geometric explanation of the conflict where close election tallies define radically different election rankings.

Discovering new statements about $Sup(\mathbf{p})$ now is a game. Just draw lines in the representation triangle and examine how they cross the various ranking regions. Thus, while the conclusions of the following theorem are deep, the approach to find and prove them mimics a child's game of placing sticks on a diagram to discover which regions are crossed.

Theorem 4.2.3. a. *The jth election ranking is in $Sup(\mathbf{p})$ if and only if $PL(\mathbf{p}) \cap \mathcal{R}(j) \neq \emptyset$.*

---

[2]Suppose $f(\mathbf{p}, \mathbf{w}_0)$ and $f(\mathbf{p}, \mathbf{w}_s)$, $s \neq 0$ are at $\mathcal{I}$. Solving Eq. 4.2.3 for $f(\mathbf{p}, \mathbf{w}_{\frac{1}{2}})$ leads to the conclusion that the antiplurality outcome is $\mathcal{I}$. Substituting the plurality and the antiplurality outcomes into Eq. 4.2.3 leads to the stated conclusion.

b. For integer k, $1 \le k \le 7$, there is a profile **p** so that $Sup(\mathbf{p})$ has precisely k rankings. Conversely, if $Sup(\mathbf{p})$ has k rankings, then $1 \le k \le 7$. If either the plurality or the antiplurality ranking involves a tie, then $Sup(\mathbf{p})$ has, at most, six rankings.

c. For integer k, $0 \le k \le 4$, there is a profile **p** where $Sup(\mathbf{p})$ has precisely k strict rankings. Conversely, if $Sup(\mathbf{p})$ has k strict rankings, then $0 \le k \le 4$. The number of rankings in $Sup(\mathbf{p})$ with a tie satisfies $0 \le k \le 3$.

d. If the plurality and the antiplurality rankings are the reversal of each other, then $Sup(\mathbf{p})$ has either one, three or seven entries. In the first case, all entries are $\mathcal{I}$, in the second case the $Sup(\mathbf{p})$ entries are the rankings of the plurality vote, the antiplurality vote, and $\mathcal{I}$.

e. The election ranking for **p** is the same for all choices of $\mathbf{w}_s$ iff the plurality and the antiplurality ranking agree. Indeed, for any ranking β, there is a line of profiles so that not only is β the common ranking for all $\mathbf{w}_s$ elections, but the normalized election tally is the same specified value for all procedures.

This answers the question about the size of $Sup(\mathbf{p})$; according to part b, $Sup(\mathbf{p})$ can have anywhere from one to seven entries. Part e offers good news; it specifies necessary and sufficient conditions so that all voting procedures record the same election ranking. Contrary to intuition, a unanimity profile does *not* satisfy this condition!

Proof. Part a is immediate as $PL(\mathbf{p}) \cap \mathcal{R}(j) \ne \emptyset$ iff there is a $\mathbf{w}_s$ so that $f(\mathbf{p}, \mathbf{w}_s) \in \mathcal{R}(j)$ iff the jth ranking is in $Sup(\mathbf{p})$.

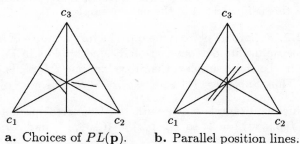

a. Choices of $PL(\mathbf{p})$.   **b.** Parallel position lines.

Fig. 4.2.6. Various positions of the position line

To prove parts b and c, just experiment with the positioning of line segments in $Si(3)$ to see how many and few ranking regions the segment intersects. For instance, $PL(\mathbf{p}_1)$ in the left-hand side of Fig. 4.2.6 borders on two indifference lines and intersects five regions so $Sup(\mathbf{p}_1)$ consists of the five rankings $\{c_1 \sim c_2 \succ c_3, c_1 \succ c_2 \succ c_3, c_1 \succ c_2 \sim c_3, c_1 \succ c_3 \succ c_2, c_1 \sim c_3 \succ c_2\}$. The other line segment, $PL(\mathbf{p}_2)$, is in $\mathcal{R}(5)$, so $Sup(\mathbf{p}_2) = \{c_2 \succ c_3 \succ c_1\}$. The proof of the theorem follows immediately because any line segment (in the $\mathbf{w}_0$, $\mathbf{w}_{\frac{1}{2}}$ disk) is a procedure line for some profile.

To prove d, let the plurality ranking be in $\mathcal{R}(1)$ and the antiplurality ranking in $\mathcal{R}(4)$. The associated procedure line either passes through $\mathcal{I}$, which forces

$PL(\mathbf{p})$ to meet $\{\mathcal{R}(1), \mathcal{R}(4), \mathcal{I}\}$, or $PL(\mathbf{p})$ passes on one side of $\mathcal{I}$, so it meets seven regions. These two situations are depicted in Fig. 4.2.6.

For part e, all election rankings agree iff $PL(\mathbf{p})$ is in a single ranking region iff the plurality and the antiplurality rankings agree. Similarly, the normalized election tallies all agree iff $PL(\mathbf{p})$ is a point $\mathbf{q}$. This situation holds iff $f(\mathbf{p}, \mathbf{w}_0) = f(\mathbf{p}, \mathbf{w}_{\frac{1}{2}}) = \mathbf{q}$. According to Theorem 4.2.2, for any $\mathbf{q}$ in the described disk, there is a line of profiles defining this outcome. Because the disk is centered at $\mathcal{I}$, $\mathbf{q}$ can be chosen in any of the 13 ranking regions.   □

4.2.4 Using the Procedure Line

To review: the mystery why different election outcomes can arise with the same profile is answered by using Sect. 1.4. For a given profile $\mathbf{p}$, the mapping $f(\mathbf{p}, -)$ picks up the line of election vectors and repositions it as the procedure line defined by $\mathbf{p}$. Using the parametric representation $PL(\mathbf{p}) = \{(1-2s)f(\mathbf{p}, \mathbf{w}_0) + 2sf(\mathbf{p}, \mathbf{w}_{\frac{1}{2}}) \mid s \in [0, \frac{1}{2}]\}$, the different points on $PL(\mathbf{p})$ manifest the changing emphasis a procedure places on a second-ranked candidate. The only issue is the positioning of $PL(\mathbf{p})$; here, algebra allows considerable freedom in the choice of the endpoints $f(\mathbf{p}, \mathbf{w}_0), f(\mathbf{p}, \mathbf{w}_{\frac{1}{2}}) \in \mathcal{B}(\mathcal{I}, \rho)$. Once $PL(\mathbf{p})$ is specified, all related properties, such as the rankings in $Sup(\mathbf{p})$, which voting methods give rise to which rankings, etc., follow immediately. Moreover, because the $Sup(\mathbf{p})$ rankings are determined by the straight line segment $PL(\mathbf{p})$, the entries of $Sup(\mathbf{p})$ are related. All of this is illustrated in the next example.

Example 4.2.2. For profile $\mathbf{p}'$ from the introductory example of this section, the plurality and antiplurality outcomes are indicated by dots in Fig. 4.2.1. When both dots are in the same simplex, the procedure line $PL(\mathbf{p}')$ is the connecting line segment. Thus $Sup(\mathbf{p}') = \{c_1 \succ c_2 \sim c_3, c_1 \succ c_2 \succ c_3, c_1 \sim c_2 \succ c_3\}$.

The introductory example starts with the Condorcet profile $\mathbf{p}_m$ for which $f(\mathbf{p}_m, \mathbf{w}_0) = f(\mathbf{p}_m, \mathbf{w}_{\frac{1}{2}}) = \mathcal{I}$, so $PL(\mathbf{p}_m) = \{(\frac{1}{3}, \frac{1}{3}, \frac{1}{3})\}$ and $Sup(\mathbf{p}_m) = \{c_1 \sim c_2 \sim c_3\}$.

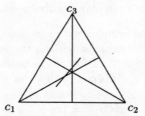

Fig. 4.2.7. An example of the procedure line

To find $Sup(\mathbf{p})$, $PL(\mathbf{p})$ for $\mathbf{p} = (0, \frac{7}{18}, 0, \frac{5}{18}, \frac{6}{18}, 0)$, notice that all voters rank c_3 in either first or second position. (See Fig. 4.2.2.) As $f(\mathbf{p}, \mathbf{w}_0) = (\frac{7}{18}, \frac{6}{18}, \frac{5}{18})$

and $f(\mathbf{p}, \mathbf{w}_{\frac{1}{2}}) = (\frac{7}{36}, \frac{11}{36}, \frac{18}{36})$, we have that

$$PL(\mathbf{p}) = \{(1 - 2s)(\frac{7}{18}, \frac{6}{18}, \frac{5}{18}) + 2s(\frac{7}{36}, \frac{11}{36}, \frac{18}{36})$$

(4.2.5)
$$= (\frac{14(1 - s)}{36}, \frac{12 - 2s}{36}, \frac{10 + 16s}{36}) \mid s \in [0, \frac{1}{2}]\}.$$

The geometric positioning of this line (Fig. 4.2.5) requires

$$Sup(\mathbf{p}) = \{c_1 \succ c_2 \succ c_3, c_1 \succ c_2 \sim c_3, c_1 \succ c_3 \succ c_2, c_1 \sim c_3 \succ c_2,$$
$$c_3 \succ c_1 \succ c_2, c_3 \succ c_1 \sim c_2, c_3 \succ c_2 \succ c_1\}.$$

Observe that the $Sup(\mathbf{p})$ rankings are related according to the straight line geometry of $PL(\mathbf{p})$. For instance, the relative rankings of two adjacently ranked candidates are reversed by first going through a tie vote.

Using elementary algebra and Eqs. 4.2.3, 4.2.5, we can determine which $\mathbf{w}_s$ define which rankings from $Sup(\mathbf{p})$. For instance, for $\mathbf{w}_s$ to define $c_1 \succ c_2 \succ c_3$, the components of $\mathbf{q}$ must satisfy $q_1 > q_2 > q_3$. So, according to Eq. 4.2.5, s satisfies $\frac{14(1-s)}{36} > \frac{12-2s}{36} > \frac{10+16s}{36}$, or $s \in [0, \frac{1}{9})$. The complete listing is

s for $\mathbf{w}_s$	Ranking	s for $\mathbf{w}_s$	Ranking
$s \in [0, \frac{1}{9})$	$c_1 \succ c_2 \succ c_3$	$s \in (\frac{2}{15}, \frac{1}{6})$	$c_3 \succ c_1 \succ c_2$
$s = \frac{1}{9}$	$c_1 \succ c_2 \sim c_3$	$s = \frac{1}{6}$	$c_3 \succ c_1 \sim c_2$
$s \in (\frac{1}{9}, \frac{2}{15})$	$c_1 \succ c_3 \succ c_2$	$s \in (\frac{1}{6}, \frac{1}{2})$	$c_3 \succ c_2 \succ c_1$
$s = \frac{2}{15}$	$c_1 \sim c_3 \succ c_2$		

This listing identifies which $\mathbf{w}_s$ support which of the seven rankings admitted by $\mathbf{p}$. Notice that (for this particular $\mathbf{p}$) the more emphasis $\mathbf{w}_s$ places on the identity of a voter's second-ranked candidate, the better c_3 (everyone's top or second-ranked candidate) fares. In particular, procedures providing increased recognition of a voter's second-ranked candidate force the rankings to approach $c_3 \succ c_2 \succ c_1$. So, while the $\mathbf{w}_0$ (plurality) ranking of $c_1 \succ c_2 \succ c_3$ relegates c_3 to last place, the $(7, 1, 0) \approx \mathbf{w}_{\frac{1}{8}}$ ranking of $c_1 \succ c_3 \succ c_2$ advances c_3 to a middle ranking, and the BC $(2, 1, 0) \approx \mathbf{w}_{\frac{1}{3}}$ ranking of $c_3 \succ c_2 \succ c_1$ finally elevates c_3 to the top status. $\square$

This example makes it clear that the normalized plurality and antiplurality election outcomes uniquely determine the properties and entries of $Sup(\mathbf{p})$. The following assertion stating how $Sup(\mathbf{p})$ can change is based on this fact.

Corollary 4.2.4. a. *Because $f(-, \mathbf{w}_0)$ and $f(-, \mathbf{w}_{\frac{1}{2}})$ are continuous functions of the profile, the procedure line varies continuously with $\mathbf{p}$.*

b. With changes in $\mathbf{p}$, there are two ways the entries of $Sup(\mathbf{p})$ can change.

i. The plurality ranking is the reverse of the antiplurality ranking and the procedure line passes through the point of complete indifference $\mathcal{I}$.

ii.   The plurality and/or the antiplurality ranking changes. This requires passing through a ranking involving tie votes.

Proof. Part a is obvious, so only b needs to be proved. If the plurality and/or the antiplurality ranking change, then the end-points of the procedure line move into different regions. This creates new entries for $Sup(\mathbf{p})$.

The proof of the rest of this assertion involves the geometry of the ranking regions; they are either triangles, line segments, or $\mathcal{I}$. By experimenting with the positioning of line segments in $Si(3)$, notice that if the end-points are in ranking regions that are not the reverse of one another, then most of the procedure line always intersects the same ranking regions. Another way a procedure line changes ranking regions is if its end-points are in ranking regions that are the reverse of one another. Here, the union of the ranking regions meeting $PL(\mathbf{p})$ is *not* convex. With the loss of convexity, the line can pass through the point $\mathcal{I}$. This completes the proof. $\square$

Example 4.2.3. Suppose all we know about a profile $\mathbf{p}$ for a large number of voters is that $\mathcal{I} \in Sup(\mathbf{p})$; thus, some $\mathbf{w}_s$ has a complete tie outcome. We want to determine what can happen if another voter arrives. This voter, then, slightly changes $\mathbf{p}$ to the profile $\mathbf{p}'$. (See Eq. 4.2.1.)

Using Theorem 4.2.3d, $Sup(\mathbf{p})$ has one, two, or three entries depending on whether the procedure line is the point $\mathcal{I}$, has an endpoint on $\mathcal{I}$, or has $\mathcal{I}$ as an interior point. In the first case, the new voter breaks the tie; as in the introductory example, the new $Sup(\mathbf{p}')$ admits precisely three entries. In the second case ($|Sup(\mathbf{p})| = 2$)), either the plurality or the antiplurality outcome must be a complete tie while the other is not. If the new voter is of type j, then this endpoint will move either in the direction $[\mathbf{w}_0]_j$ or $[\mathbf{w}_{\frac{1}{2}}]_j$. By experimenting with possible choices for $PL(\mathbf{p})$, it can be seen that $Sup(\mathbf{p}')$ can have anywhere from one to five entries. Finally, in the last case, $|Sup(\mathbf{p}')| = 3, 7$. The reader should verify these assertions with pictures. $\square$

The Size of the Region. The positioning of profile lines is described next.

Theorem 4.2.5. *Let $\mathbf{q}_0, \mathbf{q}_{\frac{1}{2}} \in Si(3)$. For a profile $\mathbf{p}$ to exist so that $f(\mathbf{p}, \mathbf{w}_s) = \mathbf{q}_s$, $s = 0, \frac{1}{2}$, it is necessary and sufficient that the following two conditions are satisfied.*

i. Each $\mathbf{q}_{\frac{1}{2}}$ component is bounded above by $\frac{1}{2}$.

ii. Each $\mathbf{q}_{\frac{1}{2}}$ component is at least as large as half the corresponding $\mathbf{q}_0$ component.

Thus, there does not exist a profile supporting both $\mathbf{q}_0 = (0.2, 0.4, 0.4)$, $\mathbf{q}_{\frac{1}{2}} = (0.45, 0.15, 0.4)$ because the c_2 component of $\mathbf{q}_{\frac{1}{2}}$ is smaller than half of the corresponding $\mathbf{q}_0$ component. However, there are profiles supporting the nearby outcomes $\mathbf{q}_0 = (0.2, 0.4, 0.4)$, $\mathbf{q}_{\frac{1}{2}} = (0.4, 0.2, 0.4)$. As another illustration, to find all admissible $\mathbf{q}_{\frac{1}{2}} = (x, y, z)$ when $\mathbf{q}_0 = (0.4, 0.1, 0.5)$, the constraints are

$$0.5 \geq x \geq 0.2 \quad 0.5 \geq y \geq 0.05$$
$$0.5 \geq z \geq 0.25 \quad x + y + z = 1.$$

This example illustrates the enormous flexibility to choose a procedure line even when one endpoint is fixed, and it eliminates the final obstacle for their design.

Idea of the proof. The first condition on $\mathbf{q}_{\frac{1}{2}}$ merely requires $\mathbf{q}_{\frac{1}{2}} \in \mathcal{CH}(\mathbf{w}_{\frac{1}{2}})$. The rest of the proof considers what happens when $\mathbf{e}_2 = (0,1,0)$ is admitted as an voting vector. (Here, only the second ranked candidate receives points.) With computations, it can be shown that election outcomes exist for a profile $\mathbf{p}$ as long as each $f(\mathbf{p}, \mathbf{e}_1) + f(\mathbf{p}, \mathbf{e}_2)$ component is bounded by unity. Namely, existence is ensured as long as this condition is satisfied by $\mathbf{q}_0 + [2\mathbf{q}_{\frac{1}{2}} - \mathbf{q}_0] = 2\mathbf{q}_{\frac{1}{2}}$. The conclusion follows after some computations. (See [S20].) $\square$

4.2.5 Robustness of the Paradoxical Assertions

Are these assertions of practical concern, or "Gee Whiz" facts to be invoked as an attempt to salvage a boring cocktail conversation. The answer, suggested by Theorems 4.2.2, 4.2.5, is that the immense freedom to choose the tallies of the plurality and antiplurality outcomes makes the conclusions robust and likely. In fact, extrapolating from Example 4.2.2, only profiles with a remarkable uniformity of views among the voters are immune from the conclusions. A more practical test is to determine whether actual election examples can be found to illustrate Theorems 4.2.1, 4.2.2. This is easy; in fact, practical examples should be expected from most closely contested election among three (or more) candidates.

Example 4.2.7. A plurality method favors a candidate who is top-ranked among a sizable, unified portion of the electorate, while other methods favor more subtle distinctions of the electorate. So, depending upon the demographics and political unity, different political groups will find different choices of $\mathbf{w}_s$ to be to their political advantage. But, election procedures are mathematical tools without an ideological bias. Thus, an advantage a procedure grants a group can change with the demographics and the degree of political unity.

To illustrate, the 1983 primary election for the Mayor of Chicago was closely contested among Jane Byrne, Richard Daley and Harold Washington. The polls indicated that Washington would lose a "head-to-head" election with either other candidate. Yet, because of unified Afro-American support and because the plurality method does not recognize a voter's second-ranked candidate, Washington became the first Afro-American Mayor of Chicago. Choices of $\mathbf{w}_s$ with increased recognition to a voter's second-ranked candidate, such as the BC, may have forced Washington to lose.

In 1987, Mayor Washington appeared to be sufficiently popular to beat any competitor with almost any method; he easily won reelection. Unfortunately, he died soon after. The resulting political scramble for a successor divided the Afro-American community into two factions supporting either Evans or Sawyer. Consequently in the election to fill the remainder of Washington's term, the plurality vote with its inability to reflect "second-choices" now worked against this same community; Richard Daley won. It is arguable that had a different positional method been used, such as the BC, an Afro-American would have been elected. So, in the short time span of five years, the voting method that initially showered success upon the united Afro-American community, now worked against the divided group. Indeed, the need for a single candidate to emerge with the plurality vote appears to be keeping this community divided.

Incidentally, just before the 1987 election, there was a "reform movement" to change the procedure to a runoff. The Black and Liberals viewed this as an attempt to defeat Mayor Washington, and they defeated it. But, suppose they lost. Washington was so popular he would have won with a runoff. In the election to fill the remainder of his term, either Evans or Sawyer might have won.

A 1991 example comes from the "crook or klan" Louisiana gubernatorial race. Former Governor Edwards was labeled a "crook" and a womanizer, while David Duke had been a leader of the Ku Klux Klan and a member of the neo-Nazi party. It is reasonable to suspect that the incumbent Governor Roemer would have beaten either of them in a head-to-head race – even though he changed political parties and made controversial decisions during his term. But, the plurality method does not recognize a voter's second-ranked candidate, so Roemer came in last. In the highly publicized "crook or klan" runoff, Edwards beat Duke. □

More Candidates. With more than three candidates, the number of possible election outcomes accompanying a fixed profile grows at a disturbingly fast rate. Replacing the procedure line is the *procedure simplex* ([S15]); it is the convex hull of the election outcomes when the $n - 1$ procedures $(1, 0, \ldots, 0)$, $(1, 1, 0, \ldots, 0)$, $\ldots, (1, 1, \ldots, 1, 0)$ are used with **p**. To provide insight into how bad the situation deteriorates, there is a ten-candidate profile where 84,830,767 *different* election rankings emerge just by varying the choice of the positional method. (That is, the procedure simplex for this profile crosses 84,830,767 ranking regions.) Moreover, each candidate can be top-ranked with some procedures and then bottom-ranked with others! So, which of these 84 million different rankings best reflect the "true views" of these voters? Clearly, the choice of a procedure matters! Thus, it is critical to understand potential flaws of these methods so an appropriate procedure can be identified!

4.2.6 Proofs

Proof of Theorem 4.2.2 a We need to examine the five equations in six unknowns with matrix form $A(\mathbf{p}^t) = (q_1^1, q_2^1, q_1^2, q_2^2, 1)^t$ where the transpose $\mathbf{p}^t$ is a column vector, q_i^j is the ith component of $\mathbf{q}_j$, and

$$
(4.2.6) \qquad A = \begin{pmatrix} s_1 & 0 & 0 & s_1 & 1 - s_1 & 1 - s_1 \\ 1 - s_1 & 1 - s_1 & s_1 & 0 & 0 & s_1 \\ s_2 & 0 & 0 & s_2 & 1 - s_2 & 1 - s_2 \\ 1 - s_2 & 1 - s_2 & s_2 & 0 & 0 & s_2 \\ 1 & 1 & 1 & 1 & 1 & 1 \end{pmatrix}.
$$

As $s_1 \neq s_2$, one s_j value is not zero and the other is not $\frac{1}{2}$. So, assume that $s_1 \neq 0$, $s_2 \neq \frac{1}{2}$. By moving the fifth row to become the second row and the fourth row to become the third row, the matrix equation is

$$
\begin{pmatrix}
s_1 & 0 & 0 & s_1 & 1-s_1 & 1-s_1 \\
1 & 1 & 1 & 1 & 1 & 1 \\
1-s_2 & 1-s_2 & s_2 & 0 & 0 & s_2 \\
1-s_1 & 1-s_1 & s_1 & 0 & 0 & s_1 \\
s_2 & 0 & 0 & s_2 & 1-s_2 & 1-s_2
\end{pmatrix}
(\mathbf{p}^t) =
\begin{pmatrix}
q_1^1 \\
1 \\
q_2^2 \\
q_1^2 \\
q_2^1
\end{pmatrix}.
$$

By using elementary row operations on this matrix (which corresponds to standard algebraic manipulations of the five original algebraic equations), the matrix is reduced to the form

$$
(4.2.7) \qquad
\begin{pmatrix}
1 & 0 & 0 & 1 & \frac{1-s_1}{s_1} & \frac{1-s_1}{s_1} \\
0 & 1 & 1 & 0 & \frac{-1}{s_1} & \frac{-1}{s_1} \\
0 & 0 & 2s_2-1 & s_2-1 & 1-s_2 & 1 \\
0 & 0 & 0 & \frac{s_1-s_2}{2s_2-1} & \frac{s_2-s_1}{2s_2-1} & \frac{2(s_2-s_1)}{2s_2-1} \\
0 & 0 & 0 & 0 & \frac{s_1-s_2}{s_1} & \frac{s_1-s_2}{s_1}
\end{pmatrix}.
$$

It follows from the reduced matrix of Eq. 4.2.7 that a solution exists for any $\mathbf{q}_1$, $\mathbf{q}_2$. For instance, from the last row, we have that $p_5 = -p_6 + c_5$ where c_5 is a scalar depending on the row reduction and the values of $\mathbf{q}_j$, and where the p_6 value can be varied. Similarly, from the fourth row, we have that $p_4 = -p_5 + 2p_6 + c_4 = 3p_6 + c_4 + c_5$. The equations for the remaining variables can be read off in a similar manner. The resulting solution defines a line in R^6 where the defining variable is p_6. The slope of this line is uniquely determined by the values of s_1, s_2, while the positioning of the line is determined by $s_1, s_2, \mathbf{q}_1, \mathbf{q}_2$. Also notice that for s_1 close to s_2, some of the coefficients are either very small or very large.

The one problem is that some solutions require a negative number of type-five voters. Independent of one's opinions about them, this is not permitted for a profile. Therefore, we need to verify that with appropriate restrictions[3] on the $\mathbf{q}_1, \mathbf{q}_2$ values, there are solutions with non-negative coefficients.

The resolution is simple. As shown, the algebraic system

$$
(4.2.8) \qquad F(\mathbf{p}) = (f(-, \mathbf{w}_{s_1}), f(-, \mathbf{w}_{s_2}) : Si(6) \to Si(3) \times Si(3)
$$

has maximum rank, so solutions exist for any $(\mathbf{q}_1, \mathbf{q}_2)$. Now, $\mathbf{p}' = (\frac{1}{6}, \frac{1}{6}, \ldots, \frac{1}{6})$ is the barycentric point of $Si(6)$ and solves the equation $F = (\mathcal{I}, \mathcal{I})$. By continuity, if $(\mathbf{q}_1, \mathbf{q}_2)$ is near $(\mathcal{I}, \mathcal{I})$, a solution is near the interior point $\mathbf{p}'$. This completes the proof.

---

[3] These restrictions explain why the profile sets are small for s_1 close to s_2.

Re-expressing the last argument geometrically, notice that $\mathbf{p}' = (\frac{1}{6}, \frac{1}{6}, \ldots, \frac{1}{6})$ is an interior point of the $Si(6)$ hull, so its image $F(\mathbf{p}') = (\mathcal{I}, \mathcal{I})$ is in the interior of the F image set. Either the F image is a lower dimensional linear space passing through this point, or it is a higher dimensional space with $\mathcal{F}(\mathbf{p}') = (\mathcal{I}, \mathcal{I})$ as an interior point. If the later holds, there is a ball of profiles about $\mathbf{p}'$ that is mapped to the image space. The latter case does hold from the analysis of Eq. 4.2.7. $\square$

Proof of Theorem 4.2.1. Theorem 4.2.2a asserts that $\{\mathbf{q}_i\}_{i=1}^{2}$ can be chosen in an arbitrary fashion from $B(\mathcal{I}, \rho)$. But, $B(\mathcal{I}, \rho)$ intersects all 13 ranking regions, so for any choice of β_1, β_2 a value of $\mathbf{q}_1, \mathbf{q}_2$ can be selected from that ranking region. $\square$

4.2.7 Exercises

1. Show that while $f(\mathbf{p}, \mathbf{w}_0) = (1, 0, 0)$ and $f(\mathbf{p}, \mathbf{w}_{\frac{1}{2}}) = (0, \frac{1}{2}, \frac{1}{2})$ have common solutions, no solution allows all coefficients to be non-negative. Namely, prove there exist admissible plurality and antiplurality outcomes that cannot be obtained simultaneously. Does this example satisfy Theorem 4.2.5?

2. Suppose $\mathbf{p}$ and $\mathbf{w}_s$, $s \neq 0, \frac{1}{2}$, satisfy $f(\mathbf{p}, \mathbf{w}_s) = \mathcal{I}$. Prove that no more than two other rankings are possible with any other positional voting method.

3. a. Suppose $f(\mathbf{p}, \mathbf{w}_0) = (\frac{5}{10}, \frac{4}{10}, \frac{1}{10})$ and $f(\mathbf{p}, \mathbf{w}_{\frac{1}{2}}) = (\frac{4}{10}, \frac{5}{10}, \frac{1}{10})$. Find $f(\mathbf{p}, \mathbf{w}_{\frac{1}{3}})$.

b. Suppose $f(\mathbf{p}, \mathbf{w}_0) = (\frac{3}{8}, \frac{3}{8}, \frac{2}{8})$ and $f(\mathbf{p}, \mathbf{w}_{\frac{1}{3}}) = (\frac{6}{16}, \frac{5}{16}, \frac{5}{16})$. Find $f(\mathbf{p}, \mathbf{w}_{\frac{1}{2}})$ and $f(\mathbf{p}, \mathbf{w}_{\frac{1}{4}})$.

c. Suppose $f(\mathbf{p}, \mathbf{w}_{\frac{1}{4}}) \in \mathcal{R}(c_1 \succ c_3 \succ c_2)$ and that $f(\mathbf{p}, \mathbf{w}_{\frac{1}{3}}) \in \mathcal{R}(c_3 \succ c_1 \sim c_2)$. Find all admissible rankings for $f(\mathbf{p}, \mathbf{w}_{\frac{1}{2}})$ and $f(\mathbf{p}, \mathbf{w}_0)$.

4. a. Suppose $f(\mathbf{p}, \mathbf{w}_0) \in \mathcal{R}(c_3 \succ c_2 \succ c_1)$ and $f(\mathbf{p}, \mathbf{w}_{\frac{1}{2}}) \in \mathcal{R}(c_1 \succ c_2 \succ c_3)$. By varying the choice of the $\mathbf{w}_s$ there may be three different listing of rankings associated with $\mathbf{p}$. Find them. Suppose that $f(\mathbf{p}, \mathbf{w}_{\frac{1}{2}}) = (\frac{4}{15}, \frac{5}{15}, \frac{6}{15})$ and $f(\mathbf{p}, \mathbf{w}_0) = (\frac{13}{30}, \frac{9}{30}, \frac{8}{30})$. List all possible rankings that could occur with any $\mathbf{w}_s$. Find choices of $\mathbf{w}_s$ that support each possible ranking.

b. Show it is possible for the plurality ranking of $\mathbf{p}$ to be $c_2 \succ c_3 \succ c_1$ while the antiplurality ranking is $c_1 \succ c_2 \succ c_3$. Find all possible remaining rankings for $\mathbf{p}$ when other positional methods are used.

c. Show that if $|Sup(\mathbf{p})| > 1$, there is at least one ranking with a tie vote.

5. Carry out the details of the row reduction part of the proof of Theorem 4.2.2, by carrying the values of q_i^j. In this way, find the equations for the line of profiles in terms of the values of p_6 and $\{q_i^j\}_{i,j=1}^{2}$.

6. a. Instead of using the plurality and antiplurality endpoints for define a procedure line, show that is can be defined by one of these endpoints and the BC outcome. Show, for instance, that the procedure line is defined by extending the line $f(\mathbf{p}, \mathbf{w}_0)$ and $f(\mathbf{p}, \mathbf{w}_{\frac{1}{3}})$ half again as far. Use this approach to find all admissible rankings for $f(\mathbf{p}, \mathbf{w}_0) = (\frac{1}{3}, \frac{5}{12}, \frac{1}{4})$ and $f(\mathbf{p}, \mathbf{w}_{\frac{1}{3}}) = (\frac{1}{3}, \frac{1}{3}, \frac{1}{3})$.

b. Use Fig. 4.2.2 to explain the beverage paradox from the fable. That is, show how certain profiles using these three voter types will place the BC and anti-plurality outcomes in the $c_3 \succ c_2 \succ c_1$ region while the same profile places the plurality outcome in the $c_1 \succ c_2 \succ c_3$ region. Show that no profile involving these three types allows $c_1 \succ c_2 \succ c_3$ for $s \geq \frac{1}{3}$.

c. Follow the lead of Fig. 4.2.2 to compare the possible plurality, BC, and antiplurality outcomes when profiles are restricted to types one and five; to types one, three, and five; to types one, four, and five; and to types one, two, and five.

7. Show that the optimal choice of ρ in the statement of Theorem 4.2.2 depends upon the choice of the s_1, s_2 values. Show that the maximum ρ value occurs with $s = 0, \frac{1}{2}$.

8. For the beverage example, we know that the BC and the antiplurality rankings are consistent with the pairwise rankings. For this profile, find all $\mathbf{w}_s$ with this property. Find all $\mathbf{w}_s$ where the ranking agrees with the plurality ranking.

9. Suppose the $\mathbf{p}$ ranking for $\mathbf{w}_{s_1} \neq \mathbf{w}_{s_2}$ have a tie vote between c_1 and c_2. Show for this profile that *all* positional rankings have a tie vote between these candidates.

10. Show there is a profile where each candidate is top-ranked with some $\mathbf{w}_s$. Show there is a profile where each candidate is bottom-ranked depending on which $\mathbf{w}_s$ is used. Show there is a profile where c_3 always is bottom-ranked, but some positional methods have c_1 top-ranked, while others have c_2 top-ranked.

11. a. If $f(\mathbf{p}, \mathbf{w}_0) = (0.2, 0.5, 0.3)$, find all admissible values for $f(\mathbf{p}, \mathbf{w}_{\frac{1}{2}})$.

b. The 1992 plurality vote for U.S. President was $(0.43, 0.38, 0.19)$. Find all procedure lines that could accompany this outcome.

c. For a given $f(\mathbf{p}, \mathbf{w}_{\frac{1}{2}}) = \mathbf{q}_{\frac{1}{2}}$, find a relationship specifying all admissible $\mathbf{q}_0$.

4.3 Positional Versus Pairwise Voting

We now know why election outcomes can vary with the choice of the positional voting method and why the paradoxical cycles occur with pairs of candidates. In this section, these ideas are combined to compare positional with pairwise vote outcomes. This material, then, is a step toward understanding the kinds of difficulties introduced in the fable.

To start, I compare positional voting outcomes with the pairwise ranking of a particular pair of candidates. One result is that *all* positional methods allow "anything to happen" – the $\{c_i, c_j\}$ pairwise and positional rankings need not have anything to do with one another. This negative assertion holds for all $\mathbf{w}_s$, so more delicate ways are needed to compare procedures. One way is to develop profile coordinates. By doing so, we discover that the plurality method is more apt to cause such chaotic behavior, while the BC is the unique method to impose a tone of temperance. But, watch out; more kinds of troublesome election outcomes exist than one might expect. As true throughout this book, while the goal is to understand the informational reasons for electoral problems, the analysis depends on developing appropriate geometric representations.

4.3.1 Comparing Votes With a Fat Triangle

Comparing a positional and a majority ranking outcome of the pair $\{c_1, c_2\}$ involves comparing a point in the representation triangle $Si(3)$ – the positional election outcome – and a point in $[-1, 1]$ – the $\{c_1, c_2\}$ majority vote outcome. The analysis, then, is modeled as the mapping

(4.3.1) $$F_4(-, \mathbf{w}_s) : Si(6) \to Si(3) \times [-1, 1]$$

defined by

$$F_4(\mathbf{p}, \mathbf{w}_s) = (f(\mathbf{p}, \mathbf{w}_s), f_{\{c_1, c_2\}}(\mathbf{p})).$$

To visualize $Si(3) \times [-1, 1]$, follow the lead of Sect. 3.2 by passing in an orthogonal direction an interval of pairwise vote outcomes, $[-1, 1]$, through $\mathbf{q} \in Si(3)$. By varying the choice of $\mathbf{q} \in Si(3)$, a "fat" equilateral triangle is traced out.

The F_4 image is the convex hull defined by the six unanimity F_4 election outcomes. The identification is easy because $F_4(\mathbf{E}_j, \mathbf{w}_s) = ([\mathbf{w}_s]_j, \pm 1)$, $j = 1, \ldots, 6$, where the choice of 1 or -1 depends, respectively, on whether the jth voter type has $c_1 \succ c_2$ or $c_2 \succ c_1$. The image hulls for the plurality and antiplurality methods are depicted in Fig. 4.3.1.

The plurality and antiplurality methods can account for all six unanimity outcomes by using only four points from $Si(3) \times [-1, 1]$. This is due to a "doubling up" effect where, for instance, the type-one and two unanimity outcomes agree, $F_4(\mathbf{E}_1, \mathbf{w}_0) = F_4(\mathbf{E}_2, \mathbf{w}_0) = ((1, 0, 0), 1)$; i.e., $[\mathbf{w}_0]_1 = [\mathbf{w}_0]_2 = (1, 0, 0)$ and both voter types have the same $c_1 \succ c_2$ ranking of the pair. (This F_4 point is the dot at the bottom, back, and left of Fig. 4.3.1a. I reversed the usual geometric representation of the line interval $[-1, 1]$ to make the picture easier to analyze – at least for me.) All other $\mathbf{w}_s$, $s \in (0, \frac{1}{2})$, define six distinct F_4 unanimity election points. (See Fig. 4.3.2a.)

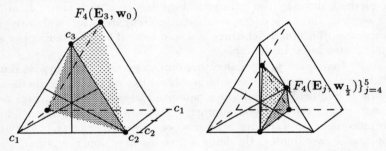

a. The F_4 plurality hull.   **b.** The F_4 antiplurality hull

Fig. 4.3.1. Extreme hulls

Fig. 4.3.1 shows that the region of complete indifference, $((\frac{1}{3}, \frac{1}{3}, \frac{1}{3}), 0)$, is an interior point for the plurality and the antiplurality image sets. As shown later and as suggested by Fig. 4.3.2a, the same geometry holds for all positional methods. Some consequences are captured by the next statement.

Theorem 4.3.1. *For* $\mathbf{w}_s$, $s \in [0, \frac{1}{2}]$, *the indifference point* $((\frac{1}{3}, \frac{1}{3}, \frac{1}{3}), 0)$ *is an interior point of the image of* $F_4(-, \mathbf{w}_s)$; *the image set meets all ranking regions in* $Si(3) \times [-1, 1]$. *Thus, for any ranking of* $\{c_1, c_2\}$ *combined with any (of the 13 possible) positional election ranking of the three candidates, there is a profile* $\mathbf{p}$ *where the majority vote of* $\{c_1, c_2\}$ *and the* $\mathbf{w}_s$ *election outcome are the chosen ones. Indeed, an election point* $\mathbf{q}$ *in the interior of the* $F_4(-, \mathbf{w}_s)$ *image set is supported by a two-dimensional set of profiles.*

Well, there it goes again! Flaunting our expectations, Theorem 4.3.1 asserts that anything can happen when comparing a positional election outcome with the majority vote outcome of a particular pair. The statement does not even provide a scapegoat to blame a particular positional method; instead, for *any* $\mathbf{w}_s$, there exist profiles where the positional ranking of $c_1 \succ c_3 \succ c_2$ is distinctly at odds with the same voters' pairwise ranking of $c_2 \succ c_1$. This means that the ranking of a scholarship competition could be Arvid $\succ$ Andrew $\succ$ Adam, even though most voters really prefer Adam to Arvid. As these examples involve strict rankings, the outcomes are likely, robust events.

The proof of the theorem depends upon the geometry of the F_4 image set; but this is complicated! For example, the wedged surface to the left and back of Fig. 4.3.2a (partially outlined by hidden, dashed lines), W_s^1, is the convex hull defined by the three points $\{([\mathbf{w}_s]_j, 1)\}_{j=1}^3$ while the wedge to the right and front, W_s^2, is the convex hull of $\{([\mathbf{w}_s]_j, -1)\}_{j=4}^6$. The six remaining surface wedges connect the front and back faces of the fat triangle.

4.3.2 Positional Group Coordinates

To understand and prove Theorem 4.3.1, it helps to know which profiles define which F_4 outcomes; i.e., we need to invent another coordinate representation for the profiles. Here, it is natural to group the voters according to how they rank the pair $\{c_1, c_2\}$. Thus, the *liberals*, or voter types $\{1, 2, 3\}$ that are to the left of $c_1 \sim c_2$ line, have the relative ranking $c_1 \succ c_2$ while the *conservatives*, or types $\{4, 5, 6\}$, are to the right of the $c_1 \sim c_2$ indifference line.

If only liberals vote, the outcome is in the convex hull W_s^1 defined by the vertices $\{F(\mathbf{E}_j, \mathbf{w}_s)\}_{j=1}^3$; similarly, the election outcome when only conservatives vote is in W_s^2. So, let $(\alpha_s \in W_s^1, \beta_s \in W_s^2, d \in [0, 1])$ represent, respectively, the $\mathbf{w}_s$ election outcome if only the liberals vote, if only the conservatives vote, and the proportion of all voters that are liberals. The analytic definition is

$$d = \sum_{j=1}^3 p_j, \quad a_i = \frac{p_i}{d}, \, i = 1, 2, 3; \quad \alpha_s = (\sum_{j=1}^3 a_j [\mathbf{w}_s]_j, \, 1) \in W_s^1$$

$$b_j = \frac{p_j}{1-d}, \, j = 4, 5, 6; \quad \beta_s = (\sum_{j=4}^6 b_j [\mathbf{w}_s]_j, \, -1) \in W_s^2$$

$$(4.3.2) \qquad F_4(\mathbf{p}, \mathbf{w}_s) = d\alpha_s + (1-d)\beta_s.$$

As in Sect. 3.2, a profile is represented as a line segment connecting α_s, β_s, and a designated point on the segment that is d of the distance from β_s to α_s. If $s \neq 0, \frac{1}{2}$, there is a smooth invertible relationship between $\mathbf{p} \in Si(6)$ and the *positional group coordinate representation*, (α_s, β_s, d), of the profile. Unfortunately, the invertibility does not extend to the plurality and antiplurality methods; instead, these extreme procedures assign a *subset* of profiles to *each* (α_s, β_s, d) value. While this annoying fact makes it improper to call (α_s, β_s, d) a "coordinate representation" when $s = 0, \frac{1}{2}$, I do so anyway. (A similar singularity situation occurs with spherical coordinates when the radius of the sphere is zero.)

Even with these coordinates, the geometry remains too complicated to use. The easiest part of the geometry is the majority vote outcome; if $d > \frac{1}{2}$, then $c_1 \succ c_2$; if $d < \frac{1}{2}$, then $c_2 \succ c_1$. Geometrically, then, $d > \frac{1}{2}$ forces $\mathbf{q}_s$ to be closer to α_s than to β_s. (The converse relationship holds for $d < \frac{1}{2}$.) Thus, all information about who wins the $\{c_1, c_2\}$ pairwise vote and by how much is captured by how close $\mathbf{q}_s$ is to α_s or β_s. This information is retained if we view the fat triangle through the front triangular surface.

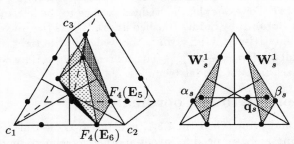

a. The image set of $F_4(-, w_s)$ **b.** The collapsed region

Fig. 4.3.2. Reducing the dimension

Stated in practical terms, as the geometry allows us to ignore the pairwise vote direction, we can collapse the fat triangle to the front surface. Fig. 4-3-2b is the result where the shaded areas are the wedges W_s^1, W_s^2. A potential problem is the effect on the d value. I suggested that the relative distances among $\mathbf{q}$, α_s, and β_s remain the same whether they are compared in the fat triangle, or projected to the front surface. This assertion is true. (The reader can check this by using standard properties of similar triangles. See the exercises.)

This liberal-conservative coordinate representation is particularly easy to use and interpret with the collapsed fat triangle.

1. *The point α_s can be any point in W_s^1. The closer α_s is to the ith vertex of W_s^1, the stronger the dominance of the ith voter type among the liberals. Similar statements apply to the conservatives for $\beta_s \in W_s^2$.*

2. *A profile $\mathbf{p}$ is represented by the line segment α_s - β_s and a designated point that is d of the distance from β_s toward α_s. As the designated point identifies $\mathbf{q}_s$, the $\mathbf{w}_s$ election ranking is the ranking region containing $\mathbf{q}_s$.*

3. *The c_1, c_2 majority vote ranking is determined by the value of d; e.g., if the designated point $\mathbf{q}_s$ is closer to α_s than to β_s, the majority ranking is $c_1 \succ c_2$.*

Triangle Abuse. The power of the coordinate representation is that it allows us to "see" what profiles define which election outcomes. As true for the cyclic representation, the designated outcome $\mathbf{q}_s$ serves as a pivot creating a balance between the types of liberals and conservatives needed to support $\mathbf{q}_s$. In particular, it is interesting to see how this pivoting action and the triangular geometry of $Si(3)$ shape the possible election outcomes. Indeed, several paradoxes are consequences of the pointy head – fat bottom geometry of the representation triangle.

The plurality vote is particularly easy to use because the wedges W_0^1, W_0^2 are, respectively, the left and right side edges of $Si(3)$. Thus *any line segment connecting the side edges of the representation triangle represents a α_0 - β_0 profile line.* Recall, a plurality vote ignores a voter's second-ranked candidate while the pairwise vote ignores the intensity of pairwise comparisons. Surrounded by this wealth of ignorance, we must expect all sorts of paradoxical situations to arise. This happens, and the geometry displays them.

Start with $d = \frac{1}{2}$; this d value requires the pairwise ranking to be $c_1 \sim c_2$. Geometrically, $d = \frac{1}{2}$ requires $\mathbf{q}_0$ to be the midpoint of the α_0 - β_0 profile line. If α_0, β_0 are the same height above the base of the representation triangle, then the connecting line segment is parallel to the base. Using the properties of similar triangles, this positions $\mathbf{q}_0$ on the $c_1 \sim c_2$ indifference line (see Fig. 4.3.3) where the relative ranking of $\{c_1, c_2\}$ for the pairwise and plurality votes agree. Of course, the status of c_3 in the plurality ranking varies through three possible choices of $c_3 \succ c_1 \sim c_2$, $c_3 \sim c_1 \sim c_2$, $c_1 \sim c_2 \succ c_3$ by changing the common height of α_0 and β_0.

These consistent outcomes are due to "canceling errors." As α_0 shares the same height with β_0, the geometry requires the α_0 and β_0 ends of the profile to have a reasonably similar mix of strong and weak $\{c_1, c_2\}$ intensity comparisons with a similar frequency of having c_3 top-ranked by the liberals and conservatives. It is this careful balance of the kind of information ignored by a pairwise vote (the intensity factor) and dropped by the plurality procedure (a voter's second-ranked candidate) that cancels out any artificial advantage shown to one candidate over the other. So, the geometry allows the plurality and pairwise $\{c_1, c_2\}$ rankings to agree.

A geometrically more interesting case is if α_0 or β_0 is the higher point. Such a profile presents a different mix for the intensity of the $\{c_1, c_2\}$ comparisons (for the pairwise vote) and a different distribution of how often c_3 is the second-ranked candidate (for the plurality vote). Without balancing the "lost" information, we must expect paradoxes.

To see the consequences, observe that when one endpoint is higher than the other, the resulting slant of the α_0 - β_0 profile line forces its midpoint off of the $c_1 \sim c_2$ indifference line; thus the pair's relative plurality ranking disagrees with the $c_1 \sim c_2$ pairwise ranking. For instance, the higher a liberal point is on W_0^1, the closer α_0 is both to the pointy head and the $c_1 \sim c_2$ indifference line. Similarly, the closer the conservative point approaches the fat bottom of the representation triangle, the farther β_0 strays from the indifference line. Thus, elementary geometry (or observation) ensures that the midpoint of the connecting line is in the $c_2 \succ c_1$ region. Consequently, if β_0 is lower than α_0 while $d = \frac{1}{2}$, then $\mathbf{q}_0$ is pulled to the right forcing the pair's relative plurality ranking to be $c_2 \succ c_1$. Similarly, if α_0 is lower than β_0, then $\mathbf{q}_0$ is pulled to the left creating the plurality ranking $c_1 \succ c_2$. By varying the relative α_0, β_0 heights the midpoint can be forced into any of the thirteen regions of the representation triangle. Thus *any of the thirteen plurality rankings can accompany a pairwise outcome of* $c_1 \sim c_2$. Fig. 4.3.3a depicts three different situations.

Extending beyond the pairwise tie vote $c_1 \sim c_2$ where $\mathbf{q}_0$ is the midpoint of the α_0 - β_0 line segment, similar statements hold for most other d values. If, for example, c_1 beats c_2 by receiving 60% of the vote, then $d = 0.6$. This d value requires $\mathbf{q}_0$ to be closer to α_0 than β_0. Consequently, to obtain the contradictory plurality relative ranking of $c_2 \succ c_1$, α_0 must be close to the pointy head while β_0 is near the fat bottom; we need an extreme slant to force the designated point into the $c_2 \succ c_1$ region. On the other hand, should the profile line be horizontal, or slant in the other direction, the liberal beats the conservative in both the plurality and pairwise $(d > \frac{1}{2})$ elections. Using similar arguments and varying the height of α_0 and β_0, it is clear that Theorem 4.3.1 holds for the plurality method.

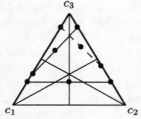
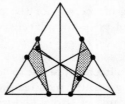

a. Plurality $(s = 0)$ voting.   **b.** For $0 < s < \frac{1}{2}$

Fig. 4.3.3. Liberals and conservative coordinates

One way to appreciate the geometry is to use it to describe actual election behavior. As soon as Ross Perot entered the race for the 1992 US Presidency, there was considerable speculation about which of the other two candidates, George Bush or Bill Clinton, would be hurt the most. For example, if a voter has (c_3) Perot top-ranked and (c_2) Bush second-ranked, then Bush loses the vote. Geometrically, the more voters there are of this type, the closer β_0 moves to the c_3 vertex. From the geometry, the resulting slant of the profile line could force a (c_1) Clinton victory even if more people preferred Bush to Clinton (as indicated by the polls in Spring, 1992). As a response, in June of 1992, the Bush forces tried to instill doubt about Perot's reliability. The goal, of course, was to convert voters indecisive between Bush and Perot to vote for Bush (to push β_0 closer to the base of the representation triangle). Expressed geometrically, they tried to put an appropriate slant on the profile line to allow a Bush victory even should more voters prefer Clinton. In July, 1992, Perot withdrew (for a couple of months) leaving a two-person race.

The geometry changes if $0 < s < \frac{1}{2}$ as the wedges W_s^i become two-dimensional triangles instead of simple lines (because $F_4(\mathbf{E}_1, \mathbf{w}_s) \neq F_4(\mathbf{E}_2, \mathbf{w}_s)$). The extra direction in the wedges, which manifest the recognition accorded to a second-ranked candidate, allows α_s, β_s to be moved horizontally as well as vertically. (See Fig. 4-3-3b.) Consequently, even when $d = \frac{1}{2}$ and α_s and β_s have the same height, the designated point need not be on the $c_1 \sim c_2$ indifference line.

By using the horizontal freedom to move α_s more to the left, the $\mathbf{w}_s$ election outcome $\mathbf{q}_s$ is forced into the liberal region with its relative ranking of $c_1 \succ c_2$. By varying the vertical and horizontal positions of α_s, β_s, the position of $\mathbf{q}_s$ can be radically changed. It is this flexibility that almost encourages the pairwise and $\mathbf{w}_s$ rankings of c_1, c_2 to disagree.

There is a trade-off; accompanying the new found freedom where α_s, β_s can be moved horizontally, a limit is imposed on the vertical movement – only for $s = 0$ is the pointy head of the representation triangle accessible. In particular, the upper limit for W_s^1 is determined by the c_3 value of $f(\mathbf{E}_3, \mathbf{w}_s) = [\mathbf{w}_s]_3 = (s, 0, 1 - s)$. This upper limit, of course, restricts the slant of a profile line. As we have seen, the greater the slant, the more likely it is for a pairwise winner to be ranked *below* her opponent in the positional ranking. Thus, the geometric upper bound has implications about election outcomes; they are developed later.

Even though the height of the wedges W_s^j, $j = 1, 2$, is limited, enough flexibility remains to choose α_s, β_s to construct profiles to support any combination of election outcomes. After all, the bottom of a wedge is on the base of the representation triangle while the top is at height $1 - s > \frac{1}{2} > \frac{1}{3}$. The vertical range between 0 and $1 - s > \frac{1}{3}$ provides ample room to manipulate the α_s - β_s line above and below $\mathcal{I}$. With all of this freedom, $\mathbf{q}_s$ can be moved into any ranking region – anything can happen with $d = \frac{1}{2}$. Again, it is clear that other values of d – particularly those sufficiently close to $\frac{1}{2}$ – can be accompanied with any of the 13 positional rankings. This is a geometric proof of Theorem 4.3.1 for $\mathbf{w}_s$, $s \in [0, \frac{1}{2})$.

For the remaining procedure, $\mathbf{w}_{\frac{1}{2}}$, the wedge $W_{\frac{1}{2}}^1$ degenerates to the line connecting the midpoints of the left and bottom edges of $Si(3)$; similarly, $W_{\frac{1}{2}}^2$ is the line connecting the midpoints of the right and bottom edges. As true for the plurality method, the wedges form a pointy head and fat bottom, but in the reversed direction. The geometric arguments justifying the theorem are similar to those used for the plurality vote.

4.3.3 Profile Sets

To complete Theorem 4.3.1, we need a geometric way to demonstrate that a $F_4(-, \mathbf{w}_s)$ interior election point (i.e., a specified $\mathbf{q}_s$ and a specified majority $\{c_1, c_2\}$ outcome) is supported by a two-dimensional set of profiles. The construction uses the fact that a given $\{c_1, c_2\}$ majority vote uniquely defines $d = \sum_{j=1}^{3} p_j \in [0, 1]$.

Each profile line in the cone of profiles supporting a designated $\mathbf{q}_s$ (and, hence, passing through $\mathbf{q}_s$) can be described as wiggling lines being held at $\mathbf{q}_s$. The points $\mathbf{q}_s$ and β_s (the W_s^2 endpoint) determine the slope of the line while the specified d explains how much it is stretched; it uniquely determines α_s, the W_s^1 endpoint. Consequently, with a specified d, the two-dimensional profile set is represented by the cone of all line segments passing through $\mathbf{q}_s$; the two-dimensional parameterization of the lines is given by the ways $\beta_s \in W_s^2$ can vary. (Alternatively, use $\alpha_s \in W_s^1$.)

As true with the earlier coordinate representations, the cone of β_s values is found by wiggling the profile lines to find extreme settings. Thus, it is a convex set defined by its vertices. These vertices are the three profile lines defined when α_s is a vertex of W_s^1. (See Fig. 4.3.4.) If $d > \frac{1}{2}$, the pivoting role of $\mathbf{q}_s$ makes the smaller set, the cone in W_s^1, a more descriptive set of supporting profiles.

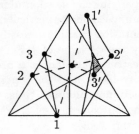

Fig. 4.3.4. The β_s profile values for a specified outcome

Example 4.3.1. In Fig. 4.3.4, $s = \frac{2}{5}$, $\mathbf{q}_s = (0.2, 0.3, 0.5)$ and $d = 0.4$ defines the $\mathbf{w}_{\frac{2}{5}}$ outcome of $c_3 \succ c_2 \succ c_1$ and the pairwise outcome is $c_2 \succ c_1$. Because $\mathbf{q}_s$ is closer to $W_{\frac{2}{5}}^2$ than to $W_{\frac{2}{5}}^1$ (as $d < \frac{1}{2}$), the pivoting action of $\mathbf{q}_s$ on the profile lines makes $W_{\frac{2}{5}}^2$ the better indicator of the size of the cone of profiles.

To find the vertices of the $\beta_{\frac{2}{5}}$ cone, start with $\alpha_{\frac{2}{5}} = [\mathbf{w}_{\frac{2}{5}}]_1 = (\frac{3}{5}, \frac{2}{5}, 0)$; this vertex of the wedge $W_{\frac{2}{5}}^1$ is labeled 1 in Fig. 4.3.4. According to Eq. 4.3.2, the corresponding $\beta_{\frac{2}{5}}$ value satisfies the equation

$$0.4(\frac{3}{5}, \frac{2}{5}, 0) + 0.6\beta_{\frac{2}{5}} = \mathbf{q}_{\frac{2}{5}} = (0.2, 0.3, 0.5),$$

or

$$\beta_{\frac{2}{5}} = (\frac{-2}{30}, \frac{7}{30}, \frac{25}{30}).$$

The negative component, $\frac{-2}{30}$, is meaningless in a profile representation; therefore no profile supports $\mathbf{q}_{\frac{2}{5}}$ where $\alpha_{\frac{2}{5}} = (\frac{3}{5}, \frac{2}{5}, 0)$. Nevertheless, plot this value as point $1'$ in the figure.

To find $1'$ geometrically, draw the dashed line from 1 (the vertex $[\mathbf{w}_{\frac{2}{5}}]_1$) through $\mathbf{q}_{\frac{2}{5}}$; point $1'$ is on this line. (See the figure.) By the definition of d,

$$d = \frac{\|1' - \mathbf{q}_{\frac{2}{5}}\|}{\|1' - \mathbf{q}_{\frac{2}{5}}\| + \|\mathbf{q}_{\frac{2}{5}} - [\mathbf{w}_{\frac{2}{5}}]_1\|}$$

where $\|1' - \mathbf{q}_{\frac{2}{5}}\|$ is the distance from the sought after $1'$ to the designated outcome $\mathbf{q}_{\frac{2}{5}}$. So, $1'$ is on the dashed line a distance $\frac{1}{1-d}\|[\mathbf{w}_{\frac{2}{5}}]_1 - \mathbf{q}_{\frac{2}{5}}\|$ from $[\mathbf{w}_{\frac{2}{5}}]_1$.

Similarly, the vertices $2'$, $3'$, correspond, respectively, to $\alpha_{\frac{2}{5}} = [\mathbf{w}_{\frac{2}{5}}]_2$, $[\mathbf{w}_{\frac{2}{5}}]_3$. The intersection of the triangle formed by $1', 2', 3'$ with the wedge $W_{\frac{2}{5}}^2$ is the cone of $\beta_{\frac{2}{5}}$ values. By using these vertices of the $\beta_{\frac{2}{5}}$ cone, the corresponding $\alpha_{\frac{2}{5}}$ cone is determined. □

The profile line also can be used to "see" the three-dimensional set of profiles defining a specified $\mathbf{q}_s$. Because the outcome of the pairwise vote is not specified, let the d value vary. Therefore, the set of profiles is given by *all* profile lines passing through $\mathbf{q}_s$ with one endpoint in W_s^1 and the other in W_s^2. In other words, just wiggle the profile lines without worrying the length as defined by d.

For the above $\mathbf{q}_{\frac{2}{5}}$, this set is determined by the three boundary lines passing through $\mathbf{q}_{\frac{2}{5}}$ and a vertex $\{[\mathbf{w}_{\frac{2}{5}}]_j\}_{j=1}^3$; i.e., just extend the dashed lines in the figure to the boundary of the representation triangle. Here, only the 3 - 3' dashed line need to be extended, so the admissible β_s values are all points in W_s^2 above this extended line. The profiles are given by any line segment passing through $\mathbf{q}_{\frac{2}{5}}$ with β_s in this region and $\alpha_s \in W_{\frac{1}{5}}^1$. The significant advantage of this geometric approach is that we can "see" what profiles lead to specified election outcomes, and we can compare the sets of supporting profiles for different results. (See the exercises.) Also, from the profile representation, we can "see" for each profile which candidate wins the pairwise election – just check whether α_s or β_s is closer to $\mathbf{q}_s$.

How Bad It Can Get. Can c_1 trounce c_2 in a majority vote election and still be plurality ranked below c_2? How decisive of a victory does c_1 need over c_2 to ensure she is not $\mathbf{w}_s$-ranked below c_2? Do the answers change with the choice of $\mathbf{w}_s$? What profile restrictions ensure compatibility between the majority vote and how the pair is $\mathbf{w}_s$-ranked? Answers for these kinds of questions follow from the coordinate representation.

Start by finding the pairwise vote needed by c_1 to ensure that she is plurality ranked above c_2. For instance, if c_1 beats c_2 with 80% of the pairwise vote, will she be ranked above c_2 in the plurality contest? Remember, the pairwise vote is uniquely determined by d. So, the goal is to find a $d = d_0^*$ value where, for all α_0, β_0, the election outcome $\mathbf{q}_0$ is to the left of the $c_1 \sim c_2$ line. So, if it turns out that $d_0^* < .8$, then with an 80% vote, c_1 is assured of being ranked over c_2. However, if $d_0^* > .8$, then there are profiles where c_1 is plurality ranked below c_2.

We know from the geometry that for a given $d \geq \frac{1}{2}$, c_1 can be $\mathbf{w}_0$-ranked below c_2 only if the profile line has a sufficiently steep slant. The more extreme the slant, the easier it is for the pairwise ranking to be reversed by the plurality vote. Therefore, to compute d_0^*, find the profile line segment with the steepest slant. This is where $\alpha_0 \in W_0^1$ is as close as possible to the $c_1 \sim c_2$ indifference line while $\beta_0 \in W_0^2$ is as far from this line as possible. If $\mathbf{q}_0$ is the point where this profile line intersects the $c_1 \sim c_2$ line, then $\mathbf{q}_0$ defines the limiting $d = d_0^*$ value. This is the sought after value because d_0^* defines the extreme situation where the $\mathbf{w}_0$ ranking of the pair is tie. As no other profile line admits such an extreme slant, on any other profile line the point corresponding to d_0^* falls on the $c_1 \succ c_2$ side of the $c_1 \sim c_2$ line.

From the geometry, the extreme slant is when $\alpha_0 = F_4(\mathbf{E}_3, \mathbf{w}_0)$ and $\beta_0 \neq F_4(\mathbf{E}_4, \mathbf{w}_0)$. This choice places α_0 at the c_3 vertex, so the α_0 - β_0 profile line is in W_0^2 (the right hand edge of the representation triangle); thus, $d_0^* = 1$. In words, *no matter how decisive the victory c_1 has over c_2 – even if she wins by as close to an unanimous vote as desired – c_2 could be plurality ranked above c_1!* The geometry of the coordinate representation dictates the profiles allowing such a biased outcome – almost all liberals are type-three.

To illustrate, suppose 9,999 of 10,000 voters have the ranking $c_3 \succ c_1 \succ c_2$ and only the last voter, who happens to be c_2, has the ranking $c_2 \succ c_1 \succ c_3$. There is no debate; the correct group ranking is $c_3 \succ c_1 \succ c_2$ and everyone, other than c_2, prefers c_1 to c_2. Yet, this obvious conclusion is flaunted by the plurality ranking of $c_3 \succ c_2 \succ c_1$. This, of course, manifests the fact that the plurality method totally ignores information about a voter's second-ranked candidate. Thus, c_1 joins a distinguished group of victims of the plurality method's elitist disregard for lower ranked candidates. Victims with better name recognition can be found in most New Hampshire Presidential Primaries.

As other positional procedures recognize lower ranked candidates, we must expect a sufficiently strong majority victory for c_1 to ensure that she is $\mathbf{w}_s$-ranked above c_2. The geometric analysis is similar; use extreme choices of $\alpha_s \in W_s^1$ and $\beta_s \in W_s^2$ to find the threshold value d_s^*. As already observed, a manifestation of the $\mathbf{w}_s$, $s \neq 0$, recognition of a voter's second-ranked candidate is the upper limit on W_s^j. This upper limit restricts the slant of the profile line, so we should expect more realistic values for d_s^*. This happens – sometimes. The following assertion simplifies the analysis.

Proposition 4.3.2. *Let $\rho(\mathbf{q})$ be the distance of point $\mathbf{q} \in Si(3)$ to the $c_1 \sim c_2$ indifference line. For*

$$(4.3.3) \qquad\qquad d = \frac{\rho(\beta_s)}{\rho(\alpha_s) + \rho(\beta_s)},$$

the election outcome for the profile (α_s, β_s, d) is on the $c_1 \sim c_2$ indifference line.

Proof. The proof is based on the triangle created by passing a vertical line through α_s and an horizontal line through β_s. This large triangle is similar to the smaller, darker one in the figure created by the $c_1 \sim c_2$ indifference line, the α_s - β_s profile line, and the horizontal line passing through β_s. (See Fig. 4.3.5.) If h is the length of the hypotenuse of the first triangle (so h is the length of the α_s - β_s segment), then dh is the length of the hypotenuse of the smaller triangle; it is the distance from β_s to the point on the $c_1 \sim c_2$ line. Eq. 4.3.3 follows by comparing the ratio of the base and hypotenuse of the two similar triangles; a comparison that yields

$$\frac{h}{\rho(\alpha_s) + \rho(\beta_s)} = \frac{dh}{\rho(\beta_s)}. \qquad \square$$

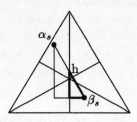

Fig. 4.3.5. Maximizing d values

With Proposition 4.3.2 and the geometry of the wedges, it is easy to find d_s^*. Let α_s be the point in W_s^1 closest to the $c_1 \sim c_2$ indifference line, and β_s the point farthest from this line. While $\beta_s = F_4(\mathbf{E}_5, \mathbf{w}_s)$, the location of α_s varies because the geometry of W_s^1 changes with the value of s. For $s \leq \frac{1}{3}$, the top vertex of W_s^1 is the closest to the indifference line; for $s \geq \frac{1}{3}$, the base vertex of the W_s^1 wedge now is the closest. Separating the two situations is the BC ($s = \frac{1}{3}$). So, for $s \in [0, \frac{1}{3}]$, choose $\alpha_s = F_4(\mathbf{E}_3, \mathbf{w}_s)$, for $s \in [\frac{1}{3}, \frac{1}{2}]$, choose $\alpha_s = F_4(\mathbf{E}_1, \mathbf{w}_s)$.

The choice of α_s, β_s defines an extreme mixture of voter types with a strong $c_2 \succ c_1$ ranking and a weak $c_1 \succ c_2$. Consequently, d_s^* *measures how* $\mathbf{w}_s$ *handles the intensity of comparison information. In particular, the smaller the value of* $1 - d_s^*$, *the less importance the procedure places upon the intensity information.* Adding force is the observation that if d_s has a value near d_s^* and if the $\{c_1, c_2\}$ pairwise ranking is reversed by the $\mathbf{w}_s$-ranking, then the profile is dominated by voters of the two identified types. Thus the reversal is caused because profile information is not being used by the pairwise and/or the positional method.

Theorem 4.3.3. *The value of d_s^* is*

$$d_s^* = 1 - s \text{ for } 0 \leq s \leq \frac{1}{3}$$

(4.3.4)
$$d_s^* = \frac{1-s}{2-3s} \text{ for } \frac{1}{3} \leq s \leq \frac{1}{2}.$$

So, suppose in a $\{c_i, c_j\}$ pairwise election, c_i receives the portion $k \in [0, 1]$ of the total vote. If $k < d_s^*$, then there are profiles where the $\mathbf{w}_s$ election ranking has c_j ranked above c_i. If $k = d_s^*$, then either c_i is $\mathbf{w}_s$-ranked above or tied with c_j. If $k > d_s^*$, then c_i must be $\mathbf{w}_s$-ranked above c_j.

Let's see what this means. The voting vector $(4, 1, 0)$ corresponds to $\mathbf{w}_{\frac{1}{5}} = (\frac{4}{5}, \frac{1}{5}, 0)$, so $s = \frac{1}{5}$. Thus, according to the theorem, even though Gina beats Dave by receiving 79% of the pairwise vote (the relevant fact is that $0.79 < d_{\frac{1}{5}}^* = 1 - s = .8$), it is possible for the $\mathbf{w}_{\frac{1}{5}}$ ranking to have Dave ranked above Gina. If this happens, however, it is because most of Gina's support comes from type-three voters (exhibiting a weak intensity in their Gina-Dave ranking), while Dave's support comes primarily from type-five votes with strong Dave-Gina preferences. Should Gina receive one more than 0.8 of the pairwise vote, she is ensured of being $\mathbf{w}_{\frac{1}{5}}$-ranked above Dave. Similarly, because the voting vector $(1,1,0)$ defines $s = \frac{1}{2}$, it can be that even though Brigid receives 99% of the votes in a contest with Adrian, Adrian is antiplurality ranked above Brigid. (This is because $0.99 < d^*_{\frac{1}{2}} = \frac{1-\frac{1}{2}}{2-3\times\frac{1}{2}} = 1$.) But if Katri beats Eric with $\frac{2}{3}$ of the vote, then, at the worse, she is at least BC tied with him. (For the BC, $s = \frac{1}{3}$, so $d^*_{\frac{1}{3}} = \frac{2}{3} = 1 - \frac{1}{3}$, or $d^*_{\frac{1}{3}} = \frac{1-\frac{1}{3}}{2-3\times\frac{1}{3}} = \frac{2}{3}$.)

Proof. To use the described choice of α_s, β_s (representing the extreme d values) with Eq. 4.3.3, we need the values of $\rho(\alpha_s)$, $\rho(\beta_s)$. The value of $\rho(\beta_s)$ is the distance between $\beta_s = (0, 1-s, s)$ and $(\frac{1-s}{2}, \frac{1-s}{2}, s)$, the closest point on $c_1 \sim c_2$.[4] For example, if $s \in [\frac{1}{3}, \frac{1}{2}]$, then

$$\rho(\alpha_s) = \rho((1-s, s, 0)) = \sqrt{((1-s) - \frac{1}{2})^2 + (s - \frac{1}{2})^2} = \sqrt{2}\frac{1-2s}{2}$$

while

$$\rho(\beta_s) = \rho((0, 1-s, s)) = \sqrt{(\frac{1-s}{2})^2 + (\frac{1-s}{2})^2 + (s-s)^2} = \sqrt{2}\frac{1-s}{2}.$$

The conclusion follows from Eq. 4.3.3. □

4.3.4 Some Comparisons

Theorem 4.3.3 is disturbing! It means that even though c_1 beats c_2 with, say, 64% of the vote, c_2 could be $\mathbf{w}_s$-ranked above c_1. (As shown in the exercises, different profiles might be needed with different methods.) On the other hand, the BC has the minimum d^*_s value; a smaller pairwise victory ensures the same ranking holds with the BC. Consequently, *if we desire maximum compatibility between how a pair is ranked in a pairwise contest and how it is ranked in a positional election, we must use the BC.* This assertion about the BC is consistent with the crude measure, $1 - d^*$, of attention paid by $\mathbf{w}_s$ to the intensity of pairwise comparisons.

Corollary 4.3.4. *If c_i beats c_j with two-thirds of the vote, then, at the worse, she is ensured of being BC tied with c_j. With any other $\mathbf{w}_s$, it could be that c_j is $\mathbf{w}_s$ ranked above c_i. Indeed, there are profiles where c_i can beat c_j with as close to an unanimous vote as desired, yet c_j is plurality, or antiplurality ranked above c_i.*

The positional group representation makes it easy to find profiles where the plurality and antiplurality outcomes are indefensible – the election outcome denies what is obviously the group's true ranking. An example for the plurality

---

[4] For a point to be on the indifference line, the c_1, c_2 values must agree. To define the shortest distance, the selected point and β_s define a line orthogonal to the indifference line. This condition requires both points to have the same c_3 value of s.

ranking is given above; similar examples hold for the antiplurality method. For instance, it follows from the geometry that antiplurality extreme situations involve type-two and six voters. So, suppose 9,999,999 of the 10,000,000 voters have the conservative ranking $c_2 \succ c_1 \succ c_3$, and the last voter has the ranking $c_1 \succ c_3 \succ c_2$. While the group's ranking should be $c_2 \succ c_1 \succ c_3$, the antiplurality ranking is $c_1 \succ c_2 \succ c_3$.

Upon reflection, these assertions about the plurality and antiplurality outcomes should not be surprising. While the plurality vote totally ignores the distinction between a voter's second and third-ranked candidates, the antiplurality method discards all information differentiating a voter's top and second-ranked candidate. Therefore, whenever the discarded information dominates or is critical for the profile, the outcome is suspect. (For each method, $1 - d^* = 0$.)

The symmetry of the s values defining d_s^* indicates that the BC ($s = \frac{1}{3}$) serves as a pivot point for positional voting methods. Methods for s near zero place little stock on the distinctions between a voter's second and third-ranked candidates; methods for s near $\frac{1}{2}$ place little value on distinctions between a voter's first and second-ranked candidates. Moreover, each admissible d^* value is attained by a $s \in [0, \frac{1}{3}]$, and a $s' \in [\frac{1}{3}, \frac{1}{2}]$; in fact, $\mathbf{w}_s^r = \mathbf{w}_{s'}$. (See the exercises.)

4.3.5 Comparisons

Common sense dictates that procedures with large d_s^* values admit larger sets of profiles that cause these election anomalies; i.e., there is a stronger probability that the $\{c_1, c_2\}$ pairwise and $\mathbf{w}_s$-rankings disagree. Conversely, the BC (with its minimum d_s^* value) should minimize the likelihood that such contradictory outcomes occur. This intuition is accurate and it can be proved from the coordinate representation.

Further Comparisons. As also shown by the geometry, the profiles, such as a division between type-one and five voters, define the extreme setting for positional voting method; these situations combine extreme differences between the intensity of a particular pairwise comparison and who is top-ranked. Hence, another way to compare positional voting methods is to compare the threshold required with such extreme profiles before c_1 is ranked above c_2.

(4.3.5)

Procedure	Vote
Pope Selection	One more than $\frac{2}{3}$
Condorcet Improvement	One more than $\frac{2}{3}$
Borda Count	One more than $\frac{2}{3}$
$\mathbf{w}_s, s \in [0, \frac{1}{3})$	One more than $1 - s > \frac{2}{3}$
$\mathbf{w}_s, s \in (\frac{1}{3}, \frac{1}{2}]$	One more than $\frac{1-s}{2-3s} > \frac{2}{3}$

Thus the Catholic Church, Borda, and the Condorcet Improvement agree; *the other procedures impose stricter requirements upon the type-one voters before c_1 can prevail.* Again, this should be expected because these other methods place less value upon the intensity information.

As noted, the BC makes it easier for the pairwise winner to be BC ranked in the same way. Therefore, the arguments used to criticize the plurality and antiplurality methods do not apply to the BC. In fact, by use of the linearity of voting processes, it follows that each positional voting method is a weighted compromise between the desirable manner the BC handles profiles and the deplorable way the plurality (or antiplurality) method can disregard voters' beliefs.

The Two-Thirds Rule. Sure, c_1 can win 99% of the majority vote over c_2 and still be plurality ranked below c_2, but when this happens, the plurality ranking *must* be $c_3 \succ c_2 \succ c_1$. After all, the only way $\mathbf{q}_0$ can be kept to the right of the $c_1 \sim c_2$ indifference line with $d = 0.99$ is if both α_0 and $\mathbf{q}_0$ are near the c_3 vertex. So, even if c_1 beats c_2 by a large margin, she may be $\mathbf{w}_s$-ranked below c_2. On the other hand, her pairwise victory margin may be sufficiently large to preclude certain $\mathbf{w}_s$-rankings from occurring. A natural issue, then, is to determine which pairwise votes prevent all 13 $\mathbf{w}_s$-rankings from occurring.

The geometric way to resolve this problem is to find an extreme profile with the steepest slant that just barely satisfies the conditions. This means the profile line must pass through $\mathcal{I}$. On such a line with an extreme slope, find the $d = d^{\#}$ value where $\mathbf{q}_s = \mathcal{I} = (\frac{1}{3}, \frac{1}{3}, \frac{1}{3})$. By finding the extreme $d^{\#}$ value, $d > d^{\#}$ can never realize $\mathcal{I}$, or any ranking that requires the profile line to move toward one side or the other of the indifference point. Similarly, if $d = d^{\#}$, then any positioning of the profile line does not allow the distinguished point $\mathbf{q}_s$ to fall below $\mathcal{I}$ – not all rankings can be obtained.

This critical $d^{\#}$ value is found the same way as above; set β_s at $F_4(\mathbf{E}_5, \mathbf{w}_s)$, pass the profile line through $\mathbf{q}_s = (\frac{1}{3}, \frac{1}{3}, \frac{1}{3})$, and let α_s be the first boundary point of ∂W_s^1 that meets the profile line. The values of α_s, $\mathbf{q}_s$ determine the threshold $d^{\#}$ value. Surprisingly, the value is independent of the choice of s.

Theorem 4.3.5. *If c_i beats c_j in a majority vote by receiving at least $\frac{2}{3}$ of the vote, then there are restrictions on the associated $\mathbf{w}_s$-ranking. If c_i receives at least one vote more than $\frac{2}{3}$ of the total majority vote, then it is impossible for the $\mathbf{w}_s$-ranking to be $\mathcal{I}$. On the other hand, for any choice of $\mathbf{w}_s$, $\epsilon > 0$, and a ranking of the three candidates, there is a profile where c_i beats c_j by receiving at least $\frac{2}{3} - \epsilon$ of the vote (but less than $\frac{2}{3}$ of the vote) and the $\mathbf{w}_s$-ranking is the chosen ranking.*

Again, the geometry allows us to determine the admissible rankings when a candidate does well in a majority vote election.

So far the analysis has emphasized the variable d; similar approaches can be used with the α_s, β_s variables. For example, suppose whenever c_1 beats c_2 by winning at least 55% of the vote, we want her to be $\mathbf{w}_s$-ranked above c_2. Here the $d = .55$ value is specified, the goal is to find profile restrictions on α_s, β_s that realize the stated objective. Such restrictions are obtained in a straightforward manner.

4.3.6 How Varied Does It Get?

We know from Sect. 4.3 that different positional methods can define radically different election outcomes for the same profile. We now know that the ranking of a positional voting procedure and the majority ranking of a particular pair can be chosen at random. These results can be combined into a single statement.

Theorem 4.3.6. *Let* $\mathbf{w}_{s_1} \neq \mathbf{w}_{s_2}$ *be given. Choose any two rankings of the three candidates and any ranking of* $\{c_1, c_2\}$. *There is a profile where the* $\mathbf{w}_{s_j}$ *ranking is the* j*th selected one,* $j = 1, 2$, *and the pairwise outcome is the selected ranking of a pair. Indeed, there exists a positive value* ρ *so that for* $\mathbf{q}_i \in \mathcal{B}(\rho, \mathcal{I})$, $i = 1, 2$ *and* $q \in (-\rho, \rho)$, *there exists a (unique) profile* $\mathbf{p}$ *so that*

$$f(\mathbf{p}, \mathbf{w}_{s_1}) = \mathbf{q}_1, \quad f(\mathbf{p}, \mathbf{w}_{s_2}) = \mathbf{q}_2, \quad f_{\{c_1, c_2\}}(\mathbf{p}) = q.$$

Outline of the Proof. An easy way to see this is to choose a profile $\mathbf{p}$ satisfying the theorem for $\mathbf{w}_0$ and $\mathbf{w}_{\frac{1}{2}}$. Then, by use of Fig. 3.1.3, add a Condorcet portion to alter the pairwise outcome. This portion, of course, does not change the positional rankings. It remains to compare the position of the procedure line and the rankings of all pairs of candidates. Actually, there is a simple geometric way to do this, but this discussion is deferred to Sect. 4.6. $\square$

Election outcomes can be more random than previously suspected! Theorem 4.3.6 asserts that there need not be any relationship between the positional and $\{c_1, c_2\}$ pairwise rankings. This means, for instance, that profiles can be found so that the ranking for *all* choices of $\mathbf{w}_s$ is $c_2 \succ c_3 \succ c_1$ while the pairwise ranking is the reversed $c_1 \succ c_2$. Indeed, by choosing $\mathbf{q}_1 = \mathbf{q}_2$ in Theorem 4.3.6 (so the procedure line becomes the point $\mathbf{q}_1$), the $\mathbf{w}_s$ outcomes share the same normalized tally!

4.3.7 Exercises

1. For $\mathbf{q}_{\frac{1}{3}} = (0.3, 0.4, 0.5), d = 0.6$, find the cone of supporting profiles.

2. Find the combinations of $\alpha_s \in \partial W_s^1$, $\beta_s \in \partial W_s^2$, $d \in \{0, 1\}$ that represent boundary regions of $Si(6)$. With this identification, extend Theorem 4.3.1 to discuss the kinds of boundary regions identified with the cone of profiles defined by a $\mathbf{q}_s$.

3. In collapsing the fat triangle to the representation surface, it is asserted that no change is made in the value of d. Justify this statement. (To do so, set up a triangle inside the fat triangle given by the vertices α_s, β_s, and the point defined when α_s is projected to the front representation triangle surface. Next, set up a similar triangle formed by $\mathbf{q}_s$ and its projection to the front surface.)

4. a. Eq. 4.3.2 specifies (α_s, β_s, d) in terms of $\mathbf{p} \in Si(6)$. Find $\mathbf{p}$ as a function of α_s, β_s, d.
b. Suppose c_1 beats c_2 by winning 60% of the vote. Find the upper limit on α_0 to ensure that c_1 beats c_2 in the plurality ranking. Do the same for $\alpha_{\frac{1}{3}}$ and $\alpha_{\frac{1}{2}}$. Finally, find a general relationship between α_s and d to ensure that c_1 is $\mathbf{w}_s$ ranked above c_2.

5. Extend Theorem 4.3.1 to explain what happens with $\mathbf{q}_s$ on the boundary of the $F_4(-, \mathbf{w}_s)$ image set. For instance, suppose $d = \frac{1}{2}$ and $\mathbf{q}_s, s \in (0, \frac{1}{2})$, is on the c_1, c_2 edge of $Si(3)$. Show that the supporting set of profiles is either empty (so the outcome cannot occur), or $\mathbf{q}_s$ is the unique point $(\frac{1}{2}, \frac{1}{2}, 0)$ supported by a unique profile.

6. Caution is needed when using the plurality and anti plurality procedures where (α_s, β_s, d) is not a true coordinate representation. For instance, show that if $\mathbf{q}_0$ is on the $Si(3)$ bottom edge and $d = \frac{1}{2}$, then the set of supporting profiles is empty if $\mathbf{q}_0 \neq (\frac{1}{2}, \frac{1}{2}, 0)$, but it is a *two-dimensional* set if $\mathbf{q}_0 = (\frac{1}{2}, \frac{1}{2}, 0)$. (Compare the outcome with Prob. 5.)

7. a. Suppose c_1 beats c_2 by winning 60% of the vote. Find the upper limit on α_0 to ensure that c_1 beats c_2 in the plurality ranking. Do the same for $\alpha_{\frac{1}{3}}$ and $\alpha_{\frac{1}{2}}$. Finally, find a general relationship between α_s and d to ensure that c_1 is $\mathbf{w}_s$ ranked above c_2.

b. Suppose c_1 beats c_2 by winning 60% of the vote. Find (geometrically) all $\mathbf{w}_{\frac{1}{3}}$ normalized election *tallies* that can accompany this vote. Next, do the same for the plurality vote. Devise a technique so that if d is specified, then all associated $\mathbf{w}_s$ normalized tallies are found.

8. Find all profiles supporting the positional election outcome $\mathbf{q}_{\frac{1}{5}} = (\frac{1}{3}, \frac{1}{3}, \frac{1}{3})$. Next, find the set for $\mathbf{q}_{\frac{1}{5}} = (\frac{1}{2}, \frac{1}{4}, \frac{1}{4})$. Compare these sets and explain why the location of $\mathbf{q}_{\frac{1}{5}}$ (which determines the pivoting action) makes the second set smaller than the first. Use this argument to devise and prove a general statement about the sets of profiles supporting $\mathbf{q}_s$. Then, use the coordinate representation for profiles to describe what profiles dominate as $\mathbf{q}_s$ tends to the boundary of $\mathcal{CH}(\mathbf{w}_s)$. In doing so, explain what happens to the majority vote outcome of a particular pair.

9. In the discussion of d_s^*, it is stated that $1 - d_s^*$ serves as a crude measure of the ability of $\mathbf{w}_s$ to incorporate information about the intensity of pairwise comparisons. Justify this statement. Next, critique it by showing that if $s \neq \frac{1}{3}$, then some weak comparisons are treated more favorably than others.

10. Show that if $d^* \in (\frac{2}{3}, 1]$, then there are two s values, s_1 and s_2, that define d^*. Show that $\mathbf{w}_{s_1}^r = \mathbf{w}_{s_2}$.

11. Suppose c_1 beats c_2 by winning $d \in (\frac{1}{2}, 1]$ of the vote. Also suppose the plurality ranking has c_2 ranked above c_1. For this profile, what can you say about the antiplurality ranking? Carry this one step further; observe that the value of d_s^* in Theorem 4.3.3 is determined by a particular profile which depends on whether $s \in [0, \frac{1}{3}]$, or $s \in [\frac{1}{3}, \frac{1}{2}]$. This suggests that a profile may allow the $\mathbf{w}_s$ ranking to reverse the pairwise ranking, but the $\mathbf{w}_s^r$ ranking will preserve it. In other words, associated with d_s^* which determines what happens with $\mathbf{w}_s$, there is an associated value d_s^{*r} which indicates what happens with the same profile with $\mathbf{w}_s^r$. Find this value and explain what can occur. (Can you explain the difference in terms of the kind of information each procedure emphasizes?)

12. a. Theorem 4.3.5 specifies that if $d \geq d^\# = \frac{2}{3}$, then not all $\mathbf{w}_s$ rankings occur. Find the rankings that can occur. Namely, specify which $\mathbf{w}_s$ rankings can accompany a $c_1 \succ c_2$ pairwise victory where $d = d^\#$. What happens if $d > \frac{2}{3}$?

b. Re-do Theorem 4.3.5, but now in the context of the three threshold methods described in the exercises of Sect. 2.1. Namely, for each threshold method, find the $d^\#$ value that avoids all possible rankings. (This value must be in terms of the specified threshold values.)

4.4 Profile Decomposition

We have serious problems! Although positional methods eliminate the confused voter by demanding proof of transitive preferences, they still encounter difficulties. After all, if a three-candidate profile can admit up to seven different rankings just by changing the procedure, how do we know which one best reflects the true views of the voters? Clearly, we need to winnow out the chaff.

One way to judge procedures is to determine whether and how they bias the outcome. An unbiased procedure is one that would methodically mirror changes in voters' beliefs. When, for instance, all voters make the same change in their preferences, this should be reflected in the conclusion. Conversely, we must worry about the bias exhibited when a procedure ignores such universal changes. To explore these issues, symmetry is used.

By identifying a new kind of bias, we can decompose profiles. To explain, in Sect. 3.1 profiles are separated into the Condorcet and reduced portions. This decomposition makes it easy to understand why cycles emerge and why pairwise and positional methods can differ so radically. Similarly, the profile decomposition given here makes it easy to explain the radical difference among positional outcomes. Just as the Condorcet portion makes it possible to construct profiles illustrating pairwise voting examples, the decomposition provided here allows us to construct profiles for positional voting examples. The main tools are the procedure line and profile coordinates introduced in the previous two sections.

4.4.1 Neutrality and Reversal Bias

Neutrality is where when all voters interchange their rankings of a pair of candidates, the same change applies to the group ranking. For instance, with candidates Anneli, Katri, and Lillian, suppose all voters confused Anneli and Katri because all Scandinavians look alike. With neutrality, we do not need a new vote; we could just interchange their names in the group ranking. Neutrality also is a fairness condition; if Martha needs more than 50% of the vote to win, then so does Edna. Namely, neutrality, mandates that the outcome is independent of the candidates' names. Fortunately it is easy to show that commonly used procedures such as pairwise voting and positional methods satisfy neutrality.

To describe a natural extension of neutrality, let me explain what once happened in my department when everyone misunderstood instructions. When asked to rank three candidates, we placed our top-ranked candidate first, second-ranked candidate second, and so forth. However, our chair expected the opposite; e.g., he wanted the top-ranked candidate listed last! Consequently, tallying the ballots, he unintentionally reversed our true views; a ballot for a voter believing Martha $\succ$ Ruth $\succ$ Edna was tallied as Edna $\succ$ Ruth $\succ$ Martha. Instead of holding still another election (which we did), it was suggested that we reverse the original election outcome. After all, if everyone reverses their ranking, then surely the outcome also would be reversed. A procedure failing to satisfy this natural reversal property exhibits distinct bias.

Many methods, such as pairwise voting, BC, and CI, satisfy reversal. This is easy to prove for pairwise voting; after a profile is reversed, everyone who previously voted for c_j in a $\{c_j, c_k\}$ election now prefers c_k. The surprising fact is that *with the sole exception of the BC, all positional procedures violate reversal!* Indeed, with any $\mathbf{w}_s \neq \mathbf{w}_{\frac{1}{3}}$, the $\mathbf{w}_s$-tallies for a profile and its reversal could even be the same! To appreciate the potential conflict associated with this trait, imagine how my colleagues might have reacted had our chair announced the outcome $c_1 \succ c_2 \succ c_3$ with the misinterpreted ballots, and then later announced the same outcome with the corrected ballots![5]

---

[5] Such a problem is impossible because we use the BC.

Some Notation. With the base point $\mathcal{I}$, a reversal is something that is diametrically opposite. For instance, the reversal of a type-one ranking $c_1 \succ c_2 \succ c_3$ is the type-four ranking $c_3 \succ c_2 \succ c_1$; they have opposite ranking regions in the representation triangle. Similarly, the reversal of $\mathbf{q} \in Si(3)$ should be on the extended line from $\mathbf{q}$ through $\mathcal{I}$; it should be on the opposite side of $\mathcal{I}$ as far away as $\mathbf{q}$. This motivates the following definition.

Definition 4.4.1. For profile $\mathbf{p} = (p_1, p_2, p_3, p_4, p_5, p_6)$, the *reversed profile* is $\mathbf{p}^r = (p_4, p_5, p_6, p_1, p_2, p_3)$. The reversal of $\mathbf{q} \in Si(3)$, $\mathbf{q}^r$, is the $180°$ rotation of $\mathbf{q}$ about $\mathcal{I}$. The reversal of a ranking region $\mathcal{R} \neq \mathcal{I}$, $\mathcal{R}^r$, is the ranking region diametrically opposite $\mathcal{R}$. (So, $\mathcal{I}^r = \mathcal{I}$.) The reversal of a ranking α associated with ranking region $\mathcal{R}(\alpha)$ is the ranking identified with $\mathcal{R}^r$. $\square$

Example 4.4.1. If $\mathbf{p} = (\frac{1}{4}, 0, \frac{1}{6}, \frac{1}{12}, \frac{1}{3}, \frac{1}{6})$, then $\mathbf{p}^r = (\frac{1}{12}, \frac{1}{3}, \frac{1}{6}, \frac{1}{4}, 0, \frac{1}{6})$. Notice how the reversal process converts one Condorcet triple, $\mathbf{p}_m = (\frac{1}{3}, 0, \frac{1}{3}, 0, \frac{1}{3}, 0)$, into the other $\mathbf{p}_m^r = (0, \frac{1}{3}, 0, \frac{1}{3}, 0, \frac{1}{3})$. Thus, the "confused voter" profile set is invariant under reversal.

A reversal of a ranking is obvious; for instance $(c_2 \succ c_3 \succ c_1)^r = c_1 \succ c_3 \succ c_2$. Finding $\mathbf{q}^r$ from a given $\mathbf{q} \in Si(3)$ is almost as simple, just pass a line through $\mathcal{I}$ to find what is diametrically opposite. For instance, $\mathbf{q} = (\frac{3}{10}, \frac{1}{2}, \frac{1}{5}) \in Si(3)$ is the $t = 1$ endpoint of the line $t\mathbf{q} + (1-t)\mathcal{I}$, so the $t = -1$ point on the extended line is $\mathbf{q}^r = (\frac{11}{30}, \frac{1}{6}, \frac{14}{30})$. $\square$

To examine a special case of reversal, suppose $\mathbf{p}$ has the election outcome

$$(4.4.1) \qquad\qquad f(\mathbf{p}, \mathbf{w}_s) = \mathcal{I}.$$

Intuition suggests that the reversed profile shares the outcome

$$(4.4.2) \qquad\qquad f(\mathbf{p}^r, \mathbf{w}_s) = \mathcal{I}^r = \mathcal{I}.$$

This is true for the BC and, for any $\mathbf{w}_s$, there are profiles which satisfy this relationship. But, as shown next, when $\mathbf{w}_s \neq \mathbf{w}_{\frac{1}{3}}$ *most* profiles satisfying Eq. 4.4.1 do not satisfy Eq. 4.4.2.

To analyze this behavior, define the *reversal set* to be

$$(4.4.3) \qquad \mathcal{R}(\mathbf{q}_s) = \{f(\mathbf{p}^r, \mathbf{w}_s) \,|\, \mathbf{p} \text{ where } f(\mathbf{p}, \mathbf{w}_s) = \mathbf{q}_s\}$$

In words, for a specified $\mathbf{w}_s$-outcome $\mathbf{q}_s$, $\mathcal{R}(\mathbf{q}_s)$ specifies all $\mathbf{w}_s$-outcomes obtained by reversing the profiles supporting $\mathbf{q}_s$. To illustrate, both $\frac{1}{2}(\mathbf{E}_1 + \mathbf{E}_5)$ and $\frac{1}{2}(\mathbf{E}_1 + \mathbf{E}_6)$ define the plurality outcome $(\frac{1}{2}, \frac{1}{2}, 0)$, so $\mathcal{R}((\frac{1}{2}, \frac{1}{2}, 0)_0)$ includes the plurality outcomes of the profiles $[\frac{1}{2}(\mathbf{E}_1 + \mathbf{E}_5)]^r = \frac{1}{2}(\mathbf{E}_4 + \mathbf{E}_2)$ and $[\frac{1}{2}(\mathbf{E}_1 + \mathbf{E}_6)]^r = \frac{1}{2}(\mathbf{E}_4 + \mathbf{E}_3)$. These outcomes are, respectively, $(\frac{1}{2}, 0, \frac{1}{2})$ and $(0, 0, 1)$. The ranking of $(\frac{1}{2}, \frac{1}{2}, 0)_0$ is $c_1 \sim c_2 \succ c_3$, but the rankings for the reversed profiles are $c_1 \sim c_3 \succ c_2$ and $c_3 \succ c_1 \sim c_2$. The second is a reversal; the first is not.

Theorem 4.4.1. *A BC outcome* $\mathbf{q}_{\frac{1}{3}}$ *satisfies* $\mathcal{R}(\mathbf{q}_{\frac{1}{3}}) = \{\mathbf{q}_{\frac{1}{3}}^r\}$. *In particular,* $\mathcal{R}(\mathcal{I}_{\frac{1}{3}}) = \mathcal{I}_{\frac{1}{3}}$. *If* $s \neq \frac{1}{3}$, *then* $\mathcal{R}(\mathcal{I}_s)$ *is a convex set that meets all thirteen ranking regions. If* $s \neq \frac{1}{3}$, *there is a ball* B_s *with center* $\mathcal{I}$ *so that if* $\mathbf{q}_s \in B_s$, *then the convex set* $\mathcal{R}(\mathbf{q}_s)$ *meets all ranking regions.*

Ouch! Not only is the Eqs. 4.4.1, 4.4.2 relationship violated, but the Eq. 4.4.2 ranking can be anything! By appealing to continuity, a slight change in the $\mathcal{I}_s$ outcome impose minor changes in the $\mathcal{R}(\mathcal{I}_s)$ set. Consequently, for $\mathbf{q}_s$ near $\mathcal{I}$, the convex set $\mathcal{R}(\mathbf{q}_s)$ meets all possible ranking regions.

4.4.2 Reversal Sets

To construct $\mathcal{R}(\mathcal{I}_0)$, use our standard approach. Namely, first find the profile vertices satisfying Eq. 4.4.1. Next, compute the plurality outcomes for the reversal of these profiles. The set $\mathcal{R}(\mathcal{I}_0)$ is the convex hull of these points.

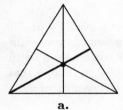 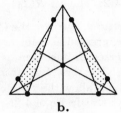 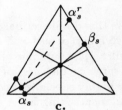

Fig. 4.4.1. Computing $\mathcal{R}(\mathcal{I}_s)$

A profile vertex is an extreme position of the profile line. So, hold a profile line at $\mathcal{I}$ and wiggle it as far as possible. As illustrated in Fig. 4.4.1a, this places one end of the profile line (for the plurality vote) at a $Si(3)$ vertex while the other is at the midpoint of a $Si(3)$ edge. Remember, the plurality vote does not admit a true coordinate system because more than one $\mathbf{p} \in Si(3)$ corresponds to each profile line. Using the position indicated in Fig. 4.4.1a, for instance, one supporting profile is $\frac{1}{3}\mathbf{E}_1 + \frac{2}{3}(\frac{1}{2}\mathbf{E}_5 + \frac{1}{2}\mathbf{E}_4)$. Alternatively, $\mathbf{E}_1$ could be replaced with $\mathbf{E}_2$ and $\mathbf{E}_5$ could be replaced with $\mathbf{E}_6$. Thus, the sought after vertices are the eight profiles obtained by using either $\frac{1}{3}\mathbf{E}_1$ or $\frac{1}{3}\mathbf{E}_2$, and either $\frac{1}{3}\mathbf{E}_3$ or $\frac{1}{3}\mathbf{E}_4$, and either $\frac{1}{3}\mathbf{E}_5$ or $\frac{1}{3}\mathbf{E}_6$. Two of these vertices are the Condorcet triplets which, as we know, satisfy the Eqs. 4.4.1, 4.4.2 relationship.

For the remaining profiles, the reversals and the plurality outcome are easy to compute. For instance, one such profile is $\mathbf{p}_1 = (0, \frac{1}{3}, \frac{1}{3}, 0, \frac{1}{3}, 0)$. As $\mathbf{p}_1^r = (0, \frac{1}{3}, 0, 0, \frac{1}{3}, \frac{1}{3})$, we have that $f(\mathbf{p}_1^r, \mathbf{w}_0) = (\frac{1}{3}, \frac{2}{3}, 0)$. So, while the plurality outcome for $\mathbf{p}_1$ is complete indifference, its reversal, $\mathbf{p}_1^r$, allows c_2 to win by a landslide (two-thirds of the vote), c_1 comes in second, and c_3 receives not a single point! Something is seriously wrong! The $\mathbf{p}_1^r$ conclusion is reasonable, but the strong support $\mathbf{p}_1$ provides c_1 and c_3 makes the $f(\mathbf{p}_1, \mathbf{w}_0) = \mathcal{I}$ ranking suspect.

The plurality outcome for all remaining reversals have the same surprising conclusion; one candidate receives two-thirds of the vote, a second candidate earns one-third, while the third receives nothing. Notice, these outcomes correspond to the $[\mathbf{w}_{\frac{1}{3}}]_j$ unanimity vectors. Once these vertices are plotted, the $\mathcal{R}(\mathcal{I}_0)$ set, as depicted in Fig. 4.4.2, agrees with the set of all (normalized) BC outcomes! In words, if $\mathbf{p}$ satisfies Eq. 4.4.1, the $\mathbf{p}^r$ plurality tally could be almost anything!

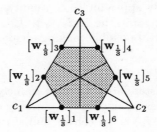

Fig. 4.4.2. The set $\mathcal{R}(\mathcal{I}_0)$

As this profile set has eight vertices, (two are the Condorcet triplets), a profile satisfying $f(\mathbf{p}, \mathbf{w}_0) = \mathcal{I}$ can be expressed as a linear combination of these eight profiles. The outcome of the reversed profile, then, is a linear combination (with the same coefficients) of the $[\mathbf{w}_{\frac{1}{3}}]_j$ vectors. But, from Fig. 4.4.2, it follows that only highly specialized combinations allow the $\mathcal{I}$ conclusion. Consequently, most profiles satisfying Eq. 4.4.1 fail to satisfy Eq. 4.4.2.

Other Procedures. While the profile line approach can be used with all $\mathbf{w}_s$ methods, the algebra is messy. After taking a couple of paragraphs to convince the reader that this is true; a geometric argument is developed.

To use this approach with Fig. 4.4.1b, wiggle a profile line held at $\mathcal{I}$. The extreme settings depend upon whether $s \leq \frac{1}{3}$ or $s \geq \frac{1}{3}$. To see why, notice for $s \leq \frac{1}{3}$ that an extreme choice is $\alpha_s = [\mathbf{w}_s]_1$ but $\alpha_s = [\mathbf{w}]_3$ is impossible (because the profile line misses W_s^2). For $s \geq \frac{1}{3}$, the situation is reversed. From the geometry, we find that there are eight vertices; two are the Condorcet triplets.

For $s \leq \frac{1}{3}$, $\alpha_s = [\mathbf{w}_s]_1$ allows two extreme β_s positions; they are on the lines connecting $[\mathbf{w}_s]_4$ and $[\mathbf{w}_s]_5$ and connecting $[\mathbf{w}_s]_4$ and $[\mathbf{w}_s]_6$. The first case defines the equations

$$(4.4.4) \qquad d[\mathbf{w}_s]_1 + (1-d)\beta_s = \mathcal{I}, \quad \beta_s = (1-y)[\mathbf{w}_s]_4 + y[\mathbf{w}_s]_5$$

After computing d and y, the profile vertex is $d\mathbf{E}_1 + (1-d)[(1-y)\mathbf{E}_4 + y\mathbf{E}_5]$ with the reversed profile of $d\mathbf{E}_4 + (1-d)[(1-y)\mathbf{E}_1 + y\mathbf{E}2]$. Eq. 4.4.4 can be expressed as the six equations (one for each coordinate)

$$d(1-s, s, 0) + (1-d)(0, u_2, u_3) = (\frac{1}{3}, \frac{1}{3}, \frac{1}{3})$$

$$(4.4.5) \qquad (1-y)(0, s, 1-s) + y(0, 1-s, s) = (0, u_2, u_3) = \beta_s$$

with the solution $d = \frac{1}{3(1-s)}, \beta_s = (0, \frac{1-2s}{2-3s}, \frac{1-s}{2-3s}), y = \frac{1}{2-3s} - \frac{s}{1-2s}$. Notice, that $y = 0$ iff $s = \frac{1}{3}$. Indeed, y has a forbidden negative value when $s > \frac{1}{3}$; this reflects the assertion that the BC, $s = \frac{1}{3}$, divides the s-values into two sets with geometrically different extreme positions for profile lines.

This vertex is found with uninspiring algebra (which is carried out in a later section for a different purpose). So, lets examine the geometry. Notice from Fig. 4.4.1c where $s < \frac{1}{3}$ that the profile line from $\alpha_s = [\mathbf{w}_s]_1$ through $\mathcal{I}$ hits the edge of the representation triangle between $[\mathbf{w}_s]_4$ and $[\mathbf{w}_s]_5$. When this β_s endpoint of the profile is reversed, β_s^r, an endpoint for the reversed profile, is on the $[\mathbf{w}_s]_1$-$[\mathbf{w}_s]_2$ line As $\mathbf{E}_1^r = \mathbf{E}_4$, the other endpoint is $\alpha_s^r = [\mathbf{w}_3]_4$. Both endpoints of the $\beta_s^r - \alpha_s^r$ line (the dashed line in Fig. 4.4.1c) are above the original profile line, so the reversed profile line misses $\mathcal{I}$. Compare this geometry with what happens to the BC; here the original line has $\beta_{\frac{1}{3}} = [\mathbf{w}_{\frac{1}{3}}]_4$, so the dashed and the original lines coincide.

To find a geometric estimate for d, notice that $[\mathbf{w}_{\frac{1}{3}}]_1$, $[\mathbf{w}_{\frac{1}{3}}]_4$, and the c_2 vertex define an equilateral triangle. Therefore, when $s = \frac{1}{3}$, we have that $d = \frac{1}{2}$. Superimposing the $s < \frac{1}{3}$ line on this triangle shows that $\mathcal{I}$ is closer to β_s than α_s. Thus, the distinguished point on the dashed reversed profile line is closer to β_s^r; the outcome is in the $c_1 \succ c_3 \succ c_2$ region. Using a similar geometric argument with the remaining vertices, it follows that $\mathcal{R}(\mathcal{I}_s)$, $s \neq \frac{1}{3}$, has a vertex in each strict ranking region. The conclusion now follows. $\square$

4.4.3 Cancellation

If Eric and Adrian have precisely opposing views, why should they vote; their ballots would just cancel. In other words, if their ordinal rankings are $c_1 \succ c_2 \succ c_3$ and $c_3 \succ c_2 \succ c_1$, we should expect a tie. (This happens, of course, with pairwise voting.) This describes a decomposition; remove the supposedly neutral reversal portion from a given profile. For instance, most of the integer profile $(7, 5, 1, 7, 3, 6) = (0, 2, 0, 0, 0, 5) + (7, 3, 1, 7, 3, 1)$ involves reversals which should not affect the final ranking. If this reduction can be justified, the remaining $2\mathbf{E}_2 + 5\mathbf{E}_6$ portion is easier to analyze.

To justify this profile decomposition, we need to understand the consequences of the reversal portion. To simplify the notation, gather the opposing voter types to define $\mathbf{r}_1 = \frac{1}{2}(\mathbf{E}_1 + \mathbf{E}_4)$, $\mathbf{r}_2 = \frac{1}{2}(\mathbf{E}_2 + \mathbf{E}_5)$, $\mathbf{r}_3 = \frac{1}{2}(\mathbf{E}_3 + \mathbf{E}_6)$; e.g., the normalized version of $(7, 3, 1, 7, 3, 1)$ is $\frac{7}{11}\mathbf{r}_1 + \frac{3}{11}\mathbf{r}_2 + \frac{1}{11}\mathbf{r}_3$. The reversal portion of a profile always is a combination of the $\{\mathbf{r}_j\}_{j=1}^3$ vectors.

These reversal vectors have the nice property $\mathbf{r}_j^r = \mathbf{r}_j$. As each $\mathbf{r}_j$ vector is invariant under reversal, so is a linear combination; e.g. if $\mathbf{p} = \sum_{j=1}^3 \lambda_j \mathbf{r}_j$, then $\mathbf{p} = \mathbf{p}^r$. So, denoting the convex hull of $\{\mathbf{r}_j\}_{j=1}^3$ by $\mathcal{RE}$, we have that the *reversal set* $\mathcal{RE}$ is the profile set where $\mathbf{p}^r = \mathbf{p}$. To understand the (many) consequences reversal profiles impose on the $\mathbf{w}_s$-elections, compute the $\mathbf{w}_s$-image of $\mathcal{RE}$. This

is done by finding the vertices $f(\mathbf{r}_j, \mathbf{w}_s)$, or
(4.4.6)
$$f(\mathbf{r}_1, \mathbf{w}_s) = (\frac{s}{2}, 1-s, \frac{s}{2}),\ f(\mathbf{r}_2, \mathbf{w}_s) = (\frac{s}{2}; \frac{s}{2}, 1-s),\ f(\mathbf{r}_3, \mathbf{w}_s) = (1-s, \frac{s}{2}, \frac{s}{2})$$

As $\mathbf{p} \in \mathcal{RE}$ requires $\mathbf{p}^r = \mathbf{p}$, $\mathcal{RE}$ is a profile set where $f(\mathbf{p}, \mathbf{w}_s) = f(\mathbf{p}^r, \mathbf{w}_s)$ – these are the profiles with the uncomfortable property that the profile and its reversal have the exact same $\mathbf{w}_s$-tally! This property would be of no interest with a common tally $\mathcal{I}$. However, Eq. 4.4.6 tells us that $f(\mathbf{r}_j, \mathbf{w}_s) = \mathcal{I}$ iff $s = \frac{1}{3}$; namely, *only the BC converts all* $\mathbf{p} \in \mathcal{RE}$ *into complete indifference!* Therefore, by plotting the vertices of Eq. 4.4.6, we discover the $\mathbf{q}_s$ values where the reversal of a supporting profile can be the same tally.

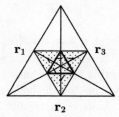

Fig. 4.4.3. The $\mathbf{w}_s$ images of $\mathcal{RE}$

To plot all sets simultaneously, use procedures lines. Recall (Prob. 6, Sect. 4.2) that these lines can be determined by the BC and plurality outcomes. (This is done by drawing a line from the plurality endpoint through the BC outcome and extending it half again as far.) What simplifies the computation is that the BC outcomes for $\{\mathbf{r}_j\}$ is $\mathcal{I}$ while the plurality outcomes are the midpoints of the edges of the representation triangle. Consequently, each $\mathbf{r}_j$ procedure line is on the appropriate indifference line. The s value tells us how far to go on each line to find the $\mathbf{w}_s$ vertex; it is the same for each line. Thus, the $\mathbf{w}_s$-image of $\mathcal{RE}$ is an equilateral triangle with an orientation depending on whether s is larger or smaller than $\frac{1}{3}$. This is depicted in Fig. 4.4.3 where the large shaded area denotes the plurality outcomes, the dashed line is the boundary for an $s < \frac{1}{3}$ value, and the heavy line defines the hull for the antiplurality procedure. From the shaded area we find that a full 25% of the plurality outcomes have this disturbing property allowing the tally for a profile and its reversal to be the same!

Beverages. Rather than getting caught up with abstractions, let me describe the critical importance of the reversal points, $\mathcal{RE}$, with the example illustrated in Fig. 4.4.4. Start, as illustrated in the triangle on the left, with an innocuous $\mathbf{E}_2 + 4\mathbf{E}_4$ profile. Using the projection method, the pairwise tallies, given along the edges, indicate the pairwise rankings $c_3 \succ c_1$, $c_3 \succ c_2$, $c_2 \succ c_1$. The normalized plurality and BC tallies are, respectively, $(\frac{1}{5}, 0, \frac{4}{5})$ and $(\frac{2}{15}, \frac{4}{15}, \frac{9}{15})$, so the procedure line in the third triangle indicates all $\mathbf{w}_s$ outcomes.

The second triangle adds reversal to the profile. Whatever the x, y, z values, they cannot impact on the pairwise rankings. (This is because the same value $x+y+z$ is added to the tally of each candidate in each pairwise election.) As the BC converts these values into a multiple of $(\frac{1}{3}, \frac{1}{3}, \frac{1}{3})$, this reversal portion just moves the normalized BC outcome closer to $\mathcal{I}$ to reflect the number of voters whose views cancel. More specifically, draw a line from the normalized BC tally to $\mathcal{I}$ (this is the dashed line in Fig. 4.4.4c); the new normalized tally is on this line.

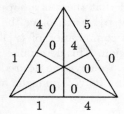 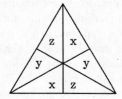 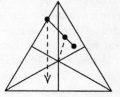

Fig. 4.4.4. Effects of reversal

From the perspective of the procedure line, the reversal portion of a profile moves the BC pivot point closer to $\mathcal{I}$. But these x, y, z choices rotate the plurality endpoint about the BC pivot point to exhibit the reversal bias. For instance, choosing $x = z = 0, y > 0$ adds a $\mathbf{r}_2$ term to the profile. Instead of moving this endpoint toward $\mathcal{I}$, it follows from Fig. 4.4.3 that the plurality endpoint moves in a $(\frac{1}{2}, \frac{1}{2}, 0)$ direction. (This is the dashed arrow in Fig. 4.4.4c.) A sufficiently large y value can even induce a plurality ranking of $c_1 \succ c_2 \succ c_3$ while the pairwise and BC rankings remain the same. Indeed, $y = 5$ defines the beverage example!

We now can create any desired paradox. For instance, choosing $y = 8$ defines the integer profile $(0, 9, 0, 4, 8, 0)$ with the same beverage consequences where the plurality ranking differs from the BC and pairwise rankings. Alternatively, to create an example where the antiplurality vote reverses the BC and pairwise rankings, twist the plurality endpoint into the type-four region. (This moves the $\mathbf{w}_{\frac{1}{2}}$ endpoint into the type-one region.) From Fig. 4.4.3, this requires a reversal bias combination of $\mathbf{r}_1$ and $\mathbf{r}_3$. One choice is $y = 0$ $x = 2$, $z = 5$.

In other words, this decomposition prescribes the design of paradoxes exhibiting any desired extension of the beverage example. Start with a profile $\mathbf{p}$ and compute the plurality, BC, and pairwise rankings. Next, place the origin of the $\mathcal{RE}$ triangle over the plurality outcome. From the triangle, determine the appropriate $\{\mathbf{r}_j\}$ directions so that the new profile has the desired plurality ranking. By choosing appropriate x, y, z values, the plurality ranking can be rotated into any desired outcome while the pairwise and BC rankings remain the same. Even more, by adding a Condorcet portion to the profiles (which does not affect the BC or positional rankings), the pairwise rankings can be rotated into something different.

As this same argument holds for any specified $\mathbf{w}_s \neq \mathbf{w}_{\frac{1}{3}}$ procedure, we have the following striking, most disturbing conclusion.

Theorem 4.4.2. *For* $\mathbf{w}_s \neq \mathbf{w}_{\frac{1}{3}}$, *choose rankings for the three pairs of candidates and a three-candidate ranking. There exists a profile* $\mathbf{p}$ *where the pairwise and the* $\mathbf{w}_s$ *rankings are as specified.*

For instance, there are profiles where the pairwise rankings crown c_1 as the Condorcet winner along with $c_2 \succ c_3$, while the reader's favorite $\mathbf{w}_s \neq \mathbf{w}_{\frac{1}{3}}$ ranking is precisely the opposite! This is a chaotic state of affairs!

To repeat the idea of the proof, we know from Sect. 3.1 that there is a supporting profile for any specified rankings of the pairs; call it $\mathbf{p}_1$. Next, place the center of the $\mathbf{w}_s$ image of $\mathcal{RE}$ on $f(\mathbf{p}_1, \mathbf{w}_s)$ to determine a combination of $\{\mathbf{r}_j\}$ terms which moves the $\mathbf{w}_s$ point into the desired ranking region. This determines $\mathbf{p}_2$. When a sufficiently large multiple of $\mathbf{p}_2$ is added to $\mathbf{p}_1$, we have the desired outcomes. This argument does not apply to the BC because its $\mathcal{RE}$ image is a point; this is a source of the favorable BC properties. $\square$

4.4.4 Basic Profiles

A profile defines a procedure line and the pairwise votes independent of how it is decomposed. But some decompositions are easier to analyze than others. To illustrate with the earlier integer profile $(7, 5, 1, 7, 3, 6)$, by separating the reversal portion we have

$$(7, 5, 1, 7, 3, 6) = (0, 2, 0, 0, 0, 5) + (7, 3, 1, 7, 3, 1)$$

The $2\mathbf{E}_2 + 5\mathbf{E}_6$ portion has c_2 as the Condorcet winner, $c_1 \succ c_3$, and the plurality and BC normalized tallies of $(\frac{2}{7}, \frac{5}{7}, 0)$ and $(\frac{9}{21}, \frac{10}{21}, \frac{2}{21})$. What unusual harmony; all three rankings agree! The reversal portion is a little more difficult to interpret. First, the reversal does not change the BC or pairwise rankings. It does, however, rotate the procedure line about the BC. With a $\mathbf{r}_1$ dominant term, this endpoint is moving to favor c_1; indeed, it is sufficiently strong to rotate the plurality endpoint into the $c_1 \succ c_2 \succ c_3$ region.

I prefer a second approach which separates the effects on the pairwise and positional rankings. First convert a profile into its reduced and Condorcet portions; for the example profile, this is $(6, 0, 0, 2, 2, 1) + (1, 5, 1, 5, 1, 5)$. Next, remove from the reduced profile any reversals; this is $(4, 0, 0, 0, 2, 1) + (2, 0, 0, 2, 0, 0)$. The remaining portion, $4\mathbf{E}_1 + 2\mathbf{E}_5 + \mathbf{E}_6$ for the example, is what I call the *basic profile*. This decomposition is indicated in Fig. 4.4.5.

To illustrate how to use this decomposition to analyze the profile, notice for the basic profile that c_1 is the Condorcet winner and that the normalized plurality and BC tallies are, respectively, $(\frac{4}{7}, \frac{3}{7}, 0)$ and $(\frac{9}{21}, \frac{10}{21}, \frac{2}{21})$. Here we have a surprising conflict; this reduction crowns different candidates as the Condorcet and plurality winners! On the other hand, the BC normalized tally remains the same! As argued later, central to an appreciation of voting procedures is an understanding of how conflict can arise with a basic profile.

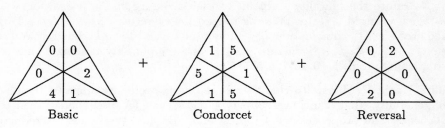

Fig. 4.4.5. Decomposition of $(7, 5, 1, 7, 3, 6)$

The remaining two portions alter the basic profile to change outcomes in a desired way. For instance, the Condorcet portion (the middle triangle) shows the portion of the profile affecting the pairwise rankings (without influencing the positional rankings) has a strong negative cycle bias. Indeed, this strong confused voter influence changes the Condorcet winner from c_1 (of the basic profile) to c_2 (for the given profile) to provide an artificial agreement with the BC winner. Finally, the reversal portion (the last triangle) indicates a weak rotation of the plurality endpoint in a direction parallel to the $c_1 \sim c_3$ indifference line.

This decomposition forces us to confront the remaining conflict between the Condorcet and BC outcomes in the basic profile; a conflict that cannot be blamed on confused voters. The Condorcet portion identifies which part of a profile loses (for pairwise rankings) the important transitivity assumption. The final decomposition identifies the portion of a profile suffering from reversal bias; it explains how much and in what direction the profile line is rotated about the BC pivot point.

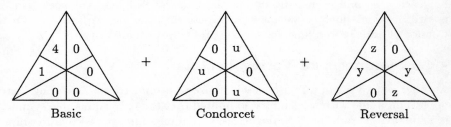

Fig. 4.4.6. A three-corner profile

Three-corners. To illustrate this decomposition, I construct a profile where c_1 is the Condorcet winner, c_2 is the plurality winner, and c_3 is the BC winner. As in Fig. 4.4.6, start with a basic profile $\mathbf{E}_2 + 4\mathbf{E}_3$ where the pairwise and all $\mathbf{w}_s \neq \mathbf{w}_{\frac{1}{2}}$ positional rankings are $c_3 \succ c_1 \succ c_2$. We need a negative cycle to rotate the pairwise outcomes to make c_1 the Condorcet winner; this requires a confused voter profile as indicated in the second triangle. This change is tight; we must have $u = 4$. This cyclic affect, of course, has no impact on the positional rankings; all but the antiplurality ranking are $c_3 \succ c_1 \succ c_2$.

To rotate the plurality endpoint of the procedure line into a region where c_2 wins, we need a vector pointing toward the c_2 vertex; (from Fig. 4.4.3) this requires a $\mathbf{r}_2$, $\mathbf{r}_3$ combination. By adding the first and third triangles, we learn that $y \geq 5$, $z > y - 3$ generates a $c_2 \succ c_3 \succ c_1$ plurality ranking. Thus, one supporting profile is $(0, 10, 7, 4, 5, 7)$.

The Basic Profiles. To characterize the basic profiles, assume (without loss of generality) that it includes some type-one voters. (A discussion of their consequences and properties is left to Sect. 4.5.) Because the Condorcet reduction leaves the reduced profile with no voters of one even and one odd type, this assumption requires that either the type-three or -five voters are removed. Also, one even voter type has no voters. The reversal reduction and the assumption about type-one voters means that all type-four voters have been removed. The worse case scenario is that if these voters have been removed with the Condorcet reduction; here, the basic profile has no type-four and (type-three and/or type five voters).

If there are type-three voters, then reversal removes all type-six voters. Similarly, type-five voters excludes type-two voters from the basic profile. When all these possibilities are charted on a representation triangle, we find that a basic profile has voters of at most three voter-types, and all of the voter types have the same pairwise ranking for one pair of candidates!

Because type-one voters are represented in the basic profile, the three possibilities are

1. Types 1, 2, 3 with the pairwise ranking $c_1 \succ c_2$
2. Types 1, 2, 6 with the pairwise ranking $c_1 \succ c_3$
3. Types 1, 5, 6 with the pairwise ranking $c_2 \succ c_3$

For each case and each pair, two of the pairwise rankings are weak and one is strong. Consequently, we must anticipate that the comparison between the Condorcet and BC rankings for a basic profile involve intensity.

4.4.5 Symmetry of Voting Vectors

Another way to relate $\mathbf{w}_s$ outcomes is to use $\mathbf{w}_s$-symmetries. The voting vectors $\mathbf{w}_s$ live on a line with a geometry so limited that the only admissible symmetry is a flip; a $180°$ rotation.[6] Nevertheless, this admits unexpected relationships.

To define a 180^0 rotation or "flip" of $\mathbf{w}_s$, we need a pivot point. However we define the flip, the plurality vector, $\mathbf{w}_0$, should be flipped to the antiplurality $\mathbf{w}_{\frac{1}{2}}$. The mechanics of converting $(1, 0, 0)$ to $(0, 0, -1)$ are obvious – reverse $(1, 0, 0)$ to obtain $(0, 0, 1)$ and then multiply by -1. To convert the vector into its standard form, add $(1, 1, 1)$ and multiply by $\frac{1}{2}$. Using this approach with $\mathbf{w}_s = (1-s, s, 0)$, first we obtain $(0, s, 1 - s)$ and then $(0, -s, s - 1)$. To change this vector into an equivalent, normalized form, add $(1 - s)(1, 1, 1)$ and multiply by the scalar $\frac{1}{2-3s}$ to obtain $\mathbf{w}_s^r$.

---

[6] But, if $n > 3$, then the positional voting methods are in the $(n - 2)$ dimensional simplex $Si(n - 1)$ with added symmetries – and more problems.

Definition 4.4.2. The *reversal* of voting vector $\mathbf{w}_s$, $\mathbf{w}_s^r$, is

(4.4.7) $$\mathbf{w}_s^r = (\frac{1-s}{2-3s}, \frac{1-2s}{2-3s}, 0). \quad \square$$

Notice the similarity between the components of $\mathbf{w}_s^r$ and β_s computed for the construction of $\mathcal{R}(\mathcal{I}_s)$. This is no coincidence; as the following statement shows, they should agree. Indeed, this assertion offers geometric support for calling $\mathbf{w}_s^r$ the *reversal* of $\mathbf{w}_s$.

Theorem 4.4.3. a. *In $Si(3)$ consider the line passing through $[\mathbf{w}_s]_1$ and $\mathcal{I}$. This line intersects the boundary of $Si(3)$ at $[\mathbf{w}_s^r]_4$.*

b. *For $\mathbf{w}_s$, we have that $(\mathbf{w}_s^r)^r = \mathbf{w}_s$.*

c. *The relationship $\mathbf{w}_s = \mathbf{w}_s^r$ holds if and only if $s = \frac{1}{3}$. Namely, only the BC voting vector is its own reversal.*

Proof. Parts a and c are exercises in Sect. 4.1. Part b follows from the geometry of part a. $\square$

Symmetry (part c of the theorem) again identifies *the Borda Count as the midpoint, the pivot point, of the positional voting methods.* It divides the $\mathbf{w}_s$ into those to the left and to the right of the BC. The connection between these vectors is the 180° flip where the BC is the pivot point. This type of assertion, where the BC is singled out for recognition when a new property is discussed, represents the favored status of the BC within positional voting.

For the reversal of voting vectors to be useful, the $\mathbf{w}_s$ and $\mathbf{w}_s^r$ outcomes should be related.

Theorem 4.4.4. *For a given $\mathbf{w}_s$, the normalized tallies satisfy*

(4.4.8) $$f(\mathbf{p}^r, \mathbf{w}_s^r) = tf(\mathbf{p}, \mathbf{w}_s) + (1-t)\mathcal{I}, \quad t = -\frac{1}{2-3s}.$$

Expressed in terms of election rankings,

(4.4.9) $$\mathcal{R}(f(\mathbf{p}^r, \mathbf{w}_s^r)) = \mathcal{R}((f(\mathbf{p}, \mathbf{w}_s))^r).$$

Notice a fascinating consequence of this theorem; it asserts that what happens with $\mathbf{w}_s$ also happens with $\mathbf{w}_s^r$! To illustrate with the beverage example of the fable, we know that $\mathbf{p} = (0, \frac{6}{15}, 0, \frac{4}{15}, \frac{5}{15}, 0)$ causes the plurality ranking $c_1 \succ c_2 \succ c_3$ to conflict with the pairwise rankings $c_3 \succ c_1, c_3 \succ c_2, c_2 \succ c_1$. Because $\mathbf{w}_{\frac{1}{2}} = \mathbf{w}_0^r$, the theorem provides another way to find profiles causing the same conclusion for the antiplurality method! Indeed, according to Eq. 4.4.9, the ranking for $f(\mathbf{p}^r, \mathbf{w}_{\frac{1}{2}})$ is $(c_1 \succ c_2 \succ c_3)^r = c_3 \succ c_2 \succ c_1$. Because pairwise voting respects reversal, the pairwise rankings of $\mathbf{p}^r = (\frac{4}{15}, \frac{5}{15}, 0, 0, \frac{6}{15}, 0)$ are $c_1 \succ c_2, c_2 \succ c_3, c_1 \succ c_3$. Therefore the pairwise and antiplurality rankings are in direct contradiction.

Stated in words, the antiplurality and plurality methods share the same ranking problems. More generally, the problems experienced by $\mathbf{w}_s$ for profile $\mathbf{p}$ are experienced by $\mathbf{w}_s^r$ with $\mathbf{p}^r$. So, the sins of a positional procedure are visited upon its reversal, and they are equally likely.

As indicated by the following proof, the value of t in Eq. 4.4.8 reflects the algebraic construction going from $\mathbf{w}_s$ to $\mathbf{w}_s^r$.

Proof. Because $[\mathbf{w}_s^r]_4$ is on the line defined by $\mathbf{w}_s$ and $\mathcal{I}$, we have from algebra and Theorem 4.4.3 that

$$[\mathbf{w}_s^r]_4 = (1-t)\mathcal{I} + t\mathbf{w}_s, \quad t = -\frac{1}{2-3s}.$$

The more general expression is

$$(4.4.10) \qquad [\mathbf{w}_s^r]_{j+3} = (1-t)\mathcal{I} + t[\mathbf{w}_s]_j, \; j = 1, \ldots 6, \quad t = -\frac{1}{2-3s}.$$

If $\mathbf{p}^r = (p_1^r, \ldots, p_6^r)$, then $p_{j+3}^r = p_j$. Using Eq. 4.4.10 and the definition of an election, we have that

$$
\begin{aligned}
f(\mathbf{p}^r, \mathbf{w}_s^r) &= \sum_{j=1}^{6} p_{j+3}^r [\mathbf{w}_s^r]_{j+3} = \sum_{j=1}^{6} p_j [\mathbf{w}_s^r]_{j+3} \\
&= \sum_{j=1}^{6} p_j \{(1-t)\mathcal{I} + t[\mathbf{w}_s]_j\} \\
&= (1-t)\mathcal{I} + t f(\mathbf{p}, \mathbf{w}_s). \quad \square
\end{aligned}
$$

Example 4.4.2. Let $\mathbf{p} = (\frac{1}{2}, 0, \frac{1}{3}, 0, \frac{1}{6}, 0)$. The plurality outcome is $c_1 \succ c_3 \succ c_2$ with the election point $\mathbf{q}_0 = (\frac{1}{2}, \frac{1}{3}, \frac{1}{6})$. The profile $\mathbf{p}^r = (0, \frac{1}{6}, 0, \frac{1}{3}, 0, \frac{1}{3})$ has the antiplurality outcome $c_2 \succ c_3 \succ c_1$. Using $s = 0$ with Eq. 4.4.8 leads to the value $t = -\frac{1}{2}$. Thus, the normalized outcome is $\mathbf{q}_{\frac{1}{2}} = (\frac{1}{4}, \frac{5}{12}, \frac{1}{3}) = -\frac{1}{2}\mathbf{q}_0 + \frac{3}{2}\mathcal{I}$. As promised by the theorem, the reversal of the antiplurality ranking is the plurality ranking. $\square$

The pivoting role of the BC, as manifested by Eq. 4.4.8, endows it with special properties.

Corollary 4.4.5. *For the BC, the normalized outcomes satisfy*

$$(4.4.11) \qquad\qquad f(\mathbf{p}^r, \mathbf{w}_{\frac{1}{3}}) = (f(\mathbf{p}, \mathbf{w}_{\frac{1}{3}}))^r.$$

For $\mathbf{w}_s \neq \mathbf{w}_{\frac{1}{3}}$, there are profiles $\mathbf{p}$ where Eq. 4.4.8 does not hold.

Proof. That Eq. 4.4.11 holds for the BC is immediate from Eq. 4.4.5 with $s = \frac{1}{3}$. The second assertion has been shown with the profile decomposition. $\square$

WGAD. The symmetry of Eq. 4.4.11 adds force to what we learned from the profile decomposition. Namely, *BC elections exhibit more regularity than any other positional method.* All other positional methods suffer a bias allowing paradoxes. In fact, by combining Corollary 4.4.5, the fact that the pairwise vote respects reversal, and the profile decomposition, it follows that *the BC has a stronger connection with the pairwise rankings than any other positional voting methods.* This is because both the BC and the pairwise rankings respect reversal symmetry while all other positional voting methods ignore it.

To see other consequences of these results, start with the naive belief that the pairwise election rankings must agree with the ranking of all three candidates. Thus, for any $\mathbf{p}$, if the $f(\mathbf{p}, \mathbf{w}_s)$ ranking is $c_i \succ c_j \succ c_k$, then the $F_3(\mathbf{p})$ rankings are the inherited $c_i \succ c_j, c_i \succ c_k, c_j \succ c_k$. But, with the exception of the BC, we cannot expect this to be true! If it were, then, because $F_3(\mathbf{p}^r) = F_3^r(\mathbf{p})$, the ranking of $f(\mathbf{p}^r, \mathbf{w}_s)$ would have to be the reversal of $f(\mathbf{p}, \mathbf{w}_s)$. But, this is not true; instead, the rankings of $f(\mathbf{p}, \mathbf{w}_s)$ and $f(\mathbf{p}^r, \mathbf{w}_s)$ could remain fixed! This suggests that, with the exception of the BC, the ranking defined by the pairs could be the reverse of the ranking defined by the positional voting method.

Similarly, suppose we find it repulsive to have the Condorcet winner bottom-ranked. This means that, when a Condorcet winner exists, there should be restrictions on the $\mathbf{w}_s$-ranking. The reversal of such a profile either defines a new Condorcet winner, or a pair of top-ranked candidates. However, the refusal of $\mathbf{w}_s$, $s \neq \frac{1}{3}$, to honor reversal symmetry means that the $\mathbf{w}_s$-outcome could be anything!

4.4.6 Exercises

1. If $\mathbf{q} = (\frac{1}{2}, \frac{1}{3}, \frac{5}{12})$, find $\mathbf{q}^r$. If $\mathbf{p} = (1, 2, 3, 4, 5, 6)$, what is $\mathbf{p}^r$? Find a $\mathbf{q}$ where $\mathbf{q}^r$ is not defined.

2. Following Eq. 4.4.5, an algebraic and geometric argument are given to find the $\alpha_s = [\mathbf{w}_s]_1$ and β_s is on the $[\mathbf{w}_s]_4 - [\mathbf{w}_s]_5$ line. With both the algebraic and geometric approach, find β_s on the $[\mathbf{w}_s]_6$ line. Then, find the reversed profile and the $\mathbf{w}_s$ outcome for this reversed profile. Which extreme profile lines define the Condorcet profiles?

3. Use Fig. 4.4.2 to find the fraction of the plurality outcomes that could result from the reversal of a profile where $f(\mathbf{p}, \mathbf{w}_s) = \mathcal{I}$. (Hint: The figure can be divided into nine equilateral triangles of the same size.)

4. In fig. 4.4.3, suppose there are twenty voters in the reversal portion. Find the BC outcome for this profile.

5. a. One reason $f(\mathbf{p}^r, \mathbf{w}_s) \neq \mathbf{q}_s^v$ is that for certain values of s, $\mathbf{q}_s^r$ need not even be in the representation triangle! Find the values of s for which this is true. For each s, find a $\mathbf{q}_s$ to illustrate this peculiar fact. Characterize those choices of $\mathbf{q}_s$ where $\mathbf{q}_s^r$ is in the representation triangle.

b. For $\mathbf{q}_0 = (0.4, 0.3, 0.3)$, find $\mathcal{R}(\mathbf{q}_0)$.

6. Suppose $\mathbf{w}_s$ has the alarming property that for any rankings of the three pairs and of the three candidates, there is a profile so that the rankings are attained by $(F_3(\mathbf{p}), f(\mathbf{p}, \mathbf{w}_s))$. Prove that the same property is satisfied by $\mathbf{w}_s^r$.

7. Directly compute both $\mathcal{R}(\mathcal{I}_{\frac{1}{2}})$ and the $\mathbf{w}_{\frac{1}{2}}$ image of $\mathcal{RE}$.

8. a. Construct a $\mathbf{p}$ where the ranking of $f(\mathbf{p}, \mathbf{w}_0)$ and $f(\mathbf{p}^r, \mathbf{w}_0)$ have the tally $(\frac{2}{3}, \frac{1}{6}, \frac{1}{6})$.

b. Show that all profile vertices in $\mathcal{R}(\mathcal{I}_0)$ have either a Condorcet or a reversal part.

c. Use the $\mathbf{w}_0$ image of $\mathcal{RE}$ and Fig. 4.4.3 to explain the set $\mathcal{R}(\mathcal{I}_0)$. (Hint: If $f(\mathbf{p}, \mathbf{w}_0) \neq \mathcal{I}$, what kind of $\mathbf{p}_1 \in \mathcal{RE}$ can be added to $\mathbf{p}$ to obtain a $\mathcal{I}$ outcome? Can you find the vertices?)

9. If $\mathbf{p}$ is such that the procedure line is a point $\mathbf{q}$, prove that the procedure line for $\mathbf{p}^r$ is the point $\mathbf{q}^r$.

10. a. Create a profile where c_1 is the Condorcet winner, c_2 is the BC winner, and the antiplurality ranking is $c_3 \succ c_1 \succ c_2$.

b. In Fig. 4.4.6, it was shown how to construct an example where c_1 is the Condorcet winner, c_3 is the BC winner, and the plurality ranking is $c_2 \succ c_3 \succ c_1$. There are six possible strict rankings for the plurality outcome; find five other profiles where the Condorcet and BC winners remain the same, but the plurality has each of the remaining five rankings.

c. Explain how to modify each of the profiles in b. so that the pairwise rankings define a positive cycle; a negative cycle.

11. a. For a profile $\mathbf{p}$ consisting of the basic portion $3\mathbf{E}_4 + \mathbf{E}_5$ and a reversed portion $6\mathbf{r}_2$, compute the normalized BC and plurality outcomes. Next, find the procedure line. Now do the same for $\mathbf{p}^r$.

b. Use what you discovered from part a. to show how the reversal portion of a profile changes the procedure line from $\mathbf{p}$ to $\mathbf{p}^r$. Can you use this to explain Theorem 4.4.4?

4.5 From Aggregating Pairwise Votes to the Borda Count

Due to its familiarity, simplicity, and the general ignorance of its serious defects, pairwise majority voting retains its status as a favored procedure. But, as we now know, these election outcomes are suspect if only because pairwise rankings drop the assumption that voters have transitive preferences. This raises an interesting question; if cycles and other problems are caused because we use only the information about who won each pairwise election, maybe acceptable conclusions emerge if we recognize how well each candidate does in each election. To illustrate, the Fig. 4.5.1 profile crowns c_2 as the Condorcet winner even though she probably is not the voters' true top-choice. (These voters have extreme views about c_2, while very few have c_1 bottom-ranked.) A hint that something must be wrong comes from c_2's close victories while c_1 wallops c_3.

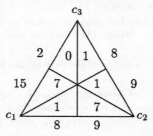

Fig. 4.5.1. Pairwise majority vote

The decomposition of this profile is $(5\mathbf{E}_2 + \mathbf{E}_1 + 6\mathbf{E}_6) + (\mathbf{r}_2) + (\mathbf{E}_2 + \mathbf{E}_4 + \mathbf{E}_6)$. Rankings of pairs are not affected by the reversal term $\mathbf{r}_2$, but they are influenced by the Condorcet factor. Indeed, manipulating this confused voter influence is that the Condorcet winner of the basic profile is c_1, not c_2. Clearly, the perverse influence of the confused voter needs to be eliminated! A hint how to do this comes from Prob. 9f, Sect. 3.1, which asked to show that the Condorcet portion of a profile requires the sum of points a candidate receives over all pairwise elections to be the same. For instance, the profile $(5, 1, 5, 1, 5, 1)$ defines the cycle $c_1 \succ c_2$, $c_2 \succ c_3$, and $c_3 \succ c_1$ where each election is won with a $11 : 7$ tally. Thus, over the two pairwise elections, the sum of votes for each candidate is 18. Namely, *an effective way to cancel the confused voter problem is to add the scores a candidate receives in all pairwise elections!*

The natural extension of the pairwise majority vote, then, is to add the tallies. This makes sense; as the pairwise tally indicates how *well* each candidate did in each contest, "adding" incorporates this information. Also, because addition cancels the Condorcet and reversed portion of a profile, the outcome depends only on the basic profile. To illustrate with Fig. 4.5.1, c_1 receives eight votes from the c_1 - c_2 election and 15 votes from the c_1 - c_3 contest for a total of 23 points. Similarly, c_2 receives 18 points, and c_3 receives a meager 10 points. Thus, the *aggregated pairwise vote* defines the more reasonable $c_1 \succ c_2 \succ c_3$ ranking with the tally $23 : 18 : 10$. The basic profile has the same ranking, but with the tally $18 : 13 : 5$; the five point difference per candidate represents the Condorcet and reversal portions of the profile. (Notice, a candidate's total is obtained by adding the pairwise totals next to her vertex.)

Definition 4.5.1. For $\{c_i, c_j\}$, let $q_{i,j}$ be the fraction of voters that prefer c_i to c_j. The *aggregated pairwise vote* procedure is where $\sum_{j \neq i} q_{i,j}$ points are assigned to c_i and the candidates are ranked according to the point totals. $\square$

This aggregation method, which provides another measure of the voters' intensity of support for one candidate over another, offers an immediate benefit; we lose the cycles! We might herald this conclusion as a major victory achieved by cleverly canceling the confused voter element from a profile. However, a more accurate and mundane explanation is that, by assigning a value to each candidate, the transitivity is inherited from the properties of numbers along a line.

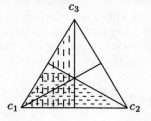

Fig. 4.5.2. c_1's aggregated vote

Keeping to the theme of this book, it is time to develop a geometric description of the aggregation procedure. The key to the geometry is depicted in Fig. 4.5.2. In a $\{c_1, c_2\}$ contest, c_1 receives the sum of terms in the triangle with the vertically shaded components; in the $\{c_1, c_3\}$ contest, she receives those points in the horizontally shaded regions. As the figure makes clear, c_1's vote total, the sum of numbers in both shaded regions, captures important aspects of a profile. For instance, c_1 enjoys a "double count" for the two ranking regions where she is top-ranked, but in regions where c_1 is second-ranked, the vote is counted only once. Finally, no points are assigned to c_1 from those regions where c_1 is bottom-ranked.

This shady reasoning provides an alternative way to compute the c_j outcome of the aggregated pairwise vote. Double count the number of voters with c_j top-ranked, count the number of voters with c_j middle-ranked, and ignore those voters with c_j bottom-ranked. Equivalently, for each voter, assign two points to his top-ranked candidate, one to his middle-ranked candidate, and zero for his bottom-ranked candidate. In other words, *the aggregated pairwise majority vote is equivalent to the BC.*

Theorem 4.5.1. *The aggregated pairwise majority vote and the BC are equivalent.*

4.5.1 Borda and Aggregated Pairwise Votes

Another way to see the connection between the pairwise contests and the BC is to consider a voter with the ranking $c_1 \succ c_2 \succ c_3$. As illustrated with the table, the BC weight he assigns to a candidate equals the sum of votes he would assign to her over the three pairwise (voting vector $(1,0)$) elections.

Method	Set of candidates	$\{c_1\}$	$\{c_2\}$	$\{c_3\}$
Majority	$\{c_1, c_2\}$	1	0	
Majority	$\{c_1, c_3\}$	1		0
Majority	$\{c_2, c_3\}$		1	0
BC	$\{c_1, c_2, c_3\}$	2	1	0

Thus, *the BC voting vector is the aggregated version of pairwise voting.* This "aggregated pairwise majority vote" interpretation, demonstrates why the BC (not the plurality vote or any other positional method) is the "natural" extension of a two candidate majority vote. A precise relationship between the BC and the aggregated pairwise vote tallies is

$$(4.5.1) \qquad f(\mathbf{p}, \mathbf{w}_{\frac{1}{3}}) = \frac{1}{3}(\sum_{j \neq 1} q_{1,j}, \sum_{j \neq 2} q_{2,j}, \sum_{j \neq 3} q_{3,j})$$

where the multiple $\frac{1}{3}$, needed to normalize the total tally to unity, arises because there are three pairwise contests.

Example 4.5.1. Suppose the pairwise election outcomes for 30 voters are as given in the following table. Because the BC agrees with the aggregated pairwise vote outcome, the sum of each column is the $(2, 1, 0)$ BC outcome for these voters. Notice, the Condorcet winner c_1 is not BC top-ranked.

	$\{c_1\}$	$\{c_2\}$	$\{c_3\}$
$\{c_1, c_2\}$	16	14	
$\{c_1, c_3\}$	16		14
$\{c_2, c_3\}$		20	10
BC tally	$\overline{32}$	$\overline{34}$	$\overline{24}$

. $\square$

This connection of the BC with pairwise votes accurately supports a suspicion that the BC respects certain properties of pairwise elections. Some important results follow.

Theorem 4.5.2. *A Condorcet winner never is BC bottom-ranked, and a Condorcet loser never is BC top-ranked.*

A Condorcet winner always receives more than a third of the assigned BC points while a Condorcet loser always receives less than a third of the assigned BC points. Therefore, a Condorcet winner always is BC ranked above a Condorcet loser.

If all pairwise votes end in a tie, then the BC ranking is $\mathcal{I}$.

With reflection, these conclusions must be expected, and some of them must have been known by Borda.[7] After all, for c_j to be a Condorcet winner, she must win both pairwise elections, so her point total on the right hand side of Eq. 4.5.1 must exceed that of at least one other candidate. This happens; the following elementary proof is fashioned from this description. Indeed, as shown next, a *Condorcet winner is favored by the BC*. Yet, while favored, Example 4.5.1 and Fig. 4.5.1 prove that if she strives to be mediocre, she need not be top-ranked.

Proof. If all pairwise elections end in a tie, it is obvious that the BC election outcome is $\mathcal{I}$, because the aggregated pairwise vote sums the same values for each candidate. If c_1 is the Condorcet winner, then

$$q_{1,j} = \frac{1}{2} + \epsilon_{1,j}, \quad q_{j,1} = \frac{1}{2} - \epsilon_{1,j}, \, j = 2, 3,$$

$$q_{2,3} = \frac{1}{2} + \alpha_{2,3}, \quad q_{3,2} = \frac{1}{2} - \alpha_{2,3}$$

where $\epsilon_{1,j} > 0$ is the amount over $\frac{1}{2}$ of c_1's victory over c_j. Similarly, the sign of fractional difference (from $\frac{1}{2}$), $\alpha_{2,3}$, determines whether c_2 or c_3 wins this pairwise contest.

Substituting these values into Eq. 4.5.1 leads to

$$(4.5.2) \qquad f(\mathbf{p}, \mathbf{w}_{\frac{1}{3}}) = \frac{1}{3}(1 + \epsilon_{1,2} + \epsilon_{1,3}, \, 1 - \epsilon_{1,2} + \alpha_{2,3}, \, 1 - \epsilon_{1,3} - \alpha_{2,3}).$$

The first component requires c_1, the Condorcet winner to receive more than a third of the total tally. Now if c_2, instead of c_1, is BC top-ranked, then the inequality

$$\alpha_{2,3} > 2\epsilon_{1,2} + \epsilon_{1,3} > 0$$

---

[7]See [D]. If $n \geq 4$, then the BC admits these and many other properties. See [S9, 11, 16-19].

determines the margin of victory c_2 needs over c_3 to overcome the favoritism shown by the BC to the Condorcet winner c_1. But the sign of $\alpha_{2,3} > 0$ relegates c_3 to be BC bottom-ranked, and she receives less than $\frac{1}{3}$ of the total vote. Consequently, a Condorcet winner never can be BC bottom-ranked.

(As a simpler argument, because the Condorcet winner receives over one-third of the vote, she has more than the average number of points. Thus, some other candidate must receive less than one-third of the vote; that candidate is ranked below the Condorcet winner.)

A similar argument proves the other assertions such as the Condorcet winner must be BC ranked strictly above a Condorcet loser, and that a Condorcet loser cannot be top-ranked. $\square$

It is interesting that the BC is the only positional method to enjoy these reasonably favorable properties.

Theorem 4.5.3. *If $\mathbf{w}_s \neq \mathbf{w}_{\frac{1}{3}}$ then $\mathbf{w}_s$ doesn not posses any of the Theorem 4.5.2 properties. Indeed, for any ranking of the pairs and for any ranking of three candidates, there is a profile where the pairwise and $\mathbf{w}_s$ rankings are as specified.*

The proof of this important theorem is an immediate application of the profile decomposition of Sect. 4.4. The fault, of course, is that all other procedures are swayed, in one direction or the other (depending on the sign of $s_{\frac{1}{3}}$, by the reversal portion of a profile while this portion is ignored by the pairwise rankings.

The next statement completes a listing of equivalent methods.

Theorem 4.5.4. *The BC and the aggregated pairwise majority vote are Condorcet Improvement procedures.*

Proof. It suffices to show that the profiles leading to each election outcome agree with that of the Condorcet Improvement. Using the notation of Sect. 3.2, recall that the $x \in [1, -1]$ component measures the c_1, c_2 pairwise vote where $x = 1, 0, -1$ corresponds, respectively, to c_1 getting all votes, a tie, and c_2 getting all votes. Indeed, because $q_{i,j} = 1 - q_{j,i}$, we have that $x = q_{1,2} - q_{2,1} = 2q_{1,2} - 1$. Similarly, $y = q_{2,3} - q_{3,2} = 2q_{2,3} - 1$, $z = q_{3,1} - q_{1,3} = 2q_{3,1} - 1$. With these equations, the CI requirement for the $c_1 \succ c_2$ relative ranking, $2x > y + z$, is $2q_{1,2} > q_{2,3} + q_{3,1}$.

According to Eq. 4.5.1, the BC admits the relative ranking $c_1 \succ c_2$ iff $q_{1,2} + q_{1,3} > q_{2,1} + q_{2,3}$. By expressing this relationship in terms of the three chosen variables, the BC condition also is $2q_{1,2} > q_{2,3} + q_{3,1}$. The proof is completed by observing that the equivalence of the procedures follows from neutrality and the fact that each gives the same relative (strict) ranking for c_1, c_2 for a profile. $\square$

The CI of Sect. 3.4 captures the intensity information about pairwise comparisons. This connection between the BC and CI allows these comparisons to be assigned number values. Namely, in a $\{c_i, c_j\}$ pairwise election where a voter's ranking is $c_i \succ c_j$, the CI (or BC) assigns a differential of one point to c_i (over c_j) if the comparison is weak but two points if it is strong.

4.5.2 Basic Profiles

As we now know, the BC ranking is uniquely determined by the basic portion of a profile! Another way to prove this statement is to use the identification of the BC with the aggregated pairwise vote. With Fig. 4.5.3, for instance, it follows by adding the pairwise scores on each side of a vertex that the only impact the Condorcet and reversed portions have on the BC outcome is to add the same number of points to each candidate's tally. Only the basic portion of a profile determines the BC ranking.

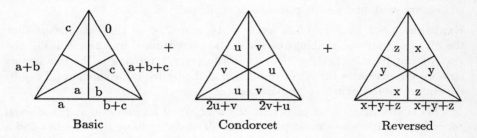

Fig. 4.5.3. BC properties

This is powerful information! It asserts that once we understand how the BC and pairwise rankings differ with a basic profile, we can immediately comprehend the consequences of any profile for all pairwise and positional procedures! In other words, the previously complicated analysis of voting reduces to simple computations with basic profiles.

A Further Simplification. The basic profile of Fig. 4.5.3 requires all voters to have a $c_2 \succ c_3$ ranking, but (because of symmetry of changing the names of candidates) anything we learn from this example holds for all basic profiles. So, Fig. 4.5.3 is used as a prototype to characterize differences between pairwise and BC rankings of pairs. In this analysis, remember that a pairwise procedure only recognizes the relative rankings of pairs while the BC provides a differential of points depending on whether the pairwise ranking is strong or weak.

To further simplify the basic profile, consider what happens with a $\{c_1, c_2\}$ comparison. Here, two voter types (one and six) weakly rank this pair, so both the BC and pairwise voting treat this portion of the profile the same. Indeed, these voter types bottom-rank c_3; they view the election as a majority vote between c_1 and c_2 for top-place. Consequently, by pairing a voter from each type, there is a natural cancellation.

To illustrate the cancellation, either $b \geq a$ or $a > b$. The first possibility defines the separation $a[\mathbf{E}_1 + \mathbf{E}_6] + [(b-a)\mathbf{E}_6 + c\mathbf{E}_5]$. The term in the first bracket does not affect the $\{c_1, c_2\}$ outcome; indeed, both the BC and pairwise voting just add a points to each candidate's tally. Consequently, the outcome is determined by the profile in the second bracket which is an unanimous $c_2 \succ c_1$ preference. Here, the BC and pairwise rankings agree. The $a > b$ case, on the other hand, separates the basic profile as $b[\mathbf{E}_1 + \mathbf{E}_6] + [(a - b)\mathbf{E}_1 + c\mathbf{E}_5]$. As common sense and intuition dictate, the first bracket is a cancellation, so the outcome depends on the second bracket. Here, the comparison involves conflicting weak (type-one) and strong (type-five) $\{c_1, c_2\}$ preferences. This difference makes a difference in the BC and pairwise rankings!

As a basic profile requires everyone to have the same ranking for some pair (in Fig. 4.5.3 it is $c_2 \succ c_3$), only the $\{c_1, c_3\}$ pair remains. Again, after a natural cancellation of voters with conflicting weak $\{c_1, c_3\}$ rankings (types five and six), the decision on this pair is either unanimous, or it involves a comparison between conflicting weak and strong preferences of the pair!

Example 4.5.2 In Fig. 4.5.3, let $a = 14$, $b = 2$, $c = 10$. This means that the BC and pairwise rankings of $\{c_1, c_2\}$ are determined by $12\mathbf{E}_1 + 10\mathbf{E}_5$, the $\{c_1, c_3\}$ rankings by $14\mathbf{E}_1 + 8\mathbf{E}_5$, while the $\{c_2, c_3\}$ ranking is the unanimous $c_2 \succ c_3$. Observe how the effective portion of the basic profile changes (iff $b \neq 0$) depending on the pair being considered. □

This is stunning! *It implies that the analysis of all pairwise and positional procedures reduces to the simple problem of understanding how the BC and a pairwise vote treat conflicting $\{c_j, c_k\}$ rankings when one is strong and the other weak!* The answer is trivial; the BC gives twice as much weight to the strong comparisons as does the pairwise vote. In Example 4.5.2, for instance, both pairwise rankings of $c_1 \succ c_2$ and $c_1 \succ c_3$ are reversed by the BC.

Example 4.5.3 These ranking differences are the same type-one and -five intensity comparisons discussed in Sects. 3.4 and 4.3.5. To review, consider a profile where five million voters believe that Toini $\succ$ Vivian $\succ$ Joyce, and five million have the ranking Vivian $\succ$ Joyce $\succ$ Toini. Surely Joyce is bottom-ranked; the voters only differ whether she should be bottom- or middle-ranked. Contentious Toini, on the other hand, splits the voters where half love her and half hate her. Everyone has easy-going Vivian ranked at least second, while half have her top-ranked. Thus, the ranking should be a robust "Vivian $\succ$ Toini $\succ$ Joyce." This intensity is accurately reflected by the BC ranking; but the pairwise ranking is a tie "Toini $\sim$ Vivian $\succ$ Joyce."

Suppose just one more Toini voter arrives; the BC rankings reflects the obvious intensity of the voters opinions by remaining the same. This pairwise ranking further manifests the procedure's inability to gauge voters' beliefs and sentiments; it now is "Toini $\succ$ Vivian $\succ$ Joyce." As the three figures of this section demonstrate, because the BC is an aggregated pairwise vote, it captures this intensity of preferences while retaining the assumption of transitive preferences; the pairwise vote does not. Incidentally, in a conflicting weak-strong pairwise comparison of $\{c_j, c_k\}$, the BC requires the weakly preferred candidate to have one more than two-thirds of the vote to beat the strongly preferred candidate. Ah, the pope selection procedure and the other Sect. 4.3.5 comparisons arise again!

To create basic profile examples with conflict between the BC and the pairwise rankings, start with a $x\mathbf{E}_1 + y\mathbf{E}_5$ profile where $y < x < 2y$. (Thus c_1 is, respectively, the pairwise winner and BC loser of the two $\{c_1, c_j\}$ elections.) If b type-one and -six voters are added, the $\{c_1, c_2\}$ election remains the same, but, after the cancellation, the $\{c_1, c_3\}$ election is determined by $(x+b)\mathbf{E}_1 + (y-b)\mathbf{E}_5$. Therefore, if $2(y - b) > x + b$, or $2y - x > 3b$, then there is conflict with each pair. Example 4.5.2 was created by choosing $x = 12$, $b = 2$, $y = 10$. $\square$

One way to understand the basic profile outcomes is to list them. For instance, if the BC ranking $c_1 \succ c_2 \succ c_3$ requires $a \geq b + 2c$ and the $\{c_1, c_2\}$ pairwise rankings must be $c_1 \succ c_2, c_1 \succ c_3$. Similarly, a $c_1 \sim c_2 \succ c_3$ ranking allows pairwise rankings $c_1 \sim c_2$ and $c_1 \succ c_3$ or $c_1 \succ c_2$ and anything for the $\{c_1, c_3\}$ ranking. The remaining three BC rankings can be accompanied by any combination of $\{c_1, c_2\}$ and $\{c_1, c_3\}$ rankings.

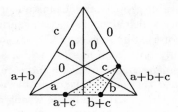

Fig. 4.5.4. Basic profiles

The Basic Procedure Line. It is easy to find the procedure line associated with a basic profile; the plurality endpoint and BC midpoints are, respectively,

$$(4.5.3) \qquad (\frac{a}{a+b+c}, \frac{b+c}{a+b+c}, 0), \quad \frac{1}{3}(\frac{2a+b}{a+b+c}, 1 + \frac{a+b}{a+b+c}, \frac{c}{a+b+c}).$$

The plurality endpoint, then, is on an edge of the representation triangle agreeing with the $\{c_1, c_2\}$ normalized pairwise tally, while the BC midpoint is in the shaded region of Fig. 4.5.4 which is the convex hull of $\{[\mathbf{w}_{\frac{1}{3}}]\}_{j=1,5,6}$. Adding a Condorcet portion to the profile changes the pairwise rankings (it slides the procedure line closer to $\mathcal{I}$ without changing any positional rankings), while a reversal component rotates the procedure line about the BC point.

To illustrate with a profile of historical interest,[8] $(13, 6, 10, 13, 0, 18)$ has basic part $6\mathbf{E}_1 + 2\mathbf{E}_6$, Condorcet part $6(\mathbf{E}_2 + \mathbf{E}_4 + \mathbf{E}_6)$ and reversal part $7\mathbf{r}_1 + 10\mathbf{r}_3$. The procedure line starts on the bottom edge of the representation triangle with the plurality and BC points $(\frac{3}{4}, \frac{1}{4}, 0)$ and $(\frac{14}{24}, \frac{10}{24}, 0)$. In other words, with the exception of the antiplurality method, the pairwise and positional rankings for the basic portion are $c_1 \succ c_2 \succ c_3$ (as they well should be because the only conflict is between weak rankings). The Condorcet portion spins the pairwise vote to make c_2 the Condorcet winner, while the reversal portion spins the profile

---

[8]This Condorcet example [M] raised questions about the *Condorcet jury theorem* with three candidates. This issue is outside the theme of this book, but these difficulties become manageable with the profile decomposition.

line in an essentially northern direction (while sliding the BC point toward $\mathcal{I}$) making c_3 the plurality winner.

The fact the plurality outcome agrees with the pairwise vote for some pair is not surprising; after all, the plurality procedure also ignores vital information about a profile. This is manifested by Fig. 4.5.4; even though the pairwise vote has its difficulties, it at least recognizes the existing support for c_3! (I leave it to the reader to show that the plurality procedure cannot distinguish between a transitive and an acyclic voter.)

A Dubious Plurality Property. To illustrate the use of the procedure line for the basic portion of a profile, I use a proposal that is periodically rediscovered with the axiomatic approach to choice theory. This approach characterizes procedures in terms of desirable properties. For instance, it may seem impossible to argue against a procedure which always selects a candidate who is top-ranked by more than half of all voters, but it is easy. To do so, I show that although *the plurality vote is the only positional method which always elects a majority candidate, the profiles ensuring this conclusion indicate that this is the wrong outcome!* This is because this seemingly desirable property holds only for profiles which indicate that the conclusion is the wrong one.

To see why, start with a basic profile $n(\mathbf{E}_1 + \mathbf{E}_5)$ where n is an integer; this is the Toini, Vivian, Joyce example when n equals five million. From Eq. 4.5.3, the plurality and BC points for the procedure line are, respectively, $(\frac{1}{2}, \frac{1}{2}, 0)$ and $(\frac{1}{3}, \frac{1}{2}, \frac{1}{6})$. (They are, respectively, the midpoints of the lines defined by $[\mathbf{w}_0]_1, [\mathbf{w}_0]_6$ and $[\mathbf{w}_{\frac{1}{3}}]_1, [\mathbf{w}_{\frac{1}{3}}]_6$.) By adding one more type-one voter, c_1 becomes both a majority and plurality winner; however, as argued, it is doubtful that this conclusion reflects the voters' beliefs. Unfortunately, for the assertion, by pulling the plurality endpoint of the procedure line into the type-one region, other $\mathbf{w}_s$ outcomes are dragged into this region. (From algebra, this is for $s < \frac{1}{n}$.) To get rid of these methods, n has to have larger and larger values.

All profiles supporting this property are obtained by adding to this basic portion. Notice that adding a $m(\mathbf{E}_1 + \mathbf{E}_6)$ portion does not change the $\{c_1, c_2\}$ ranking of anything, nor does it reduce the sting that the conclusion relies on an Example 4.5.3 profile with its dubious conclusion. Similarly, only a $\mathbf{r}_2$ reversal component can be added to the profile; any other $\mathbf{r}_j$ term endangers c_1's status of being the majority candidate. But, this $\mathbf{r}_2$ term has no impact on the $\{c_1, c_2\}$ rankings, and the basic profile remains dominant in the analysis. Finally, adding a Condorcet portion only jeopardizes c_1's standing as a majority winner. Consequently, the only profiles supporting this conclusion about the plurality vote strongly suggest that the plurality conclusion is the wrong one!

As this example shows, a severe limitation of the axiomatic approach is that, in general, we do not know if the profiles supporting a nice-sounding property are beneficial or harmful. This information now is available with the profile decomposition. Even more is possible; we can discover other properties. For instance, start with a $\mathbf{E}_1 + n\mathbf{E}_5$ basic profile that, for large n values, overwhelming suggests a $c_2 \succ c_3 \succ c_1$ ranking. The procedure line is determined by the

$(\frac{1}{n+1}, \frac{n}{n+1}, 0)$ plurality and $\frac{1}{3(n+1)}(2, 2n+1, n)$ BC defining points. To swing the plurality endpoint into the c_1 region, add a r_1 term. Notice, adding $n(E_1 + E_4)$ proves the assertion that *the plurality method is the only positional method that can allow the election of a candidate even though almost two-thirds of the voters have her bottom-ranked!* So, one swing of the procedure line reveals w_s-properties that sound attractive, but another swing brings out the ugly side of a procedure; only the BC avoids this Dr. Jekyll and Mr. Hyde change.

4.5.3 Geometric Representation

An alternative way to compare BC and pairwise outcomes is to use the mapping

$$(4.5.4) \qquad F_{\frac{1}{3}} = (F_3, f(-, w_{\frac{1}{3}})) : Si(6) \to [-1, 1]^3 \times Si(3).$$

Namely, for a given profile, compute each of the three pairwise election tallies and then determine the BC tally. Just as the three pairwise elections can be viewed as defining a point in $[-1, 1]^3$, a cube (see Sect. 3.2), the four elections can be viewed as defining a point in the space $[-1, 1]^3 \times Si(3)$.

We could figure out what the five-dimensional object $[-1, 1]^3 \times Si(3)$ looks like, but it is not necessary. This is because the pairwise rankings determine the BC rankings according to the equation

$$(4.5.5) \qquad (x, y, z; \frac{x-z}{6} + \frac{1}{3}, \frac{y-x}{6} + \frac{1}{3}, \frac{z-y}{6} + \frac{1}{3})$$

where

$$(x, y, z) \in [-1, 1]^3, \quad -1 \le x + y + z \le 1.$$

These equations just reinforce the assertion that the BC is a CI procedure. Therefore, in the representation cube, the BC outcomes are as given in Fig. 4.5.5.

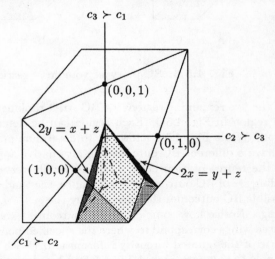

Fig. 4.5.5. The shaded region is the BC ranking $c_1 \succ c_2 \succ c_3$. Not all of the hidden lines are included.

To analyze the BC outcomes, the approach remains the same. As the set of outcomes leading to a specified ranking is a convex set, we want to find the vertices. It follows from Eq. 4.5.5 that when the BC outcomes are characterized in the representation cube, the region has nine vertices. Thus, the region for the BC ranking of $c_1 \succ c_2 \succ c_3$ is the convex hull of the vertices

Vertices for the BC region $c_1 \succ c_2 \succ c_3$

$$(1, -1, -1), \ (0, 1, -1), \ (\frac{1}{3}, -\frac{1}{3}, -1), \ (1, 0, -1),$$

(4.5.6)
$$(-\frac{1}{3}, \frac{1}{3}, -1), \ (\frac{1}{3}, 1, -\frac{1}{3}), \ \pm(\frac{1}{3}, \frac{1}{3}, \frac{1}{3}), \ (1, \frac{1}{3}, -\frac{1}{3}).$$

Finding these vertex values is an algebraic exercise using the equations for the boundaries of the F_3 image set (e.g., $x + y + z = \pm 1$) along with the equations defining indifference for pairs in the BC ranking. For instance, for the BC ranking $c_1 \sim c_2$, we have from Eq. 4.5.5 that the defining equations are $x - z = y - x$ or $2x = y + z$. Similarly, the other boundary set with the BC ranking $c_2 \sim c_3$ is $2y = x + z$. Consequently the BC region for $c_1 \succ c_2 \succ c_3$ is defined by the two inequalities

(4.5.7)
$$2x > y + z, \quad 2y > z + x.$$

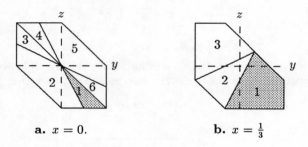

a. $x = 0$. **b.** $x = \frac{1}{3}$

Fig. 4.5.6. BC-pairwise vote cross sections

Each of the five remaining regions for BC strict rankings is geometrically similar to the region in Fig. 4.5.5. Each region can be determined with a similar computation. While Fig. 4.5.5 allows us to determine precisely which pairwise outcomes have a different BC outcome, an alternative approach is to take a region from the representation cube, find the profile vertices, and compute the corresponding set of BC outcomes. For instance, the shaded region of Fig. 4.5.6a has all possible BC outcomes that accompany the $c_1 \succ c_2$, $c_1 \succ c_3$, $c_2 \succ c_3$ pairwise rankings. Notice how some of the BC outcomes extend into other ranking regions; these wings correspond to where the specified pairwise rankings are suspect because of the ignored intensity information. (With this hint, the readoer should be able to compare Figs. 4.5.5, 4.5.6a.) Similarly, Fig. 4.5.6b are the BC outcomes that can accompany a pairwise cycle. (Which triangle corresponds to the positive cycle?)

4.5.4 The Borda Dictionary

To understand the BC, we must determine which pairwise rankings can accompany a BC ranking.

Definition 4.5.2. For a profile $\mathbf{p}$, the election outcome $F_{\frac{1}{3}}(\mathbf{p})$ defines a unique election ranking for each of the sets $\{c_1, c_2\}$, $\{c_2, c_3\}$, $\{c_1, c_3\}$, $\{c_1, c_2, c_3\}$; the *word* defined by $\mathbf{p}$ is the listing of these four rankings. The *Borda Dictionary*, $\mathcal{D}(\mathbf{w}_{\frac{1}{3}})$, is a collection of all words that occur for some profile. The *Universal Set*, U^3, is the set of all $3^3 13 = 351$ ways to list a ranking for each of the four sets of candidates.   □

Example 4.5.4. The listing $(c_1 \succ c_2, c_2 \succ c_3, c_1 \succ c_3, c_1 \succ c_2 \succ c_3)$ is a word in the Borda Dictionary $\mathcal{D}(\mathbf{w}_{\frac{1}{3}})$ because these are the election rankings associated with, say, the profile $\mathbf{E}_1$. Somewhat less obvious is that $(c_1 \succ c_2, c_2 \succ c_3, c_3 \succ c_1, c_1 \succ c_2 \succ c_3)$ also is a word in the BC Dictionary. To see why, observe that these pairwise rankings define the sign listing $(x, y, z) = (+, +, +)$ in the representation cube; this point is in the positive orthant. But, the shaded region of Fig. 4.5.5 (representing the BC ranking $c_1 \succ c_2 \succ c_3$) has a portion in the positive orthant of the representation cube. Thus, there are profiles leading to this list of outcomes. Alternatively, observe how easy it is to find positive x, y, z values where $x - z > y - z > z - y$. The conclusion now follows from Eq. 4.5.5.

The listing $(c_1 \succ c_2, c_3 \succ c_2, c_3 \succ c_1, c_1 \succ c_2 \succ c_3)$ is *not* a word in the Borda Dictionary because the pairwise rankings define the orthant with the sign pattern $(x, y, z) = (+, -, +)$; this particular orthant misses the shaded region of Fig. 4.5.5. Alternatively, the $(x, y, z) = (+, -, +)$ sign pattern and Eq. 4.5.5 requires the BC rankings to satisfy $x - z > 0, y - x < 0, z - y > 0$. (The negative value requires that candidate to receive less than $\frac{1}{3}$ of the total vote. Conversely, positive values indicate that a candidate receives over $\frac{1}{3}$ of the vote.) This requires c_2 to be BC bottom ranked, rather than the specified middle-ranking.

As another example, $(c_2 \succ c_1, c_2 \succ c_3, c_3 \succ c_1, c_1 \succ c_2 \succ c_3) \notin \mathcal{D}(\mathbf{w}_{\frac{1}{3}})$. Thus, this is a listing of election rankings that never can occur with a BC election. There are several ways to prove this assertion; one is to note that it allows the Condorcet loser to be top-ranked (which violates Theorem 4.5.2). As another approach, use the geometry of Fig. 4.5.5. A third approach is to use Eq. 4.5.5.

Just the fact that one listing cannot be in the Borda Dictionary proves that

$$(4.5.8) \qquad\qquad\qquad \mathcal{D}(\mathbf{w}_{\frac{1}{3}}) \subsetneqq U^3. \quad \square$$

4.5.5 Borda Cross-Sections

While Fig. 4.5.5 provides a convenient way to determine what BC rankings can, and cannot accompany various pairwise rankings, it is not sufficiently refined to extract subtle features because Fig. 4.5.5 is a two-dimensional representation of a three-dimensional object. To remove the complexity, find two-dimensional slices. This is done next.

To see what words can occur in the BC Dictionary, we can take sections of Fig. 4.5.5. For example, for $x = 0$ (a $c_1 \sim c_2$ pairwise outcome), the relevant regions from Fig. 4.5.5 is the intersection of the figure with the y-z plane. This intersection is given in Fig. 4.5.6a where the numbers indicate the BC ranking regions and the shaded area is where the BC ranking is $c_1 \succ c_2 \succ c_3$. (To find these regions, first substitute the $x = 0$ value into the boundary equations $x + y + z = \pm 1$, $2x = y + z$, $2y = x + z$, $2z = x + y$, and then plot the resulting equations.)

To use this cross-section, notice that the positive orthant (determined by the dashed lines) is strictly included in the BC ranking of type-5. Thus, the only BC ranking that can accompany $c_1 \sim c_2$ ($x = 0$), $c_2 \succ c_3$ ($y > 0$), and $c_3 \succ c_1$ ($z > 0$) is $c_3 \succ c_2 \succ c_1$. Other information from this cross-section is that the pairwise rankings represented by $x = 0$, $y < 0$, $z > 0$ can be accompanied by four different strict BC rankings; these are BC rankings of types 2, 3, 4, or 5. On the other hand, if the pairwise rankings define the sign pattern $(0, -, -)$ then the only possible choice for the BC outcome is the type-two ranking $c_1 \succ c_3 \succ c_2$.

Another interesting cross-section is where $x = \frac{1}{3}$; this x value corresponds to c_1 winning two-thirds of the vote in her contest against c_2. As indicated in Fig. 4.5.6b, this x value is a bifurcation point; it is the smallest x value that does not admit BC rankings where $c_2 \succ c_1$. In fact, with this $x = \frac{1}{3}$ value, the BC ranking can be one of three strict rankings or one of four rankings with a tie vote, or $\mathcal{I}$. When $x > \frac{1}{3}$, several of these BC options immediately disappear. (These are all BC rankings where $c_1 \sim c_2$.)

Entries of the Borda Dictionary. To list all words in a Borda Dictionary, start with Eq. 4.5.5 or Fig. 4.5.5 to find all words where the BC ranking is $c_1 \succ c_2 \succ c_3$. Out of the 27 possible rankings of the pairs, only seventeen can occur. These pairwise rankings can be characterized by their (x, y, z) sign patterns

$$
\begin{gathered}
(+, \text{ any, any}), (0, +, -), \\
(0, 0, -), (0, -, -) \\
(-, +, -), (-, 0, -), (-, -, \text{ any }).
\end{gathered}
$$

(4.5.9)

Changing names (neutrality), we find all strict words in the Borda Dictionary.

If the BC ranking is $\mathcal{I}$, the admissible pairwise rankings are found either from the geometry or Eq. 4.5.5. For instance with the geometry the $\mathcal{I}$ region is the line in the representation cube connecting the points $\pm(\frac{1}{3}, \frac{1}{3}, \frac{1}{3})$. The only three words in the BC dictionary of this type, then, are

$$
\begin{gathered}
(c_1 \succ c_2, c_2 \succ c_3, c_3 \succ c_1, \mathcal{I}), (c_1 \sim c_2, c_2 \sim c_3, c_3 \sim c_1, \mathcal{I}) \\
(c_2 \succ c_1, c_3 \succ c_2, c_1 \succ c_3, \mathcal{I})
\end{gathered}
$$

(4.5.10)

Next consider the BC rankings with one tie; e.g., the BC ranking region $c_1 \succ c_2 \sim c_3$ is on the left hand side of Fig. 4.5.3 passing through the five vertices $(1, 0, -1), (1, \frac{1}{3}, -\frac{1}{3}), \pm(\frac{1}{3}, \frac{1}{3}, \frac{1}{3}), (\frac{1}{3}, -\frac{1}{3}, -1)$. From the geometry or Eq. 4.5.5, the five combination of pairs that accompany this BC ranking can be determined. Similarly, the slanted region on the right-hand side of the shaded region corresponding to the BC ranking $c_1 \sim c_2 \succ c_3$ meets five regions defined by the pairs. (Identifying these regions is an exercise.) The following theorem is based on these assertions.

Theorem 4.5.5. *The Borda Dictionary, $\mathcal{D}(\mathbf{w}_{\frac{1}{3}})$ has 135 words. Thus, it contains 38.5% of the 351 entries in U^3.[9]*

4.5.6 Exercises

1. a. If the pairwise votes are $c_2 \succ c_2$ by $21 : 19$, $c_1 \succ c_3$ by $22 : 18$ and $c_3 \succ c_2$ by $35 : 5$, find the BC ranking.
b. Find a BC ranking where the Condorcet-loser is in second place. Analyze the geometry of the profile to determine whether the BC ranking, or the Condorcet designation, is more appropriate.

2. Complete the proof of Theorem 4.5.2.

3. Find an example of a Condorcet Improvement procedure that does not always agree with the BC outcome.

4. Equation 4.5.5 provides the vertices for the BC region $c_1 \succ c_2 \succ c_3$. Find the vertices for the BC region $c_2 \succ c_3 \succ c_1$.

5. Find the $x = \frac{1}{2}$ section of the BC-pairwise vote. The $x = \frac{1}{3}$ section of Fig. 4.5.4b allows the BC ranking of $c_1 \succ c_3 \succ c_2$ to be accompanied by four strict pairwise ranking regions. Is there an x section where this BC ranking meets fewer pairwise regions?

6. a. Use the techniques leading to Theorem 4.5.5 to find all pairwise rankings that can accompany $c_1 \sim c_2 \succ c_3$. Do the same for the ranking $c_1 \succ c_2 \sim c_3$. With the help of neutrality, find the number of BC words that can occur if there is one tie vote in the ranking of all three candidates.
b. Find all the pairwise rankings that can accompany the BC ranking $c_3 \succ c_1 \succ c_2$. For instance, one might use Eq. 4.5.9 and a name change.

7. a. By use of the BC cyclic coordinates, find a profile for $\mathbf{q}_{\frac{1}{3}} = (\frac{1}{2}, \frac{1}{6}, \frac{1}{3})$ where the odd voter outcome is as cyclic as possible.
b. Let $\mathbf{p} = (\alpha_{\frac{1}{3}} = (\frac{5}{18}, \frac{4}{9}, \frac{5}{18}, \beta_{\frac{1}{3}} = (\frac{1}{6}, \frac{1}{2}, \frac{1}{3}), d = \frac{3}{5})$. Find the pairwise vote for c_1, c_2.
c. Impose the Black's single peakedness condition on profile. Does this restrict the BC election rankings?

8. a. Is $(0.2, 0.3, 0.5, \frac{17}{60}, \frac{21}{60}, \frac{22}{60})$ an admissible BC outcome? Use the BC vector space to prove your answer.
b. Suppose c_1 is the BC winner but not the Condorcet winner; c_2 is. Find a bound on the c_1 pairwise victory over c_3 in terms of the c_1, c_2 vote and the c_2, c_3 outcome.

---

[9] With more candidates, the BC Dictionary uses very few of the entries from the universal set. For instance, with $n \geq 6$ candidates, the BC dictionary has fewer than $\frac{1}{10^{50}}$ of the admissible entries of U^n. As 10^{50} is much larger than 6^{15}, this number admits all sorts of "Gee Whiz!" statements of the type used in Sect. 2.1 to indicate the number of libraries required just to hold the listings of how one BC word can be varied to get all of the paradoxes admitted by other procedures.

9. a. Use the cross-section approach to find all BC rankings that can accompany the pairwise ranking $c_1 \sim c_2$, $c_3 \succ c_2$, and $c_3 \succ c_1$.

b. Suppose a pairwise vote is on the boundary of the negative cyclic region because one pairwise ranking is a tie. Identify the corresponding BC ranking by using a cross-section approach.

c. It is asserted that the $c = \frac{1}{3}$ section is a bifurcation. Prove this assertion by finding the cross-sections for x slightly less than and slightly greater than $\frac{1}{3}$. How many BC rankings can occur in each case?

10. The point $c = \frac{1}{2}, y = \frac{1}{3}, z = 0$ defines what BC outcome? By use of profile decomposition, find the cone of profiles leading to this outcome.

4.6 The Other Positional Voting Methods

Some of the BC properties are developed, but how should they be interpreted? Are these conclusions coveted properties that become justifiable BC bragging rights, or are they embarrassing flaws that underscore BC inadequacies? After all, the universal set U^3 admits 351 different listings of rankings, and the BC realizes about 38% of them. Is this 38% figure large or small relative to other positional voting methods?

From the profile decomposition we know the answer. Nevertheless, we offer another geometric approach based on analyzing the image set of

$$F_s = (F_3, f(-, \mathbf{w}_s)) : Si(6) \to [-1,1]^3 \times Si(3), \quad s \in [0, \frac{1}{2}].$$

In the previous section I showed that the image of $F_{\frac{1}{3}}$ is three-dimensional. As proved below, if $s \neq \frac{1}{3}$, then the F_s image set is *five-dimensional and it meets all possible combinations of rankings regions*. This reinforces what we learned from the profile decomposition; namely, that unless the BC is used to tally an election, "anything can happen!"

Theorem 4.6.1. *The image of F_s is five-dimensional iff $s \neq \frac{1}{3}$. In particular, the ranking region $(c_1 \sim c_2, c_2 \sim c_3, c_1 \sim c_3, \mathcal{I})$ is an interior point of the image set. Thus, for $\mathbf{w}_s \neq \mathbf{w}_{\frac{1}{3}}$,*

$$(4.6.1) \qquad\qquad \mathcal{D}(\mathbf{w}_s) = U^3.$$

So, while the BC realizes about 38% of the entries in the universal set U^3, all other positional voting methods include 100% of the 351 different listings! Thus, *all non-BC methods admit all possible election paradoxes*. As an example, the troubling beverage paradox holds not only for the plurality and antiplurality methods, but for all non-BC procedures. This means that

$$(4.6.2) \qquad\qquad \mathcal{D}(\mathbf{w}_{\frac{1}{3}}) \subsetneq \mathcal{D}(\mathbf{w}_s) = U^3, \quad \forall s \neq \frac{1}{3}.$$

To describe Eq. 4.6.2 in a different manner, suppose a BC critic argues that a conflict between a particular BC ranking and the associated pairwise rankings demonstrates a potential flaw of the BC. (As we've discovered, a more careful analysis probably would show the flaw is in the pairwise rankings, not the BC outcome.) According to Eq. 4.6.2, the same argument using the same listing of rankings holds for all choices of positional voting methods! Thus, if the BC has a flaw, it is universal; it is suffered by all positional methods.

On the other hand, all other positional procedure have words that never occur with the BC. These are the listings of election rankings that are proscribed for the BC in Sect. 4.5. As examples, listings that allow a Condorcet loser to be top-ranked are permitted by any other positional method; only the BC outlaws such an event. A listing indicating that the Condorcet winner is bottom-ranked, or that a Condorcet winner is ranked below a Condorcet loser are admissible election outcomes for all $\mathbf{w}_s$, $s = \frac{1}{3}$; only the BC prohibits such annoying embarrassments. Namely, other procedures admit flaws that never occur with the BC. Actually, this is to be expected from the discussion of reversal bias.

Example 4.6.1. a. Use the numbers from the weekly lotto game to select rankings for the three pairs of candidates and the three-candidate set. Next, assign a non-BC positional method $\mathbf{w}_s$ to the three-candidate subset. According to Theorem 4.6.1, there is a profile where the randomly selected outcome is the sincere election outcome. Now, how can such randomly assigned rankings accurately reflect the voters' beliefs?

b. For $\mathbf{w}_s$, $s \neq \frac{1}{3}$, there exists a profile where the election rankings are

$$\{c_1 \succ c_2, c_2 \succ c_3, c_1 \succ c_3, c_2 \succ c_3 \sim c_1\}.$$

There are two reasons this listing could occur with the BC. The first is that the Condorcet winner, c_1, is (tied for) bottom-ranked, and the second is that the Condorcet loser, c_3, is not strictly ranked below the Condorcet winner.

c. According to the results of the last section, it is impossible for the BC to admit a beverage paradox. Namely, it is impossible for the BC ranking to be $c_1 \succ c_2 \succ c_3$ when the pairwise rankings are $c_3 \succ c_2, c_3 \succ c_1, c_2 \succ c_1$. On the other hand, according to Theorem 4.6.1, for any non-BC positional voting method, there is a profile supporting this outcome. In particular, this conclusion holds for $s = \frac{1}{3} + 0.00000000001$, a system that is essentially the BC.

This last comment is intended to generate skepticism about Theorem 4.6.1. After all, if two voting systems are essentially the same, then differences in outcomes should be apparent only with specially constructed profiles employing a cast of thousands. Yes, and the following shows how to prove this. □

To understand whether these problems are rare anomalies or serious concerns, we need a geometric description of the F_s image set. Following the scheme of Sect. 1.4, the image set is the convex hull of the unanimity profile outcomes

$$\{F_s(\mathbf{E}_j, \mathbf{w}_s) = (F_3(\mathbf{E}_j), f(\mathbf{E}_j, \mathbf{w}_s))\}_{j=1}^6.$$

A straightforward algebraic argument establishes that any five of these vectors are independent if $s \neq \frac{1}{3}$; this proves the first part of Theorem 4.6.1. Multiplying the sum of these vectors by $\frac{1}{6}$ defines the complete indifference ranking, which clearly is an interior point. This completes the proof. $\square$

In describing the geometry, again we stumble upon the problem of representing a higher dimensional object in a lower dimensional picture. To understand what positional election tallies can accompany specified pairwise election tallies, we adopt the approach of the last section. Instead of examining the full five-dimensional space, concentrate on sections representing an issue of particular interest. As this construction is a valuable tool, it is carried out in detail. For example, we know from Sect. 4.5 that if the three pairwise elections end in tie votes, then the BC ranking also is a tie vote. What happens for other positional voting methods?

4.6.1 What Can Accompany a F_3 Tie Vote?

To analyze the profile set $\mathbf{p} \in Si(6)$ where $F_3(\mathbf{p}) = (0,0,0)$, we must expect a two-dimensional set of profiles,

$$F_3^{-1}(\mathbf{0}) = \{\mathbf{p} \mid F_3(\mathbf{p}) = (0,0,0)\}.$$

Because pairwise voting satisfies the reversal property, we have that

(4.6.3)   if $\mathbf{p} = \mathbf{p}^r$, then $\mathbf{p} \in F_3^{-1}(\mathbf{0})$.

Namely, $\mathcal{RE}$ (see Sect. 4.4) is in $F_0^{-1}0$. A basic or Condorcet profile destroys this conclusion, so we have that

Proposition 4.6.2. *The convex set $F_3^{-1}(\mathbf{0}) \subset Si(6)$ is the convex hull $\mathcal{RE}$ defined by $\{\mathbf{r}_j\}_{j=1}^3$.*

For any $\mathbf{w}_s$ we now know all $\mathbf{w}_s$-positional election outcomes, $P_0(s)$, that accompany tie votes for all pairwise elections. Namely, $P_0(s)$ is the $\mathbf{w}_s$ image of $\mathcal{RE}$. Again, the importance of the reversal profiles is highlighted.

The three vertices of $P_0(s)$ are given by the three vectors that can be constructed from the entries $\frac{1-s}{2}, s, \frac{1-s}{2}$. As illustrated in Fig. 4.6.1, each vertex is the intersection of an indifference line with the dashed line connecting $f(\mathbf{E}_i, \mathbf{w}_s)$ and $f(\mathbf{E}_i^r, \mathbf{w}_s)$; these vertices form an equilateral triangle.

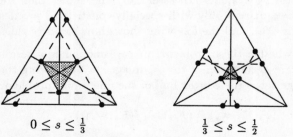

$$0 \leq s \leq \tfrac{1}{3} \qquad\qquad \tfrac{1}{3} \leq s \leq \tfrac{1}{2}$$

Fig. 4.6.1. The $\mathbf{w}_s$ outcomes with ties for the three pairs

Observe how the size of $P_0(s)$ decreases as s approaches $\frac{1}{3}$. The largest regions (corresponding to the largest deviation in election outcomes) occur for $s = 0, \frac{1}{2}$, the plurality and antiplurality vote. Also, observe the interesting reversal when s passes through the BC value of $\frac{1}{3}$; if $s < \frac{1}{3}$, the vertices are along one set of indifference regions, but if $s > \frac{1}{3}$, the vertices are along the remaining set of indifference regions. This bifurcation point where $P_0(s) = \mathcal{I}$ is the BC voting vector. The collapse of $P_0(s)$, of course, illustrates the BC symmetry.

With minimal effort, we can see how this interesting inversion is due to the twisting effect of teh reversal bias on the procedural line.

Example 4.6.2. a. It is easy to design examples by just using the reversal portion of a profile. For example, find the profile where each pair is tied and the $\mathbf{w}_s$ election tally is as extreme as possible while supporting the ranking $c_1 \succ c_2 \sim c_3$. The choice of a profile depends upon whether $s < \frac{1}{3}$, or $s > \frac{1}{3}$. If $s < \frac{1}{3}$, it follows from Fig. 4.6.1a that the election outcome is where the $c_2 \sim c_3$ indifference line meets the left edge of the shaded triangle. This point is midway between $\mathbf{r}_1$ and $\mathbf{r}_2$. Thus, the desired profile is $(\frac{1}{4}, \frac{1}{4}, 0, \frac{1}{4}, \frac{1}{4}, 0) = \frac{1}{2}(\mathbf{r}_1 + \mathbf{r}_2)$. A similar argument, but now using Fig. 4.6.1b., shows that the profile for $s > \frac{1}{3}$ is $\mathbf{r}_3$.

More generally, using the $\{\mathbf{r}_j\}$ vertices of $F_3^{-1}(\mathbf{0})$, it follows that a profile where the pairwise elections end in a tie is given by

$$(4.6.4) \qquad \sum_{j=1}^{3} \lambda_j(\mathbf{r}_j), \quad \lambda_j \geq 0, \sum_{j=1}^{3} \lambda_j = 1.$$

By varying the λ_j values, different $\mathbf{w}_s$-outcomes are created.

b. *Proof of Theorem 4.6.1.* Figure 4.6.1 (and the supporting analysis) can be used to prove Theorem 4.6.1. First, if $s \neq \frac{1}{3}$, the set of $\mathbf{w}_s$-positional election outcomes that accompany a complete pairwise tie vote is given by the non-degenerate triangle which meets all 13 ranking regions of the representational triangle. Thus, any $\mathbf{w}_s$-positional ranking can accompany the pairwise rankings $c_1 \sim c_2, c_2 \sim c_3$, $c_1 \sim c_3$. By the continuity and linearity of F_s, slight changes in the profile off of the set $F_3^{-1}(\mathbf{0})$ lead to slight changes in the outcomes. An appropriate slight change in the profile changes the pairwise rankings to any specified choice. (Only ties are being broken, so not much of a change is required.) However, a sufficiently small change (in normalized profiles), alters the $\mathbf{w}_s$ triangle only slightly. So, the triangle still meets all 13 $Si(3)$ ranking regions; this proves that $\mathcal{D}(\mathbf{w}_s) = U^3$.

The size of the shaded positional election triangle determines the maximum size of a profile change. For instance, the plurality shaded region is so large that even vast changes in a profile keeps the new profile in the shaded region. However, for $s = \frac{1}{3} + 0.000001$, the shaded region is so small that only an incredibly small change in a profile keeps the outcome in the shaded zone. Now, if $\|\mathbf{p}_1 - \mathbf{p}_2\|$ is small, the common denominator of all terms is very large in value. This means that an accompanying integer profile must involve an enormous number of voters. Consequently, *for all outcomes to occur for s values close to $\frac{1}{3}$, a very large number of voters may be required.*

The assertion that the F_s image set is five-dimensional for $s \neq \frac{1}{3}$ also follows from the geometry. At each point (at least around $(0,0,0)$) in the three-dimensional space $[-1,1]^3$, the associated set of possible $\mathbf{w}_s$-positional election outcomes is a two-dimensional equilateral triangle. The conclusion follows by a dimension count. $\square$

4.6.2 A Profile Coordinate Representation Approach

Instead of a tied vote, let $P_{\mathbf{q}}(s)$ be the $\mathbf{w}_s$ outcomes accompanying a $F_3(\mathbf{q}$ pairwise outcome. To illustrate how to compute $P_{\mathbf{q}}(s)$, consider the special case where c_1 beats each of the other candidates by winning two-thirds of the vote and c_2 and c_3 end up in a tie; these pairwise outcomes define $\mathbf{q} = (\frac{1}{3}, 0, -\frac{1}{3})$. We need to determine the cone of profiles supporting this outcome.

By use of elementary algebra, the three (α, β, d) vertices for the $(\frac{1}{3}, 0, -\frac{1}{3})$ cone are

$$((-\frac{1}{3}, 1, \frac{1}{3}), (1, -1, -1), \frac{1}{2}), ((1, 1, -1), (-\frac{1}{3}, -1, \frac{1}{3}), \frac{1}{2}),$$
$$(1, -\frac{1}{3}, \frac{1}{3}), (-\frac{1}{3}, \frac{1}{3}, -1), \frac{1}{2}).$$

When expressed in $Si(6)$ coordinate representation, the vertices are

(4.6.4) $(\frac{1}{6}, \frac{1}{2}, 0, 0, \frac{1}{3}, 0), (\frac{1}{2}, \frac{1}{6}, 0, \frac{1}{3}, 0, 0), (\frac{1}{6}, \frac{1}{6}, \frac{1}{3}, 0, 0, \frac{1}{3}).$

Once the vertices of the cone of profiles is known, the $P_{\mathbf{q}}(s)$ set is determined by the $f(-, \mathbf{w}_s)$ outcome for each vertex. They are

$$(\frac{2}{3}(1-s), \frac{1}{3} - \frac{s}{6}, \frac{5s}{6}), (\frac{2}{3}(1-s), \frac{5s}{6}, \frac{1}{3} - \frac{s}{6}), (\frac{1}{3}(1+s), \frac{1}{3} - \frac{s}{6}, \frac{1}{3} - \frac{s}{6}).$$

The set $P_{(\frac{1}{3}, 0, -\frac{1}{3})}(0)$ (plurality outcomes) is displayed in Fig. 4.6.2a while the antiplurality outcomes, $P_{(\frac{1}{3}, 0, -\frac{1}{3})}(\frac{1}{2})$, are given in Fig. 4.6.2b. The BC outcome for this pairwise outcome is a single, decisive point; the plurality and antiplurality outcomes offer indeterminacy of a set of possible values. This large set, of course, corresponds to all ways reversal bias can be added to the procedure.

Figure 4.6.2b displays other $P_{\mathbf{q}}(s)$ properties. Each dashed line is a procedure line for the appropriate vertex of the profile cone; these lines intersect at the BC outcome. (Remember, the BC outcome is uniquely determined by the pairwise election tallies, so it is a point.) Thus, again, the geometry of the $P_{\mathbf{q}}(s)$ regions changes corresponding to $s < \frac{1}{3}$ and $s > \frac{1}{3}$. The rules of finding outcomes on the procedure line (see Sect. 2.4) determines the set $P_{\mathbf{q}}(s)$. Notice, the pairwise outcome defines a cone of procedure lines where each procedure line passes through the unique BC outcome.

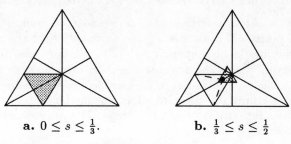

a. $0 \le s \le \frac{1}{3}$.   **b.** $\frac{1}{3} \le s \le \frac{1}{2}$

Fig. 4.6.2. Sections when $F_3 = (\frac{1}{3}, 0, -\frac{1}{3})$

More specifically, for a given $\mathbf{q}$ of pairwise outcomes, compute the unique BC outcome (see Sect. 3.2) $\mathbf{q}_{\frac{1}{3}}$ and the vertices $f(\mathbf{p}, \mathbf{w}_0)$, representing the plurality outcomes. Draw lines passing through the plurality vertices and the BC outcome. Each line contains a vertex for $P_{\mathbf{q}}(s)$; it is the point

$$(4.6.5) \qquad f(\mathbf{p}, \mathbf{w}_s) = (1 - 3s)f(\mathbf{p}, \mathbf{w}_o) + 3s\mathbf{q}_{\frac{1}{3}}.$$

From the three vertices, the set $P_{(\frac{1}{3}, 0, -\frac{1}{3})}(s)$ can be determined.

Some conclusions using the geometry of the two figures and from the method of construction are listed next.

Theorem 4.6.3. a. *Suppose the pairwise election tallies are given by* $\mathbf{q}$.
   a. $P_{\mathbf{q}}(\frac{1}{3})$ *is a point in* $P_{\mathbf{q}}(s)$ *for all* s.
   b.   *If* $s_1 < s_2 \le \frac{1}{3}$ *or if* $\frac{1}{3} \le s_2 < s_1 \le \frac{1}{2}$, *then*

$$(4.6.6) \qquad\qquad P_{\mathbf{q}}(s_2) \subsetneqq P_{\mathbf{q}}(s_1).$$

   c.   *If* $s \ne \frac{1}{3}$, *then the dimension of* $P_{\mathbf{q}}(s)$ *equals the dimension of* $F_3^{-1}(\mathbf{q})$.
   d.   *For any* $\mathbf{q}$, *there is a profile* $\mathbf{p}$ *so that*

$$(4.6.7) \qquad F_3(\mathbf{p}) = \mathbf{q}, \; f(\mathbf{p}, \mathbf{w}_s) = f(\mathbf{p}, \mathbf{w}_{\frac{1}{3}}), \quad \forall s.$$

Part d asserts that *for any BC election tally, there is a profile so that this is the normalized tally for all possible positional election outcomes.* This conclusion is a consequence of part a and the positional line. Because the BC outcome is in $P_{\mathbf{q}}(s)$ for all choices of s, choose the plurality outcome to agree with the BC outcome. By the properties of the procedure line, this is the common outcome for all possible positional election processes.

What we have seen so far is that *only the BC ranking is related, in any manner, with the rankings of the pairs.* The ranking for any other choice of a positional procedure need not reflect in any manner whatsoever the rankings of the pairs. Instead, there is a set of possible outcomes. When this set meets other ranking regions, we have paradoxes! However, the closer a $\mathbf{w}_s$ resembles the BC, the faster it sheds its troubles.

4.6.3 What Pairwise Outcomes Can Accompany a w_s Tally?

Instead of starting with teh pairwise outcome $\mathbf{q}$ and then computing the accompanying set of positional outcomes $P_{\mathbf{q}}(s)$, we could select the $\mathbf{w}_s$-election outcome $\mathbf{q}_s$ and compute the accompanying set of binary outcomes $B_{\mathbf{q}}(s)$. Start with the special setting where the $\mathbf{w}_s$-outcome is $\mathcal{I}$; extensions to the general value of $\mathbf{q}_s$ follow in the same manner, so they are left to the reader.

The issue is to interpret the meaning of a $\mathbf{w}_s$ outcome of $\mathcal{I}$; what kinds of binary (pairwise) election outcomes can arise? The approach follows that developed above. Namely,

$$B_{(\frac{1}{3},\frac{1}{3},\frac{1}{3})}(s) = \{F_3(\mathbf{p}) \,|\, \mathbf{p} \in (f(-, \mathbf{w}_s))^{-1}(\mathcal{I})\}.$$

In words, find the profile vertices defining the $\mathbf{w}_s$-outcome of $\mathcal{I}$, and then compare the pairwise elections for these vertices.

A vertex of $f(-, \mathbf{w}_s))^{-1}(\mathcal{I})$ is a profile with as few voter types as possible. Only the BC allows a profile with only two voter types to support $\mathcal{I}$, so a profile vertex for any other $\mathbf{w}_s$ must involve three voter types. Two such profiles are immediate; they are the Condorcet portion of a profile, $\mathbf{p}_m = (\frac{1}{3}, 0, \frac{1}{3}, 0, \frac{1}{3}, 0)$, $\mathbf{p}_m^r = (0, \frac{1}{3}, 0, \frac{1}{3}, 0, \frac{1}{3})$, which define the two $B_{(\frac{1}{3},\frac{1}{3},\frac{1}{3})}(s)$ vertices

$$(4.6.8) \qquad\qquad (\frac{1}{3}, \frac{1}{3}, \frac{1}{3}), \quad -(\frac{1}{3}, \frac{1}{3}, \frac{1}{3}).$$

The set $f(-, \mathbf{w}_s))^{-1}(\mathcal{I})$ has six more vertices; due to reversal portion of a profile. The idea is simple; if $\mathbf{p}_b$ is a basic profile with outcome $f(\mathbf{p}_b, \mathbf{w}_s) \neq \mathcal{I}$, then by adding an appropriate reversal term, $\mathbf{r}_j$, the new $\mathbf{w}_s$ outcome is moved to $\mathcal{I}$. A way to find this basic profile is to find the extreme values for $f(t\mathbf{p}_b + (1-t)\mathbf{r}_j) = \mathcal{I}$ for each j. Then, the pairwise elections for these points are computed.

A geometric way to accomplish the same conclusion follows. If $s < \frac{1}{3}$, the line of profiles $t\mathbf{E}_1 + (1-t)\mathbf{E}_4$ defines a line of election results that misses $\mathcal{I}$; this is the dashed line starting from the left corner of Fig. 4.6.1a. To pull the election ranking to $\mathcal{I}$, we need a voter of type-five or six. A direct computation shows that if a profile $\mathbf{p} = (p_1, 0, 0, p_4, p_5, 0)$ leads to the $\mathbf{w}_s$ outcome of $\mathcal{I}$ with tally $(\frac{1}{3}, \frac{1}{3}, \frac{1}{3})$, then

$$p_1 = \frac{1}{3(1-s)}, p_4 = \frac{1}{3} + \frac{s^2}{3(1-s)(1-2s)}, p_5 = \frac{1/3 - (p_1+p_4)s}{1-s},$$

$$(4.6.9) \qquad\qquad 0 \leq s \leq \frac{1}{3}.$$

These values make sense. For instance, when $s = 0$, the profile reduces to $(\frac{1}{3}, 0, 0, \frac{1}{3}, \frac{1}{3}, 0)$ which clearly defines the plurality outcome of $\mathcal{I}$. At the other extreme, when $s = \frac{1}{3}$, we have that $p_5 = 0$ and the profile $(\frac{1}{2}, 0, 0, \frac{1}{2}, 0, 0)$ associated with the BC outcome of $\mathcal{I}$ is recovered. Thus, the expression for p_5 truly measures the degree to which a basic profile needs to be modified to create a profile vertex for $(f(-,\mathbf{w}_s))^{-1}(\mathcal{I})$.

We now can obtain all of the remaining six vertices for $(f(-,\mathbf{w}_s))^{-1}(\mathcal{I})$ should $0 \le s \le \frac{1}{3}$. To see how to do this, notice that type-five voters help the type-four voters force the election outcome toward the right-hand edge of the representation triangle. (See a representation triangle.) If the profile had involved the voter types one, four, and six, then the type-six voters would assist the type-one voters in moving the outcome toward the bottom edge of $Si(3)$. Thus, to get the $\mathcal{I}$ outcome, just interchange names of candidates. The following gives the list of all profile vertices where any voter type not mentioned has zero voters.

Types	Vertices $a = \frac{1}{3(1-s)}$	$0 \le s \le \frac{1}{3}$ $b = \frac{1}{3} + \frac{s^2}{3(1-s)(1-2s)}$	$1-(a+b)$ $= \frac{2}{3} - \frac{1-2s+s^2}{3(1-s)(1-2s)}$
$1,4,5$	p_1	p_4	p_5
$1,4,6$	p_4	p_1	p_6
$2,4,5$	p_2	p_5	p_4
$2,3,5$	p_5	p_2	p_3
$1,3,6$	p_3	p_6	p_1
$2,3,6$	p_6	p_3	p_2

(4.6.10)

These are the profile vertices for $(f(-,\mathbf{w}_s))^{-1}(\mathcal{I})$ for $0 \le s \le \frac{1}{3}$.

The vertices for $\frac{1}{3} \le s \le \frac{1}{2}$ can be obtained from the above table by using the reversal properties of Theorem 4.5.6.

Types	Vertices $a = \frac{2-3s}{3(1-s)}$	$\frac{1}{3} \le s \le \frac{1}{2}$ $b = \frac{3s^2-3s+1}{3s(1-s)}$	$1-(a+b)$ $= \frac{-3s^2+4s-1}{3s(1-s)}$
$1,2,4$	p_4	p_1	p_2
$1,3,4$	p_1	p_4	p_3
$1,2,5$	p_5	p_2	p_1
$2,5,6$	p_2	p_5	p_6
$3,4,6$	p_6	p_3	p_4
$3,5,6$	p_3	p_6	p_5

(4.6.11)

With these vertices for $f(-,\mathbf{w}_s))^{-1}(\mathcal{I}), s \in [0,\frac{1}{2}]$, it is an exercise to determine the pairwise election outcomes that can accompany a $\mathbf{w}_s$-ranking of $\mathcal{I}$. Namely, determine the F_3 image of each vertex; $B_{\mathcal{I}}(s)$ is the convex hull of the eight F_3 image points. The set $B_{\mathcal{I}}(s)$ for $s = 0, \frac{1}{2}$ is illustrated in Fig. 4.6.3.

The shaded region $B_{\mathcal{I}}(s)$ for $s = 0, \frac{1}{2}$ given in Fig. 4.6.3 is the cube with vertices $(\pm\frac{1}{3}, \pm\frac{1}{3}, \pm\frac{1}{3})$. This cube dramatically indicates how widely the pairwise tallies can deviate from the plurality ranking of $\mathcal{I}$. (Again, this manifests the

extremes introduced by the reversal portion of a profile.) For example, because
$(\frac{1}{3}, -\frac{1}{3}, -\frac{1}{3}) \in B_{\mathcal{I}}(0)$, it follows that there are profiles where, even though c_1
beats both c_2 and c_3 in pairwise competitions by winning two-thirds of the vote
in each case, and c_3 beats c_2 by getting two-thirds of the vote, the plurality
election ends in a complete tie vote! As this point is a vertex, it is trivial to show
that $(0, \frac{1}{3}, \frac{1}{3}, 0, 0, \frac{1}{3})$ is the supporting profile. It is difficult to justify the complete
tie plurality outcome as reflecting the views of the voters! When decomposed
as $\frac{1}{3}\mathbf{E}_1 + \frac{2}{3}\mathbf{r}_3$ we find, again, that the dubious outcome is caused by the severe
reversal bias. The general case is described next.

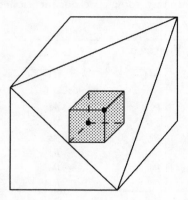

Fig. 4.6.3. The pairwise vote outcomes with plurality ranking $\mathcal{I}$

Theorem 4.6.4. a. For $0 \leq s \leq \frac{1}{3}$,

$$(4.6.12) \qquad\qquad B_{\mathcal{I}}(\mathbf{w}_s) = B_{\mathcal{I}}(\mathbf{w}_s^r).$$

b. The points $\pm(\frac{1}{3}, \frac{1}{3}, \frac{1}{3})$ are vertices of each $B_{\mathcal{I}}(\mathbf{w}_s)$. The remaining six
vertices of $B_{\mathcal{I}}(\mathbf{w}_s)$, $0 \leq s \leq \frac{1}{3}$, are

	Voter types	F_3 image
	1, 4, 5	$(2a - 1, 1 - 2b, 1 - 2a)$
	1, 4, 6	$(2b - 1, 1 - 2a, 2a - 1)$
(4.6.13)	2, 4, 5	$(2a - 1, 2b - 1, 1 - 2a)$
	2, 3, 5	$(1 - 2a, 2a - 1, 1 - 2b)$
	1, 3, 6	$(1 - 2b, 1 - 2a, 2a - 1)$
	2, 3, 6	$(1 - 2a, 2a - 1, 2b - 1)$

where the values of a and b are given in Eq. 4.6.11, 4.6.12. The remaining six *vertices of $B_\mathcal{I}(\mathbf{w}_s^r)$ are*

(4.6.14)

Voter types	F_3 image
$1, 2, 4$	$(1 - 2a, 2b - 1, 2a - 1)$
$1, 3, 4$	$(1 - 2b, 2a - 1, 1 - 2a)$
$1, 2, 5$	$(1 - 2a, 1 - 2b, 2a - 1)$
$2, 5, 6$	$(2a - 1, 1 - 2a, 2b - 1)$
$3, 4, 6$	$(2b - 1, 2a - 1, 1 - 2a)$
$3, 5, 6$	$(2a - 1, 1 - 2a, 1 - 2b)$

c. *If $s \neq \frac{1}{3}$, then $B_\mathcal{I}(\mathbf{w}_s)$ is a three-dimensional object. The set $B_\mathcal{I}(\mathbf{w}_{\frac{1}{3}})$ is the line connecting the two points $\pm(\frac{1}{3}, \frac{1}{3}, \frac{1}{3})$.*

Proof. Equations 4.6.12, 4.6.13 follow from a direct computation. As to be expected from $F_3(\mathbf{p}^r) = (F_3)^r(\mathbf{p})$, the vertices in Eq. 4.6.14 are obtained by reversing the value for the corresponding entry of Eq. 4.6.13. Equation 4.6.12 is a direct consequence of this reversal operation. $\square$

The interpretation of this theorem is clear. By showing that there are an abundance of pairwise tallies that can accompany a non-BC positional voting ranking of $\mathcal{I}$, we find the pernicious influence of the reversal bias. As the value of s gets closer to $\frac{1}{3}$, the six variable vertices of $B_\mathcal{I}(\mathbf{w}_s)$ start approaching the point $(0, 0, 0)$, so the three-dimensional region approximates a straight line. In other words, the closer $\mathbf{w}_s$ is to being the BC, the stronger the restrictions on the choices of the pairwise tallies that can accompany the $\mathbf{w}_s$ ranking $\mathcal{I}$. (With the above argument, this means that to create a "paradox," a large number of voters may be needed.) But this, too, is to be expected. It just assumes that the more a procedure emulates the BC, the less it is influenced by reversal bias. This is shown in Fig. 4.6.1.

4.6.4 Probability Computations

It is obvious that with any reasonable probability distribution and enough voters, the BC is the most likely to respect any condition requiring consistency with the pairwise rankings. After all, the cones illustrate the many profiles where the $\mathbf{w}_s$ rankings differ from the pairwise rankings once $s \neq \frac{1}{3}$. Indeed, from these cones, the profile vertices of the associated set of profiles is a straightforward computation. Then, with any probability distribution, calculus techniques provide the actual values for the probability.

Because of the ease, I was tempted to report this analysis, but I did not for two reasons. This first is that we already know what the answer will be from the cones and geometric techniques developed here. Anyway, probability comparisons are crude measures; a more useful approach is to be able to "see" the actual set of profiles defining different outcomes and to understand the source of the problem. This more refined approach is described with the coordinate representations and the problem is caused by the reversal portion of a profile that the BC ignores. So, why invest in hamburger when prime steak is available?

Extensions. There are many other issues that require finding the pairwise votes that can accompany the outcome $f(\mathbf{p}, \mathbf{w}_s) = \mathbf{q}_s$. As an illustration, for the procedure $(3, 1, 0)$ $(s = \frac{1}{4})$, we might wish to determine the $\mathbf{q}$ normalized pairwise election tally for a ranking $c_1 \succ c_2 \succ c_3$ that will ensure that c_1 could win both pairwise elections. More generally, we might be interested in finding all pairwise tallies, $B_{\mathbf{q}_s}(\mathbf{w}_s)$, that accompany a $f(\mathbf{p}, \mathbf{w}_s) = \mathbf{q}_s$ outcome.

The approach is the same; as

$$B_{\mathbf{q}_s}(\mathbf{w}_s) = \{F_3(\mathbf{p}) \,|\, \mathbf{p} \in (f(-, \mathbf{w}_s))^{-1}(\mathbf{q}_s),$$

we must determine the vertices for the profile set $(f(-, \mathbf{w}_s))^{-1}(\mathbf{q}_s)$. These vertices are found by using the same three voter type profiles used above. Now, however, certain profile vertices can drop out depending on the value of $\mathbf{q}_s$. For instance, it is impossible to find a profile $(p_1, 0, 0, p_4, p_5, 0)$ if $\mathbf{q}_s$ is not in the convex hull defined by $\{[\mathbf{w}_s]_j\}_{j=1,4,5}$. Thus, as $\mathbf{q}_s$ approaches extreme regions, a radical difference in the geometry of $B_{\mathbf{q}_s}(\mathbf{w}_s)$ emerges. These issues are left for the reader to explore.

4.6.5 Exercises

1. If a procedure line is a point $\mathbf{q}$, then this point has all of the properties of the BC outcome. (Why?) Use this argument to prove and extend Theorem 2.6.9.

2. Find the set of $\mathbf{w}_s$ outcomes for the pairwise vote $(\frac{1}{4}, 0, 0)$. Which choices of s allow all 13 outcomes to occur? Find the cone of all profiles supporting this outcome.

3. Find the values of $(x, 0, 0)$ which restrict the accompanying plurality outcomes to only three rankings. What values of $(x, y, 0)$ reduce the outcome to one ranking? In both cases, compare the plurality outcome with the BC outcome.

4. Compare the cones of profiles supporting $B_{\mathcal{I}}(\mathbf{w}_s)$ for $s = 0, \frac{1}{3}$.

5. Show that for any $\mathbf{q}$, $B_{\mathbf{q}}(\mathbf{w}_{\frac{1}{3}})$ is a line parallel to $B_{\mathcal{I}}(\mathbf{w}_{\frac{1}{3}})$. Show for any $\mathbf{q}$ and $s \neq \frac{1}{3}$ that $B_{\mathbf{q}}(\mathbf{w}_{\frac{1}{3}}) \subsetneq B_{\mathbf{q}}(\mathbf{w}_s)$ and that if $0 < s < \frac{1}{3}$, then $B_{\mathbf{q}}(\mathbf{w}_s) \subsetneq B_{\mathbf{q}}(\mathbf{w}_0)$. What does this say about the sets of supporting profiles?

6. (For those readers comfortable with calculus.) Show that $a(s), b(s)$ as defined in Eq. 4.6.11 are increasing functions on $[0, \frac{1}{3}]$. Then, use Eq. 4.6.14 to show that if $0 < s_1 < s_2 \leq \frac{1}{3}$, then

$$(4.6.16) \qquad\qquad B_{\mathcal{I}}(\mathbf{w}_{s_2}) \subsetneq B_{\mathcal{I}}(\mathbf{w}_{s_1}).$$

What is the relationship for $\frac{1}{3} \leq s_2 < s_1 \leq \frac{1}{2}$? Show that Eq. 4.6.16 holds in general; that is, it holds when $\mathcal{I}$ is replaced by $\mathbf{q}$. What do these relationships mean about supporting sets of profiles?

4.7 Multiple Voting Schemes

So far, I assumed that each voter has a *strict* transitive ranking of the candidates. But, anyone who has stood in an election booth confronted with pages of names of obscure candidates while silently wondering *"Who are these people?"* recognizes the conflict between reality and this convenient assumption. To compound the problem, even should everyone have a strict ranking, we all can cite examples of an obstinate voter who accompanies his refusal to rank the candidates with advice about where to spend eternity. Finally, there are situations when a voter doesn't want to rank all candidates.

What do we do? We could insist that the equivocating voters "get off the fence" and make a decision by choosing a strict ranking. This is easy to enforce; just invalidate ballot not complying with the rules. The virtue of this "tough love" approach is to force the voters to think through the issues. But, let's be honest; it is important to understand what to do if voters do not use strict rankings. Anyway, this question introduces a nice theoretical issue.

The strict ranking assumption restricts attention to six voter types, so a new theory requires extending the earlier ideas to all 13 transitive rankings. So, which "extended positional voting procedures" best capture the voters' true wishes? Because the analysis utilizes the geometric techniques developed in the previous sections, I only outline the issues and questions; the technical details are left to the reader.

4.7.1 From Multiple Methods to Approval Voting

Labels for the seven new voter types are defined in Fig. 4.7.1 where the one missing region, $\mathcal{R}(13) = \mathcal{I}$, characterizes a voter who is either totally confused or an indifferent wimp. While such voters exist, they should not (in a reasonable system) affect the outcome. So, by ignoring such studied indifference, the following six new types emerge.

Voter type	Ranking	Unanimity profile
7	$c_1 \succ c_2 \sim c_3$	$\mathbf{E}_7$
8	$c_1 \sim c_3 \succ c_2$	$\mathbf{E}_8$
9	$c_3 \succ c_2 \sim c_1$	$\mathbf{E}_9$
10	$c_2 \sim c_3 \succ c_1$	$\mathbf{E}_{10}$
11	$c_2 \succ c_1 \sim c_3$	$\mathbf{E}_{11}$
12	$c_1 \sim c_2 \succ c_3$	$\mathbf{E}_{12}$

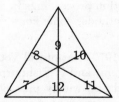

Fig. 4.7.1. The added voter types

The six new voter types can be subdivided into the "singleton-type" (types $\{7, 9, 11\}$) where one candidate is preferred while the other two are treated with indifference, and the "binary-type" (types $\{8, 10, 12\}$) where no difference is seen between the two top-ranked candidates. The assignment of voting vectors to each of the three types is

(4.7.1)

Voter type	Voting vector
Strict ranking	$\mathbf{W}_0 = (w_1, w_2, w_3)$
Singleton	$\mathbf{W}_1 = (w_1^1, w_2^1, w_3^1),\ w_2^1 = w_3^1$
Binary	$\mathbf{W}_2 = (w_1^2, w_2^2, w_3^2),\ w_1^2 = w_2^2$

The listing illustrates that three kinds of voting vectors are needed to accommodate the three classes of voter types. Such a system is imaginatively called *a multiple positional voting system*.

Example 4.7.1. a. *Truncated voting.* Multiple voting systems emerge even when not intended. A typical situation involves an obstinate voter who casts a truncated ballot listing only his top choice. We could toss these ballots out. But, to avoid ill will or a broken nose, it might be wiser to tally them. If the voting vector is $\mathbf{W} = (3, 1, 0)$, then maybe the truncated ballots could be tallied by crediting the lone candidate with 3 points and zero points for the others. Such a benign attitude defines the vector $\mathbf{W}_1 = (3, 0, 0)$. Alternatively, one might divide the remaining point among the bottom two candidates to define $\mathbf{W}_1' = (3, \frac{1}{2}, \frac{1}{2})$. To further complicate the election, suppose some voters can't or won't choose between their top choices of say, Martha and Helvi. Such ballots can be handled by "splitting the difference" of the four available points to define $\mathbf{W}_2 = (2, 2, 0)$.

b. Cumulative voting. The State of Illinois, among other places, experimented with "cumulative voting." (See [SMR].) To illustrate this procedure, let each voter have three points to split among the candidates in units of either integers or $\frac{3}{2}$. The assignment of points, of course, reveals the voter's preferences. For instance, a voter with strict preferences for the candidates uses $\mathbf{W}_0 = (2, 1, 0)$; a voter of the singleton type chooses $\mathbf{W}_1 = (3, 0, 0)$, and a binary type voter uses $\mathbf{W}_2 = (\frac{3}{2}, \frac{3}{2}, 0)$. (A voter using $(1, 0, 0)$ or $(1, 1, 0)$ is called a fool; such voters are ignored here.) Incidentally, while this is an old, widely used procedure that was even endorsed by the conservative Bush and Reagan administrations, when it was discovered during confirmation proceedings in the US Senate that Ms. Lani Guinier had suggested such methods, some conservatives quickly labeled her a dangerous radical.

c. *Approval voting.* In the late 1970's, Approval Voting (AV) was independently invented by R. Weber, by S. Brams and P. Fishburn, and by others. Since then, AV has been carefully analyzed and widely promoted by Brams and Fishburn [BF1, BF2]. Because AV requires a voter to choose either "Yes" or "No" for each candidate, it follows that $\mathbf{W}_1 = (1, 0, 0)$ and $\mathbf{W}_2 = (1, 1, 0)$. On the other hand, it is not clear how a voter with strict preferences should vote; consequently, with AV, $\mathbf{W}_0$ is not well-defined.

Just from the clever choice of the name, approval voting has to sound attractive: a voter can either approve or disapprove of each candidate. Yet, when this freedom is combined with the undefined $\mathbf{W}_0$, new kinds of election difficulties crop up.[10] After all, without a $\mathbf{W}_0$, AV forces a decisive voter to climb back on the fence and start equivocating. Namely, with a positional method, an undecided voter is forced to clarify his views; with AV, a voter with a clear ranking of the candidates is forced to develop indifference among them. These comments are supported by the emphasis in the AV literature describing strategies, such as "a voter's mean utility," which are needed even to vote "sincerely."

To analyze AV, the set of the voters with a strict ranking of type j is split into two subgroups; those adopting the singleton type, j_1, and those who use a binary persuasion, j_2. For AV, then, there are $12 + 6 = 18$ voter types. (For the same reasons described earlier, the ranking region $\mathcal{I}$ is ignored.) □

We now encounter a technical problem; the voting vectors must be normalized. (This reduces an infinite number of choices into a single equivalent one.) As true for positional voting methods, "equivalence" means that the election ranking is preserved for all profiles.

There is no problem normalizing the vector $\mathbf{W}_0$; convert $\mathbf{W}_0$ into a standard $\mathbf{w}_s$, $s \in [0, \frac{1}{2}]$ form. To demonstrate the difficulty in normalizing $\mathbf{W}_1$ and $\mathbf{W}_2$, suppose for the truncated voting example $\mathbf{W}_0 = (3, 1, 0)$ is identified with $\mathbf{w}_{\frac{1}{4}} = (\frac{3}{4}, \frac{1}{4}, 0)$. With a truncated ballot, the voter only identifies his top-ranked candidate. So, $\mathbf{W}_1 = (3, 0, 0)$. But if the normalized form of this $\mathbf{W}_1$ is $\mathbf{w}_0 = (1, 0, 0)$, the normalization *increases* the power of this voter's ballot. To see this, the $\mathbf{W}_0$, $\mathbf{W}_1$ outcome for the profile $\frac{7}{13}\mathbf{E}_1 + \frac{6}{13}\mathbf{E}_9$ is $c_1 \succ c_3 \succ c_2$ with the tally $(\frac{21}{13}, \frac{7}{13}, \frac{18}{13})$, but the normalized $\mathbf{w}_{\frac{1}{4}}$, $(1, 0, 0)$ outcome is $c_3 \succ c_1 \succ c_2$ with the tally $(\frac{21}{52}, \frac{7}{52}, \frac{24}{52})$. As the ranking is not preserved, the normalization is incorrect.

As an example, with the AV, suppose $\mathbf{W}_1 = (1, 0, 0)$ is normalized to $\mathbf{w}_0 = (1, 0, 0)$ and $\mathbf{W}_2 = (1, 1, 0)$ to $\mathbf{w}_{\frac{1}{2}} = (\frac{1}{2}, \frac{1}{2}, 0)$ and consider the profile $\frac{1}{2}\mathbf{E}_7 + \frac{1}{2}\mathbf{E}_{11}$. The election outcome with $\mathbf{W}_1$, $\mathbf{W}_2$ is $\mathcal{I}$ with the tally $(\frac{1}{2}, \frac{1}{2}, \frac{1}{2})$, but if $\mathbf{w}_0$, $\mathbf{w}_{\frac{1}{2}}$ are used, the election ranking is $c_1 \succ c_2 \sim c_3$ with the tally $(\frac{1}{2}, \frac{1}{4}, \frac{1}{4})$. The normalization does not preserve the ranking, so it is wrong.

Normalization process. *Let $\mathbf{W}_0$, $\mathbf{W}_1$, $\mathbf{W}_2$ be the multiple voting vectors assigned to the three kinds of voter types. Let the scalars a and b define the normalized voting vector $\mathbf{w}_s = a\mathbf{W}_0 + b(1, 1, 1)$. The normalized form for the singleton and binary voter types are, respectively, $\mathbf{w}^1 = a\mathbf{W}_1 + b(1, 1, 1)$ and $\mathbf{w}^2 = a\mathbf{W}_2 + b(1, 1, 1)$.*

In other words, the scalars used to normalize one voting vector are used to normalize all of them. It is left to the reader to show that the normalization process preserves the election rankings.

Example 4.7.2. For the truncated voting example, the normalized voting vectors are $\mathbf{w} = (3, 0, 0) \approx \mathbf{w}_{\frac{1}{4}} = (\frac{3}{4}, \frac{1}{4}, 0)$, $\mathbf{W}_1 = (3, 0, 0) \approx \mathbf{w}^1 = (\frac{3}{4}, 0, 0)$, and

---

[10] For instance, the AV inherits the susceptibility of the plurality and the antiplurality methods to reversal bias of a profile. Arguably, these profile characteristics cause a procedure to choose the incorrect election rankings, so the AV uses the worse part of both.

$\mathbf{W}_1' = (3, \frac{1}{2}, \frac{1}{2}) \approx \mathbf{w}^1 = (\frac{3}{4}, \frac{1}{8}, \frac{1}{8}), \mathbf{W}^2 = (2, 2, 0) \approx \mathbf{w}^2 = (\frac{1}{2}, \frac{1}{2}, 0)$. For AV, the vectors specified above are in a normalized form. For the cumulative voting example, $\mathbf{W}_0 \approx \mathbf{w}_{\frac{1}{3}}$, $\mathbf{w}^1 = (1, 0, 0)$, and $\mathbf{w}^2 = (\frac{1}{2}, \frac{1}{2}, 0)$. $\square$

4.7.2 No Good Deed Goes Unpunished

"Fairness" often is used to promote multiple voting systems. After all, why discard a colleague's truncated ballot? An attractive argument used to motivate cumulative voting and AV is that multiple systems appear to create a fairer, more responsive procedure because a voter can more accurately represent his true preferences. Clearly, a better approximation is obtained by using cardinal rather than ordinal rankings. A closely related third theme, coming from Chap. 3, is that the pairwise vote has problems because it ignores vital information. Are other kinds of information being ignored by non-multiple procedures? Why not use methods that incorporate as much information as possible? There is no debate; these noble arguments and positive intentions are "good deeds." Consequently we should understand the promised punishment.

Often (but not always) multiple systems introduce new kinds of problems. What I find particularly disturbing is that these troubles are direct consequences of the good intentions motivating the adoption of a multiple system! After all, the added opportunities for voters to better express themselves suggest that, in some way, multiple systems promote basic democratic principles. Yet, these additional options vitiate the noble objectives by forcing election outcomes that distinctly violate the voters' wishes! These added options permitting a voter to better express his or her views can distort the outcome so that it violates the voters' beliefs. What a paradox!

To understand this problem, we can use standard algebraic intuition. As even elementary school students learn, when the number of variables increases, so does the complexity of the system – extra variables introduce new problems and difficulties. With two equations in two unknowns, the image sets and solution sets are reasonably simple. But, nobody would expect a similar statement to apply for two equations in five unknowns. Instead, with five unknowns, we must anticipate new complexities to torment the analysis.

This algebraic intuition is relevant because, as developed here, voting theory is intimately connected with algebra and geometry. In fact, this intuition, while not expressed in terms of variable counting, already is firmly established in choice theory. Support comes from profile restrictions used to obtain election relationships. As shown in Chap. 3 with single peakedness conditions, etc., "nice" election relationships emerge. This is because effective profile restrictions are equivalent to decreasing the number of variables.

Armed with this common sense, observe that for multiple systems, the number of variables is *increased*, not decreased. Instead of a profile restriction, we have a profile addition. Thus, instead of realizing sharper election relationships, we must expect the added variables to cause new problems. For example, a positional voting system is based on six variables; with a multiple system the number of variables is doubled to twelve. (So, a positional method is a profile restriction of a multiple system.)

Must There Be Problems? The Causes. A multiple system need not cause problems. To illustrate, there is not much difference between the image sets of $f_1(x,y) = x + 2y$, $f_2(x,y) = 2x - y$ and $g_1(x,u,v) = x + 2(u+v)$, $g_2(x,u,v) = 2x - (u+v)$, because the second system comes from the first by substituting $y = u+v$. Indeed, this kind of algebraic dependency creates the election relationships enjoyed by the BC. (Technically, these dependencies reduce the number of effective equations.) Therefore, it is worth wondering whether multiple systems enjoy a similar phenomenon with carefully coordinated choices of $\mathbf{w}_s, \mathbf{w}^1, \mathbf{w}^2$. They can, and when they do we must anticipate that the advantages of a multiple system can be bought at a minimal extra cost.

Some Voters Are More Equal than Others. It is not really the number of variables that creates problems; as demonstrated in Example 3.2.1, it is the geometry of the image set. In a sense already described in this chapter, the "smaller" the dimension and size of the image set, the more consistency we can expect among the election relationships. The problem with admitting more variables, then, is that they tend to force the image set to grow. This must be expected with multiple systems; after all, we are trying to force a higher dimensional space of profiles into the usual $[-1, 1]^3 \times Si(3)$ range space.

The "size" problem emerges dramatically with multiple voting systems because the image can be larger than the representation triangle! To see why, start with the election mapping

$$(4.7.2) \quad f(\mathbf{p}_j, \mathbf{w}_s, \mathbf{w}^1, \mathbf{w}^2) = \sum_{j=1}^{6} p_j [\mathbf{w}_s]_j + \sum_{j=7,9,11} p_j [\mathbf{w}^1]_j + \sum_{j=8,10,12} p_j [\mathbf{w}^2]_j$$

where $[\mathbf{w}^k]_j$ has the obvious definition. The domain is

$$(4.7.3) \quad Si(12) = \{\mathbf{p} = (p_1, \ldots, p_{12}) \in R_+^{12} \,|\, p_j \geq 0, \sum_{j=1}^{12} p_j = 1\}.$$

Proposition 4.7.1. *If the sum of the components for each of* $\mathbf{W}, \mathbf{W}_1, \mathbf{W}_2$ *are the same, then the image set of Eq. 4.7.2 is a subset of the two-dimensional representation triangle. In the contrary case, the image set is a three-dimensional convex set.*

Proof. The proof is simple; the image set is the convex hull defined by the twelve points

$$\{[\mathbf{w}_s]_j\}_{j=1}^{6}, \{[\mathbf{w}^1]_j\}_{j=7,9,11}, \{[\mathbf{w}^2]_j\}_{j=8,10,12}.$$

If all vectors are in the representation triangle, then the convex hull is two-dimensional. If the sum of the components of either $\mathbf{w}^1$ or $\mathbf{w}^2$ differ from unity, then the permutations of these particular vectors are either above (where the sum is greater than unity), or below (where the sum is less than unity) the representation triangle. This forces the convex hull to be three-dimensional. □

Example 4.7.3. To illustrate, the truncated voting example has all of the $[\mathbf{w}_{\frac{1}{4}}]_j$ and $[(\frac{3}{4}, \frac{1}{8}, \frac{1}{8})]_j$ terms on $Si(3)$ (because the sum of the components adds to unity), but the three vectors $[(\frac{3}{4}, 0, 0)]_j$ are below the representation triangle because the sum of the components equals $\frac{3}{4}$. Consequently, if truncated ballots are counted as $(\frac{3}{4}, \frac{1}{8}, \frac{1}{8})$, then the image is in the representation triangle, while if $(\frac{3}{4}, 0, 0)$ is used, we have a three-dimensional image with six vertices on the plane $x + y + z = 1$ and three more on the plane $x + y + z = \frac{3}{4}$.

A striking example comes from AV. Here, the vertices associated with $(1, 0, 0)$ are in the plane $x + y + z = 1$, while those vertices derived from $(1, 1, 0)$ are in the plane $x + y + z = 2$. The AV image set, given in Fig. 4.7.2, is a copy of the representation cube. □

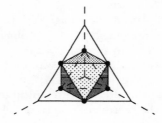

Fig. 4.7.2. The 3-dimensional image set for AV

For positional voting, the image space always is in the representational triangle; for multiple voting, it need not be. An outline of some consequences of this thickness follows. The reader is encouraged to find other issues and to develop the geometry for supporting arguments.

- With k voters, a voter of the jth type adds $\frac{1}{k}[\mathbf{w}]_j$ points toward the final outcome. The value $\frac{1}{k}$ doesn't change, but a multiple system makes the choice of $\mathbf{w}$ (in the vector ballot $[\mathbf{w}]_j$) n option for the voter. By simple geometry (or common sense), a longer vector has a greater impact on the final election ranking. For example, being able to use $(2, 0, 0)$ rather than $(1, 0, 0)$ is a legal license to vote twice. There is no question; when a multiple procedure has a three-dimensional image space, *some voters are more equal than others*. This lack of equality may be by design; e.g., to penalize voters not using a strict ranking of the candidates, choose $\mathbf{w}^1$, $\mathbf{w}^2$ so that the sum of points is less than unity.

- One way to determine whether election rankings reflect the views of the voters is to compare the rankings of the pairs of candidates with the three-candidate outcome. This is done with help from the dictionaries and cross sections of Sects. 4.5, 4.6. Recall, given the tallies of the pairwise rankings, we can compute the cross section for all positional outcomes. Correspondingly, for a specified positional election tally, the set of associated binary outcomes can be found. Now, when the image set of a multiple system is three-dimensional, it is clear that the corresponding sections are much larger. (The reader is encouraged to choose a system and compute some of these sections.) As "large" usually translates into "more paradoxes and problems," we must expect new problematic election outcomes.

4.7.3 Comparisons

Just as the plurality and antiplurality methods define the extreme limits for positional voting, AV is an extreme multiple method. Consequently, AV is an excellent choice to demonstrate the problems caused by the added variables. (These problems are shared by other multiple methods; see the exercises.) As a way to compare what can happen with the AV, assume that the plurality election outcome is $(\frac{1}{2}, \frac{1}{4}, \frac{1}{4})$; a situation where half of the voters have c_1 top-ranked, and the rest are split between the other two candidates. This point is the dot in Fig. 4.7.4a. So, who should be top-ranked?

The procedure line helps address this issue for positional voting methods, where, because c_1 is either a Condorcet winner, or very close to being one, the BC tally for c_1 is at least $\frac{1}{3}$ of the total number of points. (Thus, c_1 cannot be BC bottom-ranked.) These two points determine all associated positional outcomes. However, one must expect the added variables to allow an even larger set of outcomes. It does; the shaded region is the set of AV outcomes that can accompany this c_1 plurality outcome.[11] So, even though it is arguable that c_1 should be at least second-ranked, any of the 13 rankings are admissible AV outcomes. This conclusion, due to the added variables, is difficult to accept.

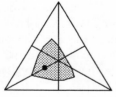 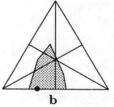

b

Fig. 4.7.3. Comparison of AV outcomes. **a.** AV outcomes for majority $\mathbf{w}_0$ vote. **b.** AV outcomes and Pope selection

(This region is created by finding the vertices of the convex hull of profiles leading to this plurality outcome. For example, one vertex is $\frac{1}{2}\mathbf{E}_1 + \frac{1}{4}\mathbf{E}_3 + \frac{1}{4}\mathbf{E}_5$. From the profile vertices, the corresponding AV outcomes are computed. The set of all AV outcomes, then, is the convex set defined by these AV vertices.)

As a more extreme example, the dot on the bottom edge of Fig. 4.7.3b corresponds to the Pope selection process where c_1 passes the two-thirds vote barrier,

---

[11] In fact, the AV outcome is three-dimensional. To simplify the viewing, all election outcomes are normalized.

c_2 is in second place, and c_3 receives no votes. This decisive sentiment of the voters, which finally sends the correct colored smoke up the chimney, need not be reflected by an AV outcome. The decisive sentiment of the voters makes it difficult to justify selecting any candidate other than c_1. However, as illustrated by the shaded area of possible accompanying AV outcomes, any of the three candidates could be top-ranked if the AV is used. Again, the large region of election outcomes is caused by the added options available to the voters.

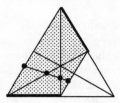

Fig. 4.7.4. Finding AV indetermancy

The above examples suggest that the AV is *indeterminate* in the sense that each profile defines not one outcome, but many of them.[12] To see why this indeterminacy occurs for *all possible* profiles, consider Fig. 4.7.4. In this figure, the profile is $\lambda \mathbf{E}_1 + (1 - \lambda)\mathbf{E}_4$ where $\lambda = 1$ is an unanimity profile; yet it supports the dark bottom line of AV outcomes that intersects three ranking regions. Thus, *even if the voters are unanimous in their beliefs, the AV outcome can be indeterminate*. A similar statement holds for $\mathbf{E}_4$ and $\lambda = 0$.

If $\lambda \in (0, 1)$, then the AV outcome is in the shaded region where one vertex is on the left edge of the shaded region (an edge of $Si(3)$), and one is on the right edge. In fact, the four vertices are determined in the following way. First, let all type-one voters and type-four voters use $(1, 0, 0)$. The value of λ determines the point on the left edge of the representation triangle. Next, let all of the voters use $(1, 1, 0)$; the λ value determines the point on the right edge of the shaded region. The remaining two vertices are determined in a similar way, but where one type uses $(1, 0, 0)$ while the other type uses $(1, 1, 0)$. The convex region defined by these four dots is the AV hull.

Incidentally, if $\lambda > 0$, then the AV hull intersects $\mathcal{R}(c_2 \succ c_1)$. Thus, even should almost all voters have the ranking $c_1 \succ c_2 \succ c_3$, it is possible for c_2 to be AV top-ranked. This, of course, is due to the extra variables made available by multiple systems. Ironically, the added options available to the voters can vitiate the good intentions motivating the design of the procedure.

4.7.4 Averaged Multiple Voting Systems

How should $\mathbf{W}_1$ and $\mathbf{W}_2$ be chosen? To keep the image space two-dimensional, the sum of the components for each vector must be the same as for $\mathbf{W}_0$. To avoid introducing undue bias for one candidate over another, the choices should

---

[12] For a discussion about the pros and cons of *indeterminacy*, see [SvN1, SvN2, BFM].

use the obvious averages. For example, with a given $\mathbf{W}_0$, a type-seven voter, with his indecision between whether he is really of type-one or type-two, should be assigned the average, or $\mathbf{W}_1 = [\mathbf{W}_1]_7 = \frac{1}{2}[\mathbf{W}_0]_1 + \frac{1}{2}[\mathbf{W}_0]_2$. Similarly, a type-twelve voter should be assigned $\mathbf{W}_2 = [\mathbf{W}_2]_{12} = \frac{1}{2}[\mathbf{W}_0]_1 + \frac{1}{2}[\mathbf{W}_0]_6$. Because all three vectors are uniquely determined by the choice of $\mathbf{w}_s$, this is called the *averaged $\mathbf{w}_s$-multiple voting system*.

With the truncated ballot example of $\mathbf{W}_0 = (3, 1, 0)$, the averaged $\mathbf{W}_0$-multiple system is $\mathbf{W}_1 = (3, \frac{1}{2}, \frac{1}{2})$ and $\mathbf{W}_2 = (2, 2, 0)$. Similarly, the averaged plurality system is where the voting vector is $\mathbf{w}_0$ and the antiplurality vector, $\mathbf{w}^2 = \mathbf{w}_{\frac{1}{2}}$, is used with indecisive voters. The improvement the averaged plurality system has over the AV is that by keeping the image set on the representational triangle, it reduces the number and kinds of paradoxes: it prohibits voter from being more equal than others. It is left to the reader to compare the geometry of averaged multiple voting systems with the original system.

It remains to determine which system "best" reflects the pairwise rankings. There are several ways to do this. First, just mimic the derivations used to relate the BC with the pairwise majority votes. The derivation of Sect. 3.2 establishes that $(2, 1, 0)$ agrees with the number of points a $c_1 \succ c_2 \succ c_3$ voter would assign each candidate over the three pairwise elections. To determine what happens for an indecisive voter, give a type-seven voter with the ranking $c_1 \succ c_2 \sim c_3$ a single point to split in each pairwise election. This leads to the following:

(4.7.4)

Set	$\{c_1\}$	$\{c_2\}$	$\{c_3\}$
$\{c_1, c_2\}$	1	0	
$\{c_1, c_3\}$	1		0
$\{c_2, c_3\}$		$\frac{1}{2}$	$\frac{1}{2}$
Total	2	$\frac{1}{2}$	$\frac{1}{2}$

Thus, $\mathbf{w}^1 = (2, \frac{1}{2}, \frac{1}{2})$. Similarly, by examining how many points a voter with the ranking $c_1 \sim c_2 \succ c_3$ assigns to each candidate, we arrive at the vector $\mathbf{w}^2 = (\frac{3}{2}, \frac{3}{2}, 0)$. This is *the Averaged BC (ABC) multiple voting system*.

All of the earlier results about the central role played by the BC within positional voting systems extend to multiple voting systems. For example,

- If the pairwise majority vote ranking is a complete tie, then the ABC outcome must be $\mathcal{I}$. No other averaged $\mathbf{w}_s$ system has this property.
- A Condorcet winner always receives over $\frac{1}{3}$ of the total number of ABC points cast; a Condorcet loser receives less than $\frac{1}{3}$. Consequently, a Condorcet winner never can be ABC bottom-ranked; a Condorcet loser never can be ABC top-ranked, and a Condorcet loser never can be ABC-ranked equal to or above a Condorcet winner. This is the only averaged positional voting method for which these statements are true. For all other averaged $\mathbf{w}_s$ systems, the Condorcet winner can be bottom-ranked while the Condorcet loser can be top-ranked.

- The ABC dictionary is a proper subset of the dictionary for any other multiple voting system.

- Choose an admissible choice of outcomes for the three binary elections. Next, compute the sections of the associated averaged $\mathbf{w}_s$ outcomes. The section of ABC outcomes is a proper subset of the section for any other averaged $\mathbf{w}_s$ outcome. Indeed, the ABC outcomes are a subset of the section for any multiple system.

- The procedure line for averaged $\mathbf{w}_s$ systems is defined in the same manner as for positional methods. Namely, the averaged plurality and antiplurality outcomes are computed; the connecting line is the procedure line for average systems. The averaged $\mathbf{w}_s$-outcome is at the point $1 - 2s$ of the length of the line measured from the averaged plurality outcome. As true for the positional procedure line, the positioning of the ABC outcome is pivotal.

The strong arguments justifying the use of the BC extend to support the use of the ABC multiple voting system when accommodationg indecisive voters. Namely, the ABC system admits fewer paradoxes and disturbing situations where the outcome violates the voters wishes. In fact, the above containment assertions require any criticism or fault of the ABC to be a fault of all multiple systems. The converse, of course, is false; many problems of the average $\mathbf{w}_s$, $s \neq \frac{1}{3}$ system are not admissible with the ABC.

A second approach is to develop a profile decomposition to discover the flaws of different methods. Adding to the Condorcet portion of a profile are mutliples of $\mathbf{E}_1 + \mathbf{E}_q + \mathbf{E}_{11}$ and $\mathbf{e}_8 + \mathbf{E})10 + \mathbf{E}_{12}$. (See Fig. 4.7.1.) A simple computation proves that this extension to the Condorcet portion of a profile has no effect on the multiple system, but it spins the paiwise vote with teh two new kinds of confused voter. Similarly, augmenting the reversal poirtion of a profile is $\mathbf{r}_j = \frac{1}{2}[\mathbf{E}_j + \mathbf{E}_{j+3}]$ for $j = 7, 8, 9$. Again, these reversal terms have no effect on the ABC reanking, but they do on other multiple methods.

4.7.5 Procedure Strips

As final suggestions how to analyze multiple systems, I show how to compare the *AV procedure strip* with the averaged procedure strip. To do so for a given profile, compute the procedure line and then the convex hull of AV outcomes. (A convex hull emerges for the AV because each strict voter type must be divided into two different groups.) This is illustrated in Fig. 4.7.5 for the beverage profile.

This drawing shows that while seven rankings can occur with different choices of $\mathbf{w}_s$, all 13 rankings are admissible outcomes for the AV. This figure suggests several relationships.

- For $\mathbf{p} \in Si(6)$, the procedure line is a subset of the AV procedure strip. Any $\mathbf{w}_s$-ranking is an admissible AV outcome. Thus the AV inherits all paradoxes and faults admitted by any positional voting system.

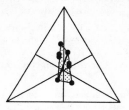

Fig. 4.7.5. The procedure line and AV procedure strip

- For all profiles the AV hull intersects at least three ranking regions. For any profile, then, the AV never can promise a single outcome; AV always has an element of indeterminacy. This is illustrated in Fig. 4.7.4, where the unanimity profile $\mathbf{E}_1$ has three different AV outcomes. It is further illustrated in Fig. 4.7.6 with the integer profile $(4, 4, 2, 2, 0, 6)$ where the *procedure line* is the single point $(\frac{4}{9}, \frac{3}{9}, \frac{2}{9})$ and the pairwise rankings are $c_1 \succ c_2, c_1 \succ c_2, c_2 \succ c_3$. Thus, *for all* $\mathbf{w}_s$, *the normalized election tally is the same fixed value with the ranking* $c_1 \succ c_2 \succ c_3$; *a ranking that coincides with the pairwise rankings.* The shaded area, which indicates the eight admissible AV outcomes for this profile, introduces a wide variety of paradoxes and troubling election outcomes. For instance, even though c_3 is the Condorcet loser and bottom-ranked for all positional methods, she can be AV tied for top spot.

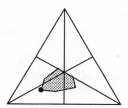

Fig. 4.7.6. The AV hull for a **p** specific tally

4.7.6 Exercises

1. Show that voters with the indifferent type-13 can influence the outcome of a threshold election.

2. Create an example where the procedure line is in $\mathcal{R}(1)$ but the AV hull is in all 13 ranking regions.

3. Find the three-dimensional set of cumulative election outcomes.

4. Find the averaged plurality and the AV hulls for $\frac{1}{2}(\mathbf{E}_1 + \mathbf{E}_2)$. To show the difference, the full three-dimensional nature of the AV hull must be displayed.

5. Prove all of the bulleted comments.

6. Show that the normalization procedure preserves election ranking.

7. Compute the set of AV outcomes described in Fig. 4.7.3 a and b. Find all positions of the procedure line. Observe how the procedure line always is a subset of the shaded region.

8. The indicated set of AV outcomes for a fixed λ in Fig. 4.7.4 appears to be a one-dimensional line segment. Show that, in general, it is two-dimensional. Find λ values where it is a line. Also show for the indicated profile that it is no accident that each of the dots is on a line defining the representation triangle. Use this geometry to find a quicker way to determine the set of AV outcomes.

9. Suppose the BC $(2,1,0)$ is used in an election where truncated voting is anticipated. There are three ways to handle such a ballot; one could use the ABC, one could assign one point to the only candidate on the ballot, or one could assign two points to this candidate. Choose a profile and compare the different outcomes. By using the methods of this section, critique the different choices.

10. Use Table 4.7.4 to show that the pairwise tallies of the pairwise elections determines the ABC outcome.

11. Compare the convex hull of election outcomes for a $\mathbf{w}_s$ procedure and an averaged $\mathbf{w}_s$ procedure.

12. a. A procedure occasionally used extends the cumulative voting method by allowing the voter to split a specified number of points in any desired manner. Thus, each voter has all $\mathbf{w}_s$ options. To analyze this method, compute the hull of outcomes for $\mathbf{p} = (0, \frac{2}{5}, 0, \frac{4}{15}, \frac{1}{3}, 0)$. Prove that this procedure has more than one ranking for each profile; and that the procedure line always is properly contained in the hull of outcomes.

b. Show that the AV does not respect reversal for $\mathbf{r}_j$, $j = 7, 8, 9$. Show that for these profiles, the AV problems arise because some voters have more power than others.

4.8 Other Election Procedures

Instead of relying on positional methods to rank and choose candidates we could use an agenda, a runoff election, create more imaginative runoffs, and on and on. Indeed, with minimal imagination all sorts of new methods can be generated. The next step, to analyze these procedures to determine what can go right or wrong, is not overly difficult for those methods based on pairwise or positional voting. I demonstrate how to do this with a sample of procedures; the reader is encouraged to invent and analyze others.

4.8.1 Other Pairwise Procedures

Traditionally, procedures are analyzed by designing profiles to demonstrate a method's strengths or failings. To show, for instance, that a Condorcet winner might lose a runoff election, we need a profile where the Condorcet winner is bottom-ranked in the first election. These two general steps are represented with the diagram

(4.8.1) $\boxed{\textbf{Profiles}} \rightarrow \boxed{\begin{array}{c}\textbf{Election} \\ \textbf{outcomes}\end{array}} \rightarrow \boxed{\begin{array}{c}\textbf{Procedure} \\ \textbf{outcome}\end{array}}$.

The main computational difficulty with this program has been to invent profiles to exhibit the desired election behavior over the subsets of candidates. This step of finding a profile no longer is necessary because we now know all possible outcomes; they are catalogued by the dictionaries and the geometry of the F_s image sets. Moreover, if we want an illustrating profile, it now is easy to create one with the profile decomposition.

Example 4.8.1. An agenda lists the order candidates are to be compared in pairwise competitions; e.g., $< c_1, c_3, c_2 >$ advances the $\{c_1, c_3\}$ majority winner to a runoff with c_2. So, to show why the last listed candidate always can win, we need a cycle. This is easy to do because we know that cycles exist and that they are caused by a strong Condorcet portion of a profile.

A $\mathbf{w}_s$–runoff advances the two $\mathbf{w}_s$ top-ranked candidates to the runoff. Choose an issue to explore; say, suppose we want to determine whether the Condorcet winner could lose. This happens only should she be bottom-ranked in the first election, so we just need election rankings like $(c_1 \succ c_2, c_1 \succ c_3, c_2 \succ c_3, c_2 \succ c_3 \succ c_1)$. But, we know from the $\mathbf{w}_s$–dictionaries that these rankings occur for all $s \neq \frac{1}{3}$. Moreover, finding profile examples is a simple exercise of adding an appropriate reversal portion to a basic profile. □

In other words, we can treat election procedures as the composition of mappings. The first one converts profiles into election tallies and rankings. The easier second mapping combines election outcomes in a way to determine the outcome. Significantly simplifying this two-step process are the results from the previous sections. Whatever the method, we now can quickly characterize basic properties.

To illustrate, start with *Copeland's method*; this procedure was invented to rectify the "sometimes it is useful, but sometimes it is not" flaw of the Condorcet winner. Here, one point is assigned to a winner of a pairwise election, half a point to each contestant in a tie, and zero to a loser; candidates are ranked according to the number of assigned points where "more is better." As each candidate is assigned a number, Copeland's method spits out transitive rankings. But, are they any good?

While analyzing Copeland's method might seem to be difficult, it is not. Indeed, as soon as issues are raised, finding answers is just an exercise. For instance, could all positional methods have the same strict ranking while the Copeland ranking is $\mathcal{I}$? or the Copeland ranking is a strict ranking that differs from the consensus positional ranking? Could, say, the plurality and Copeland rankings be the reverse of each other? All questions have an immediate yes answer. To prove the first, for instance, just note that all $\mathbf{w}_s$ dictionaries admit a word with a pairwise cycle (so the Copeland ranking is $\mathcal{I}$) and the $c_1 \succ c_2 \succ c_3$ $\mathbf{w}_s$-ranking. An illustrating profile can be created by starting with a basic profile which has $c_1 \succ c_2 \succ c_3$ as the ranking for all positional procedures. Next, add a sufficiently strong Condorcet portion to the profile to ensure that the pairwise rankings are caught in a cycle. The last assertion just involves an appropriately chosen reversal portion for the profile.

On the other hand, it is possible to show that the Copeland and "most" positional rankings cannot radically differ. Such an assertion follows because the relationship between the BC and pairwise rankings (Sect. 4.6) severely constrain how the BC and Copeland rankings can differ. For instance, because a strict Copeland ranking requires the pairwise rankings to define a Condorcet winner and loser, we have that the Copeland winner cannot be worse than BC second ranked. To complete the story, exploit the pivoting role played by the BC for the procedure line; while the reversal portion of a profile can twist part of the procedure line into any ranking region, the other half of the line cannot differ radically from the BC ranking. Pulling all of this together, Merlin and I [SM] obtained results such as the following.

Theorem 4.8.1. *If the Copeland ranking is $c_1 \succ c_2 \succ c_3$, then at least for $s \geq \frac{1}{3}$ or $s \leq \frac{1}{3}$, the $\mathbf{w}_s$-outcome has c_1 strictly ranked above c_3.*

For added discussion about Copeland's method, including how to extend these statement to $n \geq 4$, see [SM, MS].

4.8.2 Runoffs

Recall, a $\mathbf{w}_s$-*simple runoff* advances the two $\mathbf{w}_s$ top-ranked candidates to a runoff. Properties of this procedure are immediate. For instance, because $\mathcal{D}(\mathbf{w}_s) = \mathcal{U}^3$ if and only if $s \neq \frac{1}{3}$, it follows that *the only restriction on a non-BC simple runoff is that a Condorcet loser never wins.* This negative assertion holds because the two top-ranked candidates in the $\mathbf{w}_s$-election need not be related, in any manner, with the pairwise majority vote ranking. For example, the Condorcet winner could be bottom-ranked at the first stage to make her ineligible for the runoff, etc. On the other hand, if a Condorcet loser is advanced to the runoff, she loses in the pairwise comparison. Again, not only do we know this, but we know how to generate illustrating profiles. (To avoid a cycle, place the emphasis on the reversal portion of a profile.)

However, the BC does admit election relationships, so we can expect regularity with a BC runoff. As by Nanson [N] in 1884, because a Condorcet winner cannot be BC bottom-ranked, she must be advanced to the runoff. In the runoff she wins. But, even though *this assertion is true only for the BC*, we can extract more. For instance, as shown in the last section, the closer s is to $\frac{1}{3}$, the more $\mathbf{w}_s$ begins to behave like the BC. In particular, the set of profiles allowing a Condorcet winner to lose with a $\mathbf{w}_s$-runoff has to shrink. Using this observation and the techniques of the last section, Merlin and Tataru [MT] generalized Nanson's observation by characterizing the kinds of profiles and likelihood a Condorcet winner could lose.

Different Procedures; Different Outcomes. To be slightly more inventive, notice that a runoff winner is determined by the election ranking of a particular pair of candidates; we have no interest in the rankings for the other two pairs. On the other hand, the outcome of an agenda is determined by the rankings of two pairs of candidates; the ranking of the third pair is immaterial. From this statement, we must expect that rankings of the pairs can be chosen so that, for a fixed profile, the runoff and an agenda select different candidates! The following indicates the kind of possible results.

Theorem 4.8.2. a. *A Condorcet loser never can be the winner of a $\mathbf{w}_s$-runoff. If a Condorcet winner exists, she is guaranteed to be the winner of a $\mathbf{w}_s$-runoff election iff $\mathbf{w}_s$ is the BC.*

b. *If $\mathbf{w}_{s_1} \neq \mathbf{w}_{s_2}$, then there exists a profile where the winners of the two simple runoff elections do not agree. Even more, there is an agenda where the third candidate wins.*

c. *Specify an agenda and a $\mathbf{w}_s$-runoff where $s \neq \frac{1}{3}$. Choose two candidates, say c_1 and c_2. There exists profiles so that c_1 is the winner of the agenda and c_2 is the winner of the runoff. For the BC runoff, this assertion is true only for the agenda $< c_2, c_3, c_1 >$.*

Proof. Part b follows by using the procedure line. Choose rankings so that different candidates are dropped at the first stage and one dropped candidates is the winner of the other runoff election. To handle the agenda portion, with an appropriate Condorcet portion added to this profile, a cycle will emerge. So, choose an agenda with the remaining candidate last listed.

For part c and the agenda $< c_2, c_3, c_1 >$, the specified outcomes occur for the word $(c_2 \succ c_1, c_1 \succ c_3, c_3 \succ c_2, c_2 \succ c_1 \succ c_3)$ which is in all $\mathbf{w}_s$-dictionaries. For c_1 to win with the agenda $< c_1, c_3, c_2 >$ or with $< c_1, c_2, c_3 >$, she needs to beat both candidates; thus c_1 must be the Condorcet winner. So, for c_2 to win the runoff, she must avoid being compared with c_1. To avoid comparing c_1 with c_2 in the runoff, c_1 must be bottom-ranked in the first election, and, for c_2 to win, we need $c_2 \succ c_3$ in a pairwise match. Such a situation is impossible for the BC (because it forces the Condorcet winner, c_1, to be bottom-ranked), but many words of this type, such as $(c_1 \succ c_2, c_1 \succ c_3, c_2 \succ c_3, c_3 \succ c_2 \succ c_1)$, are admitted by all other choices of $\mathbf{w}_s$. $\square$

4.8.3 Scoring Runoffs

The idea behind the design of a runoff is to drop the candidate least supported by the voters so that the remaining candidates can be compared directly. Presumably the $\mathbf{w}_s$ bottom-ranked candidate has the least amount of support, so she is dropped from further consideration in a $\mathbf{w}_s$-runoff. But, there are other ways to identify who should be eliminated.

An important example is the *Coombs Runoff* which drops the "winner" of the $\mathbf{sc}_1 = (0, 0, 1)$ contest. Namely, we should have an election to determine who the voters truly dislike so she can be dropped from further consideration. But, there are alternative ways to identify the most disliked candidate; e.g., drop the winner of the $\mathbf{sc}_{\frac{1}{2}} = (0, \frac{1}{2}, \frac{1}{2})$ "scoring election" because she is viewed most often as being either mediocre or bottom-ranked. The "scoring vector" $\mathbf{sc}_{\frac{1}{6}} = (0, \frac{1}{6}, \frac{5}{6})$ imposes a compromise by placing a heavier emphasis on a voter's bottom-ranked candidate.

To analyze such methods, first notice that these scoring vectors are not voting vectors because they assign more points to lower ranked candidates. On the other hand, it is obvious how to tally such $\mathbf{sc}_s = (0, s, 1 - s)$ elections. Indeed, it is easy to show that

$$(4.8.2) \qquad\qquad f(\mathbf{p}, \mathbf{sc}_s = f(\mathbf{p}^r, \mathbf{w}_s)$$

This means, for example, that a way to determine the candidate to drop from a Coombs runoff is to hold a plurality election by using the reversal of each voter's ranking of the candidates, and then have a plurality election. Not only does this make sense, it is the intent of the procedure.

Remember the $\mathbf{w}_s$-reversal theory developed in Sect. 4.4? By using it, we have that the ranking defined by $f(\mathbf{p}^r, \mathbf{w}_s)$ is the reversal of the ranking defined by $f((\mathbf{p}^r)^r, \mathbf{w}_s^r) = f(\mathbf{p}, \mathbf{w}_s^r)$. Pulling these double negatives together leads to the useful relationship

$$(4.8.3) \qquad\qquad \mathcal{R}(f(\mathbf{p}, \mathbf{sc}_s)) = \{\mathcal{R}(f(\mathbf{p}, \mathbf{w}_s^r))\}^r$$

For instance, to find the most despised Coombs candidate, first find the antiplurality election outcome for $\mathbf{p}$ and then (Eq. 4.8.3) reverse this ranking. The top-ranked candidate from the reversal (i.e., the antiplurality bottom-ranked candidate) is to be dropped.

In general, a $\mathbf{w}_{s_1}$, $\mathbf{sc}_{s_2}$ runoff *is where if a candidate receives over half of all the $\mathbf{w}_{s_1}$ votes cast, then she is the winner. Otherwise, the winner of the $\mathbf{sc}_{s_2}$ election is dropped from further consideration, and the other two candidates are matched in a runoff.*

Among many natural questions, we should wonder whether a $\mathbf{w}_{s_1}$-runoff outcome must coincide with a $\mathbf{w}_{s_1}$, $\mathbf{sc}_{s_2}$ outcome, or whether these procedures can elect a Condorcet loser or winner.

Theorem 4.8.3. a. *The winner of a $\mathbf{w}_{s_1}$-runoff always is the same as the $\mathbf{w}_{s_1}$-$\mathbf{sc}_{s_2}$ election iff $\mathbf{w}_{s_2} = \mathbf{w}_{s_1}^r$.*

b. *A Condorcet loser never wins in a $\mathbf{w}_{s_1} - \mathbf{sc}_{s_2}$ runoff. If $s_2 \neq \frac{1}{3}$, then a Condorcet winner can lose. On the other hand, if $s_2 = \frac{1}{3}$ and a runoff is required, then the Condorcet winner (if one exists) wins.*

c. *The winner of a $\mathbf{w}_{s_1}$-$\mathbf{sc}_{s_2}$ election and an agenda need not agree.*

Thanks to Eq. 4.8.2, the proof of this theorem is an immediate application of the procedure line. This is because the candidate to be dropped is determined by reversing the ranking for the $\mathbf{w}_{s_2}$ election. To prove part a, for example, the person eliminated is the bottom ranked candidate of a $f(\mathbf{p}, \mathbf{w}_{s_2}^r)$ election. By the conditions of the theorem, this is the $\mathbf{w}_{s_1}$ bottom-ranked candidate. To further illustrate with the beverage example and Coombs method, we have that the antiplurality ranking is Wine $\succ$ Beer $\succ$ Milk. When this ranking is reversed, to find the $f(\mathbf{p}, \mathbf{sc}_0)$ outcome, we find that Milk is dropped and the runoff is between Beer and Wine; Wine is the winner.

Ouch!! Notice how this beverage example underscores the potential for serious PR problems. I sure would hate to be the person who has to explain to the public why the top-ranked candidate from the first round is eliminated from the runoff! As we know from the geometry of the procedure line and Eq. 4.8.3, this must happen whenever $\mathbf{w}_0$ and $\mathbf{w}_0^r$ have reversed rankings.

4.8.4 Comparisons of Positional Voting Outcomes

Instead of eliminating candidates, maybe they should be compared with different positional elections. A $\mathbf{w}_{s_1}$, $\mathbf{w}_{s_2}$ *comparison procedure*, $s_1 < s_2$, *is where the candidates are ranked with both procedures. If the same candidate is top-ranked in both outcomes, she is chosen. Otherwise, a runoff is held between the top-ranked candidate from each procedure.* As an illustration using the plurality, antiplurality comparison with the beverage profile, the runoff is between milk and wine where the Condorcet winner, wine, wins.

Theorem 4.8.4. a. *If $\mathbf{w}_{s_1}$, $\mathbf{w}_{s_2}$ are not the same as $\mathbf{w}_{s_3}$, $\mathbf{w}_{s_4}$, then there are profiles where the outcomes of the two comparison procedures do not agree.*

b. *For a given $\mathbf{w}_{s_1} - \mathbf{w}_{s_2}$ comparison procedure, there are examples where the Condorcet winner is not selected. A Condorcet loser cannot be selected iff $s_1 \leq \frac{1}{3} \leq s_2$.*

Proof. The proof of the theorem is based on the positioning of the procedure line. For example, if in part a it turns out that $s_1 < s_3$, then choose a procedure line so that c_1 is top-ranked in the $\mathbf{w}_{s_1}$ and $\mathbf{w}_{s_2}$ rankings, but c_2 is top-ranked in the $\mathbf{w}_{s_3}$ and $\mathbf{w}_{s_4}$ elections. If the two comparison procedures do not have this separation property, because, say, $s_3 \leq s_2 < s_4$, then choose the procedure line so that c_1 is top-ranked in the $\{\mathbf{w}_{s_j}\}_{j=1}^3$ elections, and c_2 is $\mathbf{w}_{s_4}$ top-ranked in the last election. As we know from Sect. 4.3, the procedure line can be selected to satisfy this condition while supporting the pairwise outcome of $c_2 \succ c_1$. This leads to the stated conclusion.

To illustrate the first part of part b, choose the procedure line so that the Condorcet winner is not top-ranked for either procedure. Indeed, as long as $\mathbf{w}_s \neq \mathbf{w}_{\frac{1}{3}}$, the Condorcet loser could be $\mathbf{w}_s$ top-ranked. In fact, this is true for both procedures as long as the procedure line does not require the BC to have the Condorcet loser top-ranked. Such positioning of the procedure line always can be done as long as on this line both procedures are on the same side of the BC ($\mathbf{w}_{\frac{1}{3}}$). $\square$

Theorem 4.8.4 demonstrates that even when outcomes of two particular positional methods are compared, we still have all the accompanying conflict, controversy, and other delightful forms of academic entertainment. To retire to a more settled situation, we may wish to choose those candidates supported by the rankings of all positional methods.

Definition 4.8.1. An election ranking is **p**-specific if it is the common election ranking for all choices of $\mathbf{w}_s$. A candidate is **p**-favored if she is top-ranked for all $\mathbf{w}_s$. A candidate is **p**-inferior if she is bottom-ranked in all $\mathbf{w}_s$ rankings. $\square$

Who can argue against a **p**-favored candidate? After all, whether you are pro or anti-choice for positional methods that emphasize a voter's second-ranked candidate, the same candidate emerges victorious with all procedures. This candidate, therefore, has survived the gauntlet of the infinite number of ways there are to weight preferences. What more could be required of her? Similarly, by the universal rejection of a **p**-inferior candidate, it is difficult to justify her selection. The adoption of a **p**-specific procedure seems attractive. However, what are its properties?

Theorem 4.8.5. a. *A **p**-inferior and/or favored candidate need not exist. There exist profiles where the **p**-favored candidate exists but a Condorcet winner does not. Conversely, there exist profiles where a Condorcet winner exists but a **p**-favored candidate does not.*

  b. *A **p**-favored candidate can never be a Condorcet loser; a **p**-inferior candidate can never be a Condorcet winner. There exist profiles where the **p** favored candidate is not the Condorcet winner; there exist examples where the **p**-inferior candidate is not the Condorcet loser.*

As true with the Condorcet concepts, the **p**-favored and inferior candidates are "sometime" concepts; sometime they exist, sometime they don't. And, in those situations where both solutions exist, they need not agree. However, a Condorcet winner is determined with only partial information; it does not use the assumption that voters are transitive or the intensity of pairwise rankings. On the other hand, the **p**-favored candidate survives all possible ways to use this intensity information. Therefore, those situations where a **p**-favored candidate is not the Condorcet winner should be viewed as exposing additional Condorcet faults.

The basic idea of the proof is to use results about the procedure line from the previous sections of this chapter. For example, for c_1 to be the **p**-favored candidate, the procedure line just needs to be in $\mathcal{R}(1) \cup \mathcal{R}(7) \cup \mathcal{R}(2)$ – the union of the ranking regions where c_1 is top-ranked. So, place this line in such a manner that the pairwise ranking conditions are satisfied. From profile decompositions, we know this can be done. Also observe that the positive features of a **p**-specific ranking are due to the fact that they are satisfied by the BC.

4.8.5 Plurality or a Runoff?

Every so often, a community caught in the spirit of electoral reform must decide whether to replace one procedure with another. To demonstrate how such an issue can be analyzed, consider replacing the standard plurality election with a runoff. Of course, there are preferred systems, but the question at hand is to determine which system is "better." By "better," we want the system that is more apt to represent the true view of the voters. Here, the "facts" are debatable. For instance, in an editorial urging voters to reject a runoff, the *Evanston Review* argued that the plurality system "already affords each mayoral candidate a fair chance at being elected. A runoff won't make it any fairer."[13] Can it?

---

[13] October 29, 1992, issue of the *Evanston Review*. An advertisement in this issue argued that the plurality system provided opportunities for minority and independent candidates to be elected; in a runoff they don't have a chance. Ignoring the fact that it was not clear whether "minority" meant a member of the Democratic Party or an ethnic group, is this argument true? If so, is it at the cost of frustrating the true intent of the voters? Evanston voters adopted the

It now is easy to construct arguments showing why a runoff is an improvement. The argument, of course, involves comparing the effects of the reversal and Condorcet portions of a profile. With no Condorcet portion, there is a Condorcet winner. While the reversal portion could keep the plurality ranking compatible with all other outcomes, it also could swing this part of the procedure line into a region that contradicts not only the BC and pairwise rankings but (by the position of the procedure line) the ranking of most positional methods. Namely, the plurality top-ranked candidate could be someone who most voters view as representing true inferiority; the runoff prevents this disaster from winning. In fact, without a Condorcet portion, *whenever the pairwise rankings define a transitive ranking, the runoff winner is closer to meeting the voters' beliefs than the plurality winner.*

What remains is to analyze the effects of a strong Condorcet portion on a profile. While I leave this analysis to the reader, here there are portions where the plurality outcome probably better represents the voters' beliefs than the runoff. Nevertheless, when comparing profiles leading to various outcomes, the results indicate that the runoff serves the voters better than the plurality procedure.

4.8.6 Exercises

1. By using the dictionaries and procedure lines, show that it is possible for c_1 to be the $\mathbf{w}_0$-runoff winner, c_2 to be the $\mathbf{w}_{\frac{1}{2}}$-runoff winner, and c_3 to be the winner of an agenda. By use of profile decompositions, find a set of profiles supporting these outcomes.

2. a. Show that if there is a Condorcet winner, she is Copeland top-ranked. Similarly, show that a Condorcet loser is Copeland bottom-ranked.
b. Find a profile so that all positional methods have the ranking $c_1 \succ c_2 \succ c_3$, but the Copeland ranking is $c_2 \succ c_1 \succ c_3$. Now, modify this profile to create a situation where the Copeland ranking is $c_1 \sim c_2 \sim c_3$.
c. Explain why in a it is impossible to have a Copeland $c_2 \succ c_3 \succ c_1$ ranking. (Hint: What would be the pairwise and the BC rankings?)
d. Given that the BC ranking is $c_1 \succ c_2 \succ c_3$, find all possible Copeland rankings. Next, find all possible BC rankings that can accompany a Copeland ranking of $\mathcal{I}$.
e. The representation cube is divided into ranking regions as defined by the coordinate planes. Find the Copeland tally and ranking for each ranking region. (Remember, some of these regions consist of portions of the coordinate planes or lines.)

3. a. Prove Theorem 4.8.1.
b. Suppose the Copeland and BC rankings are $c_1 \succ c_2 \succ c_3$ while the plurality ranking is $c_3 \succ c_2 \succ c_1$. What can you say about the antiplurality ranking? Suppose the BC ranking is $c_1 \succ c_2 \succ c_3$, the Copeland ranking is $c_2 \succ c_1 \succ c_3$ and the plurality ranking is $c_3 \succ c_1 \succ c_2$. What are the possible choices for the antiplurality ranking?
c. For part b, explain the components of the profile needed to exhibit each behavior. Find illustrating profiles.

4. a. By use of the dictionaries, find a word and an agenda where c_1 is the $\mathbf{w}_{\frac{1}{6}}$-runoff winner, c_2 is the agenda winner, and the Copeland ranking is $\mathcal{I}$. Find an illustrating profile.

---

runoff and when this so-called "minority-bashing" procedure was first used, L. Morton came in second in the first election (so she would have lost a plurality vote) but won the April 20, 1993, runoff to become Evanston's first Afro-American mayor and first mayor from the Democratic Party in many years.

Find a profile and an agenda so that c_1 is the plurality runoff winner, c_2 is the antiplurality runoff winner, and c_3 wins with the agenda.

5. a. Prove Eqs. 4.4.2, 4.8.3.
b. Prove Theorem 4.8.3.
c. Use the procedure line to prove that with the exception of $s = \frac{1}{3}$, the candidate dropped in a $\mathbf{w}_s$, $\mathbf{sc}_s$ election could be the $\mathbf{w}_s$ top-ranked candidate.
d. By use of Eqs. 4.8.2, 4.8.3 and the profile decomposition, find a profile where the plurality winner is c_1, the Coombs winner is c_2, and the Condorcet winner is c_3.

6. a. Find appropriate conditions on s_1 and s_2 so that it is possible for c_1 to be the Condorcet winner, c_2 to be the winner of a $\mathbf{w}_0$-runoff, and c_3, the Condorcet loser, to be the winner of a $\mathbf{w}_{s_1}$ - $\mathbf{w}_{s_2}$ comparison procedure.
b. Use the profile decomposition to create an example where the $\mathbf{w}_0$ - $\mathbf{w}_{\frac{1}{6}}$ winner is the Condorcet loser.

7. Use the geometry of Fig. 4.8.1 to explain the location of the position line whereby c_1 is the Condorcet winner and c_2 is the $\mathbf{p}$-preferred candidate. Characterize the set of profiles leading to such a conclusion. Use this geometry to prove Theorem 4.8.5.

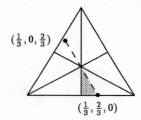

$\left(\frac{1}{3}, 0, \frac{2}{3}\right)$

$\left(\frac{1}{3}, \frac{2}{3}, 0\right)$

Fig. 4.8.1. c_2 can be $\mathbf{p}$-specific

8. Explain the role of the BC in establishing the properties of Theorem 4.8.5.

9. Carry out the geometric analysis to compare the $\mathbf{w}_0$-runoff with the plurality election. Compare the Borda outcomes with the $\mathbf{w}_{\frac{1}{3}}$-runoff outcomes.

10. As a new procedure, first find the $\mathbf{w}_{s_1}$ tally of the candidates, and then the $\mathbf{w}_{s_2}$ tally. The ranking of the candidates is based on the average outcome from these two methods. What is this procedure? Now, consider the procedure where the candidates are ranked with the average between a $\mathbf{w}_{s_1}$ and a $\mathbf{sc}_{s_2}$ election. What is this procedure?

11. Show that c_1 is a $\mathbf{p}$-favored candidate if and only if she is both plurality and antiplurality top-ranked. Extend this statement so it holds for other $\mathbf{p}$-specific properties.

12. The BC can be viewed as assigning $\sum_j G(q_{i,j})$ points to c_i where $G(x) = x$. Different choices of G define different voting procedures.
a. A natural requirement to impose is $G(\frac{1}{2}) = \frac{1}{2}$ and $G(x) = 1 - G(1-x)$. With this condition, show that the rankings always are transitive and that they satisfy the reversal property.
b. Show that if $G(x) = a(x - \frac{1}{2}) + \frac{1}{2}$, $a > 0$, then the resulting method is equivalent to the BC. Find a G choice that defines the Copeland method. Find a graph for this Copeland G and use it to explain why this is an "extreme" method of this type.
c. Let $G_t(x) = (x - \frac{1}{2})^t + \frac{1}{2}$. What t value defines the BC? What procedure is defined by $t = 0$?
d. For any t, what is the G_t outcome of a Condorcet profile? For the basic profile $y\mathbf{E}_1 + (1 - y)\mathbf{E}_5$, find the G_t outcomes. By example, show that if $t \neq 0, 1$, then the analysis cannot be easily separated how G_t treats the Condorcet and the basic portion of the profile. (That is, show how the Condorcet portion affects the G_t ranking given by the basic part of a profile.)

e. Use part d to show that if $t \neq 0, 1$, then the G_t ranking is influenced by the confused voter element. Use this to create a profile where the BC and G_2 rankings differ.

CHAPTER V

OTHER VOTING ISSUES

In addition to the single profile consequences, there are fascinating voting properties which require several profiles. A natural illustration is the Dean's Council controversy (in the fable) caused by combining the profiles for two subcommittees. Multiprofile issues are important because they help us understand what can happen if a voter votes strategically, or if he doesn't vote, or whether there are problems should new voters arrive, or when groups combine to form coalitions, or if voters change preferences, or ... In Sect. 5.1, problems such as the Dean's council are explained. In Sect. 5.2, attention turns to how "more can be less." In Sect. 5.3, the emphasis is on strategic voting. While all of these conclusions depend upon the geometry of profile sets, whenever possible, the simpler geometry of the representation triangle or cube is exploited. Then, to conclude, Sects. 5.4, 5.5 address the intriguing problems of the "list" methods and apportionment of Congressional seats.

5.1 Weak Consistency: The Sum of the Parts

The Dean's Council paradox characterizes a class of particularly troubling paradoxes. The subcommittees agree, but, when they gather as a full committee, the sincere outcome changes. Thus voting can contradict "the whole being greater than the sum of the parts." Why? How can procedures admit such inconsistent, perverse behavior? As I show, rather than being abnormal, this phenomenon where *the outcome of the whole differs from the parts must be anticipated with procedures that rely on the election rankings of more than one subset of candidates.* Such inconsistencies, therefore, must be expected with agendas, runoffs, and so forth.

To see the relevant geometry, let $\mathcal{RO}(c_j)$ be the profile set selecting c_j with a runoff, and let $\mathbf{p}_i \in \mathcal{RO}(c_j)$, $i = 1, 2$, be the normalized profile for the ith subcommittee. (So, each subgroup selects c_j in a runoff election.) The normalized profile for the full committee is

$$\mathbf{p}_\lambda = \lambda \mathbf{p}_1 + (1 - \lambda)\mathbf{p}_2$$

where $\lambda \in (0, 1)$ represents the portion of all voters that belong to the first subcommittee. Namely, the normalized profile for the full committee, $\mathbf{p}_\lambda$, is a point on the line segment connecting $\mathbf{p}_1$ and $\mathbf{p}_2$. Indeed, every point on the connecting line represents the normalized committee profile for some division of the voters (i.e., for some λ value) into two subcommittees.

The geometric explanation for paradoxes of the Dean's Council type now is immediate. If $\mathbf{p}_1$, $\mathbf{p}_2 \in \mathcal{RO}(c_1)$ but $\mathbf{p}_\lambda$ is not, then, according to the definition of convexity (Sect. 1.4), $\mathcal{RO}(c_1)$ *is not a convex set*. Conversely, if $\mathcal{RO}(c_1)$ is convex, then such disturbing events never occur! Consequently, when convexity is violated these multi-profile paradoxes arise.

Definition 5.1.1. Let the collection of nonempty subsets of three candidates be $\mathcal{P} = \{\{c_1\}, \{c_2\}, \{c_3\}, \{c_1, c_2\}, \{c_1, c_3\}, \{c_2, c_3\}, \{c_1, c_2, c_3\}\}$. A choice procedure, $f : Si(6) \to \mathcal{P}$, is *weakly consistent* if when $f(\mathbf{p}_1) = f(\mathbf{p}_2)$, then

$$f(\lambda \mathbf{p}_1 + (1 - \lambda)\mathbf{p}_2) = f(\mathbf{p}_1), \ \lambda \in [0, 1]. \quad \square \qquad (5.1.1)$$

A weakly consistent procedure prevents paradoxes of the Dean's Council type from occuring; when two groups reach the same conclusion, such as Ann from the fable, that is their joint outcome. The goal is to understand which procedures are, and are not, weakly consistent.

Weakly Consistent Procedures. The next statement, which follows immediately from Definition 5.1.1, is central for our analysis.

Proposition 5.1.1. *A choice procedure f is weakly consistent iff for each set of candidates $\alpha \in \mathcal{P}$, the profile set $f^{-1}(\alpha)$ is a convex subset in $Si(6)$.*

This proposition converts weak consistency into a geometric property about profile sets. When each outcome is supported by a convex profile set, there is no worry about weak consistency. But if even one outcome is supported by a non-convex set of profiles, weak consistency is violated!

Example 5.1.1. The natural approach of selecting the $\mathbf{w}_s$ top-ranked candidate is weakly consistent. The technical argument relies on the fact that the intersection of convex sets is convex. To use this property, observe that the outcomes where c_1 is $\mathbf{w}_s$ top-ranked, characterized by c_1 beating the other candidates, is

$$[\mathcal{C}_{c_1 \succ c_2} = \{\mathbf{q} \in Si(3) \text{ where } c_1 \succ c_2\}] \cap [\mathcal{C}_{c_1 \succ c_3} = \{\mathbf{q} \in Si(3) \text{ where } c_1 \succ c_3\}].$$

As $\mathcal{C}_{c_1 \succ c_j}$ are those representation triangle points on a side of the indifference line $c_1 \sim c_j$, $\mathcal{C}_{c_1 \succ c_j}$ is convex. Thus, $\mathcal{C}_{c_1 \succ c_2} \cap \mathcal{C}_{c_1 \succ c_3}$, where c_1 is top-ranked, is convex. There is one more constraint; as we want only outcomes realized by $\mathbf{w}_s$, restrict attention to the convex hull $\mathcal{CH}(\mathbf{w}_s)$; Thus,

$$\mathcal{C}_{c_1 \succ c_2} \cap \mathcal{C}_{c_1 \succ c_3} \cap \mathcal{CH}(\mathbf{w}_s)$$

are the normalized $\mathbf{w}_s$-election outcomes where c_1 is top-ranked. This intersection of three convex sets is convex.

The geometry of the profile set comes from the linear form of the election mapping and the comments of Sect. 1.4. Because $Si(6)$ is convex, the inverse image of a linear mapping of a convex set is convex. The election mapping $f(-, \mathbf{w}_s)$ is linear, the set of desired election outcomes $\mathcal{C}_{c_1 \succ c_2} \cap \mathcal{C}_{c_1 \succ c_3} \cap \mathcal{CH}(\mathbf{w}_s)$

is convex, so the profile set supporting c_1 is convex. A similar argument shows that this convexity assertion holds for all $\alpha \in \mathcal{P}$.

As the conditions of the proposition are satisfied, this choice function is weakly consistent. Geometrically, these comments are illustrated by the convex shaded portion of Fig. 5.1.1a which defines the election outcomes where c_1 is plurality top-ranked.

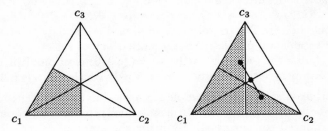

a. c_1 is plurality top-ranked. **b.** Is there convexity in a runoff?

Fig. 5.1.1. Checking for convexity

For a different procedure, suppose two members are selected for, say, the U.S.A. Olympic Frisbee Team. Presumably, they are the two $\mathbf{w}_s$ top-ranked candidates. Is this weakly consistent? Without loss of generality, assume that these top-ranked candidates are c_1 and c_2. Using the same argument, the $\mathbf{w}_s$-outcomes in the representation triangle yielding this conclusion are

$$\mathcal{C}_{c_1 \succ c_3} \cap \mathcal{C}_{c_2 \succ c_3} \cap \mathcal{CH}(\mathbf{w}_s) = \mathcal{R}(1) \cup \mathcal{R}(6) \cup \mathcal{R}(12).$$

As this set is the intersection of convex sets, it is convex. (They are given by the three ranking regions abutting the bottom edge of the representation triangle.) The convexity arguments of Sect. 1.4 ensure that the corresponding profile set is convex, so the procedure is weakly consistent.

Instead of choosing a top-ranked candidate, select the second-ranked one. Why? Well, in the newspapers, in congressional debates, and during campaign speeches we hear about the plight of the "average voter," or the "average consumer." Then, every March attention is focused on two collegiate basketball tournaments in the USA. The better teams go to the NCAA, the teams with the next level of ability go to the NIT, and, presumably, all other players return to the classroom. Instead of waiting until after the NCAA selection, suppose we want to identify who goes to the NIT. This requires identifying the middle-ranked candidates.

A natural "average candidate" is the $\mathbf{w}_s$ *middle*-ranked candidate. This procedure, however, is *not* weakly consistent because the $\mathcal{R}(3) \cup \mathcal{R}(6) \cup \mathcal{R}(13)$ region where c_1 is middle ranked is the union of two triangular regions that meet at $\mathcal{I}$. (In Fig. 5.1.1b, this is the union of the two shaded regions containing a dot.)

As this set clearly fails convexity, this middle-seeking procedure is not weakly consistent.

It is worth using this "middle-choosing" procedure to learn how to create profiles to illustrate the failure of weak consistency. This is easy; as the nonconvexity (illustrated in Fig. 5.1.1b) causes the problem, it must be used to generate examples. So, choose $q_1 \in \mathcal{R}(3)$ and $q_2 \in \mathcal{R}(6)$ around the indentation so that the connecting line passes outside of the region. (See Fig. 5.1.1b.) Any point outside of $\mathcal{R}(3) \cup \mathcal{R}(6) \cup \mathcal{R}(13)$ defines a λ value where $q_\lambda \notin \mathcal{R}(3) \cup \mathcal{R}(6)$. Obviously, there are numerous choices. The coordinate representations and q_j points can be used to compute supporting profiles. An alternative way to select the "average candidate" is to choose the "winner" of the $\mathbf{sc} = (\frac{1}{6}, \frac{5}{6}, 0)$ election. It is left for the reader to determine whether this process is weakly consistent. (It is.)

This "middle-ranked candidate" example suggests (but does not prove) why a runoff fails to be weakly consistent. In a $\mathbf{w}_s$-runoff, the two $\mathbf{w}_s$ top-ranked candidates are advanced to the runoff. By being the eventual winner, c_1 is in the runoff. The convexity problem is caused by the second ranked candidate; this set of election outcomes is $\{c_1, c_2\}$ or $\{c_1, c_3\}$. As this forked set (illustrated by the shaded region of Fig. 5.1.1b) fails to be convex, we can create examples where c_1 is one of the two top-ranked candidates for each subcommittee, but she is bottom-ranked in the committee of the whole. (This happens in the Dean's Council example.) This geometry, however, does not explain the runoff problems because it does not indicate what happens in the pairwise elections. $\square$

As these examples suggest, the analysis of weak consistency is reasonably simple for choice procedures based on positional and scoring methods. Call such a procedure a *scoring based choice procedure*. What simplifies the analysis is that weak consistency can be verified by checking the convexity properties of sets of normalized election outcomes.

Theorem 5.1.2. *For a specified scoring based choice procedure, f, let $\mathcal{A}(\alpha)$ be the set of scoring election outcomes where the set of candidates $\alpha \in \mathcal{P}$ is selected. The procedure f is weakly consistent iff $\mathcal{A}(\alpha)$ is a convex set for all $\alpha \in \mathcal{P}$.*

The proof of this theorem, as well as illustrations, are given in Example 5.1.1.

5.1.1 Other Uses of Convexity

It is worth mentioning that these convexity arguments apply to the wide spectrum of issues that arise whenever two or more groups of voters combine forces. This occurs, for instance, when different political parties form a coalition, when new voters arrive, when the Chair can vote, etc.

To illustrate, suppose c_1 and c_2 are $\mathbf{w}_s$ top-ranked with different groups. When the groups join, which candidate will be $\mathbf{w}_s$ top-ranked? From the geometry, it could be neither; c_3 could be the candidate of choice! This is because the region where c_1 or c_2 is top-ranked fails convexity; it is everything in $\mathcal{CH}(\mathbf{w}_s)$ except

$\mathcal{R}(3) \cup \mathcal{R}(9) \cup \mathcal{R}(4)$. (It is everything except regions with c_3 as a vertex.) The nonconvexity indentation allows us to generate examples where c_3 is top-ranked.

So, whenever we need to compare how the outcomes of the parts (the choices of the different groups) relate to the whole (the outcome when the diverse groups come together), convexity prevails as a powerful, yet elementary tool of analysis. In this manner other interesting examples follow by considering what happens when many groups unite, when different groups use different procedures to reach their outcome, etc. For instance, suppose each of two groups select c_1, but one group uses the agenda $< c_1, c_2, c_3 >$ and the other uses a plurality runoff. Need the full group select c_1 as a full group with a plurality runoff? (No.) If the Chair, whose top-choice is c_1, votes to break a c_1, c_2 tie, are there procedures where the Chair's sincere participation elects c_3? (Yes.) What happens with three or more groups?

5.1.2 An L of an Agenda

While it is easy to understand the source of weak consistency, the practical problem is to determine whether a specified procedure satisfies this convexity condition. For instance, is an agenda weakly consistent?

To analyze an agenda, it suffices to consider $< c_1, c_2, c_3 >$. The analysis, of course, involves the geometric structure of the representation cube reproduced in Fig. 5.1.2. For c_1 to win, she must beat c_2 in the first election and c_3 in the second. Consequently, c_1 is the $< c_1, c_2, c_3 >$ agenda winner iff she is the Condorcet winner; $\mathcal{A}(\{c_1\})$ is the cube region where $x > 0$, $z < 0$.

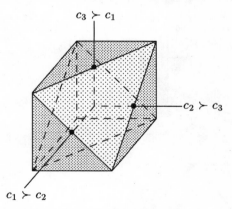

Fig. 5.1.2. The representation cube

To determine whether $\mathcal{A}(\{c_1\})$ is convex, treat each orthant of the representation cube as a child's building block. (As true with most children's toys, each block is mutilated. In our case the mutilation is caused by dropping the confused voter vertices.) The normalized outcomes selecting c_1, $\mathcal{A}(\{c_1\})$, consist of placing two blocks together along a common face. Clearly, this (somewhat) rectangular region is convex. Alternatively, because

$$\mathcal{A}(\{c_1\}) = \{\mathbf{q} \,|\, x > 0\} \cap \{\mathbf{q} \,|\, z < 0\}$$

is the intersection of convex portions of the representation cube (where each portion is half of the cube), it is convex.

This convexity ensures that if $\mathbf{p}_1$, $\mathbf{p}_2$ are profiles where c_1 wins (i.e., $f(\mathbf{p}_j) = \{c_1\}$), then $f(\lambda \mathbf{p}_1 + (1-\lambda)\mathbf{p}_2) = \{c_1\}$ for any $\lambda \in [0,1]$. Consequently, if c_1 wins with each subcommittee, she wins with the combined group. A similar assertion holds for c_2 because $\mathcal{A}(\{c_2\})$ is the convex set $\{\mathbf{q} \,|\, y > 0,\, x < 0\}$.

Now consider $\mathcal{A}(\{c_3\})$. Of the eight orthants in the representation cube, four have been claimed by the other two candidates. This places the remaining four orthants in $\mathcal{A}(\{c_3\})$. Two regions (where $y < 0$, $z > 0$) define c_3 as the Condorcet winner; the other two are the cyclic regions where, as we have seen, the last listed candidate in an agenda wins. Thus,

$$\mathcal{A}(\{c_3\}) = \{\mathbf{q} \,|\, y < 0, z > 0\} \cup \{\mathbf{q} \,|\, x > 0, y > 0, z > 0\} \cup \{\mathbf{q} \,|\, x < 0, y < 0, z < 0\}.$$

To visualize this region, notice that $\mathcal{A}(\{c_3\})$ includes three of the four orthants above the x-y plane (where $z > 0$). (This is $\{\mathbf{q} \,|\, y < 0, z > 0\} \cup \{\mathbf{q} \,|\, x > 0, y > 0, z > 0\}$.) Using the building block construction, start by placing together all four blocks (orthants) where $z > 0$ to form a convex region. Next, remove one block (where $x < 0$, $y > 0$, $z > 0$ because it is in the c_2-Condorcet region) to destroy convexity. Consequently, by adding the two cyclic regions to the c_3 victory region, the convexity of $\mathcal{A}(\{c_3\})$ and any chance for $< c_1, c_2, c_3 >$ to be weakly consistent are lost.

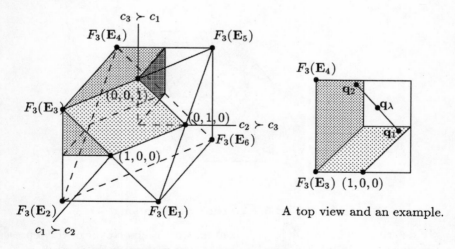

Fig. 5.1.3. The L non-convexity of $\mathcal{A}(c_3)$ for $< c_1, c_2, c_3 >$

This L of a construction proving that an agenda is not weakly consistent is illustrated in Fig. 5.1.3. (To keep the figure from becoming overly complicated, only the c_3-Condorcet and positive cyclic regions are shaded. Missing is the negative cyclic region.) The geometry makes it easy to create examples where an agenda is not weakly consistent. But, to exploit the "L" indentation of $\mathcal{A}(\{c_3\})$, *all illustrating examples must involve at least one cyclic region.*

Therefore, choose $\mathbf{q}_1$ in the positive cyclic region and $\mathbf{q}_2$ in the other L leg where $x < 0, y < 0, z > 0$. If, as illustrated in Fig. 5.1.3b, both points are chosen far enough out in the L legs (or close enough to the L boundary), the connecting line passes through the removed orthant where $x < 0, y > 0, z > 0$. An appropriate λ choice generates an example where c_3 wins with both subcommittees, but c_2 wins with the full committee. If $\mathbf{q}_1$, $\mathbf{q}_2$ are sufficiently close to the boundary, then almost any λ value suffices.

As an aside, this $\mathcal{A}(\{c_j\})$ geometry reinforces my earlier comment that the last listed candidate in an agenda is favored. The first two candidates win only by being a Condorcet winner; the last listed candidate wins by being a Condorcet winner or with a cycle. Consequently, *with any reasonable definition of a probability distribution of profiles, the last listed candidate in an agenda always has the probabilistic advantage.* For instance, for any distribution of the profiles where it is equally likely for any candidate to be a Condorcet winner, if the probability of a cycle is nonzero, the last listed candidate in an agenda has a larger chance of being selected.

5.1.3 Condorcet Extensions

If an agenda is not weakly consistent, what pairwise procedure is? Can a weakly consistent procedure be created by using only pairwise rankings? A natural condition is that such a procedure selects the Condorcet winner when one exists. A second property, imposed to avoid indecisive outcomes, is that profiles where more than one candidate is selected are in lower dimensional sets. Do such methods exist? The answer is immediate from the geometry: NO!

The argument goes as follows. If such a Condorcet extension did exist, then each open cyclic region is assigned to a $\mathcal{A}(\{c_j\})$. (This is the decisiveness requirement outlawing open sets of profiles from supporting indecisive outcomes.) But, as this generates the L problem, convexity is violated. The resulting nonconvexity of $\mathcal{A}(\{c_j\})$ proves the impossibility of constructing such a weakly consistent extension of the Condorcet winner.

Are there *any* weakly consistent extensions of the Condorcet winner? Here the answer is yes, and the actual construction is left to the reader. As a hint, notice that there are seven subsets of candidates in $\mathcal{P}$; so the 27 ranking regions (eight are the open orthants, 12 are portions of coordinate planes, six are portions of coordinate lines, and the last is $\mathcal{I}$) of Fig. 5.1.2 must be combined into seven convex regions. After partitioning the representation cube into these seven convex regions, assign each region a subset from $\mathcal{P}$.[1] The only constraint is that the singletons, $\{c_j\}$, must be assigned a region containing c_j as a Condorcet

---

[1] This holds only for $n = 3$. For $n \geq 4$, there are 2^n orthants in R^n. The geometric assignment of $n!$ orthants for the Condorcet winners leaves behind a region so divided that

winner (this is the Condorcet requirement). Other restrictions emerge from the geometry. For instance, as $\{c_1, c_2, c_3\}$ can be assigned to at most one region, at least one cyclic region must be assigned a two-candidate outcome. Consequently, this procedure is not neutral. (Why?) The reader can discover other properties.

Corollary 5.1.3. *There is no weakly consistent procedure based on the pairwise rankings of candidates that selects the Condorcet winner when one exists and that satisfies one of the following conditions.*
    a. *The procedure is neutral.*
    b. *The set of profiles assigned to a subset of more than one candidate is lower dimensional.*

This corollary demonstrates how difficult it is to extend the Condorcet winner to shed its "sometimes it can be used, sometimes it can't" limitation. Namely, the heavy price is to lose weak consistency and, say, neutrality. But, because of the doubts about the validity of a Condorcet winner, the cost is not worth it. So, rather than pairwise rankings, maybe we should modify the Condorcet concept by using the pairwise election outcomes. To preserve weak consistency, we end up, as described in Sect. 3.4, with the Condorcet Improvement procedure which is equivalent to the BC.

5.1.4 Other Pairwise Procedures

What happens if, instead of the aggregated pairwise vote (which is equivalent to the BC), a generalized pairwise method is used? (See Prob. 12, Sect. 4.8.) In other words, instead of using the rankings of the pairs, use the election tallies and a G-binary method. In what follows, while I restrict attention to smooth functions $G : [0, 1] \to [0, 1]$,[2] the result is more general and holds for $n \geq 3$. The next theorem asserts that the only choices of G admitting weak consistency are equivalent to $G(x) = x$; this is the BC.

Theorem 5.1.4. *If $G : [0, 1] \to [0, 1]$ is a smooth function defining an generalized pairwise aggregation method that is weakly consistent, then G is equivalent to $G(x) = x$ and the aggregation process is equivalent to the BC.*

One way to prove this theorem is to apply (and slightly extend) the L theorem at the end of this section. A direct approach is given next. Because this proof involves calculus, intuition is provided for the reader unfamiliar with this important technical tool.

To divide the profile space $Si(6)$ into 13 convex regions (one convex region for each ranking of the three candidates), the boundaries of each region must be defined by planes or the intersections of planes. (If not, then some region has

---

it is impossible to combine them into the required convex sets. (The problem is worse when the regions of coordinate planes and axes are introduced [S12].) Thus, constructing a weakly consistent extension of the Condorcet winner based on rankings, is doomed for $n \geq 4$.

    [2] For the reader familiar with calculus, this means that the first two derivatives of G are defined and continuous. For the reader still waiting to be initiated into the Calculus Club, treat G as a function where the graph can be smoothly drawn.

a bulge. But, one region's bulge is another region's indentation; this violates convexity.) The idea is that the linear boundaries force G to be linear. But, a linear G is equivalent to $G(x) = x$. Only the assertion that G is linear requires calculus. Therefore, only skeptics are encouraged to read the proof.

Proof. To show that G' is a constant, notice that the $c_1 \sim c_2$ boundary is

$$F = G(q_{1,2}) + G(q_{1,3}) - [G(q_{2,1}) + G(q_{2,3})] = 0.$$

As the properties of the level set $F^{-1}(0)$ are determined by ∇F evaluated along the boundary, we have that

$$\nabla F = G'(q_{1,2})(1,1,1,0,0,0) + G'(q_{1,3})(1,1,0,0,0,1) -$$
$$[G'(q_{2,3})(1,0,0,0,1,1) + G'(q_{2,1})(0,0,0,1,1,1)].$$

By collecting terms and using $G'(x) = G'(1 - x)$ (from $G(x) = 1 - G(1 - x)$), we have

$$\nabla F = (G'(q_{1,2}) + G'(q_{1,3}) - G'(q_{2,3}), G'(q_{1,2}) + G'(q_{1,3}), G'(q_{1,2}),$$
$$-G'(q_{1,2}), -G'(q_{1,2}) - G'(q_{2,3}), G'(q_{1,3}) - G'(q_{1,2}) - G'(q_{2,3})).$$
$$(5.1.2)$$

The boundary is a linear set, so on each component $\nabla F/\|\nabla F\|$ is a constant unit vector. Thus, each ∇F component is a multiple of the other components; e.g., by comparing the second and third components, we have that on the boundary $G'(q_{1,2}) = mG'(q_{1,3})$ for some scalar m. Similarly, $G'(q_{1,2})$, $G'(q_{1,3})$, and $G'(q_{2,3})$ are all fixed scalar multiples of the others.

The $q_{i,j}$ variables are independent variables so, by keeping $q_{1,3}$ fixed and varying $q_{1,2}$, it follows from $G'(q_{1,2}) = mG'(q_{1,3})$ that G' is a constant over certain domain values. Similarly, we find from the other relationships that G' is constant over all domain values represented by this $c_1 \sim c_2$ boundary. Thus, it suffices to show that all $[0, 1]$ points are needed for G to support $F = 0$. To do this, consider profiles $x[\mathbf{E}_1 + \mathbf{E}_6] + y[\mathbf{E}_2 + \mathbf{E}_5] + z[\mathbf{E}_3 + \mathbf{E}_4]$ where $x + y + z = \frac{1}{2}$, $x, y, z \geq 0$. (By neutrality, they are in the profile set supporting $F = 0$.) As such a profile defines $q_{1,2} = q_{2,1} = \frac{1}{2}$ and $q_{2,3} = q_{1,3} = 2x + y$, the profiles supporting $F = 0$ correspond to the $2x + y$ values allowed by the constraint $x + y + z = \frac{1}{2}$. This includes all values in $[0, 1]$, so the proof is completed. $\square$

5.1.5 Maybe "if's " and "and's", But No "or's" or "but's"

Figure 5.1.4 geometrically demonstrates that the intersection of convex regions is a convex set, but the union of convex sets need not be convex. (The heavily shaded region is the convex intersection. The totally shaded area, including the inward dents near the top and bottom where the circles join, is the union.) A point surviving an intersection satisfies the membership requirements of both groups as signaled by the connecting word "and". Similarly, a union allows a qualified point to be in one set *or* in the other, so *"or"* is a reasonable indicator that a geometric union is involved. So, while not infallible, we should question the weak consistency of a procedure requiring an *"or"* to describe how to select candidates.

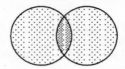

Fig. 5.1.4. Convex sets

Example 5.1.2. For the agenda $< c_1, c_2, c_3 >$, c_1 wins {if she beats c_2 } *and* { if she beats c_3 }. This $\mathcal{A}(\{c_1\})$ region is convex. On the other hand, c_3 wins { if c_1 beats c_2 *and* c_3 beats c_2 } *or* { if c_2 beats c_1 *and* c_3 beats c_2 }. The "and" in the two bracketed conditions makes each a convex set; the lone "or" destroys convexity along with weak consistency.

An extension of a Condorcet winner may involve a union; e.g., if a cyclic region is assigned to a particular candidate, say c_1, the connecting word "or" is needed to describe how to select c_1. Namely, c_1 wins { if $c_1 \succ c_2$ *and* $c_1 \succ c_3$ } *or* { if $c_1 \succ c_2$, $c_2 \succ c_3$, and $c_3 \succ c_1$. } The distribution of weak consistency is suggested by the "or."

To choose c_1 as the second-ranked candidate, the description is { the $\mathbf{w}_s$ ranking is $c_2 \succ c_1 \succ c_3$ } *or* { the $\mathbf{w}_s$ ranking is $c_3 \succ c_1 \succ c_2$ }. These procedures are not weakly consistent. On the other hand, it is easy to describe how the top (or bottom) ranked candidates are selected by using only "and". Hence, one can correctly guess that these are weakly consistent methods. Alternately, by listing the names of all admissible ranking regions, the description of a weakly consistent procedure uses the connecting "or" word. Thus, an "or" only suggests that weak consistency is absent; it is not a proof. $\square$

Runoffs and But's. c_1 is the $\mathbf{w}_s$-runoff winner { if c_3 is $\mathbf{w}_s$ bottom-ranked and $c_1 \succ c_2$ in the pairwise election } *or* { if c_2 is $\mathbf{w}_s$ bottom-ranked and $c_1 \succ c_3$ in the pairwise election }. The "or" suggests that showing why a $\mathbf{w}_s$-runoff is not weakly consistent requires showing that the bracketed (convex) sets have a non-convex union. This is correct, and I leave it to the reader to construct this argument. Instead, I use a related argument to illustrate the importance of *"but"* – a term signaling that part of a set has been removed. (Clearly, removing a portion a convex set can destroy convexity.)

The convex hull of profiles supporting a pairwise $c_1 \sim c_2$ is defined by the nine profile vertices $\{\mathbf{v}_{i,j} = \frac{1}{2}[\mathbf{E}_i + \mathbf{E}_j]\}_{i,=1,2,3,j=4,5,6}$. The corresponding positional election outcomes, the convex hull defined by $\{f(\mathbf{v}_{i,j}, \mathbf{w}_s)\}$, is illustrated by the darkly shaded region in Fig. 5.1.5 for the plurality and BC methods. Because this dark region indicates which positional outcomes can accompany a pairwise $c_1 \sim c_2$ outcome, associated with any *point* inside the region are profiles supporting both the pairwise outcome $c_1 \succ c_2$ and others supporting $c_2 \succ c_1$. To "see" this important fact, add a Condorcet portion to break the tie. Alternatively, notice from profile coordinates that any $\mathbf{q}$ in the shaded area admits many supporting profiles where α_s and β_s permit $d > \frac{1}{2}$ (so they support the positional outcome $\mathbf{q}$ and the $c_1 \succ c_2$ pairwise vote) while others support $d < \frac{1}{2}$.

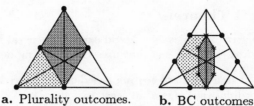

a. Plurality outcomes.   **b.** BC outcomes

Fig. 5.1.5. The outcomes associated with pairwise $c_1 \succ c_2$

The lightly shaded regions are where an election outcome must be accompanied by the pairwise ranking $c_1 \succ c_2$. Consequently, with the possible exception of boundary line segments, any point in a shaded region can be supported by a profile with a pairwise ranking $c_1 \succ c_2$.

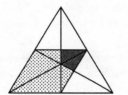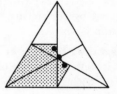

Fig. 5.1.6. The Dean's Council

The same argument (or use a "name change") establishes a symmetric region of election outcomes that can be supported by a profile with the pairwise outcome $c_1 \succ c_3$. The intersection of these regions defines a convex region where points can be supported by a profile with the pairwise outcome $c_1 \succ c_2$ and/or $c_1 \succ c_3$. For the plurality vote, this is the shaded region in Fig. 5.1.6a.

For c_1 to win a $\mathbf{w}_s$-runoff, she must avoid being $\mathbf{w}_s$ bottom-ranked. Thus, the $\mathbf{w}_s$-outcome cannot be in the heavily shaded part of Fig. 5.1.6a. But, by removing the heavily shaded region, the remaining region (indicated in Fig. 5.1.6b) looses all claims to convexity! This loss of convexity forces the runoff to violate weak consistency, and it shows how to construct illustrating examples. Geometrically, an example is given by the dots and the connecting line near the inward dent of the shaded region in Fig. 5.1.6b. The upper dot is assigned a profile with the pairwise ranking $c_1 \succ c_3$ while the lower dot is assigned a profile where $c_1 \succ c_2$. Indeed, this is how the profiles for the Dean's Council example were derived. Use either coordinate representations or the profile decomposition to find profiles for the endpoints of the line segment.

To extend this proof to all $\mathbf{w}_s$, modify the argument by including the $\mathcal{CH}(\mathbf{w}_s)$

set, and the regions where the pairwise outcome can be $c_1 \sim c_2$. As this set is the smallest for the BC, the same proof applies. $\square$

Theorem 5.1.5. *Let* $\mathbf{w}_{s_1}$ *and* $\mathbf{sc}_{s_2}$ *be given. The* $\mathbf{w}_{s_1}$*-runoff and the* $\mathbf{w}_{s_1}$, $\mathbf{sc}_{s_2}$ *runoff are not weakly consistent.*

5.1.6 A General Theorem

From this abundance of examples, we should expect a general theorem based on "or", "but" comments. There is one that uses the following definition.

Definition 5.1.2. A non-constant scoring based choice procedure is *varied* if its outcomes use the ordinal rankings of at least two subsets of candidates so that the following is true. There is an $\alpha \in \mathcal{P}$, and subsets of candidates S', S'' where α can be selected in one of two ways. First, α can be selected independent of how the S' candidates are ranked if the ranking of the S'' candidates satisfies an appropriate restriction. Alternatively, the selection of α requires restrictive rankings of the S' candidates. $\square$

Example 5.1.3. One way to select c_3 with the agenda $< c_1, c_2, c_3 >$ is if $c_1 \succ c_2$ and $c_3 \succ c_1$; as the $\{c_2, c_3\}$ ranking is immaterial, let $S' = \{c_2, c_3\}$. Alternately, c_3 can be elected by restricting the $\{c_2, c_3\}$ ranking; if $c_2 \succ c_1$ we need $c_3 \succ c_2$. Thus, an agenda is varied. $\square$

A runoff is varied because c_1 can be elected with the rankings $c_1 \succ c_2 \succ c_3$ and $c_1 \succ c_2$ without restriction on the rankings of $\{s' = c_1, c_3\}$. Similarly, c_1 can be selected only with restrictions on the $\{c_1, c_3\}$ ranking; if $c_3 \succ c_1 \succ c_2$ then we need $c_1 \succ c_3$. $\square$

So to determine whether a choice procedure is, or is not varied; just check the rankings; we need not determine whether the rankings can occur.

Theorem 5.1.6. *A varied positional choice procedure is not weakly consistent.*

While powerful, this theorem fails to characterize all procedures that violate weak consistency. For instance, because the procedure that selects the second-ranked candidate of a $\mathbf{w}_s$-election only involves the $\{c_1, c_2, c_3\}$ rankings, it is *not* varied; yet it is not weakly consistent. (A complete characterization of weakly consistent methods can be obtained by using the techniques of Sect. 5.2.)

The reason for Theorem 5.1.6 is that a varied procedure creates an L in some $\mathcal{A}(c_j)$; the L destroys the convexity of $\mathcal{A}(c_j)$ and the weak consistency of the procedure. To illustrate with *Black's procedure*, recall that D. Black argues [Bl] that a Condorcet winner should be selected if she exists. If not, then the BC winner should be selected.[3] The close relationship between pairwise and BC rankings suggests that Black's procedure might be weakly consistent; it is not.

---

[3] Of course, Black was unaware of the confused voter bias of the Condorcet winner; a bias that casts serious doubt on his procedure.

Corollary 5.1.7. *Black's procedure is varied. Therefore, Black's procedure is not weakly consistent.*

Proof. If c_1 is the Condorcet winner, the BC ranking of $S' = \{c_1, c_2, c_3\}$ is irrelevant. If no Condorcet winner exists, c_1 must be BC top-ranked; this restricts the S' rankings. The conclusion follows from Theorem 5.1.6. $\square$

To see the non-convexity of Black's method, compare the regions in the representational cube where c_1 is BC top-ranked and where c_1 is the Condorcet winner. (See Fig. 5.1.7.) The shaded region represents the BC ranking $c_1 \succ c_2 \succ c_3$ while the dashed lines outline the boundary of the c_1-Condorcet region. The obvious non-convexity is created because part of the c_1-Condorcet region is removed from the BC region and parts of the cyclic pairwise rankings are assigned to this BC ranking. Again, this geometry makes it easy to design supporting examples. Let $\mathbf{q}_1$ be in the c_1-Condorcet region near $(0, 1, 0)$ and $\mathbf{q}_2$ be near $\mathcal{I}$ and the $c_1 \sim c_2$ BC boundary in the $c_1 \succ c_2 \succ c_3$ BC region. For $\mathbf{q}_1$, $\mathbf{q}_2$, the Black method outcome is c_1. However, for many λ values, the $\mathbf{q}_\lambda$ outcome is c_2.

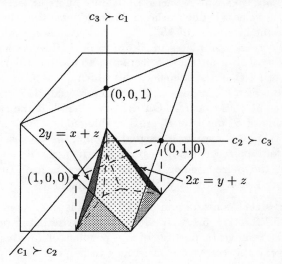

Fig. 5.1.7. The shaded region is the BC ranking $c_1 \succ c_2 \succ c_3$. The dashed lines have this ranking for pairwise votes.

An alternative approach to visualize the non-convexity involves the fat triangle (the product of the representation triangle with [-1,1]). If c_1 is the Condorcet winner, she beats c_2, so the point is in the back half of the fat triangle. In the BC election, she receives at least one-third of all votes, so the BC tally is on the c_1-side of a line passing through $\mathcal{I}$. Thus, points selecting c_1 are represented in Fig. 5.1.8a by the triangular region in the back of the fat triangle.

With a negative cycle, c_1 is BC top-ranked. This region is represented by the front half of the triangle; only representation triangle points where c_1 is BC top-ranked can be used. The L non-convexity is evident; creating examples is simple.

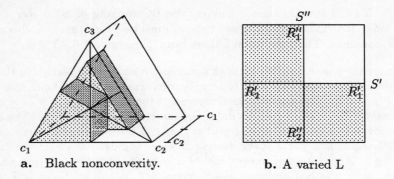

a. Black nonconvexity.   **b.** A varied L

Fig. 5.1.8. Varied procedures

Proof of the Theorem. A varied procedure offers at least two scenarios to select $\alpha \in P$. One selects α due to the rankings of sets other than S'; maybe it depends upon specified rankings of $\{S'', \ldots, S^*\}$. With these rankings, α occurs independent of how the candidates in S' are ranked. The second scenario restricts the rankings of S'; but for these S' rankings to matter, the rankings of $\{S'', \ldots, S^*\}$ must be other than the specified ones which make S' irrelevant. Namely, there is a S'' where, if the rankings of S' are immaterial, then the ranking of S'' cannot be R_1'', but it could be R_2''. On the other hand, if the ranking R_1'' occurs, then the ranking of S' must be R_1', rather than R_2'.

The "L" non-convexity is created through the Cartesian product $S' \times S$ defining the four paired ranking regions (R_i', R_j''), for $i, j = 1, 2$. For α to be the outcome, the paired region (R_2'', R_1') cannot occur. But, excising this region creates the L non-convexity. See Fig. 5.1.8b. □

The abstract construction of Fig. 5.1.8b is illustrated with specific examples in Figs. 5.1.3, 5.1.7, 5.1.8. In all cases, a restriction imposed upon the rankings of one set removes a portion of the product of ranking regions; the resulting non-convexity forces weak consistency to fail.

5.1.7 Exercises

1. Show that the threshold methods are weakly consistent.

2. By dividing the representation triangle (or the representation cube) into any seven convex sets, define a weakly consistent procedure.

3. Find a profile demonstrating that Coombs method is not weakly consistent. Is Copeland's method weakly consistent?

4. Take G to be 0 at 0, and 1/2 for all points between 0 and 1. Determine whether the resulting G-binary aggregation method (Prob. 12, Sect. 4.8) is weakly consistent.

5. Find conditions on $\mathbf{w}_s$-elections so that if c_1 is the top-ranked for group 1 and c_2 for group 2, then one of these two is top-ranked for the full group. Do the same for the agenda $< c_1, c_2, c_3 >$.

6. For the middle-ranked procedure, consider a vector $(0, s, 1 - s)$; find s values so that the "winner" indicates, in some sense, the average person. Is the method weakly consistent?

7. Suppose a procedure asserts that, in pairwise elections, if c_1 beats c_2, then c_3 wins; otherwise, c_3 must beat c_2. If not, then c_2 wins. Show by the geometry that this is not weakly consistent. Show it is varied.

8. Prove by emphasizing the union of sets that a simple runoff or a runoff with $\mathbf{sc}_s$ elimination is not weakly consistent.

9. Construct a profile where the procedure line is in the region $c_1 \succ c_2 \succ c_3$ and c_2 is the runoff winner. Next, construct a procedure line with the ranking $c_3 \succ c_2 \succ c_1$ with c_2 as the runoff winner. Construct the first procedure line so it is near the $c_1 \sim c_2$ boundary and the second one near the $c_2 \sim c_3$ boundary. Thus, for an interval of λ choices, c_2 is bottom-ranked in a combined election. This one example proves Theorem 5.1.5 for all positional voting methods.

10. Show when a $\mathbf{p}$-favored candidate exists, it defines a weakly consistent method.

11. Show that the $\mathbf{w}_{s_1}$, $\mathbf{w}_{s_2}$ comparison method is not weakly consistent.

12. Extend Theorem 5.1.6 to more general procedures where the outcome depends upon the tallies.

13. Use the procedure line to show it is possible for two subcommittees to have c_1 top-ranked, where one uses $\mathbf{w}_o$ and the other uses the BC, but c_2 is the plurality top-ranked candidate for the full committee.

14. Use orthogonality arguments from the proof of Theorem 5.1.6 to find a shorter proof that a $\mathbf{w}_{s_1}$-runoff is not weakly consistent.

15. Suppose c_1 is the plurality runoff winner of two subcommittees. Find a sufficient condition on the plurality rankings to ensure that c_1 is in the runoff for the full group. Need she win the runoff? Use the geometry of the representation cube to show the new non-convexity.

5.2 From Involvement and Monotonicity to Manipulation

Among the fascinating multiple profile consequences that can be understood with geometry are the counter-intuitive important "responsiveness" issues such as *monotonicity* and *manipulability*. Here we learn that the common sense notion that added support helps a candidate need not be true. Instead, voters can wreak planned and/or unintentional damage upon the group outcome. To let the geometry do the talking, geometric intuition coming from the representation triangle and cube is used when possible. In the second half of this section, the geometry of the profile space $Si(6)$ is needed.

5.2.1 Positively Involved

A candidate works the precincts to get out the vote because, "clearly," her chances improve with added support. Stated in another way, when a voter joins a group, he expects his sincere vote to advance, not hinder his beliefs. If by voting a voter's ballot changes the group decision from an acceptable outcome (had he abstained) to a personally worse one, then we must severely question the legitimacy of the procedure! Yet, such procedures are commonly used. When such a method is used, one can imagine scenarios where a voter is overjoyed with his good fortune – his car got a flat tire on a busy street during a heavy rainstorm; consequently, he did not vote!

Definition 5.2.1. A procedure is *positively involved* if when c_j is the selected outcome for a profile and when a group of new voters, all of the same voter type with c_j top-ranked, join the group, c_j remains the selected candidate. □

Upon reflection, we should expect procedures where a person's vote is counter-productive. After all, a similar troubling election phenomenon occurs with pro-cedures that are not weakly consistent. Here, each group reaches the same con-clusion, but their joint outcome is something different. Now, should one group consist of voters of the same type, positive involvement is violated. Consequently, all procedures failing weak consistency are on the suspect list as potential positive involvement violators.

Example 5.2.1. An agenda fails to be weakly consistent, and, as shown next, *an agenda is not positively involved.* The villain is the same L geometry causing the weak consistency problems; we just need to explain how the L nonconvexity allows q_1 to be an unanimity outcome for a subgroup.

Assume, as in Sect. 5.1, that the agenda is $< c_1, c_2, c_3 >$. As shown in Fig. 5.2.1, one L leg forcing the $\mathcal{A}(c_3)$ nonconvexity contains $F_3(E_4)$, the unanimity outcome for the ranking $c_3 \succ c_2 \succ c_1$. Let $q_1 = F_3(E_4)$ and choose q_2 in the other L leg so that the line connecting q_1 and q_2 passes through the c_2-Condorcet region. (For instance, choose q_2 close to the part of the $x = 0$ coordinate plane separating the positive cyclic region and the c_2-Condorcet region.) The portion of the line in the c_2-Condorcet region defines a rich selection of λ values (indicating how many type-four voters have been persuaded to vote) requiring q_λ to be in the c_2-Condorcet region. So, if they had stayed home to watch basketball on TV instead of voting, the reward for these type-four voters would be the election of their top-choice c_3; by being good citizens and voting, their punishment is the selection of a lesser good: c_2.

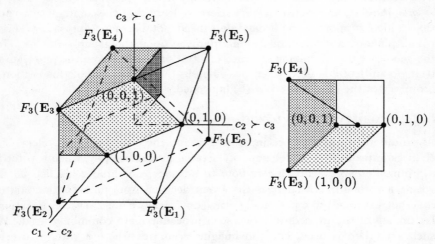

Fig. 5.2.1. Lack of positive involvement for $< c_1, c_2, c_3 >$

How bad can it be? How many, or how few type-four voters are needed to create examples? The answer, again, comes from the L geometry. First, only one type-four voter might be enough! According to the geometry, a lower bound for λ requires q_2 to be as close to the c_2-Condorcet region as possible (so that small λ values force $q_\lambda \in \mathcal{A}(c_2)$). To locate q_2, start with q on the $x = 0$ coordinate plane separating the positive cyclic region from the c_2-Condorcet region. The q rankings are $c_1 \sim c_2$, $c_2 \succ c_3$, $c_3 \succ c_1$.

A profile supporting q creates agenda headaches with its tie vote on the first pairwise election; a conflict resolved with a tie-breaker. If the tie-breaker chooses c_1 for q (or for a profile supporting q^4), then c_1 advances to the next election where c_1 loses to c_3. Consequently, with the tie breaker, either $q \in \mathcal{A}(c_3)$ or a profile defining q leads to the selection of c_3. By choosing $q_2 = q$, any $\lambda > 0$ - even a λ corresponding a single voter - suffices to establish the conclusion.

If the q tie-breaker favors c_2, then c_2 beats c_3 in the second election; thus $q \in \mathcal{A}(c_2)$. To allow a single type-four voter to change the election outcome, go one voter "deeper" into $\mathcal{A}(c_3)$. Namely, choose an integer profile p with type-four voters that supports q. (From the profile coordinate representation, such profiles exist.) Let p' be the integer profile obtained by removing a type-four voter from p, and let $q_2 = F_3(p')$. (If p requires n voters, then q_2 is defined by the equation $q = \frac{n-1}{n}q_2 + \frac{1}{n}q_1$.) By construction, the $F_3(p') = q_2$ outcome is where, by adding a single type-four voter back to the profile (which returns us to p), the outcome shifts from c_1 to c_2. This type-four voter breaks c_1's back.

So, with an agenda using tie breakers, it is easy to create examples where a *single voter can, unintentionally, act against his best own interest by voting*. If we wish to ignore tie breakers, the same analysis proves there are many q_2 choices where only two type- four voters suffice for an example.

The Other Extreme. The other λ extreme concerns the maximum number of type-four voters that can be added without forcing the outcome back to c_1. Again, the answer comes from the geometry; this bound is determined by choosing q_2 so that the longest possible portion of the q_1 - q_2 connecting line is in $\mathcal{A}(c_2)$. The geometry is obvious; start with $q = (0, 1, 0)$ and use an argument similar to the above to find q_2. By examining the λ values that keep the y component of $q_\lambda = \lambda(-1, -1, 1) + (1 - \lambda)(0, 1, 0)$ positive (so $q_\lambda \in \mathcal{A}(c_2)$), the upper bound of $\lambda = \frac{1}{2}$ is found. $\square$

An Agenda Theorem. Some facts learned from the example are:

Proposition 5.2.1. *The agenda* $< c_1, c_2, c_3 >$ *is positively involved for* c_1 *and* c_2; *it is not positively involved for* c_3. *Namely, there exist profiles where the group outcome is* c_3, *and, if joined by new voters of the same voter type with* c_3 *top-ranked, the outcome no longer is* c_3. *If tie breakers for pairwise elections are involved, the number of voters in this new group can be anywhere from one*

---

[4] A tie breaking scheme depending on vote totals rather than ranking requires us to examine the set of supporting profiles.

to one fewer than the number of the original group. If there are more voters in the new group than in the original group, the outcome is c_3.

The agenda lessons extend to other procedures. In particular, should a procedure with tie breakers fail to be positively involved, there are examples where a single voter of a particular voter type exhibits the lack of positive involvement. On the other hand, finding upper bounds on the number of voters is a more subtle computation that depends on the geometry of the $\mathcal{A}(c_j)$ regions defined by the procedure.

Sly Manipulators. Just imagine the opportunities – and dangers – offered by a procedure that is not positively involved. It allows a person to be "one of the boys" while working against their interests. To see this, call a procedure *slyly manipulable* if a voter can manipulate the outcome to his true choice of c_2 by *voting as though* he supports the group's choice of c_1. This manipulating voter can summon all possible self-righteousness, even announcing and openly voting for the group's choice of c_1, safe in the knowledge that his actions have sabotaged c_1's chances to the advantage of c_2. The above results prove that a *procedure that is not positively involved can be slyly manipulated!*

Weak Consistency Versus Positive Involvement. It is tempting to conjecture that all procedures failing to be weakly consistent also fail positive involvement. This is false; to prove so, we need a procedure where a unanimity outcome cannot exploit the nonconvexities. So, suppose a Condorcet winner is selected if one exists; otherwise the outcome is $\{c_1, c_2, c_3\}$. Because the union of the cyclic regions is not convex, this procedure fails weak consistency. But the regions creating the nonconvexity have no unanimity outcomes, so positive involvement is satisfied by default.

Because positive involvement is more selective about what new outcomes $\mathbf{q}_1$ are admitted, there are positively involved procedures that are not weakly consistent. Upon reflection, this makes sense. Positive involvement requires the outcome to remain the same after adding selective types of new voters. On the other hand, with its more liberal admissions policy, weak consistency must accommodate new voters of these selective types and those of more general types. As it is more difficult for a procedure to be weakly consist, we reach the conclusion of Proposition 5.2.2 which uses a useful definition introduced by P. Young [Y2].

Definition 5.2.2. A procedure is *faithful* if it selects the top-ranked candidate of an unanimity profile. □

Proposition 5.2.2. *A faithful, weakly consistent scoring based procedure is positively involved, but a faithful, positively involved scoring based procedure need not be weakly consistent.*

To underscore the essential geometric differences between weak consistency and positive involvement, recall that weak consistency requires all points on the profile line connecting any two supporting profiles to support the same outcome.

Positive involvement has the same line segment condition, but one endpoint is a unanimity profile. Thus, the stricter convexity requirements of weak consistency are replaced with a "starlike" convexity which requires only that lines starting from a unanimity profile can't leave a region and then re-enter. To appreciate the significant difference, notice that while an "L" destroys convexity, it is a starlike with respect to the vertex joining the two "L" legs.

Guided by the light of "starlike convexity," it is easy to decide whether a procedure is positively involved. For instance, if an outside surface of the $\mathcal{A}(c_j)$ region "faces" an unanimity outcome with c_j top-ranked, then a line connecting this boundary to the unanimity outcome lies, in part, outside of $\mathcal{A}(c_j)$. This is illustrated with the following.

Example 5.2.2. While Black's method is not weakly consistent, it is positively involved thanks to the positioning of the L in Figs. 5.1.7-8. In a representation cube, the two unanimity outcomes with c_1 top-ranked are $(1, \pm 1, -1)$. Neither point is in a position to exploit the L nonconvexity of the region.

Choosing "the average person" as the $\mathbf{w}_s$ second-ranked candidate is not weakly consistent. The non-convexity is created because this region is the union of opposing ranking regions. For instance, if c_1 is middle-ranked, then this region is the union of the type-three and six regions. A "unanimity outcome" having c_1 middle-ranked would be either $[\mathbf{w}_s]_3$ or $[\mathbf{w}_s]_j$. This region is not starlike with these unanimity outcomes because plenty of lines starting from each point leave the region only to re-enter again. Thus, this method is *not* positively involved. □

5.2.2 Monotonicity

To relax the positive involvement condition, which allows only voters of one type to be added, consider adding voters subject only to the restriction that they provide support for the winning candidate. For instance, suppose during the campaign some voters gain respect for the winning c_1. Can added support by their changing preferences be too much of a good thing because it causes her to lose? If so, just imagine a candidate campaigning for her opponent because the extra support will hurt her!

While these two situations – one involves new voters joining the group and the second involves voters changing their minds – are different, the geometry allows them to be analyzed together. This is because both cases involve comparing election outcomes for different profiles. As the election outcomes depend on what fraction of all voters are of each type, rather than the exact integer profiles, the only difference involves the restrictions imposed upon $\mathbf{q}_1$ relative to the positioning of $\mathbf{q}_2$.

All responsiveness questions can be analyzed with "starlike" geometry, but it is time to do something new. Following the starlike analysis, choose $\mathbf{q}_2$ and *the possible directions of the connecting line*. We want to determine whether the admissible directions admit adverse outcomes for the endpoint $\mathbf{q}_1$.

Definition 5.2.3. A choice procedure is *monotonic* if when c_j is chosen with profile **p**, and the only voters to change preferences change them to give c_j a higher ranking (but, preserving the original relative ranking of the other candidates), then c_j is elected with the new profile **p'**. □

Just imagine what can happen with a non-monotonic procedure. After the polls trumpet the inevitable election of c_1, a bandwagon effect sets in where previously reluctant voters, in an attempt to finally be on a winning side, rank c_1 higher. This added support causes her to lose!

Monotonicity restricts how voters can change their minds to rank c_1 higher; the possibilities are listed in the following table where each row and column indicates, respectively, the current and changed voter type. An "o" indicates no change; an "x" is an admissible change satisfying monotonicity. For example, the "x" in the third row indicates that a type-three voter can change into a type-two voter to give c_1 a higher ranking. There is no entry under this row in the 1 column because changing a type-three voter to type-one alters the relative ranking of c_2 and c_3.

$$
\begin{array}{c|cccccc}
 & 1 & 2 & 3 & 4 & 5 & 6 \\
\hline
1 & o & & & & & \\
2 & & o & & & & \\
3 & x & & o & & & \\
4 & x & x & & o & & \\
5 & x & & & & o & x \\
6 & x & & & & & o \\
\end{array}
\qquad (5.2.1)
$$

When a $\mathbf{w}_s$ positional method is used, the changes of Eq. 5.2.1 create the geometry indicated by the arrows in Fig. 5.2.2a. For example, the arrows from $[\mathbf{w}_s]_4$ indicate that a type-four voter could change to type-two or three (compare this with Table 5.2.2.) to cast either the ballot $[\mathbf{w}_s]_2$ or $[\mathbf{w}_s]_3$.

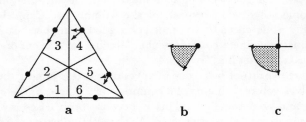

Fig. 5.2.2. Profile changes admitted with monotonicity

To further refine the Fig. 5.2.2a geometry, notice how a $\mathbf{w}_s$-outcome varies with monotonic changes in preferences that favor c_1. ¿From base outcome $\mathbf{q}_2$, the direction lines of monotonic changes from $\mathbf{q}_2$ are given by the "b-cone" (Fig. 5.2.2b) of all admissible changes in $[\mathbf{w}_s]$-votes allowed by Fig. 5.2.2a. The boundaries of the b-cone are independent of $\mathbf{w}_s$. Indeed, one cone edge is horizontal (corresponding to the voter type changes $4 \to 3$, $6 \to 1$) and pointing to the left while the other one points downwards and to the left at 60° (caused by changes of voter types $5 \to 6$, $3 \to 2$). Using various combinations, any directional change in the cone is possible.

For the pairwise rankings, the possible directions of change in the representation cube are indicated the "c-cone"of Fig. 5.2.2c. There is no possible change in the y direction (because the relative rankings of c_2 and c_3 are held fixed). The changes along the x axis correspond to where *only* c_1 and c_2 are interchanged (changes in types $4 \to 3$, $6 \to 1$) while changes downward along the vertical axis require only c_1 and c_3 to be interchanged ($3 \to 2$, $5 \to 6$).

What Is Monotonic? From the figure and the cones of admissible directions[5] for the connecting line, we can use the geometry of the $\mathcal{A}(c_j)$ regions to determine which procedures are, and are not, monotonic. For procedures failing monotonicity, the geometry determines profiles which force this unfortunate change in the outcome, so, it is easy to generate examples.

Example 5.2.3. To illustrate the geometry, suppose a procedure selects the $\mathbf{w}_s$ top-ranked candidate c_1. This $\mathcal{A}(c_1) = [\mathcal{R}(1) \cup \mathcal{R}(7) \cup \mathcal{R}(2)] \cap CH(\mathbf{w}_s)$ involve the three regions sharing the c_1 vertex; it is the shaded region of Fig. 5.2.3a to the left of the vertical boundary line ($\mathcal{R}(12)$) and below the upward slanting boundary line ($\mathcal{R}(8)$). As it is obvious that $\mathbf{q}_2 \in \mathcal{A}(c_1)$ requires the b-cone of admissible monotonicity changes to be in this region, (the dark region is one such cone), this procedure is monotonic.

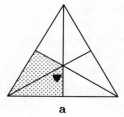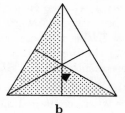

a   b

Fig. 5.2.3. Responsiveness of the cone

The procedure that selects the two top-ranked candidates from a $\mathbf{w}_s$-election also is monotonic. For example, if c_1 is one of the two top-ranked candidates and the target for an analysis of monotonicity, then we are interested in the geometry of $\mathcal{R}(1) \cup \mathcal{R}(2) \cup \mathcal{R}(3) \cup \mathcal{R}(6)$ (and the obvious indifference regions) which is the shaded region of Fig. 5.2.3b. The boundary of this region is a vertical line ($\mathcal{R}(9)$) and a line sloping downward and to the right ($\mathcal{R}(11)$), so a base point in this region requires the b-cone to remain in this region.

Next, consider the agenda $< c_1, c_2, c_3 >$ which has failed all other responsiveness criteria. To see that monotonicity is preserved, at least for c_1 and c_2, recall

---

[5] For the reader who knows the terms, observe that specifying a line emanating from a point and analyzing the changes corresponds to the "directional derivative" of the procedure.

that $\mathcal{A}(c_1)$ is the c_1-Condorcet region $z < 0$, $x > 0$. Starting from any point in this region, it is clear that a "c - cone" (a sector of the type given by Fig. 5.2.2c) remains in this region. A similar argument holds for c_2.

If monotonicity difficulties plague $< c_1, c_2, c_3 >$, they must be caused by the cyclic regions in $\mathcal{A}(c_3)$. (See Fig. 5.1.3.) The monotonicity cone for c_3 requires the x value to remain fixed (because the relative rankings of c_1 and c_2 are held fixed) while $z \geq 0$, $y \leq 0$. Starting from any point in the c_3-Condorcet region ($z > 0$, $y < 0$), the c-cone only enhances c_3's victory. In the positive cyclic region ($x > 0, y > 0, z > 0$), changes admitted by the cone have no effect on the x value; they improve upon (or leave untouched) the z values, but they can decrease the y values. However, smaller y values push the outcome into a c_3-Condorcet region. A similar argument holds for the negative cyclic region. Consequently, *an agenda is monotonic.* $\square$

As shown, the geometry makes it easy to determine the monotonicity of a procedure. To further illustrate, I show that Black's method, and all obvious $\mathbf{w}_s$-modifications, are monotonic.

Definition 5.2.4. *The $\mathbf{w}_s$-Black's method is where c_j is the winner if she is a Condorcet winner. Otherwise, select the top-ranked candidate from a $\mathbf{w}_s$ election.* $\square$

This "either/or" aspect is what preserves monotonicity. To start, suppose $\mathbf{p}$ requires the selection of c_1. If she wins by being a Condorcet winner, then any c-cone change provides a more imposing victory. If $\mathbf{p}$ is in a cyclic region, then, as shown above, a c-cone change either keeps the outcome in the same cyclic region, or it forces the outcome toward the c_1-Condorcet region where c_1 has a guaranteed victory. If the outcome remains in the cyclic region, we need to consider the impact of the b-cone. However, these changes just add to c_1's $\mathbf{w}_s$ victory margin. Consequently, *all $\mathbf{w}_s$- Black's methods are monotonic.*

What Isn't Monotonic? To find procedures that are not monotonic, we need to create a procedure where combined movements of the types indicated in Fig. 5.2.2b and c lead to c_1's defeat. An obvious choice is a $\mathbf{w}_s$-runoff.

A runoff is monotonic if c_1 is the winner of a $\mathbf{w}_s$-runoff and if the profile defines a point in the c_1-Condorcet region because an admissible monotonic change still selects c_1. This is because the b-cone keeps c_1 as a top-ranked candidate and the c-cone forces the pairwise outcome deeper into the c_1-Condorcet region. Similarly, if $\mathbf{q}_2$ is positioned so that the cone of admissible changes allows the same two candidates to be top-ranked, c_1 will remain the winner. (The $\mathbf{w}_s$ change of a b-cone advances the same two candidates to the runoff; the c-cone pairwise change improves c_1's standing.)

What remains is if the original outcome $\mathbf{q}_2$ is such that:

a. $\mathbf{q}_1$ and $\mathbf{q}_2$ have different candidates top-ranked.

b. The pairwise outcome is cyclic for both profiles.

These conditions can be satisfied simultaneously. For instance, in Fig. 5.2.4a, the shaded regions are where the $\mathbf{w}_s$-outcomes can be accompanied with a negative cycle. (The profile vertices for the negative cycles are $\frac{1}{2}(\mathbf{E}_i + \mathbf{E}_j)$ where i and

j are even. Each vertex of the shaded region, the midpoint between $[\mathbf{w}_s]_i$, $[\mathbf{w}_s]_j$ where i and j are even integers, is the $\mathbf{w}_s$-image of a profile vertex.) So, choosing a profile for such a $\mathbf{q}_2$ outcome in $\mathcal{R}(2)$ advances c_1 and c_3 to the runoff where the negative cycle anoints c_1 as the winner.

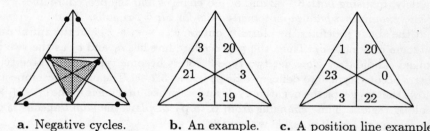

a. Negative cycles.   **b.** An example.   **c.** A position line example

Fig. 5.2.4. Monotonicity and runoffs

The key is that the $c_2 \sim c_3$ indifference line $\mathcal{R}(7)$ defines a 30° angle while the bottom edge of the b-cone forms a 60° angle – this difference in angles begs to be exploited. So, to violate monotonicity, choose $\mathbf{q}_2 \in \mathcal{R}(2)$ sufficiently close to $\mathcal{I}$ and the $c_2 \sim c_3$ indifference line to allow the b-cone to enter $\mathcal{R}(1)$. With $\mathbf{q}_1 \in \mathcal{R}(1)$, the runoff is between c_1 and c_2 where the negative cycle favors c_2. In other words, c_1's additional support sabotages her winning position!

Example 5.2.4. The geometry makes it an exercise to construct illustrating examples; I describe the one illustrated in Fig. 5.2.4b. We need a negative cycle, so start with a strong Condorcet profile such as $(0, 19, 0, 19, 0, 19)$. This profile needs to be modified so that a negative cycle is preserved, and the plurality outcome is in $\mathcal{R}(2)$.

To change the plurality outcome from $\mathcal{I}$, add an appropriate basic profile, such as $2\mathbf{E}_2 + \mathbf{E}_4$. Monotonicity is defied by exploiting the 60° slope of the b-cone. According to Table 5.2.2 or Fig. 5.2.2a, this slope requires changes in voter types from $3 \to 2$ and/or $5 \to 6$. However, before changing their types, they need to exist. So, add a small Condorcet odd profile to obtain the profile of Fig. 5.2.4b, $\mathbf{p} = (3, 21, 3, 20, 3, 19)$, with the plurality outcome $c_1 \succ c_3 \succ c_2$.

If only two type-three votes from $\mathbf{p}$ convert to type-two's, then the "c_1 improved profile" is $\mathbf{p}_1 = (3, 23, 1, 20, 3, 19) = (1, 19, 1, 19, 1, 19) + (2, 4, 0, 1, 2, 0)$. Clearly the Condorcet part preserves the negative cycle and the remaining portion of $\mathbf{p}_1$ defines the plurality outcome $c_1 \succ c_2 \succ c_3$. As c_2 wins the runoff, monotonicity is violated. $\square$

Example 5.2.4 uses a $3 \to 2$ voter change because a $5 \to 6$ change has no impact on the outcome ($[\mathbf{w}_0]_5 = [\mathbf{w}_0]_6$). Similarly, a $3 \to 2$ voter change doesn't affect a $\mathbf{w}_{\frac{1}{2}}$ antiplurality outcome, whereas a $5 \to 6$ voter change does with $\mathbf{w}_{\frac{1}{2}}$. The effect of a voter change, then, depends on who changes types and which $\mathbf{w}_s$ is being used. Thus, if $\delta_{i,j}$ represents the votes changing from type-j to type-i, the impact upon the $\mathbf{w}_s$ election outcome is

$$\delta_{i,j}[[\mathbf{w}_s]_j - [\mathbf{w}_s]_i]. \tag{5.2.2}$$

Namely, *by using both* $3 \to 2$ *and* $5 \to 6$ *changes and the procedure line, we can create examples where monotonicity fails for all* $\mathbf{w}_s$-*runoffs.* To do so, observe that the above $\mathbf{p}$ defines the plurality outcome $c_1 \succ c_3 \succ c_2$ and the antiplurality outcome $c_3 \succ c_1 \succ c_2$. Thus, the $\mathbf{p}$ procedure line has c_1 and c_3 as the two top-ranked candidates. Now, let two type-3 voters become type-2 and three type-5 voters become type-6 to define profile $\mathbf{p}_2$ in Fig. 5.2.4c. The profile decomposition shows that $\mathbf{p}_2$ keeps the negative cycle and its procedure line is in the $c_1 \succ c_2 \succ c_3$ ranking region. Thus *changing from* $\mathbf{p}$ *to* $\mathbf{p}_2$ *displays the simultaneous lack of monotonicity for all possible* $\mathbf{w}_s$-*runoffs.*

5.2.3 A Profile Angle

To introduce a new tool, recall those suppressed memories about tormenting a younger sibling with a water pistol. Think of the nozzle as an original profile, the way the pistol is held as the direction of profile change, and the shot water as the new profile. As your principal goal was to soak your young sister, you placed the nozzle sufficiently near her shirt (i.e., the original profile is near a particular surface), aimed it toward the shirt (the change in the profile is toward the surface), and pulled the trigger. If you were successful, (the new profile is through the surface), your parents yelled at you. Instead of a shirt, the surface in these multiprofile concerns is the boundary separating profile sets with different outcomes.

A convenient way to handle the angle formed by two profiles, $\mathbf{p}_1$, $\mathbf{p}_2$ (i.e., the aimed direction the water pistol) is to use the *scalar* or *dot* product between the two n-dimensional vectors $\mathbf{a} = (a_1, a_2, \ldots, a_n)$ and $\mathbf{b} = (b_1, b_2, \ldots, b_n)$ defined as

$$(\mathbf{a}, \mathbf{b}) = \sum_{j=1}^{n} a_j b_j = \|\mathbf{a}\| \|\mathbf{b}\| \cos(\theta), \tag{5.2.3}$$

The summation, which defines the scalar product, is easy to compute; just add the indicated products. What makes the scalar product particularly powerful is the standard, yet amazing fact captured by the second equality; *this sum equals the product of the lengths of the two vectors times the cosine of the angle,* θ, *between them.* Of particular concern is the *sign* of the scalar product; if it is zero, the vectors are orthogonal ($\theta = 90^o$), if it is positive, the vectors point in the same general direction ($|\theta| < 90^o$; they form an acute angle); and if it is negative, the vectors point in widely different directions ($|\theta| > 90^o$; they form an obtuse angle).

As immediate examples, the orthogonality of vectors $\mathbf{e}_1$, $\mathbf{e}_2$ is reflected by the zero value of the scalar product $((1,0,0),(0,1,0)) = 1 \cdot 0 + 0 \cdot 1 + 0 \cdot 0 = 0$. Likewise, the fact that $\mathbf{a} = (1,0)$ and $\mathbf{b} = (-1,0)$ point in opposite directions is in accord with the negative value of $(\mathbf{a}, \mathbf{b}) = (1)(-1) + (0)(0) = -1$. The power of the inner product is reflected by choosing $\mathbf{a} = (3, 6, 7)$ and $\mathbf{b} = (2, -1, 0)$. It is not obvious that $\mathbf{a}$ and $\mathbf{b}$ are orthogonal; yet, the computation $(\mathbf{a}, \mathbf{b}) = (3)(2) + (6)(-1) + (7)(0) = 0$ proves that they are.

5.2.4 A General Theorem Using Profiles

The responsiveness of positive effectiveness and monotonicity emphasizes the geometry of the representation triangle and cube. The real issue, however, concerns changes in profiles. Namely, the natural setting is the space of normalized profiles $Si(6)$. There is a tradeoff; when these issues are considered in the profile space, $Si(6)$, we lose natural geometric insight, but we gain techniques that extend to any number of candidates. Moreover, even for three candidates, the technical proofs are simpler.

The idea is to start with a base profile, $\mathbf{p}_2 \in f^{-1}(\mathcal{A}(c_j))$, in the profile set supporting c_j. A specified responsiveness property is violated if an admissible change to the profile, $\mathbf{p}_1$, is such that $\mathbf{p}_2 + \mathbf{p}_1 \notin f^{-1}(\mathcal{A}(c_j))$. For this to occur, the direction of change (i.e., how the water pistol is aimed) passes through the boundary of $f^{-1}(\mathcal{A}(c_j))$. Therefore, by understanding what admissible directions pass through the boundary, we can determine whether a specified responsiveness property is preserved.

Using the water pistol story, it is clear the pistol should be aimed perpendicular to the surface. Similarly, we want to find a vector perpendicular to a boundary set. What simplifies the analysis is that the $f^{-1}(\mathcal{A}(c_j))$ boundaries typically are expressed as linear equations set equal to zero. This means that the coefficients of the boundary equation define the desired normal vector (an orthogonal vector) to the boundary. To see why, observe that the equation $\sum a_j p_j = 0$ can be re-expressed as a scalar product $(\mathbf{a}, \mathbf{p}) = 0$ where $\mathbf{a} = (a_1, \ldots, a_6)$. As the scalar product is zero, it follows from Eq. 5.2.3 that the vectors $\mathbf{a}$ and $\mathbf{p}$ are orthogonal.

If $\mathbf{a}$ is perpendicular to a surface, then so is $-\mathbf{a}$. (This is equivalent to pointing the water pistol either directly toward the shirt or away from it.) One of these vectors points to the inside of the $\mathcal{A}(c_j)$ region; call it an *inner normal vector*. By virtue of pointing toward the interior of $\mathcal{A}(c_j)$, the inner normal indicates the direction of profile changes that assist, rather than hurt, the selection of c_j. So, how can we use all of this to our advantage? Well, suppose the current profile $\mathbf{p}_2$ is in a profile set $\mathcal{A}(c_j)$ near a boundary. We want to learn whether a small change in the profile, admitted by a responsiveness issue being analyzed, will change the c_j outcome or keep it the same. If the change moves toward the interior of $\mathcal{A}(c_j)$, then the outcome remains the same. That is, if the scalar product of the change, $\mathbf{p}_1$ and the inner normal is positive, then the same c_j conclusion holds. On the other hand, if this scalar product is negative, then the profile change is trying to leave $\mathcal{A}(c_j)$. Thus, if the original profile is close enough to the boundary, the admissible profile change will lead to a new outcome.

Thus

the dot product between the inner normal and the admissible directions of changes in profiles forms a powerful tool for the analysis of responsiveness; a tool that is technically easy to use.

Example 5.2.5. To illustrate the dot product technique, consider positive responsiveness. If c_1 is the winner, the only two admissible directional changes for a profile are $(1,0,0,0,0,0)^6$ or $(0,1,0,0,0,0)$. These vectors are not profiles; they indicate directional changes in profiles. As such, $(1,0,0,0,0,0) \neq \mathbf{E}_1$. Nevertheless, with an abuse of notation, identify $(1,0,0,0,0,0)$ with $\mathbf{E}_1$ and $(0,1,0,0,0,0)$ with $\mathbf{E}_2$. Similarly, the profile directions for c_2 and c_3 are indicated, respectively, as $\mathbf{E}_5$ or $\mathbf{E}_6$ and as $\mathbf{E}_3$ or $\mathbf{E}_4$.

For the agenda $< c_1, c_2, c_3 >$, one $\mathcal{A}(c_1)$ boundary is the $x = 0$ coordinate plane (or $c_1 \sim c_2$ region). A profile on this boundary satisfies

$$p_1 + p_2 + p_3 - p_4 - p_5 - p_6 = 0,$$

so its coefficients define the inner normal vector $\mathbf{N}_{1,2} = (1,1,1,-1,-1,-1)$. (This is an "inner" normal vector, because the positive components identify the voter types where more of them help c_1 defeat c_2.) Because $(\mathbf{N}_{1,2}, \mathbf{E}_1) = (\mathbf{N}_{1,2}, \mathbf{E}_2) = 1 > 0$, all admissible unanimity changes in profiles move in the general direction of the inner normal – toward the interior of the region electing c_1. This supports positive involvement. Similar simple computations hold for the other boundary.

Next consider the fate of c_3. Any profile with a cyclic outcome crowns c_3 as the winner. Boundaries for cyclic regions include profiles where $c_1 \sim c_2$, so $\mathbf{N}_{1,2}$ is a normal vector for this portion of the boundary. In fact, using the above argument, $\mathbf{N}_{1,2}$ is an inner normal for the positive cyclic region because it has the ranking $c_1 \succ c_2$. (The positive components determine the voter types where more of them improve the outcome.)

The two unanimity profiles for c_3 are $\mathbf{E}_3$ and $\mathbf{E}_4$. Even though $(\mathbf{N}_{1,2}, \mathbf{E}_3) = 1 > 0$, we have that $(\mathbf{N}_{1,2}, \mathbf{E}_4) = -1 < 0$. Thus, by choosing the original profile close to this boundary and then adding type-four voters to the original profile, the outcome crosses the boundary to defeat c_3. Indeed, this is the earlier example.

For the negative cyclic region, the inward normal vector is $-\mathbf{N}_{1,2}$. With this change in sign, $(-\mathbf{N}_{1,2}, \mathbf{E}_3) = -1 < 0$, so positive involvement can be violated by starting with a profile sufficiently near this boundary and adding type-three voters. Namely, *analyzing positive involvement for a procedure reduces to checking the signs of certain components of the inner normal vectors!*   □

Theorem 5.2.3. *A sufficient condition for a procedure to be positively involved is if the scalar product of all the inner normals for the boundaries of $f^{-1}(\mathcal{A}(c_j))$*

---

[6] More accurately, the sum of the components of a directional change in $Si(6)$ must add to zero because the sum of the components of the defining difference $\mathbf{p}_1 - \mathbf{p}_2$ do. Therefore, a more accurate choice is $(\frac{5}{6}, -\frac{1}{6}, -\frac{1}{6}, \ldots, -\frac{1}{6})$. It is easy to prove, however, nothing is changed by using the simpler choice given above. See the exercises.

have a positive scalar product with the two unanimity profiles having c_j top-ranked. A sufficient condition for a procedure to violate positive involvement is if one of these scalar products is negative.

Example 5.2.6. This theorem makes it easy to show that a w_s-runoff is not positively involved. To do so with c_1, just show that the inner normal vector for some boundary has a negative value for either the first or second component. The boundary dividing whether c_2 or c_3 is advanced to the runoff is in the plane of profiles with the c_2, c_3 relative ranking $c_2 \sim c_3$; with c_1 it is given by the equation $[p_1 s + p_4 s + p_5(1-s) + p_6(1-s)] - [p_2 s + p_3(1-s) + p_4(1-s) + p_5 s] = 0$. After collecting terms, the normal vector is

$$\mathbf{S}_{2,3} = (s, -s, s - 1, 2s - 1, 1 - 2s, 1 - s). \tag{5.2.4}$$

Whether $\mathbf{S}_{2,3}$ or $-\mathbf{S}_{2,3}$ is the inner normal vector depends upon whether the pairs are in the positive or negative cyclic region. If the pairs define a positive cycle (so $c_1 \succ c_2$, $c_3 \succ c_1$), then it is to c_1's advantage to be in the runoff with c_2. Thus, $\mathbf{S}_{2,3}$ is the inward normal. As the second component is negative for $s \neq 0$, positive involvement can be violated by starting with a profile near this boundary and adding type-two voters. With a negative cycle, the inward normal is $-\mathbf{S}_{2,3}$ with its negative first component. Consequently, *with the exception of the plurality system, positive involvement of a runoff is violated by using type-one voters.*

For the plurality system, consider the boundaries of the w_s relative rankings $c_1 \sim c_2$ and $c_1 \sim c_3$ where c_1 is struggling to be one of the two top-ranked candidates. For example, $\mathbf{S}_{1,3} = (1 - 2s, 1 - s, s, -s, s - 1, 2s - 1)$, is the inward normal for the region with boundary $c_2 \succ c_1 \sim c_3$. As the first two components are positive, positive involvement cannot be violated. Indeed, by checking the remaining boundaries, it follows that *although the w_0 simple runoff is not weakly consistent, it is positively involved; it is the only w_s simple runoff that is positively involved.* □

To analyze monotonicity, we just need to determine the admissible directions of profile changes. The directions associated with an "improvement" for c_1 can be read off from Table 5.2.1 or Fig. 5.2.2; they are linear combinations (with non-negative scalar multiples indicating how many voters change) of the vectors

$$\mathbf{d}_{3 \to 2} = \mathbf{E}_2 - \mathbf{E}_3, \ \mathbf{d}_{4 \to 2} = \mathbf{E}_2 - \mathbf{E}_4, \ \mathbf{d}_{4 \to 3} = \mathbf{E}_3 - \mathbf{E}_4$$
$$\mathbf{d}_{6 \to 1} = \mathbf{E}_1 - \mathbf{E}_6, \ \mathbf{d}_{5 \to 1} = \mathbf{E}_1 - \mathbf{E}_5, \ \mathbf{d}_{5 \to 6} = \mathbf{E}_6 - \mathbf{E}_5,$$

where $k \mathbf{d}_{i \to j}$ means that k voters of type-i, adhering to their firm evanescent standards, now count themselves among the type-j voters.

To illustrate, with the agenda $< c_2, c_3, c_1 >$, a typical inner normal for the $y = 0$ (or $c_2 \sim c_3$) coordinate plane, which is a boundary for the positive cyclic region, is

$$\mathbf{N}_{2,3} = (1, -1, -1, -1, 1, 1, 1). \tag{5.2.5}$$

The scalar product of $(\mathbf{N}_{2,3}, \mathbf{d}_{i \to j}) = 0$; geometrically, this zero value occurs because all changes of voter types keep the relative ranking of c_2, c_3 invariant. These are the only interesting boundaries, so we have reestablished the monotonicity of the agenda.

With a runoff, however, a simple computation proves that $(\mathbf{S}_{2,3}, \mathbf{d}_{6 \to 1}) = 2s - 1 < 0$ if $s \neq \frac{1}{2}$). The vector $\mathbf{S}_{2,3}$ is an inner normal for regions with a positive cycle (it points to the direction where c_2 is selected over c_3, and we need $c_1 \succ c_2$ in the runoff). Consequently, with the exception of the antiplurality runoff, examples are easy to design to show the lack of monotonicity for $\mathbf{w}_s$-runoffs (Just use voter changes $6 \to 1$.) To create an antiplurality example, we find from the dot product that a $4 \to 2$ change is needed. On the other hand, because $(\mathbf{S}_{2,3}, \mathbf{d}_{5 \to 1}) = 3s - 1 < 0$ if $s < \frac{1}{3}$, the voter change $5 \to 1$ demonstrates this conclusion only with a limited number of $\mathbf{w}_s$-runoffs. The same analysis extends to the $\mathbf{sc} - \mathbf{w}_s$ runoffs.

5.2.5 Other Admissible Directions

Responsiveness issues start with an election outcome, specify the admissible changes for supporting profiles, and then examine whether desired goals for the new profiles are met. This general statement makes it clear that there are all sorts of questions and issues that can be raised. For example, what happens with ties? Presumably, added support in favor of one of the candidates would lead to her selection; but will it? This statement defines the starting configurations (profiles leading to tie votes), the directions of change (adding more support for c_i), and the goal (the selection of c_i). Using the scalar product analysis, it is not difficult to characterize all procedures that do, and do not, satisfy these objectives.

Indeed, with sufficient imagination, it is possible to start with almost any specified set of directions to change a base profile, and invent an interesting story to justify its importance for voting theory. For instance, instead of admitting changes of unanimity profiles where c_1 is top-ranked, how about what happens with a change involving unanimity profiles where she is bottom ranked? Where she is middle-ranked? The immediate response should be "why! WGAD!" Actually, with slight experimentation, a story can be fashioned to justify such an investigation.

To illustrate with a middle-ranked change, suppose c_1 is elected with profile $\mathbf{p}$. Now, a type-three voter trying to decide whether to vote, is not overly pleased because c_1 is his second-place candidate; yet, this outcome is preferable to c_2's selection. So, to show support for c_3, this voter votes; c_2 is selected!

To show that this disturbing situation can occur with the $\mathbf{w}_s$-runoff, we just need a setting where the pairwise votes are $c_1 \succ c_2$, $c_2 \succ c_3$. So, if the runoff is between c_1 and c_2, c_1 wins, but a runoff between c_2 and c_3 allows the feared c_2 to be victorious. This means we need to investigate the boundary between selecting c_1 and c_3 for the runoff; the inner normal (favoring c_1) is

$$\mathbf{S}_{1,3} = (1 - s, 1 - 2s, 2s - 1, s - 1, -s, s).$$

As $(\mathbf{S}_{1,3}, \mathbf{E}_3) = 2s - 1 < 0$ for $s < \frac{1}{2}$, the above scenario can occur. To design an example, just choose $\mathbf{p}$ sufficiently near this boundary with a positive cycle, and the behavior is ensured.[7] Even though the plurality runoff is positively involved, it does suffer middle-ranked involvement problems. Such problems must be expected from the runoff, the agenda, and other varied procedures because their many boundaries provides all sorts of opportunities for changes in profiles to have an unexpected effect!

As another example, add voters with c_1 bottom-ranked. Common sense dictates that these new voters must hurt c_1's chances. To see that this need not be so, consider $\mathbf{S}_{2,3}$ – an inner normal for the boundary of a $\mathbf{w}_s$-runoff with a positive cycle. Because $(\mathbf{S}_{2,3}, \mathbf{E}_5) = 1 - 2s > 0$ if $s \neq \frac{1}{2}$, we have that if a type-five voter, votes, he can *assist* the election of his bottom-ranked candidate c_1! To create an example, choose a profile on the side of the boundary where c_2 is elected. With this base profile, if this type-five voter ($c_2 \succ c_3 \succ c_1$) stays home on election day, the runoff is between c_1 and c_3, and his second-ranked candidate, c_3 wins. So, by casting his ballot our type-five voter's day is ruined with the selection of the candidate he despises, c_1.

Notice that examples are easy to design for any procedure where an inner normal for a region selecting c_j has a positive value for a component corresponding to a voter type with c_j bottom ranked. Indeed, this provides a quick way to determine whether a procedure suffers the *negative involvement*.

This inner product approach makes it easy to understand why responsiveness problems arise once there are three or more candidates. The more candidates there are, the more profile sets we have. More profile sets means we have more boundaries and a wider selection of "inner normals." But a rich selection of inner normals means it is easier to find directions of profile change where the scalar product has the wrong sign – the responsiveness issue is violated. Also notice that if a procedure uses several subsets of candidates, like an agenda, Copeland's method, runoffs, etc., then it offers a wide selection of inner normals; it should not be surprising to find that many responsiveness conditions are not satisfied.

A Simple Analysis. To review, this inner normal vector argument makes it obvious that the more directions of change admitted by a responsiveness condition, the more difficult it is to find procedures which satisfy the specified goal. For instance, for a procedure to be positively involved for c_1, no inward normal for $f^{-1}(\mathcal{A}(c_1))$ can have a negative first or second component. Monotonicity supplements these two conditions with a larger list of other restrictions. For instance, to ensure that the admissible direction $\mathbf{E}_2 - \mathbf{E}_3$ does not suffice, the second component of an inward normal must be at least as large as the third component; the admissible directions of change, $\mathbf{E}_1 - \mathbf{E}_5$, $\mathbf{E}_1 - \mathbf{E}_6$ require the first component of all inward normals to be at least as large as the fifth and the sixth; etc.

---

[7] This "middle-ranked involvement" includes the "abstention" paradox which seems to have been discovered by Smith [Sm], significantly advanced for the plurality runoff by Brams and Fishburn [BF3], and then described in more general settings by Saari [S9].

This geometry reduces the responsiveness analysis to a simple game. To illustrate, suppose an hypothetical procedure has $(1, 2, 3, -1.4, -3.2, -1.4)$ as an inward normal for $f^{-1}(\mathcal{A}(c_1))$.

- The first two components are positive, so, at least with respect to this inner normal, the hypothetical procedure is positively involved for c_1.
- If the profile is on the boundary between c_1 and c_3, then the procedure is not positively involved for c_3. (The third component is positive, so a type-three voter improves c_1's chances.)
- The third coefficient is larger than the second, so this procedure is not monotonic.
- The third coefficient is larger than the first, so this procedure would not survive a responsiveness issue allowing a $3 \to 1$ voter type change. As this is a change from $c_3 \succ c_1 \succ c_2$ to $c_1 \succ c_2 \succ c_3$, it does not fall under the category of monotonicity (because the c_2, c_3 ranking is changed). However, $3 \to 1$ change does provide added support to c_1, so just invent a responsiveness issue that admits a $3 \to 1$ type change. For instance, if we allow type changes from where c_1 is middle-ranked to where c_1 is top-ranked, we are in business.
- The first three components are larger than the last three in sign, but not in magnitude, so we don't want to encourage any voter changes from the first three types to the last three. However if this boundary is between c_1 and c_3, a type-3 voter would be inspired to pretend to be a type-4 because the change $\mathbf{E}_4 - \mathbf{E}_3$ would ensure a c_3 victory. On the other hand, if the boundary is between c_1 and c_2, if a type-six voter acts like type-five, c_2 becomes the victor.

So, with a given inner normal, all sorts of scenarios considering responsiveness issues can be invented. Moreover, responsiveness problems occur with procedures that use the rankings from different subsets of candidates. Each set of candidates defines its own boundaries, so with several subsets, there are more boundaries. More boundaries yield more choices of inner normals. More kinds of inner normals provide more opportunities for something to go wrong with respect to responsiveness issues. Finally, when issues, such as the ones considered in Sects. 5.1-5.3 are considered, they usually are considered as separate topics. With the method developed here, all can be considered simultaneously.

5.2.6 Exercises

1. For the agenda $< c_1, c_2, c_3 >$, what choices of the unanimity profiles force positive involvement to fail? Find a general statement identifying the kinds of unanimity profiles that can, and cannot cause a profile to show positive involvement.

2. Find a profile and an agenda where c_1 loses, but if two voters who have c_1 top-ranked did not vote, then c_1 would have won. Do the same with a BC runoff.

3. Start with a $(0, 21, 0, 20, 0, 19)$ profile and subdivide the voters with c_3 top-ranked into two groups to get $(0, 21, 2, 18, 0, 19)$. Show that a $3 \to 2$ change creates an example where monotonicity is violated. Are there changes of this kind where an antiplurality method also leads to an example? Find the minimum number of voters needed to create an example illustrating that a $\mathbf{w}_0$-runoff is not monotonic. Find the minimum number of voters needed so that the same example proves that all $\mathbf{w}_s$-runoffs are not monotonic.

4. For Example 5.2.1, only one boundary surface for the cyclic regions was considered. Determine what happens with the other surfaces.

5. Use a "starlike" argument to show that a w_s-Black method is monotonic.

6. Once $n \geq 4$, the cyclic regions of pairs are replaced by even more adventurous possibilities for pairs, for rankings of the different triplets, etc. While geometry is higher dimensional, ideas and lessons from $n = 3$ apply. In particular, don't expect weak consistency, positive involvement, monotonicity, etc. for procedures that higher dimensionality of profiles comes into being; when procedures involve rankings of subsets of different numbers of candidates, boundaries can force unusual orientations. It is these different orientations that lead to conclusions. For $n = 4$, analyze the runoff $< c_1, c_2, c_3, c_4 >$.

7. Characterize the scoring rule runoffs with respect to the responsiveness issues.

8. Suppose G is a smooth nonlinear function. What responsiveness properties does the corresponding G binary procedure satisfy?

5.3 Gibbard-Satterthwaite and Manipulable Procedures

We learned from Sect. 5.2 that by examining the inner normals for $f^{-1}(\mathcal{A}(c_j))$, we can decide what responsiveness issues will and will not be satisfied. Alternatively, we can start with a specified responsiveness issue and design a procedure to satisfy it. This is because a chosen responsiveness issue restricts the admissible inner normals, the inner normals define the boundaries of profile sets, and the profile sets define a procedure. I illustrate this approach with the responsiveness issue of sincere voting.

Definition 5.3.1. A choice procedure is *strategy proof* if there do not exist situations where a voter can obtain a more preferred outcome by voting as though his voter type is different than his actual voter type. □

Does there exist a strategy proof procedure? This issue has been resolved in a general setting by Gibbard [Gi] and Satterthwaite [Sa], where, essentially, they proved the stunning conclusion that either a procedure is dictatorial, or it is not strategy proof – it can be manipulated. This important result is proved here for and "smooth" procedures.

The idea of this new proof is simple; the ways voters can change preferences determine the admissible inner normals of any procedure. For instance, if a voter pretends to be of a different type, he changes the sincere profile to a manipulated one. To ensure that the change is not to the voter's advantage, admit only those inner normals where the manipulative change is not beneficial. But, because there are so many ways voters can try to change preferences, this seriously restricts the choice of admissible inner normals. Now, with three or more candidates the space of profiles must be divided into at least three regions, $\{f^{-1}(\mathcal{A}(\{c_j\}))\}_{j=1,2,3}$. The geometry of profile space imposes a second constraint; partitioning a space into three or more regions requires using a minimal number of inner normals. The two sets of restrictions about the inner normals conflict, so the Gibbard-Satterthwaite conclusion follows.

To determine the properties a procedure needs to satisfy to be strategy proof, notice that a voter assumes a different voter type only if it improves his outcome.

So, if we consider inner normal vector $\mathbf{n} = (n_1, n_2, \ldots, n_6)$ for $f^{-1}(\mathcal{A}(c_1))$ on the boundary separating $f^{-1}(\mathcal{A}(c_1))$ and $f^{-1}(\mathcal{A}(c_2))$, then only those voters preferring $c_2 \succ c_1$ would be inspired to examine their strategies. These are the voters of types 4, 5, 6. If any of the last three components of $\mathbf{n}$ is positive (indicating a vote from a voter of this type helps c_1 over c_2), e.g. suppose $n_6 < 0$. Then, by not voting, a type-six voter creates a $(\mathbf{n}, -\mathbf{E}_6) = -n_6 < 0$ situation which hurts c_1. Thus, to be strategy-proof, the last three n_j values are negative.

Similarly, to insure that these voters cannot gain advantage just by changing their ranking of c_2 and c_3, it must be that

$$n_4 = n_5 = n_6 < 0.$$

For instance, if $n_4 > n_6$, a $4 \rightarrow 6$ change defines the direction $\mathbf{E}_6 - \mathbf{E}_4$ and the scalar product $(\mathbf{n}, \mathbf{E}_6 - \mathbf{E}_4) = n_6 - n_4 < 0$, so an example can be created where this strategic vote leads to c_2's victory instead of c_1's – exactly what a type-four strategic voter prefers.

Of course, $-\mathbf{n}$ is the inner normal for $f^{-1}(\mathcal{A}(c_2))$. The same argument applied to how supporters with $c_1 \succ c_2$ would vote indicates that $n_1 = n_2 = n_3 > 0$. But, a direction change for profiles in $Si(6)$ must have the components add to zero, so we can choose

$$\mathbf{n} = \mathbf{N}_{1,2} = (1, 1, 1, -1, -1, -1). \tag{5.3.1}$$

This computation proves that when the choice is between c_1 and c_2, a strategy-proof procedure must have inner normal $\mathbf{n}$ everywhere on the boundary of the profile set separating c_1 and c_2. Namely, all such procedures are determined by the sign of

$$p_1 + p_2 + p_3 - (p_4 + p_5 + p_6) + a$$

where a is some constant. If $a = 0$, then we have the usual pairwise majority vote scheme between c_1 and c_2 where a positive value means that c_1 wins and a negative value supports c_2. If $a \neq 0$, we still have a pairwise vote, except the sign of a means that the procedure has a bias for a particular candidate.

If a procedure also must allow c_3 to win, we need to consider the inner boundaries between c_1 and c_3 and between c_2 and c_3. The same arguments show that, to be strategy proof, the normal vectors must be $\mathbf{N}_{1,3}$ and $\mathbf{N}_{2,3}$. Thus, for some choice of scalars $a_{i,j}$, all possible strategy proof procedure must be based on the signs of the outcomes of

$$((\mathbf{N}_{1,2}, \mathbf{p}) - a_{1,2}, (\mathbf{N}_{2,3}, \mathbf{p}) - a_{2,3}, (\mathbf{N}_{3,1}, \mathbf{p}) - a_{3,1}) = F_3(\mathbf{p}) - (a_{1,2}, a_{2,3}, a_{3,1}).$$
$$\tag{5.3.2}$$

For example, if the first component is positive and the third is negative, c_1 is selected. If the first component is negative and the second is positive, c_2 is selected.

So, *if a strategy proof procedure exists, it must be a translated version of the Condorcet winner!* That is, the outcome is in terms of the pairwise votes, where bias is introduced. Namely, the image of the sought after procedure is in the representation cube where the division between the different sets $\mathcal{A}(c_j)$ need not be at the origin; it is at $\mathbf{a} = (a_{1,2}, a_{2,3}, a_{3,1})$. Call this an $\mathbf{a}$-*biased Condorcet winner*. It remains to choose $\mathbf{a}$.

If $\mathbf{a}$ is in the interior of the representation cube, then the division creates eight open regions; two correspond to translated versions of the cyclic regions. This geometry returns us to the essence of the agenda problem; each cyclic region needs to be assigned to a candidate c_j. If one cyclic region is assigned to c_1, it has three sides, so it has three different inward normals. In $Si(6)$ this means that either $\mathbf{N}_{2,3}$ or $-\mathbf{N}_{2,3}$ is an inward normal for $f^{-1}(\mathcal{A}(c_1))$. But this leads to a contradiction because, to be strategy proof, the only admissible inner normals are $\mathbf{N}_{1,2}$ or $-\mathbf{N}_{3,1}$.

The only way out of this problem is to choose $\mathbf{a}$ on a boundary of the representation cube, and this must be done so that both the positive and negative cyclic regions are eliminated. As this is geometrically impossible, no strategy proof mechanism exists.

The above argument used the assumption that the procedure selects only a single candidate. This is not necessary; we can assume it selects any number of them. All we need is an agreement that a voter with $c_j \succ c_i$ prefers $\{c_j\}$ over $\{c_i, c_j\}$, and $\{c_i, c_j\}$ over $\{c_i\}$. What emerges are the same kinds of boundary conditions.

Theorem 5.3.1. *Consider the procedure $f : Si(6) \to \mathcal{P}$ where the boundaries between profile sets supporting different outcomes are smooth. If for each c_j one outcome of f does not contain c_j and one other does, then f is not strategy proof.*

For example, if the admissible outcomes of a procedure include the sets

$$\{c_1, c_2\}, \{c_2, c_3\}, \{c_3\},$$

then it is not strategy proof.

Proof. If the boundaries are smooth, they can be represented as $F(\mathbf{p}) = 0$ with inner normal vectors $\nabla F(\mathbf{p})$. The above argument shows that $\nabla F(\mathbf{p})/\|\nabla F\| = \mathbf{N}_{i,j}$. Thus, the boundaries are linear. The proof follows from the above argument. $\square$

It is easy to extend this proof to where the separating boundaries are not smooth and to $n \geq 3$ candidates. After all, the lack of smoothness and/or more candidates introduces more "directions," and more opportunities to manipulate the system.

5.3.1 Measuring Suspectibility to Manipulation

The departmental election for a Chair from the fable, where all but one voter adopted a strategic approach, demonstrates how to manipulate the BC. That the BC can be manipulated has been recognized since the days of Condorcet and Borda in the 1780s. Periodically, this BC defect is resurrected to argue against the adoption of the BC. But, as the Gibbard-Satterthwaite Theorem and Theorem 5.3.1 prove, *all* methods have this defect. So, is some procedure less susceptible to being manipulated than the others? This question is answered next.

One way to understand which positional methods are less susceptible to being manipulated is to examine what happens when a small percentage of the voters try to change the outcome. This *micromanipulation* is in the spirit of a Nash equilibrium which examines what happens when a single voter changes strategy. In some sense, this "small percentage" approach allows more general conclusions; by concentrating on a small percentage rather than a single voter, the coordinated actions of voters are included. On the other hand, one out of three voters is not a small percentage.

The basic approach is natural. Count those profiles where a small percentage of the voters could successfully manipulate the outcome. Obviously, the more profiles that permit the outcome to be successfully manipulated, the more susceptible the system. What we need is a mathematically tractable technique to measure this level of *susceptibility to manipulation*.

To be successfully manipulated, a sincere profile, $\mathbf{p}_s$, must be in the set of profiles supporting the sincere outcome, while the manipulated profile, $\mathbf{p}_m$, is the profile set supporting a different (the manipulated) outcome. The profile difference,

$$\mathbf{v} = \mathbf{p}_m - \mathbf{p}_s, \tag{5.3.3.}$$

determines what voter types are involved in the manipulative attempt. Since only a small number of strategic voters are allowed, the magnitude $\|\mathbf{v}\|$ must be small. This requires $\mathbf{p}_s, \mathbf{p}_m$ to be on opposite sides but near the profile boundary separating these outcomes. Thus, the above count only involves profiles near the boundary.

The Choice of $\mathbf{w}_s$. In analyzing a successful manipulation, there are two factors. The first is the choice of a voting system, $\mathbf{w}_s$, and the second concerns the abundance of opportunities for a successful manipulation. Both issues can be illustrated with the departmental election of the fable (which involves a massive, highly coordinated strategic action) by comparing $f(\mathbf{p}_s, \mathbf{w}_s)$ and $f(\mathbf{p}_m, \mathbf{w}_s)$ where $\mathbf{p}_s = (\frac{7}{15}, 0, \frac{1}{15}, 0, 0, \frac{7}{15})$ and the manipulated profile $\mathbf{p}_m = (0, \frac{7}{15}, \frac{1}{15}, 0, \frac{7}{15}, 0)$. The plurality vote acknowledges only a voter's top-ranked candidate, so both profiles define the same outcome $A \sim B \succ C$ with the same normalized vote $(\frac{7}{15}, \frac{7}{15}, \frac{1}{15})$. On the other hand, as described in the fable, the BC outcomes for these profiles radically differ; while the BC sincere outcome is $A \succ B \succ C$ with the normalized tally $(\frac{22}{45}, \frac{21}{45}, \frac{2}{45})$, the BC manipulated outcome is $C \succ A \succ B$ with the normalized tally $(\frac{15}{45}, \frac{14}{45}, \frac{16}{45})$.

To see what happens with other $\mathbf{w}_s$, use these two $\mathbf{w}_s$-tallies to determine the procedure line. As demonstrated in Fig. 5.3.1, if $\mathbf{w}_s$, $s \geq \frac{1}{3}$, is used, the difference between the sincere and the coordinated manipulation is exaggerated with the extreme occurring at the antiplurality outcome. Different $\mathbf{w}_s$ choices make dramatic differences in the outcomes. (In the figure, the sincere procedure line is the small dash protruding into $\mathcal{R}(1)$, while the procedure line for the manipulated profile is the longer line ending in $\mathcal{R}(3)$.)

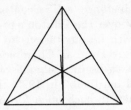

Fig. 5.3.1. Manipulated and sincere procedure lines

The choice of $\mathbf{w}_s$ determines what constitutes a *successful strategic action*. For instance, suppose the assigned procedure is the plurality vote and suppose a voter suspects that his top-ranked candidate is going to lose. Rather than "wasting a vote," he might vote for his second- ranked candidate. In the fable, for instance, had the plurality vote been used and had our Chair been more worldly, he would have voted for his second-ranked Abbott to ensure an outcome more to his liking. However, if the procedure is $\mathbf{w}_s$, $s > 0$, then this same voter can vote strategically by maximizing the point differential between the top two contenders. Obviously, the power of such strategic action increases with the value of $s \in [0, \frac{1}{2}]$, where the antiplurality vote offers the maximal power to block a second-ranked candidate.

Why wouldn't strategic action always be used? The answer is obvious; it depends on what you know. If you know who are the real contenders, then it may be difficult to resist voting strategically. If you do not know (or suspect) who are the true contenders, then it is irrational to vote in a manner than could empower your bottom-ranked candidate! *A prerequisite for strategic action, then, is prior knowledge or expectation about the sincere election outcome!*

Macromanipulation. More extreme conditions hold for a "successful" massive coordinated strategic action. It is worth exploring these problems because they serve as part of my motivation for investigating micro- rather than macromanipulation.

To justify a micro analysis we only need to believe that at least a few voters know, or suspect what is the sincere election outcome. With only a few voters, it is reasonable to expect them to design and discharge a coordinated strategic action. A macro-strategic analysis, on the other hand, requires us to believe that:

1. *There is wide-spread prior knowledge of "who are the real competitors."*
2. *There is a coordinator to ensure that the correct number of voters vote strategically (After all, by not voting sincerely, too many votes can lead to an undesired outcome – as in the fable).*

3. There is a way to impose discipline so that the designated strategic voters obediently carry out the planned action.

Situations, such as legislative bodies, almost beg for macromanipulation. With a public, rather than secret ballot, the vote of a person is known. Discipline is imposed by withholding favors. (For instance, a US Senator from Alabama embarrassed Vice President Gore on TV over the Clinton's proposed 1993 budget; one way he was "disciplined" was with his invitations to the Presidential reception for the 1992 National Collegiate Football Champions, the University of Alabama. Anyone fortunate enough to be in Alabama on a "football Saturday" recognizes that this is "political hardball." In 1995, this Senator changed political parties.) However, other than in such open forums, I find it difficult to believe that such carefully disciplined, coordinated action can be sustained. Remember strategic voting requires a voter to vote for someone other than his or her top choices. Consequently, macromanipulation is not the same as "bloc voting" by environmental groups, labor organizations, and other special interest groups. Rather than voting strategically, it is arguable that these groups try to increase the number of sympathetic voters.

Perhaps the most serious difficulty in accepting the importance of macromanipulation is the required obedience where large numbers of voters vote *strategically* as instructed. Instead, with the secret ballot and as events reported by the news media suggest (but do not prove), the solidarity of bloc voting tends to be inversely proportional to the level of political awareness and independence of the voters. Indeed, the coordination and discipline problems are so severe that it is difficult to believe that such carefully arranged strategic actions can be common events.

Opportunities for Micromanipulation. Finally, we arrive at the issue about the availability of opportunities. As noted, the choice of strategic action depends on the choice of $\mathbf{w}_s$. A more subtle and significantly more important aspect concerns the geometry of the profile boundaries separating different outcomes. Neutrality ensures that each $\mathbf{w}_s$ has the same proportion, $\frac{1}{6}$, of the profiles in $Si(6)$ supporting a specified ranking $c_i \succ c_j \succ c_k$. But this profile set changes with the choice of $\mathbf{w}_s$. Consequently, the geometry of the boundary separating different profile sets varies with $\mathbf{w}_s$.

The importance of this geometry is clear; the micromanipulability of a system depends upon how many profiles are near the boundary. Obviously, a smaller boundary admits fewer near-by profiles. Therefore, this geometry limits the number of situations where a small percentage of voters can successfully manipulate the outcome.

This difference is geometry is demonstrated in Fig. 5.3.2 where a unit square is divided into four equal parts in two different ways. In each setting, a sector has area $\frac{1}{4}$, but the perimeter dividing the sectors is smaller (by a factor of $\sqrt{2}$) in the division on the right. (To see this, superimpose the second square upon the first to define several right triangles. The hypotenuse of these triangles define the two segments of a boundary for the division on the left, while two legs are used for the division on the right.) Thus, if these divisions corresponded to profile regions, the procedure on the right, with its shorter boundary, offers fewer opportunities for a micromanipulation.

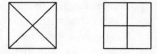

Fig. 5.3.2. Equal areas; different perimeters

Which $\mathbf{w}_s$ has the smallest boundary? Intuition comes from mathematics where a standard problem to find the region with the smallest perimeter with a specified area. The answer is clear for rectangles. If the area is 9, then a 1×9 box satisfies the area constraint, but its perimeter is 20. On the other hand, a 3×3 square has perimeter 12. Common sense suggests (and mathematics confirms) that the more symmetric the figure, the smaller the perimeter. Hence, solutions to this mathematical problem are squares, cubes, circles, spheres, etc. In voting, we should expect the minimal boundary area – the minimal exposure of opportunities to be successfully manipulated – to be associated with the $\mathbf{w}_s$ with the greater symmetry. This happens; the most symmetric procedure is, of course, the BC.

Assumptions for the Theorems. Central to an analysis of manipulation are the questions "Who knows what?" (prior information) and "Who is saying what to whom?" (coordination). To see how different answers affect the outcome, suppose an architect of a "one time only" system is confronted with an electorate similar to that of the departmental election in the fable. She knows that c_1 and c_2 will closely contest the election, and that either few voters have c_3 top-ranked, or everyone with c_3 top-ranked will vote sincerely. As demonstrated, the plurality vote, $\mathbf{w}_0$, is the method that optimally encourages a sincere vote, while the worse system in the antiplurality vote $\mathbf{w}_{\frac{1}{2}}$. Conversely, if nobody ranks c_3 in last place, then a plurality system encourages voters with c_3 top-ranked to vote strategically, while the antiplurality system encourages a stronger sincere vote. This theme generalizes; it turns out (Theorem 5.3.2) that for any $\mathbf{w}_s$, distributions of profiles can be found where $\mathbf{w}_s$ minimizes the susceptibility to manipulation. Namely, with appropriate assumptions, with a correctly constructed scenario, any system can be justified as being strategically the best. Consequently, we must treat with suspicion any assertion about the manipulability of a system that relies on a finite number of examples or on restrictive assumptions.

The above comments concern a "one-shot voting system;" we want to design a system for long term usage. Here, we do not know the distribution of the profiles, how it will evolve, how many voters are involved, or what pair of candidates are the target of a manipulation. This leads to the first assumptions.

1. *All profiles from $Si(6)$ are equally likely.*
2. *Each pair of alternatives is equally likely to be the target of an attempted*

manipulation.

Using neutrality and these assumptions, assume that *the strategic voters attempt to change the sincere relative ranking of $c_2 \succ c_2$ to $c_1 \succ c_2$*. Thus, the only voters wanting to change this relative ranking have the relative ranking $c_1 \succ c_2$, so they are of types one, two, or three. Now, a type-one voter, with his $c_1 \succ c_2 \succ c_3$ ranking can maximize the differential of his vote for these two candidates by pretending to be of type-two with $c_1 \succ c_3 \succ c_2$. The same argument hold for a type-three voter. As the type-two voter already maximizes the point differential, he must vote sincerely. So, which kind of voter is manipulative? Keeping to the theme of neutrality, we obtain the third assumption.

3. *It is equally likely for a manipulating voter to be of any strategic type. Such a voter assumes a strategy to maximize the effect of the manipulation.*

Averaging over the actions of the two types, leads to the *Expected Manipulation Vector (EMV)*

$$\lambda \mathbf{v} = \lambda(-\frac{1}{2}, 1, -\frac{1}{2}, 0, 0, 0). \tag{5.3.3}$$

where λ indicates the proportion of all voters acting strategically, and the $\mathbf{r}$ components indicate that half of the strategic voters are of type-one, half of type-three, and their best choice is to pretend to be of type-two. (For the reader concerned about situations, such as the departmental election with a plurality vote, where a type-one voter has no realistic strategic options, don't worry; this comes out in the analysis. At this point, $\mathbf{v}$ only indicates who would want to manipulate the outcome.)

Definition 5.3.2. For m voters and a specified $\lambda\mathbf{v}$, let $\mu(\mathbf{w}_s, \lambda\mathbf{v}, m)$, *the m voter measure of binary susceptibility of $\mathbf{w}_s$*, be the number of m voter profiles, $\mathbf{p} \in Si(6)$, where the relative ranking of $f(\mathbf{p}, \mathbf{w}_s)$ is $c_2 \succ c_1$ but the relative ranking of $f(\mathbf{p} + \lambda\mathbf{v})$ is $c_1 \succ c_2$.

A positional voting method $\mathbf{w}^*$ is *susceptibility efficient* if

$$\mu(\mathbf{w}^*, \lambda\mathbf{v}, m) \leq \mu(\mathbf{w}_s, \lambda\mathbf{v}, m), \forall s \in [0, \frac{1}{2}]. \quad \square$$

While this definition appears to model our objective, it has flaws. For instance, it allows an infinite number of answers where the answer changes with the number of voters. To illustrate, with 100 voters, there is no difference in the election rankings of $(1, 0, 0)$ and $(0.9999, 0.0001, 0)$, but there can be a significant difference with 10,000 voters. To discover a single answer, we use the following definition which, essentially, requires a susceptibility efficient procedure to hold for all values of m. (This is different from and more inclusive than considering the limit as $m \to \infty$; the limit only emphasizes large numbers of voters.)

Definition 5.3.3. For sufficiently small values of λ, let $\mu(\mathbf{w}_s)$ be the volume of $\{\mathbf{p} \in Si(6) | f(\mathbf{p}, \mathbf{w}_s)$ has the relative ranking $c_2 \succ c_1$ while $f(\mathbf{p} + \lambda\mathbf{v}, \mathbf{w}_s)$ has the relative ranking $c_1 \succ c_2\}$. $\square$

Susceptibility Theorems. We now come to a main conclusion.

Theorem 5.3.2. *For* $s \in [0, \frac{1}{2}]$, $\mu(\mathbf{w}_s) = \mu(\mathbf{w}_s^r)$, *and for* $0 \leq s_1 < s_2 < \frac{1}{3}$,

$$\mu(\mathbf{w}_{\frac{1}{3}}) < \mu(\mathbf{w}_{s_2}) = \mu(\mathbf{w}_{s_2}^r) < \mu(\mathbf{w}_{s_1}) = \mu(\mathbf{w}_{s_1}^r). \tag{5.3.4}$$

In words, *the BC is the unique method which is the least susceptible for micromanipulations.* Moreover, the more a procedure differs from the *BC*, the more its susceptibility measure increases. (As the proof shows, this is because the boundary area where profiles are vulnerable to manipulation increases in size.) The two procedures most susceptible to manipulation are the plurality and antiplurality votes.

The plurality vote does not fare very well by this theorem. Moreover, by examining the profiles which can be plurality manipulated, it becomes clear that many of them provide a strong incentive to vote strategically because the sincere outcome severely violates the true beliefs of the voters! We've already seen this with the beverage paradox from the fable. Practical examples can be found by examining the New Hampshire Presidential primarily election outcomes from almost any election year where it is not unusual for a candidate second-ranked by most voters to do poorly.

One might (accurately) complain that Theorem 5.3.2 includes situations where the close election is between second and third place. Second place is interesting in horse races, but not in an election where the "winner takes all." The next statement asserts that nothing changes when only the top-ranked candidates are considered.

Theorem 5.3.3. *When attempted manipulations involve only the two top-ranked candidates, a comparison of the levels of susceptibility of different* $\mathbf{w}_s$ *choices remains as asserted in Theorem 5.3.2*

One way to indicate how changes in the profile or assumptions about what voters are "strategic," is to redefine the *EMV* $\mathbf{v}$ so that c of the strategic voters, instead of $\frac{1}{2}$, are of type-one. This defines the *EMV* $\lambda \mathbf{v}_c = \lambda(-c, 1, 1 - c, 0, 0, 0)$; c *is the electorate's manipulation characteristic.* Using $\lambda \mathbf{v}_c$, changes the susceptibility efficient method. The choice is based on finding the $\mathbf{w}_s$ which, for a sufficiently small $\lambda \mathbf{v}_c$, minimizes the volume of

$\{\mathbf{p} \in Si(6) | f(\mathbf{p}, \mathbf{w}_s)$ has the relative ranking $c_2 \succ c_1$ while $f(\mathbf{p} + \lambda \mathbf{v}_c)$ has the relative ranking $c_1 \succ c_2\}$.

Actually, c can be chosen to "prove the superiority" of any $\mathbf{w}_s$.

Theorem 5.3.4. *For each* $\mathbf{w}_s$ *there exists a value of* c, *the electorate's manipulation characteristic, so that* $\mathbf{w}_s$ *is the least susceptible for manipulation.*

In words, this statement proves that with isolated examples and carefully constructed assumptions, any $\mathbf{w}_s$ can be justified as "being the best." When exposed to such arguments, watch your wallet.

As a related issue, how about *sensitivity?* This can be defined as where a small group of voters can alter the election outcome. Sensitivity differs from manipulation in that the outcome need not benefit these voters. Thus, this term captures the danger of the lunatic fringe, where small numbers of voters can alter the outcome; it captures the effects of an outcome changing when small numbers of voters just plain screw up their ballots and vote for the wrong person. Consequently, highly sensitive systems generate serious unintended problems. A fairly accurate measure of sensitivity is the number of profiles subject to such a change. This is, of course, measured by the size of the profile boundary separating different ranking regions.

Theorem 5.3.5. *The methods* $\mathbf{w}_s$ *and* $\mathbf{w}_s^r$ *are equally sensitive. The least sensitive procedure is the BC. Indeed, as the value of s increases its distance from $\frac{1}{3}$, the degree of sensitivity increases.*

Taking all of these factors into account, the conclusion is, again, that the BC is the optimal system.

Proof of the Susceptibility Theorem. Replace the notation of $\mathbf{w}_s = (1 - s, s, 0)$, with $(1, u, -1)$. Here, the BC, the plurality vote, and the antiplurality vote are given, respectively, by $u = 0, -1, 1$. In general, $\mathbf{w}_s$ has the representation

$$\mathbf{w}_s \approx (1, \frac{3s-1}{1-s}, -1),$$

and, if $\mathbf{w}_s \approx (1, u_1, -1)$, then $\mathbf{w}_s^r \approx (1, -u_1, -1)$.

An inner normal vector for c_1 on the boundary defining a $c_1 \sim c_2$ outcome is

$$\mathbf{N}_u = (1 - u, 2, u + 1, -(1 + u), -2, -(1 - u)).$$

The goal is to find the volume of $\mathbf{p}$'s close enough to this profile boundary so that $\mathbf{p} + \lambda\mathbf{v}$ crosses it. Only the ratio of measures for different $\mathbf{w}_s$ needs to be computed, so common multiples, including the value of λ, are ignored. This reduces the effective computation to the product of the surface area of the boundary plane, $S(H_u)$, with the length of the component of $\mathbf{v}$ orthogonal to it. (This orthogonality identifies which voter types have a true ability to influence the outcome.) As such,

$$\mu((1, u, -1)) \propto <\frac{\mathbf{N}_u}{|\mathbf{N}_u|}, \mathbf{v} > S(H_u). \tag{5.3.5}$$

An elementary computation proves that

$$<\frac{\mathbf{N}_u}{|\mathbf{N}_u|}, \mathbf{v} > = \frac{3}{2\sqrt{3 + u^2}}. \tag{5.3.6}$$

It remains to compute the four-dimensional surface area $S(H_u)$. This is done with two changes of variables to reduce the problem to one of integration over a region in R^4. The first change uses the defining equation for $Si(6)$, $\sum_{j=1}^{6} p_j = 1$, to define

$$y_1 = p_1, y_2 = p_2, y_3 = p_3, y_4 = p_4, y_5 = p_6, p_5 = (1 - \sum_{k=1}^{5} y_k).$$

The reason p_5 is eliminated is that the corresponding component in $\mathbf{N}_u$ is a scalar. The integrating factor for this change of variables is a constant $(\sqrt{6})$, so it is suppressed. The domain for the new variables is

$$y_k \geq 0, \quad \sum_{k=1}^{5} y_k \leq 1$$

and the boundary equation $< \mathbf{N}_u, \mathbf{p} >= 0$ becomes

$$< \mathbf{N}_u^*, \mathbf{y} >= 2; \quad \mathbf{N}_u^* = (3 - u, 4, u + 3, 1 - u, 1 + u).$$

The only scalar component of $\mathbf{N}_u^*$ is the second one, so use a change of variables to eliminate y_2. The new variables are

$$x_1 = y_1, x_2 = y_3, x_3 = y_4, x_4 = y_5,$$

and y_2 is found by solving $< \mathbf{N}_u^*, \mathbf{y} >= 2$ for y_2. The integrating factor is a scalar multiple of $\sqrt{9 + u^2}$, so the functional part is retained. The geometry of the domain for the $\mathbf{x} = (x_1, x_2, x_3, x_4)$ variables is given by

$$x_i \geq 0, \quad < \mathbf{N}_u^j, \mathbf{x} >\leq 2, \tag{5.3.7}$$

where $\mathbf{N}_u^1 = (1 + u, 1 - u, 3 + u, 3 - u)$ and $\mathbf{N}_u^2 = (3 - u, 3 + u, 1 - u, 1 + u)$.

The volume of the region defined by Eq. 5.3.7 can be determined by elementary techniques. If $\mathbf{e}_j$ is the unit vector with unity in the jth component, then the convex region defined by $< \mathbf{N}_u^1, \mathbf{x} >\leq 2$ has the profile vertices

$$\mathbf{0}, \frac{2\mathbf{e}_1}{1 + u}, \frac{2\mathbf{e}_2}{1 - u}, \frac{2\mathbf{e}_3}{3 + u}, \frac{2\mathbf{e}_4}{3 - u}$$

while the convex region $< \mathbf{N}_u^2, \mathbf{x} >\leq 2$ is defined by the profile vertices

$$\mathbf{0}, \frac{2\mathbf{e}_4}{1 + u}, \frac{2\mathbf{e}_3}{1 - u}, \frac{2\mathbf{e}_2}{3 + u}, \frac{2\mathbf{e}_1}{3 - u}.$$

As the domain defined by Eq. 5.3.7 is the intersection of these regions, it is the union of two congruent regions where one is the convex hull of the vertices

$$\mathbf{0}, \frac{2\mathbf{e}_1}{3 - u}, \frac{2\mathbf{e}_2}{3 + u}, \frac{1}{2}(\mathbf{e}_1 + \mathbf{e}_4), \frac{1}{2}(\mathbf{e}_2 + \mathbf{e}_3).$$

The four-dimensional volume is a scalar multiple of $(9 - u^2)^{-1}$, so, when the integrating factors are included, we have that

$$\mu((1, u, -1)) \propto \left\{ \frac{3 + u^2}{(9 - u^2)(81 - u^4)} \right\}^{\frac{1}{2}}.$$

The conclusion now follows. $\square$

Proof of Theorem 5.3.4. Replace $\mathbf{v}$ with $\mathbf{v}_c$, $< \mathbf{N}_u, \mathbf{v}_c > = 3 + u(1 - 2c)$. In turn,

$$\mu_c((1, u, -1)) \propto \frac{(3 + u(1 - 2c))\sqrt{3 + u^2}}{\sqrt{(9 - u^2)(81 - u^4)}}.$$

For $c = 1, \frac{1}{2}, 0$, the minimum value is, respectively, $u = 1$ (the antiplurality method), $u = 0$ (the BC), and $u = -1$ (the plurality method). The minimum point is a continuous function of c, so it follows from the intermediate value theorem that any choice of u is the optimal choice for some value of $c \in [0, 1]$. $\square$

5.3.2 Exercises

1. For a $\mathbf{w}_s$-election, find example showing how a voter can manipulate the outcome. By use of the inner product, investigate whether it is possible for a voter to manipulate the outcome from his bottom-ranked candidate to his top-ranked candidate.

2. For each $\mathbf{w}_s$, design a profile distribution where $\mathbf{w}_s$ is the least susceptible to manipulation.

3. Find an agenda and a profile where the sincere outcome is c_1, the outcome is c_2 if certain voters abstain, and c_3 if certain voters try to manipulate the outcome.

4. Analyze the strategic actions admitted by Copeland's method.

5.4 Proportional Representation

Proportional representation (PR) is the "fair division problem" that arises when more than one person, party, or alternative is to be selected from a given list. The noble intention guiding PR is to ensure that the division is in accord with what the voters want. The idea is that only when the division of power within a country matches its diversity of beliefs are the legislative outcomes representative. But, as often true, while the motivation may be to establish "fairness," the resulting procedure could introduce an intriguing selection of paradoxes and new inequities. Indeed, proportional representation has a delightfully emotional history full of charges and counter charges arguing the pros and cons. Supporting examples are easy to find in the many books written on this topic between 1860 and 1945; for more recent controversy, read the news accounts of the Lani Guinier 1993 confirmation fight for Asst. Attorney General.

The intent of PR is to select candidates in proportion to the number of voters supporting them. While there are many ways to do this, one fact is clear. Should candidates be chosen in this manner from a general group (as opposed to selecting the winners from "winner takes all" district races), candidates from minority groups have a better chance to be selected. Historically, persuasive arguments of this type have been advanced to promote various PR procedures.

A humbling yet appealing aspect about politics is that its rich history provides numerous examples to serve as counterarguments for almost any claim. This is because procedures have no ideology; they are agnostic to the changing nature of practical politics. With identical force, a PR procedure protects the minority rights of ethnic, racial, and special interest groups, as well as empowering fringe groups, such as the one formed by A. Hitler, that intend to abridge these same rights. The fact is, with repeated failure at the election booth, minorities tend to be absorbed by major groups. "There is every reason to believe that in the absence of PR [this absorption effect] would have been the same outcome so far as Hilter's party was concerned. All that kept it alive was its chance to obtain some measure of success in every election in which it participated. Otherwise it would probably have disbanded, and Hitler might have resumed the peaceful profession of painting houses."[8]

There are many examples where PR appears to work as intended, and others where it does not. Indeed, in early 1993 the PR effect of encouraging small parties was blamed for the scandals of the Italian Government. In reaction, an overwhelming 82.7% referendum vote on April 20, 1993 changed procedures. The thought was that "[t]he new method would end the strict proportional representation that gave Italy 51 post-war governments and as many political parties as there are varieties of pasta. ... This would revolutionize politics by eliminating small parties that have always fluttered around democracy's flame: no more Party of Love led by porno stars, no more electoral victories for Mussolini's granddaughter." (New York Times, April 21, 1993, p.3) Clearly, the philosophical debate as to whether the objective of an election is to achieve consensus or (PR) divide according to census continues.

What motivates our analysis are the fears that "The vague phrases which [PR advocates] think convey fundamental truths are not analyzed. 'The rights of minorities,' 'the tyranny of majorities,' 'the necessity for men of ability in Parliament,' and many other such phrases, are used as bases not to be questioned." [Ho] Echoing my earlier "No good deed goes unpunished" warning about the design of election procedures is the worry that "[PR supporters] advocate changes without calculating the effect on the abstract ideas for which they profess love unless and until a crisis arises."

These concerns are not restricted to PR; before springing any procedure upon a trusting, unsuspecting public, it should be carefully analyzed to determine what can go right, and what can go wrong. Toward this end, I introduce some of the interesting geometry needed to describe certain PR methods. (Even the dynamical instabilities of "Chaos" play a role.) As we should expect, the geometry exposes and explains hidden but fascinating faults about widely used procedures. Some of these faults have led to Presidential vetoes (e.g., by George Washing-

---

[8] [He] It is clear from the publication date of this book (1940) that this warning was written before the true consequences of these comments were known.

ton), court cases, and even helped determine the current size of the US House of Representatives. To indicate that passions remain high even today, in Sect. 5.5 I briefly describe recent US Supreme Court cases involving apportionment procedures.

5.4.1 Hare and Single Transferable Vote

A sizable portion of the emotional PR history centers around the various modifications of the Hare procedure also called the "single transferable vote." By modifying the geometric constructions already developed in this book, it is not difficult to create a geometric theory for this procedure, so I just introduce the method, suggest issues to investigate, and then move on.

PR is used for the selection of many candidates. Examples of the type given earlier, where 80% of the voters have the ranking $c_1 \succ c_2 \succ c_3$ while the rest have the ranking $c_3 \succ c_2 \succ c_1$, cast serious doubt whether a plurality second-ranked c_3 deserves to be one of the two selected candidates. On the other hand, we can correct the weakness of the procedure (generating the foolish outcome) with carefully coordinated strategic voting. After all, to be elected, each of two candidates needs just over one-third of the vote; all additional votes are superfluous. The extreme popularity of c_1 in this profile forces many of her supporters to "waste their vote;" the extra votes for c_1 are worse than meaningless because these voters' second-ranked candidate loses. If it were possible to coordinate the voters' actions so that half sincerely vote for c_1 while the other half strategically vote for c_2, they could achieve the reasonable choice of $\{c_1, c_2\}$ that more accurately mirrors these voters' wishes.

To recognize what is involved, consider a hypothetical small Vermont town where voting for the three candidates is done in the following quaint manner. Each candidate stands in an assigned corner of the high school gymnasium. Instead of casting ballots, her supporters stand by her when the count starts at 7 PM. If two candidates are to be selected by the 100 voters, a candidate is assured of selection once she has at least 34 votes. Now, if at 6:50 PM, Helvi has 52 voters standing around her, instead of "wasting their vote," 18 of them would be well advised to stand by their second-ranked candidate.

This illustrates where strategic action is to be applauded as it overcomes a distinct defect of the procedure. But, don't allow the noise of the applause to drown out realism; this action probably wouldn't occur in practice. Unless the voters are stuck in a snowbound Vermont gym, the severe informational and group discipline prerequisites for the success of a massive coordinated action makes it highly unlikely that it will occur outside of theory. On the other hand, if we like the process, then we could design a procedure to institutionalize the behavior. This is the Hare method.

The procedure goes as follows. After all voters rank the candidates, the candidates are plurality ranked. To be selected, a candidate needs one more than one-third of the vote. All candidates satisfying this criteria on the first ballot are selected. If only one candidate, say c_1, is selected, then all of her extra votes are proportionally distributed among the remaining two candidates where the proportion is based on voters' preferences. (This corresponds to voters migrating within the gym.) With the adjusted profile (unless a tie), two candidates are selected. When k out of n candidates are chosen, a candidate needs one more than $\frac{1}{k+1}$ of the vote, and several adjusted profiles may be required.

To illustrate with 100 ballots, suppose Helvi, c_1, receives 52 votes where 30 of the voters have the ranking $c_1 \succ c_2 \succ c_3$ and 22 have $c_1 \succ c_3 \succ c_2$. As Helvi only needs 34 votes to be selected, the extra $52 - 34 = 18$ votes are redistributed among the remaining two candidates on a proportional basis. That is, c_2 receives $\frac{30}{52} \times 18 = 10.38$ extra votes while c_3 receives $\frac{22}{52} \times 18 = 7.62$ extra votes. After the reallocation, Helvi and another candidate should receive the required quota. The reallocation can be viewed as converting 10.38 type-one voters into type-six voters, while 7.62 of the type-two voters now are of type-three.

The procedure captures the spirit of the above common sense approach by automatically moving ballots (rather than voters) from one candidate to another. So, this "institutionalized strategic voting" procedure eliminates the practical difficulties that makes coordinated strategic voting unrealistic; i.e., the gathering and coordinating of information about "who might vote for whom," enforcing coalitional agreements, as well as those complicating personality factors where a voter is too shy to move from one corner of the gym to another, etc. Of course, it is easy to invent all sorts of embellishments and modifications of this procedure, and probably all of them are already described in the literature if not actually used in practice. (For instance, another approach is to transfer all votes of a successful candidate to each voter's second preference. This is a form of a runoff, so it can be analyzed with the techniques of Sect. 5.2. Other procedures differ on how the transferred votes are selected, etc.)[9]

In fact, variations of this procedure have been used all over Europe, in various cities of the USA (e.g., Cincinnati), Japan, etc. as well as the American Mathematical Society among other organizations.

The properties of the Hare method derive from its multiprofile definition. The original profile, $\mathbf{p}_1$, is used to define the reallocation profile $\mathbf{p}_2$. More precisely, should c_1 win the first election with $\mathbf{p}_1 = (p_1, \ldots, p_6)$, the vote is reallocated in the following manner where, for simplicity, $\frac{1}{3}$ is used instead of "one vote above one-third." Of the votes for c_1, $\frac{p_1}{p_1+p_2}$ are from type-one voters and $\frac{p_2}{p_1+p_2}$ from type-two voters. Therefore, $\frac{p_1}{p_1+p_2}(p_1 + p_2 - \frac{1}{3})$ votes are transferred from type-one to type-six, with a similar expression for the transfer from type-two to type-three. Thus,

$$\mathbf{p}_2 = (\frac{1}{3}\frac{p_1}{p_1+p_2}, \frac{1}{3}\frac{p_2}{p_1+p_2}, p_3 + p_2 - \frac{1}{3}\frac{p_2}{p_1+p_2}, p_4, p_5, p_6 + p_1 - \frac{1}{3}\frac{p_1}{p_1+p_2}).$$

---

[9] In practice, the redistribution of votes is done in many ways. A silly way is to stop counting votes for a candidate as soon as she wins; on all remaining ballots her name is ignored and all candidates move up one position. Cincinnati used a clever approach; they used a formula to determine how many ballots needs to be redistributed. Then, they counted through the ballots in multiples of this number to adjust certain rankings. For details, see [].

Aha! Already the source of problems is apparent. The nonlinear nature of $\mathbf{p}_2$ promises that the inner normal on the profile boundary separating different conclusions varies through a spectrum of values. This, in turn, ensures that the theory of Sect. 5.2 can be used to extract the various responsiveness and strategic difficulties that exist. We now know, for instance, that it could be in voter's best interests not to vote! Related problems derive from the multiprofile nature of the method; similar to truncation methods, approval voting, etc., the increase in the number of variables can alter the outcomes (but, not as dramatically).

Other types of issues are immediate. Does the Hare method agree with a plurality runoff? (No.) With any positional method? (No.) How does the Hare method agree with pairwise rankings. (Better than the plurality vote, but it has problems.) What happens if $\mathbf{w}_0$ is replaced with $\mathbf{w}_s$ in the two elections? (Some problems, such as allowing the Condorcet loser to be the first selected candidate, are mitigated the closer $\mathbf{w}_s$ is to the BC; they are eliminated once the BC is used.) Issues and comparisons of these kinds can be handled by modifying the geometry of earlier sections. Therefore, after a parting comment, I turn to methods where new geometry is involved.

Related to the Hare procedure is where the BC, rather than the plurality vote, is used for the elections. To avoid the responsiveness problems caused by nonlinearities, the BC should be used directly. Thus, a quite reasonable PR procedure is the BC without any reallocation of ballots. Indeed, as developed in Chap. 4, the BC already achieves the desired proportional representation of the candidates without all of the difficulties.

5.4.2 The Apportionment Problem

The US Constitution requires *"Representatives shall be apportioned among the several states according to their respective numbers, counting the whole number of persons in each State ... ."* So, if the US House of Representatives consisted of $h = 15$ members and a state has one third of the total US population, then that state is entitled to $\frac{1}{3} \times 15 = 5$ representatives. Similarly, with $h = 16$ seats, that same state is entitled to $\frac{1}{3} \times 16 = 5\frac{1}{3}$ representatives.

The fractional part introduces a problem; how should the seats be allocated when the exact apportionment is a mixed number? Some readers may argue for fractional power; some might even argue that occasionally only a third of a representative actually goes to Congress – maybe the wrong third. Fractional representation is not the answer because current interpretations of the Constitution require an integer number of representatives from each state. The resolution is obvious; just "round off" $5\frac{1}{3}$. But, how?

The political need to "round off" an exact apportionment extends beyond the American boundaries to create problems in Europe and all other locales where the PR assignment of seats to different political parties is based on how many voters voted for each party. In what is called the *"list system,"* voters vote for the list of candidates provided by each party. Then, the number of candidates selected from each list is determined by the share of vote a party receives.[10] Fractions are to be expected, so how are they handled? Indeed, this need for rounding off is a standard complexity accompanying any integer allocation problem. As such, similar serious difficulties arise in military manpower decisions where the number of people to be conscripted from different regions must be determined, from economics where the goal is to determine the optimal number of automobiles of different styles to be ordered by a dealer, etc. But, "rounding off" looses simplicity once there are more than two parties. Moreover, "rounding off" can be an explosive political issue if it introduces an unexpected shift in power or resources. I give a recent example in Sect. 5.5.

To illustrate, suppose 25 seats are to be allocated among three states in accordance with the population figures specified in the table. The numbers total 10,000, so, a decimal point in front of a population figure specifies the fractional size of that state. The exact apportionment for a state is obtained by multiplying the decimal times the house size 25. The resulting exact apportionment, however, requires the barbaric act of cutting a representative to size. To find a resolution, start by listing the minimal integer number of representatives each state should have; this *minimal allocation* is in the next to last column.

State	Population	Exact Rep.	Min	Hamilton
A	4520	11.30	11	11
B	4136	10.34	10	10
C	1344	3.36	3	4
Total	$\overline{10,000}$	$\overline{25}$	$\overline{24}$	$\overline{25}$

(5.4.1)

The minimal allocation settles 24 of the 25 available seats; which state deserves the last one? The standard "rounding off" fails because the fractional part of the exact apportionment for each state is less than the magical $\frac{1}{2}$ division point; each state would be rounded down leaving the assignment problem unresolved.

The usual $\frac{1}{2}$ value is ineffective because there are three, not two states. So, to resolve the problem, we might exchange the cutoff value of $\frac{1}{2}$ with $\frac{1}{3}$; all states with a fractional part greater than $\frac{1}{3}$ would be rounded up. A minor flaw of this approach is that it is useless. In the above table, the fractional portion for two states exceeds $\frac{1}{3}$, yet only one can be rounded up.

The next obvious approach is to rank the states according to the fractional parts, and assign remaining seats to states with the largest fractions. The fractional parts for the example are $C(0.36) \succ B(0.34) \succ A(0.30)$, so this *Hamilton apportionment scheme* (due to the controversial American statesman Alexander Hamilton) awards C the remaining seat. The final Hamilton apportionment is listed in the last column.

---

[10] The political party usually determines the ordering of the candidates on a list. Alternatively, such as in Brazil, the voters can influence this ordering by voting for particular candidates.

Hamilton's Method seems to be reasonable, and it was used for a considerable period of time in the USA. But, when first proposed, Thomas Jefferson helped persuade George Washington to veto the bill.[11] Jefferson's method, described in Sect. 5.5, was adopted.

Hamilton's Method. Hamilton's method is closely related to our standard procedure that rounds off, say, the value 34.62 upwards to 35. The two candidates to replace 34.62 are 34 and 35; 35 is chosen because it is closest to 34.62. Similarly, Hamilton's method is equivalent to first specifying all ways to round off, and then choosing the one closest to the exact value. To illustrate with the above example where one extra seat is to be awarded, the three ways $(11.30, 10.34, 3.40)$ can be rounded off while satisfying $h = 25$ are

$$(11, 10, 4),\ (11, 11, 3),\ \text{and}\ (12, 10, 3).$$

A computation shows that $(11, 10, 4)$ is the closest to $(11.30, 10.34, 3.36)$ (with distance 0.7843). (The distances of $(11.30, 10.34, 3.40)$ from the other two points $(11, 11, 3)$ and $(12, 10, 3)$ are, respectively, 0.8094 and 0.8574.)

Thus, Hamilton's method is the natural extension of the familiar rounding off process learned as a young child. The general situation for m states (or parties, or ...) is described in the following definition where the jth component of $\mathbf{p}$ represents the fraction of all people that reside in the jth state and where h is the house size. (In the above example, $m = 3$, $\mathbf{p} = (0.4520, 0.4136, 0.1344)$, and $h = 25$.)

Definition 5.4.1. Let

$$\mathbf{p} = (p_1, p_2, \ldots, p_m) \in Si(m) = \{\mathbf{p} \mid \sum_{j=1}^{m} p_j = 1,\ p_j \geq 0.\}$$

For an integer h, the Hamilton apportionment of $h\mathbf{p} = (hp_1, hp_2, \ldots, hp_m)$ is the vector of integers $\mathbf{a} = (a_1, a_2, \ldots, a_m)$, $\sum_{j=1}^{m} a_j = h$, that is closest to $h\mathbf{p}$. □

Apportionment Cubes. To understand Hamilton's method, I describe it in terms of the geometry of the *apportionment cube* in R^3. This cube is defined by the eight vertices generated by how each component of $h\mathbf{p}$ (i.e., each state's exact apportionment) can be rounded up and down; the sum of the components of these vertices need not equal h. (So, for $m \geq 2$ parties, the apportionment cube has 2^m vertices.) In the example with $25(0.4520, 0.4136, 0.1344) = (11.30, 10.34, 3.36)$, the eight vertices are

$(11, 10, 3)$			$h = 24$	
$(11, 10, 4)$	$(11, 11, 3)$	$(12, 10, 3)$	$h = 25$	
$(12, 11, 3)$	$(12, 10, 4)$	$(11, 11, 4)$	$h = 26$	(5.4.2)
$(12, 11, 4)$			$h = 27$	

---

[11] In part, this is because with the population of the day Hamilton's method would award Connecticut more representatives than permitted by the Constitutional bound of no more than one representative per 30,000 persons. See [Mon, Mas, BY1].

The vertex in the first row, the *minimal apportionment*, is where every state is rounded down, while the entry in the last row, the *maximal apportionment* is where every state is rounded up. Each entry in the second row rounds up a single component of $h\mathbf{p}$; so these are the ways a single additional seat can be assigned to some state. The third row has two values of $h\mathbf{p}$ rounded up, so it represents situations where two additional seats are to be assigned.

The *base cube* is the apportionment cube where the eight vertices have entries of 0 or 1. Equivalently, the base cube is the apportionment cube for $\mathbf{p}$ and $h = 1$. Each apportionment cube is obtained by adding (or translating) the base cube to the minimal apportionment. For instance, the apportionment cube of Eq. 5.4.2 is given by adding the minimal apportionment, $(11, 10, 3)$, to each vertex of the base cube. In general,

Apportionment cube = Minimal apportionment + Base cube.

$$(5.4.3)$$

The vertices of the base cube designate which states receive extra seats.

Those vertices of an apportionment cube where k extra seats are allocated define the "k – *assignment triangle*." For the example, the $k = 1$ assignment triangle is defined by the vertices in the second row of 5.4.2, while the $k = 2$ assignment triangle is defined by the vertices of the third row. Thanks to Relationship 5.4.3, the geometry of a k - assignment triangle of an apportionment cube is the same as the respective assignment triangle in the base cube. In the base cube, the $k = 1$ triangle is the intersection of the base cube with the plane $x+y+z = 1$ (So its vertices are $(1, 0, 0), (0, 1, 0), (0, 0, 1)$), while the $k = 2$ triangle is given by the intersection of the base cube with the plane $x + y + z = 2$. (The region between these two planes resembles the representation cube.)

As seats are awarded to the states according to the "closer is better" principle, each assignment triangle is divided into three geometrically similar regions. Therefore, these *apportionment regions* are created by the lines of midpoints determined by different pairs of vertices. In this manner, the seat assignment for the different states is specified by the vertex of the region containing $h\mathbf{p}$. These triangles, along with the base cube, are displayed in Fig. 5.4.1.

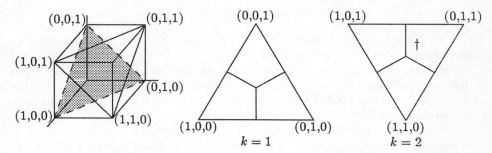

Fig. 5.4.1. The assignment triangle geometry of the base cube

Hamilton's method is based on a distance, so the apportionment regions of the assignment triangle are similar to the regions of the representation triangle where c_j, $j = 1, 2, 3$, is top-ranked. Also, the apportionment cube forces the assignment triangles for $k = 1$ and $k = 2$ to flip in a manner analogous to the "flipping" of T_1 and T_2 in the representation cube. Also observe that the barycentric points of the two assignment triangles have the fractional parts

$$k(\frac{1}{3}, \frac{1}{3}, \frac{1}{3}), \quad k = 1, 2. \tag{5.3.4}$$

Again, this comes from the geometry of a cube; a similar relationship emerged with the indifference points of T_1 and T_2 of the representation cube.

5.4.3 Something Must Go Wrong – Alabama Paradox

With three or more states (or parties), we must anticipate that the process is vulnerable to the counterintuitive peculiarities of higher dimensional geometries; peculiarities that can force unwanted consequences upon voting procedures. In more common language, "Now what goes wrong!"

In Sect. 5.2, we explored how "generosity" toward a candidate, manifested by her receiving added support, can hurt her. A similar "more can cause less" problem arises with Hamilton's apportionment procedure; when an increase in house size provides extra seats, a previously held seat can be *taken away* from a state. Congressional seats represent important political power, so this subtraction phenomenon can trigger political "chaos!"

To see the difficulties, suppose Congress changes the house size of the example to $h = 26$. The following computation shows that states A and B each receive one of the two extra seats.

State	Population	Exact Rep.	Min	Hamilton	
A	4520	11.7520	11	12	
B	4136	10.7536	10	11	(5.4.5)
C	1344	3.4944	3	3	
Total	10,000	26	24	26	

According to the last columns of 5.3.1 and 5.3.5, the generosity of increasing the house size *cost* state C 25% of its original representation! This is not just an amusing academic exercise; such problems have occurred in practice. For instance, before fixing the size of the US House of Representatives at 435, the house size could and did change. And, when the house size grew, states did lose representation!

The first US state to be victimized by the geometry of higher dimensions was Alabama; subsequently, other states such as Maine and Colorado suffered this "Alabama Paradox." Although a different apportionment method was used, the current size of the US House of Representatives, 435, derived in part from trying to avoid the Alabama Paradox with the 1910 census figures. (For all sorts of climatic, census, and political reasons, the house size remained at 435 from then until it was fixed by law in November, 1941.)

It is clear why this paradox occurs; state C has such a small population fraction that when it is added to the previous figure (from table 5.4.1), the larger fractions that are added for the other states quickly jumps their fractional part to the top of the list. To extract more subtle properties, we need a geometric explanation.

The Alabama Paradox can be understood with the algebraic expression

$$(h + 1)\mathbf{p} = h\mathbf{p} + \mathbf{p}. \qquad (5.4.6)$$

The exact apportionment $25\mathbf{p}$ is in the $k = 1$ assignment triangle region defined by the vertex $(11, 10, 4) = (11, 10, 3) + (0, 0, 1)$. For the paradox to occur, the point $(25 + 1)\mathbf{p}$ must be in the $k = 2$ assignment triangle region with vertex $(12, 11, 3) = (11, 10, 3) + (1, 1, 0)$. By examining the alignment of two assignment triangles, it is clear how this can happen. (See Fig. 5.4.1.) First, the base point $25\mathbf{p}$ must be near the barycentric point of the $k = 1$ assignment triangle. (So, the fractional values of $25\mathbf{p}$ are close to $(\frac{1}{3}, \frac{1}{3}, \frac{1}{3})$.) Then the strong "tilt" $\mathbf{p}$ acquires from the smaller population of state C forces the point $25\mathbf{p} + \mathbf{p}$ to slide into the $(11, 10, 3) + (1, 1, 0)$ region of the $k = 2$ assignment triangle.

Swatting Flies. As an intuitive way to understand the Alabama Paradox, consider the problem of swatting a fly on the screen of a door during a hot, humid summer day. For sanitary reasons, use a jar lid instead of your left hand. To avoid cutting the screen, keep the jar lid parallel to the screen while moving it toward the screen. Fly-killing expertise is demonstrated by squashing a single fly on a lid edge. This may require an appropriate size of the jar lid.

In the apportionment problem, the screen represents S_h – the space of all apportionments with house size h (i.e., all vectors where the sum of the components equals h) and the "flies" are the integer apportionments. The center of the jar lid is moved along the *exact apportionment* line $t\mathbf{p}$ where $t \in (0, \infty)$ designates how far the lid is from the origin; when t has an integer value, it represents the house size. Aligning the orientation of the lid with the screen ensures that the moved disk is on S_h, while the radius of the lid measures how far points are from the exact apportionment $h\mathbf{p}$. The squashed fly is the Hamilton apportionment. Finding the Hamilton apportionment (the integer apportionment minimizing the distance from the exact apportionment) corresponds to choosing an appropriately sized lid to hit a single fly with the lid edge.

Now suppose there are screens on the main door and storm door, both closed. (So, the screens are parallel but separated by a distance.) Furthermore, suppose the flies are are so irritating that we will ignore the cost of repairing the destruction caused by trying to hit a particular fly on the first screen (representing the $k = 1$ assignment triangle) and, continuing the motion, to hit a specified fly on the second screen (representing the $k = 2$ assignment triangle). By carefully choosing how to move the lid, this can be done. Similarly, by choosing an appropriate "tilt" for $\mathbf{p}$, an Alabama Paradox is created.

The Mathematics of Fly Swatting. To analyze the "fly swatting – Alabama Paradox phenomenon" mathematically, we need to tilt **p** so that the jar lid starts from the $(0,0,1)$ region of the $k = 1$ assignment triangle and ends up in the $(1,1,0)$ region of the $k = 2$ assignment triangle. Start with the special case where $h\mathbf{p}$ is at the barycentric point on the $k = 1$ assignment triangle and $\mathbf{p} = (\frac{1}{3}, \frac{1}{3}, \frac{1}{3})$. The direction from one barycentric point to the other is $(\frac{1}{3}, \frac{1}{3}, \frac{1}{3})$, so, by Eqs. 5.4.4, 5.4.6, $(h+1)\mathbf{p}$ is at the barycentric point of the $k = 2$ assignment triangle. Think of this in terms of a pencil where $h\mathbf{p}$ is the eraser and $(h + 1)\mathbf{p}$ is the point. In Fig. 5.4.1, both the eraser and pointer are at the center of appropriate triangle.

A "tilt" in **p** (i.e., $\mathbf{p} \neq (\frac{1}{3}, \frac{1}{3}, \frac{1}{3})$) forces $(h + 1)\mathbf{p}$ off of the barycentric point of the $k = 2$ triangle into a region that disfavors the state with the smallest population. With the pencil example, the point is moved off the center of the triangle inot the region favoring the two large states. Indeed, exploiting the tilt, the base point, $h\mathbf{p}$, can be moved in the $k = 1$ triangle while keeping the tip, $(h + 1)\mathbf{p}$, in the designated region of the $k = 2$ triangle. Of course, a stronger tilt of **p** (i.e., a greater divergence in the populations of the states), defines a larger region for the base point $h\mathbf{p}$. (Try this with a pencil; with an extreme tilt, the eraser can be moved over a large region while keeping the point in the designated region.)

When moving the base point $h\mathbf{p}$ (in the $k = 1$ triangle) we want to keep it in the region where $h\mathbf{p}$ awards the state with the smallest population the sole extra seat; denote this region by $AP(\mathbf{p})$. (This is the shaded region in Fig. 5.4.2.) By construction, $h\mathbf{p} \in AP(\mathbf{p})$ forces an Alabama Paradox because at house size $h + 1$, the state with the smallest population is denied a previously held seat!

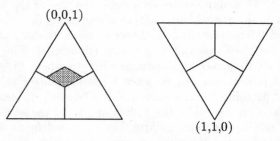

Fig. 5.4.2. The $AP(\mathbf{p})$ region

The above description (aided by the geometry of Fig. 5.4.2) shows that $AP(\mathbf{p})$ includes an open set of possibilities. Remember, the geometry of $AP(\mathbf{p})$ does not depend on h; it only depends upon the chosen **p**. As noted, the more extreme the tilt of **p** (i.e., the larger the disparity between the populations of the states), the bigger the region $AP(\mathbf{p})$. As long as $\mathbf{p} \neq (\frac{1}{3}, \frac{1}{3}, \frac{1}{3})$, $AP(\mathbf{p})$ contains an open set.

Cut and Slide. To repeat, once $h\mathbf{p} \in AP(\mathbf{p})$ in an apportionment cube, an Alabama Paradox follows. So, we might hope that only rare choices of **p** allow

$h\mathbf{p} \in AP(\mathbf{p})$ for some value of h. As the next theorem asserts, this wishful conjecture is false; for almost all choices of $\mathbf{p} \in Si(m)$, the Alabama Paradox is lurking in the background just waiting to pounce upon some unsuspecting state once an appropriate value of h is reached.

Theorem 5.4.1 [S2]). *For $m \geq 3$, almost all $\mathbf{p} \in Si(m)$ have an Alabama Paradox for some house size h.*

The technical term "almost all"[12] means that those population sizes that manage to escape the Alabama Paradox are rare; this paradoxical phenomenon is to be expected. Verifying this statement requires proving that most choices of $\mathbf{p}$ admit an integer h where $h\mathbf{p} \in AP(\mathbf{p})$ in the $h\mathbf{p}$ apportionment cube. This is demonstrated in the following plausibility argument where the missing formal details are easy to fill in. First, I show why the geometry of a donut plays a critical role for *all* integer apportionment problems. (This includes integer programming problems from economics, and so forth.)

An easy way to relate successive $h\mathbf{p}$ points is to connect them with the *exact apportionment line*

$$t\mathbf{p}, \quad t \in [0, \infty) \tag{5.4.7}$$

where the integer points, $t = h;\, h = 1, 2, \ldots$, on the apportionment line recapture Eq. 5.4.6. The rounding off process involves only the fractional parts of the exact apportionment; for instance, the fractional parts of $(23\frac{1}{3}, 45\frac{2}{3})$ and $(62\frac{1}{3}, 2\frac{2}{3})$ agree, so both terms are rounded off in the same manner. This suggests identifying points in terms of their fractional parts.

Definition 5.4.2. Two vectors $\mathbf{x} = (x_1, x_2, \ldots, x_m)$ and $\mathbf{y} = (y_1, y_2, \ldots, y_m)$ are *fractionally equivalent*, $\mathbf{x} \approx_{frac} \mathbf{y}$, if, when expressed in decimal form, the decimal portion of x_j agrees with that of y_j for $j = 1, \ldots, m$. $\square$

The theorem is proved by exploiting the equivalence relationship $\mathbf{x} \approx_{frac} \mathbf{y}$. To do so, replace a vector $\mathbf{x}$ with its fractional equivalent in the base cube. For instance, $(36\frac{2}{3}, 78\frac{3}{4}) \approx_{frac} (57\frac{2}{3}, 34\frac{3}{4}) \approx_{frac} (\frac{2}{3}, \frac{3}{4})$, so, for each of these two vectors, the same fractional point in the base cube is plotted. A geometric way to do this is illustrated in Fig. 5.4.3.

Figure 5.4.3 indicates the lattice of apportionment cubes for $m = 2$. The line $t\mathbf{p}$ leaves the base cube by passing through the horizontal line $y = 1$ at $t\mathbf{p} = (x, 1) \approx_{frac} (x, 0)$. This point of departure is plotted as $(x, 0)$. Retaining only the fractional part of $t\mathbf{p}$ is equivalent to cutting the exact apportionment line where it leaves the base cube at $(x, 1)$ and then shifting the infinite portion of the cut line downwards until it hits the x axis ($y = 0$) at the point $(x, 0)$. The shifted line, the dashed line in Fig. 5.3.3a, is parallel to the original one; it differs only by a change in the integer assignment values.

---

[12] For the mathematicians, this could be taken in the sense of Lebesgue measure, or as being an open-dense set. Actually, by examining the proof, more exacting algebraic requirements of excluding a finite number of points can be imposed.

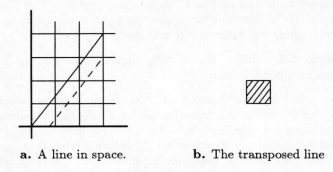

a. A line in space.   **b.** The transposed line

Fig. 5.4.3. Cutting and sliding the $t\mathbf{p}$ apportionment line

Now, trace the future of the translated dashed line. It departs the base cube at $(1, y)$ when it passes through the vertical line $x = 1$. As $(1, y) \approx_{frac} (0, y)$, use the same "cut and slide". Namely, cut the translated line where it leaves the base cube at $(1, y)$ and slide the infinite portion to the left so that its base is at the point $(0, y)$.

By continuing this process of taking a translated version of $t\mathbf{p}$, finding where it leaves the base cube, using the appropriate "cut and slide" process, and then continuing with the newly translated version of $t\mathbf{p}$, we end up with a figure similar to that given in Fig. 5.4.3b. In this figure, for instance, the small line segment in the lower right hand corner corresponds to the first cut and slide. The segment just above the diagonal represents the second cut, etc. (Another way to obtain Fig. 5.4.3b is to cut out all squares from Fig. 5.4.3a that are crossed by the apportionment line $t\mathbf{p}$ and then stack them in a pile.) Figure 5.4.3b is a geometric representation of all possible fractional parts arising from $t\mathbf{p}$. A similar geometric process applies for all values of $m \geq 3$, the only difference is that the square is replaced by a m-dimensional base cube.

The Surface of a Donut. If the parallel translates of this "cut and slide" process are sufficiently close to one another, then, clearly, some of them cut across a specified open region in the base cube; say, $AP(\mathbf{p})$. In other words, if $\mathbf{p}$ forces the parallel translates to fill in the base cube, then an Alabama Paradox probably occurs for some h. It remains is to determine how and when this happens.

One way to envision these disjoint parallel lines is to reconnect them. To see how to do this, observe from the construction that the two horizontal edges of the base cube are identified with each other; they pinpoint where a translate of the exact apportionment line $t\mathbf{p}$ is cut and slid downwards. So, by gluing these two edges together to create a cylinder, as indicated in the middle portion of Fig. 5.4.4, the horizontal cut segments of the line $t\mathbf{p}$ are reconnected.

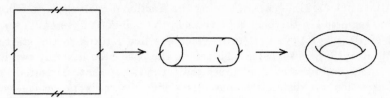

Fig. 5.4.4. Converting a square into a donut

Similarly, the side edges of the base cube establish where the exact apportionment line is cut and slid to the left. Gluing these two edges together reconnects the remaining position where translates of $t\mathbf{p}$ are cut. (This second gluing corresponds to connecting the two ends of the cylinder.) This second gluing, the figure on the right of Fig. 5.4.4, is the surface of a donut, or a torus. Now that the edges of the base are connected to form a torus, T^2, the cut parallel lines are reconnected into one long line wrapping around T^2.

A similar cut and regluing operation holds for all values of $m \geq 2$. When the exact apportionment line $t\mathbf{p}$ hits a surface of the base cube, it is cut and moved directly to the opposite surface so that the fractional part of all components remain the same. As above, the parallel translates of the line $t\mathbf{p}$ drawn in the base cube register the fractional portions for each state's exact apportionment. The lines are reconnected when opposite surfaces of the base cube are glued together to create T^m; this is an m-dimensional torus.

A problem with trying to construct the torus T^m is that, physically, it can't be done once $m \geq 3$; the folding requires us to reside in a $m + 1$-dimensional space. The reason, suggested by the folding of the square, is that at least one of the gluing steps requires moving "outwards" in a new dimension. It is this extra-dimensional movement that forces T^2 to inhabit a three-dimensional space. Similarly, for $m = 3$ the gluing requires residence in a four-dimensional space. But, we do not need the actual physical torus, the mathematical construction more than suffices. Notice, however, the amusing conclusion that

> the political apportionment problems caused by the US Constitution are subject to the geometric intricacies of a fifty-dimensional donut, T^{50}, residing in a 51- dimensional space.

No wonder there are so many difficulties! But try (as I once attempted) to explain this to your congressman!

Properties of a Torus. What remains is to show how the reconnected line wraps around the torus. These well understood properties are described in most books on modern dynamics. The explanation is critical for understanding various subtleties of the Alabama Paradox and other apportionment methods, so a brief description is offered.

For $m = 2$ assume the populations of the two states are 1000 and 2000; this defines $\mathbf{p} = (\frac{1}{3}, \frac{2}{3})$. The exact apportionment line $t\mathbf{p}$ crosses an edge of the base cube whenever tp_1 or tp_2 is an integer j; for instance, whenever $t\frac{2}{3} = j$, or $t = \frac{3j}{2}$.

Consequently, by inserting $t = \frac{3j}{2}$ into $t\mathbf{p}$ and using $j = 0, 1, 2, \ldots$, we have the points $(0,0)$, $(\frac{1}{2}, 1)$, $(1, 2)$, $(\frac{3}{2}, 3)$, ... Using the fractional equivalent, it follows that the line segments in the base cube connect the points $(0,0) \to (\frac{1}{2}, 1) \approx_{frac}$ $(\frac{1}{2}, 0)$ and $(\frac{1}{2}, 0) \to (1,1) \approx_{frac} (0,0)$. Once the line returns to the starting point $(0,0)$, everything is repeated. Therefore, the base cube has only two line segments (so the reconnected line circles the torus twice) that, measured in a horizontal direction, are distance $\frac{1}{2}$ apart. This wide separation makes it is easy for the line on the torus (or the two line segments in the base cube) to miss a fairly large open set. This typifies settings where we might expect paradoxes to be avoided.

So, to compute the "cut and slide" points for $t\mathbf{p}$ we first solve $t(p_1, p_2) = (tp_1, tp_2)$ for t values where one component is an integer. The fractional value of the other component locates the "cut and slide" point on the base cube. For example, if $t\mathbf{p}$ has an integer value j for the second state, the value of t is $tp_2 = j$, or $t = \frac{j}{p_2}$. For this value of t, the cutting point is at

$$t\mathbf{p} = \frac{j}{p_2}(p_1, p_2) = j(\frac{p_1}{p_2}, 1). \qquad (5.4.8)$$

Equation 5.4.8 offers a simple equation to determine the x values which are cut and slide points; they are at the fractional part of $j\frac{p_1}{p_2}$, $j = 0, 1, \ldots$.

To illustrate Eq. 5.4.8 with numbers from the two state example, suppose a child is born in the first state to change the population figures to 1001 and 2000. This trivial change in population unleashes a major change in the geometry and positioning of the line segments! Equation 5.4.8 now requires the $t\mathbf{p}$ line to cross the x axis in the base cube at the fractional part of the points $j\frac{1001}{2000}$; these points are

$$0, \frac{1001}{2000}, \frac{2}{2000}, \frac{1003}{2000}, \frac{4}{2000}, \frac{1005}{2000}, \ldots$$

So, instead of only two lines in the base cube, *the new population figure forces 2000 line segments to cross the x axis of the base cube, and they are only the distance $\frac{1}{2000}$ apart!* Here, the line segments are so close together that it would be difficult for all of them to miss a reasonably sized open set in the base cube. Thus, if entering a particular open set ensures the existence of a paradox (as true for the Alabama Paradox), we must expect the paradox to occur for some value of h. What a difference a birth can make; many new little paradoxes!

The same construction holds for all $m \geq 3$. For example, if $\mathbf{p} = (0.1, 0.3, 0.6)$, then we need to know how the translates of the exact apportionment line pass through, say, the bottom surface (the $z = 0$ surface) of the base cube. Following the derivation of Eq. 5.3.8, these points are the fractional equivalents of $j(\frac{1}{6}, \frac{1}{2}, 0)$. A simple computation confirms that there are only the six points,

$$(0,0,0), (\frac{1}{6}, \frac{1}{2}, 0), (\frac{2}{6}, 0, 0), (\frac{3}{6}, \frac{1}{2}, 0), (\frac{4}{6}, 0, 0), (\frac{5}{6}, \frac{1}{2}, 0)$$

which are reasonably far apart. (The minimum distance is $\frac{1}{3}$.)

Compare the above computation for **p** with the almost identical choice of **p'** = $(0.1001, 0.2999, 0.6000)$ caused by a single person moving from the second state to the first. Now the points on the bottom surface of the base cube are determined by the fractional parts of $j(\frac{1001}{6000}, \frac{2999}{6000}, 0)$. Instead of only six points, we end up with $(6000)^2 = 36,000,000$ different crossing points on the bottom of the base cube that are closer than $\frac{1}{18,000,000}$ units apart! Using **p**, it is reasonable to expect that a large open set can be chosen in the base cube which is missed by all of the line segments. Clearly, this same assertion does not hold for **p'**.

With a little thought, these statements make sense. Compare it with the "savings program" where each evening all pocket change is saved. Each day, there is only a trivial change in total savings. But, the accumulated value over a period of time can be substantial. This *"A little each day makes a lot in a week"* philosophy extends to apportionment problems. A small change in the population figures is trivial in the short run (i.e., for small h values), but the accumulated effect can be substantial in the long run (for larger h values).

Back to the Alabama Paradox. Armed with the wealth of line segments, return to the Alabama Paradox. By construction, minor changes in the value of **p** = $(0.1, 0.3, 0.6)$ introduce only trivial changes in the size and shape of the region $AP(\mathbf{p})$; consequently, $AP(\mathbf{p})$ and $AP(\mathbf{p'})$ are almost identical. Now, **p** may avoid the Alabama Paradox because $t\mathbf{p} \notin AP(\mathbf{p})$ for any $t \geq 0$. This is true if the line segments are sufficiently far enough apart so that all of them miss the open region $AP(\mathbf{p})$. On the other hand, the line segments for **p'** are so close to each other, that many of them must enter the nearly identical region $AP(\mathbf{p'})$. A population change of a single person can trigger the paradox!

In general, most **p** values pack the line segments in the torus (or base cube) close enough so that some of them must enter the open, Alabama Paradox generating region $AP(\mathbf{p})$. In fact, as indicated by the above examples, we have an amusing conclusion. The natural approach to try to avoid apportionment difficulties by using more accurate census figures can be penalized; *the added accuracy can force the exact apportionment line $t\mathbf{p}$ to unleash an Alabama Paradox.*

Theorem 5.4.2. *For $m \geq 3$, arbitrarily close to any $\mathbf{p} \in Si(m)$, there is a $\mathbf{p'}$ leading to an Alabama Paradox.*[13]

5.4.4 A Better Improved Method?

Can we find a better, improved apportionment method by inventing new procedures? Instead of choosing the integer apportionment $\mathbf{a} = (a_1, a_2, \ldots, a_m)$ which minimizes the distance $\|\mathbf{a} - h\mathbf{p}\|$, maybe the Alabama Paradox can be avoided by using another function $g(\mathbf{x})$. With such a g, the goal is to find the integer apportionment **a** which satisfies the house size and minimizes the value of

$$g(\mathbf{a} - h\mathbf{p}). \tag{5.4.9}$$

---

[13] Indeed, the set of $\mathbf{p} \in Si(m)$ that generates an Alabama Paradox includes an open dense set.

Approaches of this type have been proposed. Of course, fairness and common sense impose certain requirements upon g. The first is that, because the goal is to "round off," we only need to consider the base cube. Computationally, this means that g only needs to be defined for values in this cube.

Second, it is reasonable to assume that g is continuous. After all, a g with discontinuities allows a slight change in the value of $\mathbf{a} - h\mathbf{p}$ to force a jump, or huge change in the rounding off at a particular house size. Enough problems already occur with continuity, so there is no reason to beg for more difficulties by dropping smoothness.

Next, we require:

1. $g(\mathbf{0})$ is the unique minimum value for g and that $g(\lambda\mathbf{x})$ increases with larger values of λ.

This condition just means that when the exact apportionment for each state is an integer, that should be the apportionment. The monotonicity assumption excludes stupid choices of g where the round off favors a state when it is far from the exact apportionment but not when it is close.

A last condition, *neutrality*, ensures that each state is treated the same. Namely, if the population figures for the different states are interchanged, then so are the allocations. (Neutrality is not necessary, but it is so natural that I included it.)

Theorem 5.4.3. *Suppose the rounding off process is determined by minimizing the value of Eq. 5.4.9 in the base cube where the choice of a continuous, neutral g satisfies 1. Almost all choices of $\mathbf{p} \in Si(m)$ have an Alabama Paradox for some house size h.*

One way to think of this theorem is that the g function only changes the shape of the jar lid used to squash flies. Instead of a circle (where $g(\mathbf{x}) = \|\mathbf{x}\|$), it could be a triangle ($g(\mathbf{x}) = \sum_j |x_j|$), a square ($g(\mathbf{x}) = max(|x_j|)$), or even an object crudely resembling a snowflake ($g(\mathbf{x}) = \sum_j |x_j|^{\frac{1}{4}}$). In fact, one of the proposed procedures was $g(\mathbf{x}) = max(\sqrt{x_j(x_j + 1)})$. The motivation for this and other g choices is given in Sect. 5.5.

Whatever the choice of g, it is possible to move (i.e. by appropriately choosing $\mathbf{p}$) the newly shaped jar lid so that, in the two screen problem, designated flies on each screen can be killed even if they are in widely separated regions. In other words, don't blame the choice of a round off procedure g for the difficulties, the Alabama Paradox is caused by the enormous geometric flexibility in movement (determined by population figures) in going from one house size to another.

Outline of Proof. By neutrality, $k(\frac{1}{3}, \frac{1}{3}, \frac{1}{3})$ (or, more generally, for $m \geq 3$, $(\frac{l}{m}, \frac{l}{m}, \ldots, \frac{l}{m})$) corresponds to complete ties on a k assignment triangle. By continuity and monotonicity, there is an open set on the $k + 1$ triangle where c_j receives an extra seat and where indifference point is a boundary point. In the same manner as above, an open $AP(\mathbf{p})$ region is defined for $\mathbf{p} \neq (\frac{1}{3}, \frac{1}{3}, \frac{1}{3})$. Thus, the conclusion follows from the properties of the exact apportionment line $\mathbf{p}$. $\square$

A Chaotic Aside. As a digression intended only for readers familiar with nonlinear dynamics, let identify the apportionment problem with "chaos." The reader who has yet to become conversant with these important concepts should skip ahead to the next subsection. (See [S21].)

Of the many definitions for "chaos," most include irrational flows on a torus. So, by choosing **p** to be irrational and by considering the dynamic of Eq. 5.4.2 on a tori, it is clear that chaos occurs. However, I use a slightly different explanation based on the definition of chaos found in the seminal Li - Yorke paper [LY]. They require the system to have:

1. Sensitive dependence on initial conditions.
2. A dense set of periodic orbits.
3. A topologically transitive orbit.

Replace the traditional dynamical system with the system

$$\frac{d\mathbf{x}}{dt} = \mathbf{p}, \tag{5.4.10}$$

where $\mathbf{p} \in Si(m)$ serves both as an initial condition and the defining right-hand side. If $\mathbf{p} \neq \mathbf{p}'$, then, clearly, $t|\mathbf{p} - \mathbf{p}'|$ grows to become arbitrarily large. Consequently, arbitrarily small differences in initial conditions must lead to arbitrarily large differences in outcome. This satisfies the sensitivity property.

The second property follows from choosing **p** to have rational entries; it defines a periodic orbit on T^m. Moreover, it is known that these periodic orbits are dense.

The last condition is satisfied by any choice of **p** with completely irrational entries.

5.4.5 More Surprises, But Not Problems

Even in the relatively simplistic setting of $m = 3$ states, the assignment triangles so closely resemble the representation triangle that we must anticipate Hamilton's method to suffer problems similar to those endured by voting methods. Actually, because the assignment regions are duplicated in *each* apportionment cube, much more can happen. The approach used to discover these issues mimics that developed in Sects. 5.1, 5.2, so I just explore one unusual concern based on responsiveness.[14]

If you think the Alabama Paradox is troublesome, just wait until you learn about its other problems. To start, suppose as part of a population change, people from state 1 move to state 2. "Clearly" this migration enhances the second state's position to receive more representation. But, this need not happen; instead, state 1 could win one of state 2's representatives! This is outrageous; such intolerable behavior should disqualify Hamilton's method! Perhaps. But

---

[14]Other issues, such as when subcommittees unite, are left to the reader. Such questions have relevance for those countries using the "list" PR method. For instance, if the outcome in two regions places party 1 in the top-ranks, must the combined outcome also favor this party?

perhaps (as I argue next) Hamilton's outcome is reasonable and the misguided rage is due to how we analyze the problem.

To demonstrate this behavior with numbers, the original population in the following example awards state 1 a single representative while state 2 has 27. Now suppose after the census is corrected it is discovered that 20 of the people credited to state 1 really live in state 2. Rather than improving state 2's position, the new figures reassign one of state 2's seats to state 1!

State	Pop.	200$\mathbf{p}$	App	New Pop	200$\mathbf{p}'$	App
1	1570	1.57	1	1550	1.52	2
2	26630	26.630	27	26650	26.11	26
3	171800	171.80	172	175900	172.37	172

This is mysterious; how can a state lose a representative after its population grows? To understand why, represent the population change from $\mathbf{p}$ to $\mathbf{p}'$ by $\mathbf{v} = (v_1, v_2, v_3) = \mathbf{p}' - \mathbf{p}$. (So, $\sum_{j=1}^{3} v_j = 0$.) Following the lead of Sect. 5.2, $\mathbf{v}$ alters the apportionment iff it crosses a boundary line in the assignment triangle. (That is, iff $\mathbf{p}'$ is in a different apportionment region.) If the outer normal of the original region is $\mathbf{n}$, then the population change $\mathbf{v}$ moves toward a new region should $(\mathbf{n}, \mathbf{v}) > 0$. As we have learned from Sect. 5.2, this inequality offers ample opportunities to choose $\mathbf{v}$'s to generate paradoxes.

To illustrate, suppose $h\mathbf{p}$ is such that states 2 and 3 are rounded up while state 1 is rounded down. Geometrically, in Fig. 5.4.1, $h\mathbf{p}$ is in the region of the $k = 2$ assignment triangle with the dagger. The outer normal vectors for the two boundaries of this region are $\mathbf{n}_1 = (1, 0, 1) - (0, 1, 1) = (1, -1, 0)$ (for the vertical boundary) and $\mathbf{n}_2 = (1, 0, -1)$. Thus, should either $(\mathbf{n}_1, \mathbf{v}) = v_1 - v_2 > 0$ or $(\mathbf{n}_2, \mathbf{v}) = v_1 - v_3 > 0$ be satisfied, then when $h\mathbf{p}$ is sufficiently close to the appropriate boundary, the outcome will change to benefit state 1.

To show how to design scenarios, use the vertical boundary where the conditions are $v_1 > v_2$, $v_1 + v_2 + v_3 = 0$, and a change in outcome helps state 1 at the expense of state 2. Can state 2 lose a seat after a population increase? Yes, because $v_2 > 0$ does not preclude the possibility that $v_1 > v_2$ (which forces $v_3 = -(v_1 + v_2) < 0$.) So, even with a population increase, state 2 can lose representation! On reflection, this makes sense; state 2 lost out because its increase is relatively smaller population than other states.

A more creative situation requires $v_1 < 0$; here state 1 gains power after losing population. The responsiveness conditions requires $0 > v_1 > v_2$, so $v_3 > 0$. It now is easy to design settings where after state 1 *suffers a loss in population, it is awarded an extra representative!* This is illustrated with the following example which makes sense; although state 1 suffered a loss in population, it is relatively less than that of other states ($0 > v_1 > v_2$).

State	Pop.	100$\mathbf{p}$	App	New Pop.	% Change	v_j	100$\mathbf{p}'$	App
1	20650	20.65	20	20610	−0.19	−.00042	20.61	21
2	59670	59.67	60	59600	−0.117	−.00076	59.59	59
3	19680	19.68	20	19800	1.12	.00118	19.80	20

Notice the peculiarity where even though state 1 had a higher percentage loss than state 2 (a multiple of about 1.6), it ended up with more representatives! Actually, such a comparison is misleading; it is caused by a misuse of percentages. It is similar to a rural Northern Michigan community demanding more money for traffic control than Detroit because last year they suffered a 300% increase in traffic accidents and Detroit did not. (The year before they had one accident.) Namely, when decisions are being considered among many alternatives, the nonlinear form of percentages, with a different denominator for each state, leads to an "apple – orange" comparison. This occurs in the example where, because of its smaller size, state 1 suffers a larger percentage drop in population even though it lost fewer people. The resolution, of course, is to use a common base – this is Hamilton's method.

We now are prepared to understand why a state with an increase in population can lose a seat to a state with a declining population. The answer is that the true comparison is not between two states, but among all of them. As shown in Sect. 3.1, binary comparisons tend to discard vital information. This is what happens with the original example; state 1's loss of population is reflected by its negative v_1 value (in the following table). With only two states, state 2's position would improve with its larger population. However, state 3 enjoyed such a large increase that state 2's relative position declined (as shown by the negative v_2 value). In other words, the example combines two natural forces – a change in the relative standing of the two states, and a change in their position relative to all other states. When all states are compared with the same base, state 1's small population makes v_1 larger than $p_2 - p_2' = v_2 < 0$. So, although state 2 grew, relative to other states it declined. When viewed in terms of pairwise comparisons, something seems to be seriously wrong! When viewed in terms of the whole, the outcome is reasonable.

State	Pop.	200$\mathbf{p}$	New Pop.	% Change	v_j	200$\mathbf{p}'$
1	1570	1.57	1550	−	−.00026	1.52
2	26630	26.63	26650	.07	−.0025	26.11
3	171800	171.80	175900	2.39	.00283	172.37

(Incidentally, the above discussion underscores the dangers of the axiomatic approach that is so commonly used in choice theory. An "axiom" is a specific property, so by concentrating on specified axioms, we impose blinders to evaluate procedures strictly in terms of these properties. For instance, it is easy to package the above population responsiveness property as an appealing axiom and then use it to disqualify Hamilton's method. However, Hamilton's method is not at fault; the property is.)

With so much offered by the limited $m = 3$ assignment regions, just imagine the more imaginative examples permitted by geometry for $m > 3$ states. Using the same approach, interesting examples can be constructed, but I'll leave the fun to the interested reader. The reason more can happen is that there are even more boundaries, the representation regions no longer are triangular, and, with more states, there are more ways to vary the v_j values to satisfy the responsiveness conditions $(\mathbf{n}, \mathbf{v}) > 0$. A shameless way to generate attention about the designed paradoxes is to describe the population changes with other measures (such as percentage change within specific states, etc.) rather than in terms of v_j values.

These examples require $h\mathbf{p}$ to be sufficiently close to an appropriate boundary of assignment regions so that $h\mathbf{p}' = h(\mathbf{p} + \mathbf{v})$ crosses into another region. This suggests that such problems are rare and occur only in concocted examples. If the analysis required using only one apportionment cube, this assertion would be true. However, changes in h and $\mathbf{p}$ change which cube is of interest. When the outcomes from all possible cubes are combined, it turns out that these conclusions are quite likely. The mathematical tool permitting this analysis is my earlier discussion about the "flow on the torus." In other words, whenever a property can be described geometrically as $h\mathbf{p}$ entering an open region which is similar for all apportionment cubes, then the torus argument ensures that the property eventually (i.e., for some h) is satisfied for almost all $\mathbf{p}$.

This torus argument applies to the properties described by population changes $\mathbf{v}$, after all, $\mathbf{v}$ defines an open region near appropriate boundaries of each assignment region. (In fact, the region grows in size with the value of h.) Thus, *the above conclusions must be expected to occur for some value of h for almost all choices of $\mathbf{p}$*. There are certain restrictions; for instance, the phenomenon where a state loses population yet can win a seat requires a "large state – small state" comparison that is combined with a much larger total population growth; therefore they hold for almost all choices of $\mathbf{p}$ satisfying the appropriate inequalities. Notice, however, that since the early 1800s, these "large state – small state" conditions have been typical with the population growth in the United States; therefore it should be easy to find numerous examples from almost any stage of history. Here, $\mathbf{v}$ could reflect estimates on population growth from one year to another or errors in census (or vote) counts. (Such examples are easy to construct with the 1990 US census.)

Observation. *Let $m \geq 3$ and $\mathbf{v} = (v_1, \ldots, v_m)$, $\sum_{j=1}^{m} v_j = 0$ be such that $v_1 > v_2$. For almost all choices of $\mathbf{p} \in Si(m)$, there exists a house size h so that a change from $\mathbf{p}$ to $\mathbf{p} + \mathbf{v}$ takes a seat from state 2 and awards it to state 1.*

As a final comment, the phrase "takes a seat from state 2 and awards it to state 1" is a technically inaccurate comment of the type often used to attract attention. It is true only if there are only two states; with $m \geq 3$, there is a reallocation among all states where state 2 loses a seat and state 1 is awarded an extra one. With $m \geq 3$, everything is "relative."

5.4.6 Exercises

1. Explain why $AP((0.35, 0.34, 0.31))$ is smaller than $AP((0.6, 0.3, 0.1))$. Find a geometric description for each. (Hint: To find the $AP((0.35, 0.34, 0.31))$ boundary, consider the line $\mathbf{p} + \mathbf{d} = (0.35, 0.34, 0.31) + (d_1, d_2, d_3)$ where $\mathbf{d} \in Si(3)$. Now, set $\mathbf{p} + \mathbf{d}$ equal to a boundary point where the first and second state are awarded an extra seat, but not the first. The values of $\mathbf{d}$ describe the boundaries of $AP((0.35, 0.34, 0.31))$.)

2. Create a four-state example of an Alabama Paradox. Can an Alabama Paradox occur for $m = 2$? Use the fact there is only one assignment triangle in each apportionment cube to explain your answer.

3. The description of the Alabama Paradox describes when $h\mathbf{p}$ is in the $k = 1$ assignment triangle, and $(h + 1)\mathbf{p}$ is in the $k = 2$ assignment triangle. To develop other ways this can happen, create an example where $(h+1)\mathbf{p}$ is an integer vector, $h\mathbf{p}$ is not an integer vector, and in the process of going from h to $h+1$, an Alabama Paradox occur. This illustrates the folklore story where p_i represents the share of inheritance to be received by the ith brother, $i = 1, 2, 3$. The inheritance requires dividing up h cows. Because $h\mathbf{p}$ does not provide an integer division, two of the brothers "graciously" buy another cow to be added, free of charge, to the division so that an integer number will occur. Of course, their graciousness gives the remaining brother the "Alabama." Find a geometric representation for this description.

4. The set $A(\mathbf{p})$ is designed so that the state with the lowest population loses a representative at the next step. Can this be done so the state with the second highest population that loses a seat? What is the situation with $m \geq 4$ states?

5. For the populations of the three states specified in the introductory example, find $AP(\mathbf{p})$. Next, find the smallest integer h so that $h\mathbf{p} \in AP(\mathbf{p})$. As a more challenging problem, for a given $\mathbf{p} \neq (\frac{1}{3}, \frac{1}{3}, \frac{1}{3})$ find a way to determine a lower bound on the value of h that could cause an Alabama Paradox. As another challenging problem, which leads to an analysis of responsiveness questions, for each AP region given by the introductory example, plot the corresponding set of points on the simplex with the initial population figures.

6. Show that $\mathbf{x} \approx_{frac} \mathbf{y}$ is an equivalence relationship. Show that for any $\mathbf{x}$ and for any apportionment cube, there exists a unique $\mathbf{y}$ in the specified apportionment cube so that $\mathbf{x} \approx_{frac} \mathbf{y}$.

7. Show that Hamilton's method gives the same answer independent of the choice of the distance. Namely, we could use $d(\mathbf{a}, \mathbf{b}) = \sum |a_j - b_j|$ or, say, $(\sum [a_j - b_j]^s)^{\frac{1}{s}}$; $s \geq 1$.

8. Compare the lines in the base cube for $\mathbf{p} = (0.50, 0.50)$ and for $\mathbf{p}' = (0.49, 0.51)$. Next try $\mathbf{p}'' = (0.499, 0.501)$. Notice how a slight change in the population, or in the degree of accuracy can radically change how the base cube is filled. From this observation, create a three state example where no Alabama Paradox occurs for $\mathbf{p}$, but when just a couple people move from one state to another, a paradox does occur for some h.

5.5 House Monotone Methods

If geometry prohibits Hamilton's Method and its natural extensions from avoiding the Alabama Paradox, then we should look elsewhere. An obvious solution is to *impose* the desired monotonicity. Instead of recalculating the apportionment when a new seat is available, assign it to the most deserving state. This requires a "fairness measure" $F(a_j, p_j)$, which, presumably, indicates the level of representation enjoyed by the jth state. The idea is that the state with the minimum $F(a_j, p_j)$ value is underrepresented, so it deserves the extra seat.

To convert this common sense into a *house monotone* technique, start with an initial assignment of seats to the states. This could be zero or some other value; for instance, to satisfy the US Constitution, each state could be initially assigned a single seat. The starting apportionment of $h \geq 0$ seats provides the jth state with $a_j(h)$ representatives, $j = 1, \ldots, m$. Now, add a seat to enlarge the house size to $h + 1$; the most underrepresented state as identified by the smallest $F(a_j(h), p_j)$ value gets this seat. Next, add another seat and give it to the state with the smallest $F(a_j(h + 1), p_j)$ value. Continue until all seats are assigned. (In the USA, this is 435.) Because seats are *added* at each house size – nothing else is changed so nothing is subtracted – such methods avoid the Alabama Paradox. This appears to be a perfect scheme; but, as we now should expect, the solution of one problem gives birth to new ones.

Stability and Fairness Measures. The critical defining factor of a house monotone method is the "fairness measure" $F(a_j, p_j)$; different choices (there are an infinite number of them) distinguish among the procedures. It is natural, for instance, to equalize the number of representatives per population. Clearly, the state with the smallest $\frac{a_j(h)}{p_j}$ value is underrepresented at house size h, so it is entitled to the next available seat. Therefore, in going from house size h to $h + 1$, the *Smallest Divisors* method awards the new seat to the state j with the minimum value of

$$F_{SD}(a_j(h), p_j) = \frac{a_j(h)}{p_j}. \tag{5.5.1}$$

One might argue that "fairness" should emphasize the division of the new house size $h + 1$ rather than worrying about past inequities at smaller h values. As this forward looking philosophy requires examining what happens to each state *if* it receives the extra seat, the relevant fraction is

$$F_J(a_j, p_j) = \frac{a_j + 1}{p_j}. \tag{5.5.2}$$

$F_J(a_j, p_j)$ measures state j's level of representation at the new house size, so, in moving from house size h to $h + 1$, the *Jefferson* method (named after Thomas Jefferson) awards the extra seat to the state that minimizes $F_J(a_j(h), p_j)$.

As a compromise to try to heal the wounds of the past while seeking fairness in the future, we could use a weighted average between F_{SD} and F_J; this defines

$$F_{W,\gamma}(a_j, p_j) = \frac{a_j + \gamma}{p_j}, \quad \gamma \in [0, 1]. \tag{5.5.3}$$

Again, the state with the minimum $F_{W,\gamma}(a_j(h), p_j)$ value at house size h is entitled to the extra seat for house size $h + 1$. Different γ values define different techniques; $F_{W,0} = F_{SD}$, $F_{W,1} = F_J$, and $F_{W,\frac{1}{2}} = F_W$ is the *Webster method*.

The method currently used in the USA, *Equal Proportions,* is based upon a more sophisticated premise. E. V. Huntington [Hu1-2] reasoned that a distribution of seats is "fair" if there does not exist a reallocation that achieves a "fairer" division. Mathematically, state j has an advantage (more seats per voter) over state i should $\frac{a_j}{p_j} > \frac{a_i}{p_i}$, or, by dividing, should

$$1 > \frac{\frac{a_i}{p_i}}{\frac{a_j}{p_j}} = \frac{a_i p_j}{a_j p_i}. \tag{5.5.4}$$

This last ratio, then, measures the disadvantage experienced by state i with respect to j; the smaller the value, the more state i is underrepresented.

If state j has a relative over representation, shouldn't one of its seats be given to state i? Perhaps; but this might tip the scales to give state i an undue advantage over j! Using the same measure, the relative disadvantage state j suffers after a reallocation is $\frac{(a_j-1)p_i}{(a_i+1)p_j}$; the smaller the value, the more state j is underrepresented. Therefore, the new distribution creates an even greater disparity should

$$1 > \frac{a_i p_j}{a_j p_i} \geq \frac{(a_j - 1)p_i}{(a_i + 1)p_j}. \tag{5.5.5}$$

Stated in another way, if Inequality 5.5.5, or the equivalent $\frac{a_i(a_i+1)}{p_i^2} \geq \frac{a_j(a_j-1)}{p_j^2}$, or

$$\frac{\sqrt{a_i(a_i + 1)}}{p_i} \geq \frac{\sqrt{a_j(a_j - 1)}}{p_j}, \tag{5.5.6}$$

are satisfied, there is no reason to give state i one of j's seats; the relative relationship between these two states is stable. In turn, to achieve this stability, the goal is to make the values

$$F_{EP}(a_i, p_i) = \frac{\sqrt{a_i(a_i + 1)}}{p_i} \tag{5.5.7}$$

as equal as possible over the states. The *Equal Proportions* method used by the USA, then, awards the new seat obtained by going from house size h to $h+1$ to the state with the minimum $F_{EP}(a_j(h), p_j)$ value.

The remaining procedure that Huntington calls "workable" is the *Harmonic Mean* defined by

$$F_{HM}(a_j, p_j) = \frac{2a_j(a_j + 1)}{p_j(2a_j + 1)}. \tag{5.5.8}$$

This strange looking choice results from trying to equalize the number of citizens per representative by emphasizing the ratio $\frac{p_i}{a_i}$. State j is at a disadvantage with respect to i if $\frac{p_i}{a_j} - \frac{p_i}{a_i} > 0$, where the level of disadvantage is determined by the value of this difference. Using the stability analysis to decide which of two states is more deserving of a newly available seat in terms of the absolute differences between the fractions, state j is more deserving than i should

$$\frac{p_j}{a_j + 1} - \frac{p_i}{a_i} \geq \frac{p_i}{a_i + 1} - \frac{p_j}{a_j} > 0. \tag{5.5.9}$$

Collecting terms (and taking the reciprocal so "smaller" means "more underrepresented") leads to Eq. 5.5.8.

Each method sounds reasonable, so which one should be used? Each has serious problems. Namely, when grappling with problems based on higher dimensional geometry, be careful – "common sense" honed from experiences in our limited three-dimensional world can mislead severely. This underscores the fact that while the defining properties or axioms of a procedure may appear to be acceptable, the consequences may not be!

The Differences Make a Difference. It usually is asserted that five of the above methods are the only "workable" allocation procedures (e.g., see [Hu1, Mas]), but it takes only minimal imagination to invent an infinite number of other methods. We could, for instance, modify the derivation for F_{EP} by emphasizing the new allocation rather than the current one. Or, to combine the advantages of using relative differences (F_{EP}) and absolute differences (F_{HM}) of different a_i, p_i ratios, we might use the weighted average $F_{L,\gamma}(a_j, p_j) = (1 - \gamma)F_{EP}(a_j, p_j) + \gamma F_{HM}$, $\gamma \in [0, 1]$. Indeed, by modifying the following geometric description, the reader can invent any number of distinctly new approaches.

The main point, which we should anticipate from our discussion of positional methods, is that *different choices for F can result in significantly different apportionments.* Just as a single profile can support many different election rankings, the same population figures can define different allocations of seats as the choice of F varies. Huntington demonstrated this rich divergence with delightful examples typified by the following one where three methods define three different apportionments for three states.

State	Pop.	HM	EP	W
A	729	7	7	8
B	534	5	6	5
C	337	4	3	3
	$\overline{1600}$	$\overline{16}$	$\overline{16}$	$\overline{16}$

(5.5.10)

Huntington's examples underscore the need to understand apportionment methods. What theory has emerged is, for the most part, based on the construction of clever examples or computer simulations. (See [Hu1, Mas, BY1].) This leaves unanswered important concerns. For instance, how prevalent are these paradoxes? When should we worry about them? How can we compare methods? What else can go wrong? Why do the paradoxes occur? More generally, when a procedure is described in terms of the motivation behind its development or axioms it possesses, it may sound great. A more practical measure is to understand all of its hidden but serious consequences. This requires a careful geometric analysis.

The similarity of the examples of apportionment paradoxes with those from voting suggests that a geometric theory for apportionments can be designed – a theory closely related to that developed in Chaps. 2, 3 and 4 for voting methods. (For instance, the $F_{W,\gamma}$ methods define a version of the procedure line.) This can be done, and (because of the nonlinearities of methods such as EP) the resulting geometry is richer than that for voting. Moreover, all of the concerns from voting, such as responsiveness, comparing what happens when a new candidate or state is admitted, etc., have direct counterparts. Because of space limitations I can only hint about what is possible, enough of the geometry is described to permit the reader to develop intuition about what happens and why. In this way, we overcome Huntington confession that "crucial examples of this sort are not easy to construct, ... " Once we understand *why* something happens, constructing examples reduces to an exercise. In particular, dependence on computer simulations no longer is necessary.

5.5.1 Who Cares About Quota?

The telling clue that house monotone methods experience problems comes from Huntington's comment,

> *"Now it is a common misconception that in a good apportionment the actual assignment should not differ from the exact quota by more than one whole unit; for example, if the exact quota is 5.21 or 5.76, then it is often assumed that the actual assignment should not be less than 5 nor more than 6."*

Sure seems like a reasonable assumption to me! If my state is entitled to 62.76 seats, why should we accept only 58 seats! Yet, Huntington's comment must have its supporters; such exaggerated round-offs seem to be sanguinely accepted in Europe where allocations of seats to parties can be rounded up or down by more than unity. I am unaware of any sustained outcry of, "Foul! Foul!" Maybe they are intimidated by the mathematics.

Huntington demonstrates one such ("good"?) apportionment with the following example where state A, with its exact apportionment of 92.15, is awarded only 90 seats. This is a "large - small" state comparison, so, with the current USA population figures, citizens from California and New York should pay particular attention.

State	Pop.	EP	State	Pop.	EP	
A	9215	90	D	157	2	
B	159	2	E	156	2	(5.5.11)
C	158	2	F	155	2	
				10,000	100	

Concerned citizens from states with smaller populations, such as Vermont or Alaska, should not allow this example to lull them into smug complacency; the next Huntington example allows the EP to award a large state 90 seats although only entitled to 87.85 representatives! One must wonder which small states sacrificed seats so that A can indulge in its added political power.

State	Pop.	EP	State	Pop.	EP
A	8785	90	F	122	1
B	126	1	G	121	1
C	125	1	H	120	1
D	124	1	I	119	1
E	123	1	J	118	1
			K	117	1
				$\overline{10,000}$	$\overline{100}$

$$(5.5.12)$$

As I indicate next, much more can happen!

The Humane Way to Catch Flies. What is going on? To understand the apportionment paradoxes, return to the fly killing exercise of Sect. 5.4. Squashing flies on a screen leaves a mess, so, instead of killing flies, catch them by replacing the lid with a jar. (Surprisingly, the "shape" of the jar is the same for all F functions! Thus, by introducing new shapes, unexplored classes of methods are invented.) Holding the jar with an orientation to be specified later, move it as close as possible to the screen to catch a single fly on a side of the jar. (As before, the movement is determined by the exact apportionment line $t\mathbf{p}$.) For comfort, each jar could be held in a different manner. (How the "jar" is held distinguishes the different choices of F.) Obviously, by holding the jar in different ways, different flies can be caught. (This explains the differences in the apportionments for the same $\mathbf{p}$.)

To equate fly hunting with house monotone methods, let $F_g(a_j, p_j) = \frac{g(a_j)}{p_j}$ for function g. Of course, to be realistic, $g(0) \geq 0$ and g needs to be monotonically increasing where $\lim_{x \to \infty} g(x) = \infty$. If $F_g(a_j, p_j) \geq \lambda$, then

$$g(a_j) \geq \lambda p_j, \quad \forall j. \tag{5.5.13}$$

Equation 5.5.13 makes sense. The term $\lambda\mathbf{p} = (\lambda p_1, \ldots, \lambda p_m)$ is a point on the exact apportionment line, while $g(x)$ measures the number of representatives assigned to a state. This equation, then, asserts that the g measure should approximate the exact apportionment λp_j. (Well, if $\lambda = h$.) Indeed, for years, a closely related approach, based on Jefferson's choice of $g(a) = a + 1$, was used in the USA. After a value of λ was chosen, state j was assigned k_j seats where k_j is the first integer so that $g_J(k_j) = k_j + 1$ is greater than or equal to λp_j. By allowing the value of h to depend upon the choice of λ and $\mathbf{p}$, the house size could and did vary.

The "fly catching jar" is defined by $J_g(\mathbf{a}, \mathbf{p}, \lambda) = (g(a_1) - \lambda p_1, \ldots, g(a_m) - \lambda p_m)$ where an apportionment, $\mathbf{a}$, is "inside" the jar iff each component of J_g is nonnegative. Thus the jth side of the jar is determined by the unique x_j value

$$g(x_j) = \lambda p_j; \quad x_j = g^{-1}(\lambda p_j).$$

(All positive numbers are in the image of g, so x_j is defined; g is strictly increasing, so x_j is unique.) For example, to find the x value for EP, solve

$\sqrt{x(x+1)} = \lambda p$, or $x^2 + x - (\lambda p)^2 = 0$, to obtain (via the quadratic formula), $x = \frac{-1+\sqrt{1+4(\lambda p)^2}}{2}$, a value that is less than λp. For the methods described above, the solutions are

Method	$g(x)$	$x = g^{-1}(\lambda p)$
SD	x	$x = \lambda p$
J	$x+1$	$x = \lambda p - 1$
W, γ	$x + \gamma$	$x = \lambda p - \gamma$
EP	$\sqrt{x(x+1)}$	$x = \frac{-1+\sqrt{1+4(\lambda p)^2}}{2}$
HM	$\frac{2x(x+1)}{2x+1}$	$x = \frac{\lambda p - 1 + \sqrt{1+(\lambda p)^2}}{2}$

$$(5.5.14)$$

Example 5.5.1 For two states,[15] suppose $\mathbf{p} = (\frac{1}{5}, \frac{4}{5})$ and $\lambda = 10$. According to the table 5.5.14, the sides of the SD jar are $x = \lambda p_1 = 2$, $y = \lambda p_2 = 8$. So, the SD jar is defined by

$$J_{SD} = \{(x,y) \,|\, x \geq 2, \, y \geq 8\}.$$

In other words, the J_{SD} jar is just a translated positive quadrant where the origin now is at the point $\lambda \mathbf{p} = (2, 8)$. This is the shaded region depicted in Fig. 5.5.1.

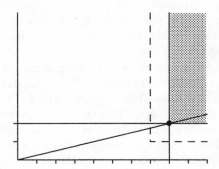

Fig. 5.5.1. Comparison between SD and Jefferson jars

For the same $\lambda \mathbf{p}$ values, the sides of the Jefferson jar are $x = \lambda p_1 - 1 = 1$, $y = \lambda p_2 - 1 = 7$. Consequently, the J_J jar for $\lambda \mathbf{p}$ is

$$J_J = \{(x,y) \,|\, x \geq 1, \, y \geq 7\}.$$

Again, J_J is a translated positive quadrant; the difference between J_{SD} and J_J is how they are held. The translated origin for J_J is at the point $\lambda \mathbf{p} - (1,1)$, rather than on the exact apportionment line! The boundaries for this J_J region

---

[15] No serious problems occur for $m = 2$, but pictures are easy to draw.

are the dashed lines depicted in Fig. 5.5.1. This means that *the J_J jar is held in a lagging, asymmetric manner as it is moved along the exact apportionment line*.

As a third example using these $\lambda \mathbf{p}$ values, J_{EP} is defined by

$$\{(x, y) \,|\, x \geq \frac{-1 + \sqrt{17}}{2} \approx 2 - 0.4384,\ y \geq \frac{-1 + \sqrt{257}}{2} \approx 8 - 0.4844\}.$$

Again, J_{EP} is obtained by sliding the positive quadrant in a lagging, asymmetric manner to a point near, but *never on* the exact apportionment line $\lambda \mathbf{p}$. In fact, with the EP, the direction and amount of translation from $\lambda \mathbf{p}$ changes with the value of $\lambda \mathbf{p}$. $\square$

For any number of states, *the jar $J_g(\mathbf{x}, \mathbf{p}, \lambda)$ always is a translated positive orthant*. The differences between F_g methods, therefore, are uniquely determined by the location of the translated origin. Expressing this point as

$$\lambda \mathbf{p} + T_g(\lambda \mathbf{p}) = \lambda \mathbf{p} + [(g^{-1}(\lambda p_1), \ldots, g^{-1}(\lambda p_m)) - \lambda \mathbf{p}],$$

the term in the brackets, $T_g(\lambda \mathbf{p})$, indicates the position of the translated origin relative to the reference point $\lambda \mathbf{p}$ on the exact apportionment line. In words, this translation term determines how the jar J_g is held as it moves. With the exception of the SD, the jar always is held in a lagging, asymmetric manner as it moves according to the exact apportionment line.

For the methods described above, all components of the translation term $T_g(\lambda \mathbf{p})$ are between -1 and 0. Therefore, if the *translation cube* is defined as $TC = [-1, 0]^m$, then *the translation term, $T_g(\lambda \mathbf{p}) \in TC$, uniquely determines the properties of F_g*. (In Fig. 5.5.1, TC is the small square defined by the dashed and solid lines; the location of the translation point in this square determines which procedure is being used.) Conversely, there are as many apportionment methods as there are ways to define the translation vector.

5.5.2 Big States, Small States

Once we recognize that the properties of a method are determined by the translation term $\mathbf{T}_g(\lambda \mathbf{p}) \in TC$, it is easy to see why different methods lead to different apportionments. Figure 5.5.1 depicts the impact of different choices of $\mathbf{T}_g(\lambda \mathbf{p})$ with the same $\lambda \mathbf{p}$ value. Obviously, certain approaches (e.g., J_a in the figure) favors states with large populations, while others (e.g., J_b in the figure) favor small population states. By positioning the orthant so that it is further along the axis representing the state with the larger population, as true with J_a, a distinct bias is interjected; for the same population figures, the large state gets more seats.

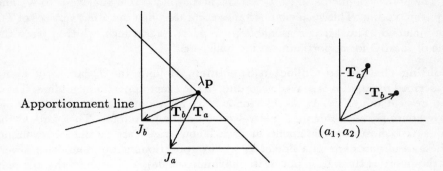

Fig. 5.5.2. A comparison of different jars

It is possible to coax an useful inequality out of the geometry that determines which methods favor large or small population states. The approach is based on comparing the (ratio of) population figures that different methods require to assign the same relative allocation (a_1, a_2), $a_1 > a_2$. To see what we are looking for, suppose method g_a assigns (a_1, a_2) with population figures $(500, 100)$ while method g_b requires $(1,000, 100)$. By awarding the large state the allocation a_1 with the smaller population figure of 500, or with the ratio $\frac{p_2}{p_1} = \frac{1}{5}$, method g_a displays its distinct bias in favor of larger states. Method g_b, on the other hand, forces a large population state to have a much larger population before justifying this allocation; here the ratio is $\frac{p_2}{p_1} = \frac{1}{10}$. So, for a given allocation, the larger the value of $\frac{p_2}{p_1}$ (where $p_1 > p_2$) required for a specific allocation (i.e., the sooner a large population state gets a particular apportionment), the more bias a method discloses toward larger states.

To describe this measure in geometric terms, place the vertex of two jars at the same (a_1, a_2) point. The exact apportionment line supporting this outcome is found by adding $-T_g$ to the origin. (See Fig. 5.5.2.) In the example, $-T_a$ locates a point above $-T_b$. This means that the exact apportionment line for g_a allows a larger slope than that g_b, $\frac{p_2^a}{p_1^a} > \frac{p_2^b}{p_1^b}$; this reinforces the earlier observation that g_a favors larger states.

Translating this description into the geometry of TC, two methods, g_a, g_b are compared in the following manner. Draw a line from $(0,0)$ through T_{g_b}. If T_{g_a} is to the south of this line, or on the line but farther along, then g_a favors large states more than g_b; otherwise g_a favors the small state. With this elementary comparison technique, it follows that *the SD favors small states more than any other procedure; the Jefferson method favors large states more than any other procedure.* Also, if $\gamma_1 > \gamma_2$, then W, γ_1 favors large states over W, γ_2. Re-expressing the geometry in terms of the g functions, g_a favors large states if for all $s > t$,

$$\frac{g_a(t)}{g_a(s)} > \frac{g_b(t)}{g_b(s)}. \qquad (5.5.15)$$

The above comments suggest that SD and J play a role analogous to $\mathbf{w}_0$ and $\mathbf{w}_{\frac{1}{2}}$ from voting. This suspicion becomes accurate when the other vertices of TC are included. Thus, it is reasonable to wonder, for instance, which g plays the role of the BC for apportionment methods, etc.[16]

Holding the Jar to Collect a Specimen. Holding the J_g jar in the above prescribed manner, it is moved according to the exact apportionment line. There is a critical value $\lambda = \lambda_h$ so that for $\lambda > \lambda_h$ all apportionments inside the jar have house sizes greater than h – we've moved the jar too far. Therefore, at the value $\lambda_h \mathbf{p}$, those apportionments in J_g with house size h are the ones we examine. These candidates are on a side of J_g (if any apportionment of house size h were in the interior, then λ_h is not at its maximum value), and usually, there is only one – this is the F_g apportionment for house size h. If there are several qualified apportionments, then there is a tie in the choice, so use a tie-breaker.

Example 5.5.2. The geometric description is invaluable for understanding the properties of an apportionment procedure, but, in practice, a computational scheme is used. As described above, the value of λ_h is such that $g(a_j(h)) = \lambda_h p_j$ for some state. For all other states, say the kth, find the smallest value of a_k satisfying $\frac{g(a_k)}{p_k} = \lambda^{(k)} \geq \lambda_h$. Then, the seats are assigned to states according to the $\lambda^{(k)}$ values where smaller values are served first.

Actual computations are fairly simple. With a spreadsheet, compute for each state the values of $\frac{g(a_i)}{p_i}$ for various consecutive choices of a_i. At house size h, λ_h must be one of the computed values. The jth state receives the smallest value of a_j so that $\frac{g(a_j)}{p_j} \geq \lambda_h$. To illustrate with the EP, $h = 100$, and the population figures of Eq. 5.5.11, suppose we thought that the accurate apportionment would assign state B a single seat. If so, then it must be that $\frac{g(1)}{0.0159} = \lambda^{(B)} = 88.944 \geq \lambda_{100}$. In turn, the ratios $\frac{g(a_j(100))}{p_j}$, $j = A, \ldots, F$, must be as close to this value as possible. With the smaller populations of states $C - F$, the inequalities $\frac{g(1)}{p_j} > \frac{g(1)}{0.0159}$ for $j = C, D, E, F$, ensures that B is entitled to a second seat before any of these four states.

For state A, $\frac{g(81)}{0.9215} = 88.4411$ while $\frac{g(82)}{0.9215} = 89.5263$. Thus, as long as B has only a single representative, state A is entitled to at most 82 seats. All together, this adds up to 87 seats; 13 more to go. The only way extra seats can be added legitimately is to relax the assumption restricting state B to only one seat. Therefore, $\lambda_{100} > \frac{g(1)}{0.0159}$, so B must be assigned another seat.

---

[16] Regional voting in Congress is becoming increasingly important for many policy factors. Indeed, for many issues, the concerns of a region overtake those of the individual states. Wendy Ramsbottom explored this question (in her 1993 Northwestern University Senior Thesis) by comparing the number of representatives from all states in a region with the number of representatives the region would receive if it were a state. In this way, she demonstrated that certain regions are short-changed in political power; a factor that can be critical on a close vote. (She identified issues where this could have been a deciding factor in several Congressional votes.) The natural question raised by her work is whether a method of the above kind can keep both kinds of apportionments – state and region – as consistent as possible. This is the Borda issue.

The much larger $\lambda^{(B)} = \frac{g(2)}{0.0159} = 154.0560$ value, obtained when B has two seats, eliminates the restricting logjam; now seats can be assigned to other states. Nevertheless, until F secures its second seat, state A's apportionment is restricted to the smallest value of a so that $\frac{g(a)}{0.9215} \geq \frac{g(1)}{0.0155} = 91.2396$, or $a_A = 84$. This leaves us still far below the designated value of $h = 100$, so F also gets a second seat.

Now that the small population states have two seats, the apportionment for state A defines the value λ_h. In fact, each new seat must be assigned to A until the first integer value of a where $\frac{g(a)}{0.9215} \geq \lambda^{(B)} = \frac{g(2)}{0.0159} = 154.0560$. With a simple computation, this means that for all house sizes from 94 to 151, states $B - F$ remain fixed at two representatives and A gets the rest. The figures for the final apportionment of 100 seats follow.

State	EP	$\frac{g_{EP}(a_j)}{p_j}$	State	EP	$\frac{g_{EP}(a_j)}{p_j}$	
A	90	98.2079	D	2	156.0185	(5.5.16)
B	2	154.0559	E	2	157.01857	
C	2	155.0400	F	2	158.0360	

¿From this computation, we have that

$$\lambda_{100} = \lambda^{(A)} = 98.2079,$$
$$\mathbf{T}_{EP}(\lambda_{100}\mathbf{p}) = -(0.4986, 0.4219, 0.4214, 0.4210, 0.4205, 0.4200).$$
$$(5.5.17)$$

In this example where the large population state is rounded down by more than unity, $\lambda_h < h$. For the population figures of Eq. 5.5.165.16, where the large population state is rounded upwards, $\lambda_{100} = \lambda^{(A)} = 103.0149$ while $\lambda^{(j)}, j = B, \ldots, K$, range in value from 112.2392 to 120.8730. □

5.5.3 The Translation Bias

The lesson learned from the example is that the F_g methods do not base the apportionment on the values of $h\mathbf{p}$, but rather on some other value $\lambda_h\mathbf{p}$ where λ_h can be larger or smaller than h. That is not all; fresh bias is manufactured by the lagging, asymmetric motion of the jar held away from the apportionment line (as established by T_g)! With all of this hidden, very real bias, something serious must go wrong. But what and why?

The answer, as always, comes from the geometry. There are only two elements; the slope of the apportionment line $\lambda\mathbf{p}$ and the translation of the jar, $T_g(\lambda\mathbf{p})$. Perhaps the easiest way to see how they interact is to run the "fly catching" film backwards. Choose the unique $\lambda = \lambda^*$ value which positions the origin of the jar right at $\mathbf{x}^*$ on the simplex $S_h = \{\mathbf{x} \in R_+^m \mid \sum_{j=1}^m x_j = h\}$. Even a slight increase in $\lambda > \lambda^*$ forces the jar to totally miss S_h. On the other hand, a $\lambda < \lambda^*$ value requires the jar to meet a portion of the simplex including $\mathbf{x}^*$. Should all components of $\mathbf{x}^*$ be integers, $\mathbf{x}^*$ is the apportionment at house size h. If not, then "back up" by choosing smaller values of λ until an integer apportionment on S_h is obtained. This backwards approach is, of course, equivalent to the earlier description.

The bias introduced by the translation term $T_g(\lambda \mathbf{p})$ permits – at times demands – the point $\mathbf{x}^*$ to be quite distant from the apportionment cube defined by $h\mathbf{p}$. With $\mathbf{x}^*$ in a different cube, this makes it easy for the backing up process to catch an apportionment that doesn't satisfy quota. Examples now become trivial to construct. For instance, for $m = 3$, choose $\mathbf{x}^* = (95, 1, 1)$; the entries are integers, so $\mathbf{x}^*$ is the apportionment for $h = 97$. All we need is to find the corresponding $\mathbf{p}$ for a specified method. To illustrate with the Jefferson method, the translation term $T_J = (-1, -1, -1)$ shows that the point on the exact apportionment line is $\mathbf{x}^* - T_J = \lambda_{97}\mathbf{p} = (95 + 1, 1 + 1, 1 + 1)$; so $\mathbf{p} = (0.96, 0.02, 0.02)$ defines fractional population figures. With this $\mathbf{p}$, the exact apportionment at $h = 97$ is $(93.12, 1.94, 1.94)$; as we might conjecture from Fig. 5.5.2, the large state is rounded up by more than one seat.

Maybe creating examples is not completely trivial; there are no population figures which allows the above $\mathbf{x}^*$ to be the basis of a paradox for the Webster or EP methods. Again, the explanation comes from the geometry. For the Webster method, the distance between $\|\lambda_{97}\mathbf{p} - \mathbf{x}^*\| = \| - T_W\| = \|(\frac{1}{2}, \frac{1}{2}, \frac{1}{2})\| = \frac{\sqrt{3}}{2}$ is insufficient to push $h\mathbf{p}$ and $\mathbf{x}^*$ into different apportionment triangles that don't share common vertices; i.e., apportionments. For $m \geq 4$ states, however, the increased value of $\|T_W\| = \frac{\sqrt{m}}{2}$ puts added distance between a chosen point $\mathbf{x}^*$ and $h\mathbf{p}$ which allows examples to be created. So, if $\mathbf{x}^* = (95, 1, 1, 1)$, then $\mathbf{x}^* - T_W = 100\mathbf{p} = 100(0.955, 0.015, 0.015, 0.015)$. The exact $h = 98$ allocation for the large state with $\mathbf{p}$ is 93.59, thus this illustrates that the Webster method can round this state up by more than one.

Of course, larger values of m increases the value of $\|T_g\|$, which allows even more extreme examples to be created. For instance, let $\mathbf{x}^* = (51, 1, \ldots, 1)$ be the $h = 100$ apportionment for $m = 50$ states. With Jefferson's method, the associated $\lambda \mathbf{p} = \mathbf{x} * - T_J = (52, 2, \ldots, 2)$, so $\mathbf{p} = (0.265, 0.015, \ldots, 0.015)$ and the exact apportionment is $(34.67, 1.33, \ldots, 1.33)$. Here, Jefferson's method rounds the large state upwards not by one, but by 17. EP does not do much better; here the exact apportionment is 42.63, so the large state is rounded upwards by 9 rather than unity.

Indeed, *the bias of $T_g \in TC$ tends to try to violate the upper quota.* As T_J is an extreme vertex of TC, it designates the upper bound on how badly upper quota can be violated. More generally, for method g, if there exists a value $\gamma > 0$ so that each component of T_g is bounded above by $-\gamma$, then examples (by choosing appropriate values of m and $\mathbf{p}$) can be created showing that instead of rounding up to the nearest integer, g can round up by a value as large as desired! Enough geometry has been described to make the proofs of these assertions an exercise.

Conversely, $T_{SD} = \mathbf{0}$, so we must expect that *the SD never violates upper quota.* The proof of this assertion also follows from the geometry. With SD, $\mathbf{x}^*$

is the exact apportionment $h\mathbf{p}$; that is, for each state $\frac{x_i^*}{p_i} = h < \frac{x_i^*+1}{p_i}$. If $\mathbf{x}^*$ is an integer vector, then it is the apportionment. If not, then the backward motion requires $\lambda_h < h$. So, for state i, the apportionment is the smallest integer a_i satisfying $\frac{x_i^*+1}{p_i} > \frac{g_{SD}(a_i)}{p_i} = \frac{a_i}{p_i} \geq \lambda_h$, or $x_i^* + 1 > a_i$. This means that a_i can be no larger than rounding x_i^* upwards.

5.5.4 Sliding Bias

By forcing the jar off the apportionment line, the translation term creates an obvious bias that attempts to violate upper quota. More subtly, but with equal force in the "other direction," the sliding action of the jar determined by the slope of the apportionment line plays a critical role.

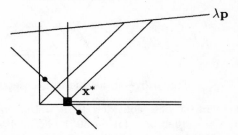

Fig. 5.5.3. The sliding bias of the apportionment line

Figure 5.5.3 demonstrates the influence (i.e., bias) the slope of $\lambda\mathbf{p}$ has on the "backing up" process for $m = 2$; even a large difference in λ values admits only a trivial change in the height of the horizontal edge (i.e., where the jar edge for the large state passes through S_h). The starting position of $\mathbf{x}^*$ is closest to an apportionment favoring the large state; the "backing-up" process forces the jar edge to hit an apportionment less favorable to the large state. This makes sense; the flatter the apportionment line is in a direction, the less change there will be in the edge of the jar in this direction. Therefore, the real change in the jar, which ends up determining the apportionment, is in the other directions. Observe who is being "helped;" by keeping the value for the larger state essentially fixed but varying the edge for the small state, the smaller population state gains an advantage!

The limited interval geometry associated with $m = 2$ forces the sliding action of the jar to hit an endpoint of the interval containing $\mathbf{x}^*$. More adventure is created once $m \geq 3$. This is illustrated in Fig. 5.5.4 with $m = 3$. Each triangle in the grid corresponds to either a $k = 1$ or $k = 2$ assignment triangle. The jar, with its edges parallel to the coordinate axis of R^3, always create a triangle with the same orientation as the $k = 1$ assignment triangle; the size of the triangle depends upon the value of λ.

The two dots in the figure represent different values of $\mathbf{x}^*$; because they are nearby, they correspond to similar population values. The two dashed triangles describe how the jar intersects with S_h; the asymmetric positioning about the respective $\mathbf{x}^*$ position is attributed to the sliding bias introduced by the apportionment line $\lambda\mathbf{p}$ as described above. In this depiction, the geometry of the expanding triangle on the right must hit a vertices of the assignment triangle containing $\mathbf{x}_2^*$. This need not be the situation with the expanding triangle on the left. Because of the assignment triangle orientation, the expanding triangle can miss all of these vertices to first hit a bottom vertex in the assignment triangle below! But, a lower vertex means the larger state is getting a smaller apportionment. Therefore, we must suspect that the sliding action might cause the apportionment to violate lower quota. This is the case!

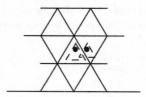

Fig. 5.5.4. Bias due to geometry and sliding

To see what can happen, consider the $h = 150$, $m = 50$, SD apportionment where the large state has population 5051 and each of the 49 small states has the population of 101. For a small state, $\frac{g_{SD}(1)}{p_1} = \frac{1}{0.0101} = 99.010$ while $\frac{2}{0.0101} = 198.020$. For the large state, $\frac{g_{SD}(51)}{0.5051} = 100.970$, $\frac{100}{0.5051} = 197.981$. Thus, when $h = 100$, we have that $\lambda_{100} = \frac{1}{0.0101} = 99.010$ leading to the quite reasonable apportionment where each small state has a single representative and the large state has 51. But, for house sizes from $h = 101, \ldots, 198$, we have that $\lambda_h = \frac{g_{SD}(51)}{0.5051} = 100.970$. In particular, the $h = 198$ apportionment has two seats for each small state and the same 51 for the large state. As the exact apportionment for the large state is 100.010, the state is rounded down not by unity, but by 49 seats! In contrast, EP would assign the large state 71 seats (some small states receive two and rest, three seats.) Here, rounding down violates lower quota by "only" 29 seats. The reasonable apportionment, where quota is met, comes from the Jefferson approach which assigns the large state 100 seats, and 2 seats for each small state.

What is going on is that the bias of the sliding action tries to violate lower quota. Countering this effect is the upward bias of the translation term T_g; if it is sufficiently large, then lower quota need not be violated. In particular, *the Jefferson apportionment never violates lower quota.* The proof of this assertion is elementary. If $\mathbf{y}^* = h\mathbf{p}$ is the exact quota, then for each i,

$$h = \frac{y_i^*}{p_i} = \frac{(y_i^* - 1) + 1}{p_i} = \frac{g_J(y_i^* - 1)}{p_i}.$$

The sum of the values $\sum_{i=1}^{m}(y_i - 1) = \sum_{i=1}^{m} y_i - m = h - m$, so the above values cannot be apportionments for house size h; that is, $\lambda_h > h$. Consequently, the

Jefferson apportionment for state i is the smallest integer a_i satisfying

$$\frac{g_J(a_i)}{p_i} = \frac{a_i + 1}{p_i} \geq \lambda_h > h = \frac{g_J(hp_i - 1)}{p_i},$$

or $a_i \geq hp_i$. This completes the proof.

Other assertions now can be proved. For instance, it turns out that if a procedure is bounded away from the Jefferson method, then values of m, h, and **p** can be chosen so that the method rounds down by any desired amount. It can be shown that if a procedure is bounded away from the boundary of TC (so, it can't be J or SD), then almost all population figures satisfying a specified ratio between the populations of densely and sparsely populated states will eventually round apportionments up and down by more than unity. With so many problems, one must wonder why these procedures are used!

Compensating Actions and Constructing Examples. What a mess! The translation term tries to violate upper quota while the sliding effect attempts to violate lower quota. This means the Jefferson - Small Divisor methods play extreme roles most similar to that played by the plurality - anti-plurality methods for positional voting. The SD favors small states by trying to abuse lower quota – Jefferson favors large states by trying to break upper quota. All other methods attempt a balance between these two evils; they combine the negatives of both approaches. So, using these methods becomes a gamble where the hope is that "compensating errors" will enable reasonable outcomes!

The following is a small sample of what else can be extracted from the geometry. Here, as above, $\mathbf{x}^*$ is the last point on S_h hit by the apportionment jar.

- Slightly changing the population can vary the location of $\mathbf{x}^*$. But, different choices can induce radically different "sliding actions." Thus, for any g, there are situations where a slight change in population can make a drastic change in apportionments.
- The admissible changes are determined by the geometry of the assignment triangles. All of the admissible, different directions defined by the boundaries between regions promise that apportionment methods are subject to all sorts of responsiveness difficulties. For instance, for any g, there are situations where, after a state has an increase in its relative population, it loses seats.
- For any g, with enough states, the rounding off process can be as bad as desired.

These two compensating elements – the translation term and the sliding effect – provides enough tools to put a grin even on Steven, the jolly anarchist, as he strokes his long, greying beard while contemplating how to construct examples to demonstrate the inadequacies of structured government. The building blocks are boundary conditions (e.g., tied outcomes) separating different outcomes. To illustrate, I show how to construct examples for a specified g where a small change in population – say, no more than two voters – can alter the allocations.

Corresponding to states A, B, C, let a, b, c be positive integers – potential numbers of seats – where $a + b + c + 1 = h$ and choose population figures so that

$$\lambda^A = \frac{g(a)}{p_a} > \lambda^B = \frac{g(b)}{p_b} = \frac{g(c)}{p_c} = \lambda^C > \frac{g(a-1)}{p_a}. \qquad (5.3.34)$$

The key is the tied outcome between B and C. There is an extra seat to be assigned, and who gets it depends upon the $g(b+1), g(c+1)$ values. On the other hand, suppose the tie vote is broken because C's population is ever so slightly increased so that $p_c^+ > p_c$; the operative inequalities now are $\frac{g(a)}{p_a} > \frac{g(b)}{p_b} = \lambda^B > \frac{g(c)}{p_c^+} = \lambda^C$. It cannot be that $\lambda_h = \lambda^C$ because this would lead to the A, B, C allocation of (a, b, c); one seat remains to be assigned. Therefore, $\lambda_h = \lambda^B > \lambda^C$, so B gets b seats, A gets a seats, and, as $\frac{g(c+1)}{p_c^+} > \lambda^B > \frac{g(c)}{p_c^+}$, C gets $c + 1$ seats. To create other scenarios, just play with the p_j values. For example, if p_c decreases, p_b increases, or p_b increases more than p_c, then B gets the extra seat. With all of this flexibility created by the radical changes in values of fractions with small changes in denominators with small values, all sorts of examples are forthcoming.

The starting point to create examples, then, is where there is equality of the $\frac{g}{p_j}$ values. Then, slight changes in the population figures can make a radical difference in the allocation. This is how I constructed the above examples demonstrating the differing bias of T_g and the sliding action. (The reader familiar with "singularity" or "catastrophe" theory will recognize similarities where qualitatively different outcomes occur with certain small perturbations from a specified singular, boundary condition. Mathematically, there is a close relationship.)

Example 5.5.3. Let $(a, b, c) = (6, 8, 5)$ and $h = 20$. For the EP, Eq. 5.3.34 becomes

$$\frac{\sqrt{42}}{p_a} > \frac{\sqrt{72}}{p_b} = \frac{\sqrt{30}}{p_c},$$

so population figures for examples can be constructed from 64750 ($< 10^4\sqrt{42}$), 84852 ($\approx 10^4\sqrt{72}$), 54772 ($\approx 10^4\sqrt{30}$). The following illustrates that when only two people move from C to A, B's apportionment can change.

State	Population	EP	Population	EP
A	64750	6	64752	6
B	84852	8	84852	9
C	54772	6	54770	5

Similarly, C would benefit if only a couple of people moved from B to A.

The same figures can be used to construct examples where even after an *increase in a state's population, the apportionment goes down.* With the first figures, suppose a mini-migration from state A has two people moving to C and five people moving to B. Before the migration, C had six seats; after the migration, even with its increased population, C is assigned only five seats. (The population figures $(64743, 84857, 54774)$ have the EP apportionment $(6, 9, 5)$.) The disturbing, but not uncommon theme from voting – more can mean less – applies again.

The remaining changes in these figures, where people move from A to just one of the states, or where people move from, say, B to C, provide no surprises. This can be corrected by admitting more states. With more states, there are more ways to move the population from one group of states to another; hence, there are more surprises. These are left for the entertainment of the reader. $\square$

Of course, EP is used above because it is the technique of choice for the USA; similar assertions hold for all choices of g. In fact, by attaching what we learned about the motion on a torus onto the above comments, it can be shown that while the construction of these assertions involves boundary values, almost all population figures eventually will satisfy these conditions. So, for instance, if only a specified ϵ percentage of the voters can change states, for almost all choices of $\mathbf{p}$, there are house sizes where certain changes within these bounds will alter the apportionments in the above indicated manner.

As for a choice of ϵ, recognize that the 1990 census of the USA was about 2.1% short. (For instance, see the discussion in the Congressional Record, July 30, 1991, S11316-S11327.) Although statistical procedures were offered (and declined) to correct the situation, an error of 2.1% was considered quite accurate. Thus, a reasonable value to use with the above comments is half of that – $\epsilon = 0.01$.

5.5.5 If Washington Had 836 More People

If changes in apportionments are likely, then why do we not observe them in practice? Actually, we do; based on the 1990 census a small change in the population of New Jersey, New York, and Massachusetts would have caused changes in the apportionment of other states. As true in giving course grades, some student is right on the dividing line between and A and B; a very slight change in the grade of even a quiz would change the grades. Similarly, for 1990 and EP, the dividing value of $\lambda_{435} = 432.5043$ is defined by Massachusetts; it has 10 seats. Other nearby values are for New Jersey, with its population of 7,730,188 and 13 seats is $\lambda_{NJ} = 432.99037$ while New York, with its population of 17,990,455 has $\lambda_{NY} = 434.35646$. Currently, Oklahoma has six seats; its EP values are $\frac{g_{EP}(6)}{p_{OK}} = 511.15877$; $\frac{g_{EP}(5)}{p_{OK}} = 432.008$. So, a slight increase in the populations of New Jersey, New York, or Massachusetts that force their λ value below 432.008 would result in Oklahoma losing a seat to that state. To assist the reader in designing examples to show how increase in populations would lead to decrease in seats, etc., a listing of the states with λ values near the division line are given below.

In this table, a_i is the current apportionment; p_j is defined by dividing the population of each state by $248, 103, 333$; the total population of the 50 states. (This excludes the population of Washington DC. Using the full population of

248, 709, 873 changes the λ_j values, but not their ordering, so it does not affect the apportionment.)

State	Pop	a_j	$\frac{g_{EP}(a_j)}{p_j}$	$\frac{g_{EP}(a_j-1)}{p_j}$
Florida	12, 937, 926	23	450.54427	431.3633
Massachusetts	6, 016, 425	10	432.5043	391.2149
Montana	799, 065	1	440.1755	∞
Mississippi	2, 573, 216	5	528.10099	431.19265
New Jersey	7, 730, 188	13	432.99037	400.87119
New York	17, 990, 455	31	434.35646	420.56384
Tennessee	4, 877, 185	9	482.59701	431.64789
Washington	4, 866, 692	9	483.63753	432.57855

These figures display the peculiar fact that *the 1990 apportionment of Congressional seats appears to be wrong!* According to the census figures (as recorded in the Congressional Record, specified by the census bureau, and listed in any number of almanacs) the state of Washington should receive 8, rather than the assigned 9 seats. In fact, $\frac{g_{EP}(9)}{p_{WA}} = 483.6375$ while $\frac{g_{EP}(8)}{p_{WA}} = 432.57855 > \lambda_{435}$. These figures require Washington to have 8, rather than 9 representatives, and that $\lambda_{435} = \frac{g_{EP}(8)}{p_{WA}} = 432.57855$. Namely, Washington is the true state on the dividing line! In turn, Massachusetts is entitled to Washington's extra seat!

¿From several perspectives, assigning Massachusetts 11 seats and Washington eight makes sense. Currently, Massachusetts has 11% more representatives than Washington (10 to 9). With the swap leading to 11 and eight seats, Massachusetts would have 25% more representatives matching its 23% larger population (6,016,425 to 4,866,692). Moreover, such representation would provide parity between Massachusetts and Virginia (pop 6,187,358). It is a close call, with only about 840 more people in Washington – no more than a reasonable turnout for a small town high school football game – the apportionment is correct! This constitutes less than $\frac{2}{100}$ of a percent change!

So, what happened? The answer is that for only the second time since 1900, the Census Bureau allocated Department of Defense's overseas employees for purposes of reapportionment. (The other time was in 1970 during the Vietnam War.) As shown above, a small change will benefit Washington at Massachusetts' expense, and it happened. Consequently, as one might expect, Massachusetts went to court. The District Court ruled that the "decision to allocate the employees and to use home of record data was arbitrary and capricious." [Mas] But, on June 26, 1992, the US Supreme Court ruled against Massachusetts on technical grounds involving "the separation of powers and the unique constitutional position of the President." (This is because the President is charged with calculating and transmitting the apportionment to Congress. See [Mas, Mon]; the decision includes a nice description of the history.)

Around the same time, Montana also issued a legal challenge prompted by the fact that the 1990 census caused it to lose one of its two representatives.

As they argued, the average population of a district in the US is 572,466 as compared to the much larger 803,655 for Montana. (The inflated number is due to the overseas employee count.) Essentially, they attacked the EP method; "Montana alleged that the 'method of the harmonic mean' or the 'method of smallest divisors' would yield a fairer result." [Mon, p4] It is no surprise to see Montana championing SD because, as shown above, it favors small states. But as demonstrated by the above discussion, for selecting a procedure, the 1990 figures are immaterial; it is easy to demonstrate other figures where the outcome is distinctly biased! Indeed, all of these procedures are subject to creating serious difficulties! Montana lost in the Supreme Court. [Mon]

5.5.6 A Solution

With so many problems generated by these procedures, what should we do? Personally, I find that the house monotone methods violate the initial intent in the design of PR methods far more than Hamilton's Method. Think about it; the serious bias pulling in both directions leaves us hostage to "compensating errors." That doesn't seem to be a reasonable way to conduct serious business. Anyway, the main reason we dropped Hamilton's method is to avoid the Alabama Paradox. This paradox requires changes in house size, so in the many situations where the house size is fixed, the political ramifications of the Alabama Paradox no longer remain relevant. Consequently, whenever the house size is fixed, as for the US Congress, Hamilton's method is most reasonable! In fact, Montana's argument about district size is an argument for a return to Hamilton.

Of course, for the intellectual challenge and for those countries using the "list system," we can develop procedures that avoid the Alabama Paradox while preserving quota but, yes, with the price of introducing still new problems. The approach I suggest is based on standard techniques from optimization theory. Before selecting an "optimal" choice, first we find all viable candidates. Similarly, before designing selection methods, we must first identify *all house monotone paths that satisfy quota*. Call this set $\mathcal{E}(\mathbf{p})$.

An entry of $\mathcal{E}(\mathbf{p})$ is a listing of apportionments starting at house size $h = 0$ and going as far as needed; even to $h = \infty$. Each apportionment in the listing differs from the previous apportionment in that one state has an extra seat (house monotone). Secondly, for each h, the apportionment for h is a vertex on the apportionment cube containing $h\mathbf{p}$ (respects quota). Once $\mathcal{E}(\mathbf{p})$ is given, then the reader's favorite method can be used to select the actual apportionment – Hamilton's method, toss of the dice, whatever. For instance, suppose $\mathbf{a}(h)$ is the apportionment at house size h. In moving to house size $h + 1$, consider all paths in $\mathcal{E}(\mathbf{p})$ that pass through $\mathbf{a}(h)$. The $h + 1$ *eligible set* are all apportionment at house size $h + 1$ that are on one of these paths. So, choose one of the eligible apportionments. This procedure eliminates all worries about the Alabama Paradox as well as the more serious concerns introduced by the normal house monotone methods.

On the other hand, once some vertices (apportionments) are eliminated (because they are not in $\mathcal{E}(\mathbf{p})$), we have changed the geometry; e.g., the boundary of $\mathbf{p}$ values dividing one type of outcome from another is significantly altered. As we have learned, changes in the boundary structure can be accompanied a host of new kinds of paradoxes. This happens; for instance, more serious "population paradoxes" than that described earlier for Hamilton's method occur; some of these problems cannot be dismissed. (To find them, apply the earlier discussion involving the inner normals to the new inner normals that are defined by the new boundaries.)

Finding the Entries of $\mathcal{E}(\mathbf{p}) \neq \emptyset$. It is easy to show for $m = 3$ that $\mathcal{E}(\mathbf{p})$ is not empty. More challenging is to prove this for $m \geq 4$. To conclude this section, I indicate why this is so.

The exact apportionment line for a given $\mathbf{p}$ passes through the interiors of various apportionment cubes. Label them in ascending order; so, cube 1 is the base cube, 2 is the second cube along the line, and so forth. For the kth cube, let $t_e(k)$ and $t_x(k)$ be, respectively, the minimum and maximum value of t with $t\mathbf{p}$ in the cube – this just identifies where the exact apportionment line enters and exits the cube. When $t_e(k)\mathbf{p}$ enters this cube, it passes through a face, an edge, or a vertex; choose the geometric construct with minimal dimension. (So, if it passes through an edge, ignore that the edge is on several faces.) Call this object the kth entering face. Similarly, $t_x(k)\mathbf{p}$ identifies where the exact apportionment line leaves the cube, so the geometric object containing this point is called the kth exiting face. What helps in this description is that the kth exiting face is the $k + 1$th entering face.

Let $[x]$ be the greatest integer function; this is the function that replaces x with the largest integer smaller than or equal to x. For instance, $[4.89] = 4$, $[7] = 7$. The candidate entering apportionments are all apportionments on the kth entering face that satisfy house size $[t_e(k)]$; similarly, the candidate leaving apportionments are all apportionments on the k exiting face that satisfy house size $[t_x(k)]$.

To illustrate with numbers, let $\mathbf{p} = (\frac{3}{12}, \frac{5}{12}, \frac{1}{12}, \frac{3}{12})$. The exact apportionment line leaves the base cube and enters cube # 2 when $t = \frac{12}{5}$ at $t\mathbf{p} = (\frac{3}{5}, 1, \frac{1}{5}, \frac{3}{5})$. Thus, the vertices of the first exiting and second entering faces are all vertices where the second component is unity, and all others are either zero or unity. As $[t_e(2)] = [\frac{12}{5}] = 2$, the entering apportionments for the second cube (and exiting apportionments for the first one) are $(1, 1, 0, 0), (0, 1, 1, 0), (0, 1, 0, 1)$.

The next time there is an integer value for $t\mathbf{p}$ is when $t = \frac{12}{3} = 4$ and the point is $4\mathbf{p} = (1, \frac{5}{3}, \frac{1}{3}, 1)$. Here, the $k = 2$ exiting face (and $k = 3$ entering face) is the set of points $(1, x, y, 1)$ where $1 = [\frac{5}{3}] \leq x \leq [\frac{5}{3}] + 1 = 2$, $0 = [\frac{1}{3}] \leq y \leq [\frac{1}{3}] + 1$. As $[4] = 4$, the exiting apportionments are $(1, 1, 1, 1)$ and $(1, 2, 0, 1)$.

The purpose of the candidate entering and exiting apportionments is to ensure that an apportionment is on the correct apportionment cube for each value of h. Clearly, an entry of $\mathcal{E}(\mathbf{p})$ crosses the kth cube from a candidate entering apportionment to a candidate exiting one. What we want to do is to construct all possible ways there are to go between them in a house monotone fashion. Any such listing is a path for the k cube. To illustrate with numbers, there are two paths going from $(1,1,0,0)$ to $(1,2,0,1)$; one has the intermediate point $(1,2,0,0)$ and the other has the intermediate point $(1,1,0,1)$. On the other hand, there are no paths going from $(0,1,1,0)$ to $(1,2,0,1)$.

In the natural way, the paths in $\mathcal{E}(\mathbf{p})$ are constructed by tying together all of the paths from the cubes. Some of these paths can end in a cube, so they cannot be continued. For instance, as shown above, there is no way to get from $(0,1,1,0)$ to $(1,2,0,1)$. It turns out that by working forwards, we can encounter many of these "dead-ends." So, the better approach mimics how some students try to do homework – start at the answer and work backwards to the problem. The trouble here is to avoid starting at the impossible $h = \infty$. Thus, we need ways to identify intermediate starting points; these are juncture points through which all paths pass.

To define an intermediate starting point, call the candidate entering apportionments *strong entering apportionments* if there is a house monotone path from *each* entering apportionment of the cube to each exiting apportionment of the cube! The advantage of these points is that they impose no complications in the construction of forward paths. Choose such an apportionment in a cube larger than needed for the problem (say, for the US Congress, in a cube where $t_e(k) > 435$), these points serve as the starting "answers" for the backwards iteration.

A sufficient condition for there to be strong entering apportionments in the kth cube is if the candidate entering apportionment is the minimal apportionment for the cube. This is satisfied whenever $\sum_{i=1}^{m}(t_e(m)p_i - [t_e(m)p_i]) < 1$. The inequality means that the exact apportionment is very close to the minimal apportionment. For theoretic purposes, observe that this inequality defines an open set about the minimal apportionment. This open set permits the earlier arguments about the line on a torus to be used to show that for all $\mathbf{p}$, *there are an infinite number of cubes with a strong entering apportionment*. In the example problem, for instance, whenever $t = 12j$, the exact apportionment passes through the minimal apportionment point, so a strong entering apportionment is defined.

Each strong entering apportionment for cube k also is an exiting apportionment for the $k-1$ cube. In this $k-1$ cube, find all paths connecting entering and exiting apportionments. All entering apportionments, then, serve as the exiting apportionments on the $k-2$ cube. Continue this process.

To demonstrate that $\mathcal{E}(\mathbf{p})$ is nonempty, we only need to construct one such path. To do this, apportionments are chosen to mimic the "cut and side" points. At house size h, initially assign each state its minimal apportionment as determined by $h\mathbf{p}$. This leave $\beta(h)$ extra seats to be assigned. We want to assign extra seats according to "need;" the states where tp_j first turns into an integer needs an extra representative to protect quota. Therefore, order the states according to the value of $t > h$ that make tp_j an integer; a state with a smaller t value needs an extra representative sooner than others. Of course, there can be ties. If so, then break them according to the "next" values of t. Use this ranking to assign $\beta(h)$ states an extra seat. To illustrate with the above example for $t = 10$, $10\mathbf{p} = (2\frac{1}{2}, 4\frac{2}{12}, \frac{10}{12}, 2\frac{3}{4})$. Thus, the initial allocation is $(2,4,0,2)$ and $\beta(10) = 2$.

The next value of $t > 10$ when tp_j is an integer for any state is $t = 12$; unfortunately, this is true for *all* four states. To invoke the tie breaker, find the smallest $t > 12$ values where tp_j is an integer. As they are $12 + 4, 12 + 2.4, 12 + 12, 12 + 4$, the second state gets one seat. The last tie cannot be broken (the states have the same population), so flip a coin to assign the next seat to get $(3, 5, 0, 2)$. At $h = 11$, the apportionment is $(3, 5, 0, 3)$, and at $h = 12$, it is $(3, 5, 1, 3)$.

The hard part is done; showing that this assignment process is in $\mathcal{E}(\mathbf{p})$ is left as an exercise.

5.5.7 Exercises

1. Carry out the details for the derviation of the Harmonic Mean method.

2. Example 5.5.1 describes the apportionment jars for two methods; find the jars for the remaining methods of Eq. 5.5.14. Notice how the W, γ methods define a line.

3. Use Eq. 5.5.14 to show that Jefferson's method favors large states more than EP. Compare g_J with HM and SD. How does HM compare with EP?

4. For each method indicated in Eq. 5.5.14, create an example where the "rounding off" for some state differs by at least five from what it should be.

5. Create examples for the main methods where when people move from one state to another, the apportionment for one state goes a direction different than what we would expect.

6. On page 280, the apportionments are give for several states based on the 1990 population figures. How do these apportionments differ from what would be the Hamilton's apportionment?

7. For $m = 3$, the k-assignment triangles are defined by three vertices in the base cube. Show that for $m \geq 4$, the k-assignment region is defined by $\binom{m}{k}$ vertices. Find the distance from the center of this object (given by $k(\frac{1}{m}, \ldots, \frac{1}{m})$) to one of these vertices. Compare this this distance to the distance between points $k(\frac{1}{m}, \ldots, \frac{1}{m})$ and $(k+1)(\frac{1}{m}, \ldots, \frac{1}{m})$. Finally, to appreciate the bias introduced by the translation $T_g(\lambda \mathbf{p})$, compute the length of T_g for EP, for J, and for W with m states.

8. Show that $\mathcal{E}(\mathbf{p}) \neq \emptyset$. To do so, show that the path constructed in the concluding subsection has all the correct properties. First, use the fact that the apportionment is defined in terms of the apportionment cube to establish quota preserving. Next, show that all apportionments within a particular cube are house monotone. Finally, show that the apportionment cannot jump by more than one seat. This takes care of the transition between cubes.

NOTES

By no means are the following references complete; they are places to start. In addition to these suggestions and their references, I recommend Kelly's *Social Choice Bibliography* [K3].

Chapter 2

The geometry of the representation triangle, ranking regions, the space of voting profiles, the normalized form for voting vectors, and the convex hull $\mathcal{CH}(\mathbf{w}_s)$ are natural, but it appears to have been first developed in [S1, 3-6, 20]. (I have not found it elsewhere. Instead, for example, most results are described with specific methods in analytic formulations rather than considering all possibilities.) This geometric approach now is my standard tool.

Chapter 3

A complete history about the rankings of pairs probably would include everybody who has written or experimented with voting! For previous work, I suggest starting with the books and survey articles by Black [Bl], Fishburn [F1], Niemi and Riker [NR], Nurmi [Nu], and Sen [Se2].

While the Money Pump argument of Sect. 3.1 is standard, it is more so in economics than choice theory. The explanation of the Condorcet cycle in terms of the irrational voter is new, but hints are in [S1, 19]. (The reader knowledgeable about algebraic group theory will find several extensions both in terms of subgroup constructions and for $n \geq 3$.) The reduced profile argument depending on removing the Condorcet portion of a profile and the use of this material to understand the Condorcet and Borda debates appears in print for the first time with this book.

The geometric argument leading to the representation cube of Sect. 3.2 and the coordinate representations first appeared in *Geometry of Voting* [S20]. Since then, they have been used in several papers by Merlin, Tataru, and others. See, for instance, [MT], [MS], [SM], [ST], [T]. The geometric description of the "confused voter" is new with this book.

When *Geometry of Voting* was written, I had planned to include a section on computing the probability of cycles and other types of voting behavior. My goal was to start with the seminal work of Gehrlein [G1,2] and his joint work with Fishburn [GF] and then show how to modify a new approach pioneered by Jill Van Newenhizen [VN] to extend this work to all values of n, a wider class of probability distributions, and all basic questions. However, then, as now, I believe that the coordinate and profile decomposition approaches developed in this chapter lead to sharper results, are more informative, and are easy to use to completely determine the profiles and profile set supporting various conclusions. Thus, we now can answer more ambitious questions than possible with the traditional approach for any number of issues in a fairly elementary manner using more general assumptions. (All of this extends to $n \geq 3$ candidates.)

Cycles arise in almost all areas involving pairwise rankings – economics, statistics, etc. The mathematical reason for these cycles is similar to the confused voter explanation. Also, a similar decomposition of the data highlights the bias of these different methods. A reader interested in reading more about this might look at [FS], [Ha], [S5-6]. For different ideas on this and related subjects, I suggest Aizerman's survey paper [A].

Black's conditions (Sect. 3.3) are well known and described in most books on this topic; in particular, see Black's classic [Bl]. The conditions developed in Sect. 3.3 seem to be more general than what is in the literature; it is the only discussion (I know about) based on geometric reasoning. The identification of the reduced profile and Black's conditions is new with this book. Again, extensions to $n \geq 3$ follow by using similar geometric arguments.

Spatial voting is an important academic growth area that provides sensitive insight into varied questions from political science. (The results of this subsection are based on arguments from [S17].) For the reader interested in learning more about this topic, I recommend starting with Steven Brams' book [Br2], progress to the book edited by Enelow and Hinich [EH], and then the references of these books. For a flavor of the serious difficulties, see the many papers and books written by Norman Schofield (e.g., [Sh1, 2]) as well as other papers on this topic such the one by Le Breton and Salles [LS]. If you want to know how many steps in an agenda manipulation it takes to get from one ideal point to another, see Maria Tataru's paper [T].

The material in Sect. 3.3 about the failings and faults of the Condorcet winners and losers was developed for this book and [S20]; all of the comments extend with even greater force to the $n \geq 3$ setting. Actually, in higher dimensions, there are even more profiles that demonstrate the serious weakness of conclusions from pairwise ordinal rankings.

When posed in its standard way, Arrow's Theorem [Ar] is so shocking that even today, at most conferences involving choice theory, several papers are presented trying to unravel the mystery. Explanations use all sorts of techniques: e.g., Barbera [Ba1] emphasizes pivotal voting while Barthelemy [Bar] describes unusual domains. Indeed, to find other earlier approaches, the reader should start with one of the many excellent books on the subject; say, the one by Kelly [K1]. As for earlier work on "possibility theorems" of the "Gene-Alfred" flavor, see the work of Kalai and his coauthors [KM, KR] and their references. However, as shown in Sect. 3.4, explanations and interpretations of Arrow's Theorem now are straightforward. Once we recognize that IIA is destroying the transitivity assumption, the conclusion of this theorem becomes easy to predict. Similarly, as I describe in [S19], by reintroducing the transitivity of the voters, reasonable procedures emerge. As one must expect, this same "intensity" approach (or modifications for those caught up in technicalities) to bring back transitive preferences answers many of the other mysteries of voting and choice procedures. For $n \geq 4$ alternatives, the same ideas hold.

The approach developed in Sect. 3.4 is a benign geometric modification of ideas developed in [S14]. This reference describes results for all values of n as well as showing how the same ideas hold for game theory, probability, economics, etc. The approach was developed to understand the "kind of information" required by certain classes of axioms. Other theorems ranging in flavor from that of Blau and Deb [BD] to Brown [Bro] can be similarly extended.

Chapter 4

Comparing the rankings of pairs and all three candidates is as old as this subject. After all, this was the force of Borda's example in 1770. Extensions to more candidates in terms of specific examples with restrictions on the choice of procedures were made by others; e.g., Fishburn. The first theory describing (in certain settings) everything that can happen is in [S1,3,4] and then, in greater generality, in papers starting with [S9]. Most everything in this chapter is new with this book and [S20]; in particular, this applies to the geometric reasoning.

Already during the exciting years of debate between Borda and Condorcet, it was understood that one profile can define different outcomes as $\mathbf{w}_s$ varies. In more recent time, others, including Steven Brams, Peter Fishburn, Herve Moulin, and Phil Straffin have created provocative and amusing examples (e.g., see [F1-3, Str]). However, this earlier discussion tends to be limited to special examples for specific procedures. The first approach to understand everything that can happen – the procedure line of Sect. 4.2 – for all $n \geq 3$ for all positional methods is [S1, 3-4]. An interesting example is in Benoit's delightful paper [Be] applying these paradoxes to the selection of the MVP in baseball.

While reversal bias is introduced in *Geometry of Voting*, the approach given here is done without the introduction to algebraic group theory. However, I recommend that the more mathematically advanced reader examine Sect. 3.1 of [S20] to learn about the different permutation subgroups in profile space. This group theory discussion underscores the source of some of the BC properties. The profile decomposition of Sect. 4.4 is new with this book. The reversal properties of voting vectors first appeared in [S20].

Some results in the first part of Sect. 4.5 probably were known by Borda. (See [D], [B]. Included among the 19th and 20th century papers contributing to the BC are Nanson [N], Smith [Sm], Young [Y1], Gehrlein and Fishburn [FG, GF]; an overview is in the expositions [Nu, Str]. For a modern approach that characterizes all of the BC properties for $n \geq 3$ candidates, see [S9, 11, 13] and the extensions to other positional systems in [S16, 17]. The arguments about the basic profiles and the connection with the profile decomposition is new with this book. The argument about the dubious positive property of the plurality vote is in the exercises of Sect. 4.5 of [S20] and it is part of my argument in

[S24] warning about the dangers of the axiomatic approach. (Reference [S24] is a written version of my comments at a 1993 conference at Columbia University; it is scheduled to appear in *Social Choice & Welfare*.) The Borda Dictionary material comes from [S9, 11]. Most of the geometric descriptions, such as the BC cross-sections, Borda cyclic coordinates, are new with this book and [S20].

Much of the material in Sect. 4.6 is a special case of statements from [S9], but with a new geometric representation; e.g., the cross-section approach has not been previously published before [S20]. The same kind of conclusion, where nothing is predicatable, holds for most positional methods for all $n \geq 3$. See [S9, 11, 16, 17]. To my chagrin, the unimaginative term of Sect. 4.7, "multiple voting systems," was coined in [SV1]. Most of the results in this section are extensions (to the restrictive setting of $n = 3$) of comments in [SV1,2]. The heavier emphasis on geometry is new. Some of the material in Sect. 4.8 is a geometric representation of conclusions from [S9, 11, 12, 13, 15] where the results were established for all $n \geq 3$.

Chapter 5

Weak consistency was introduced in [S12]. The material in this section relies upon and extends (with a greater emphasis on geometry) the results from this reference. For earlier, related statements, consult Nurmi's and Straffin's expositions [Nu, Str] as well as Moulin's work, e.g., [Mo1]. The modifier "weak" is meant to distinguish from Young's "consistency" [Y1, 2] which is a more restrictive concept.

The kind of issues described in Sects. 5.2, 5.3 have consumed much of the social choice literature. Therefore, the interested reader could start with the general books and references mentioned above as well as the work of Plott (a starting point might be the references in his paper [Pl]). It is impossible to do justice to the literature for manipulation and strategic action; after the startling, seminal work of Gibbard [Gi] and Satterthwaite [Sa], there have been many deep contributions to this topic. One starting point might be the work of Barbera [Ba2] and of Schmeidler and Sonnenschein [ScS]. Also, for almost any method, a manipulation analysis can be found; e.g., see Niemi's analysis of Approval Voting [Ni] and Chamberlin's comparison [C]. (Incidentally, many comparisons are based on computer simulations; this no longer is necessary as the method developed in [S10] and reported in this section allows an analytic analysis.) Periodically, when some organization believes they have invented a strategy-proof system, they need to be informed of the errors of their ways by others. This leads to some interesting examples; for instance, S. Brams [Br1] developed one to educate the American Mathematical Society.

Usually, the topics addressed in this section are treated separately. Thus, this geometric treatment seems to be the first to show that all of the questions from monotonicity to manipulation are so intimately connected that they can be addressed in the same general framework while obtaining sharper conclusions. Even stronger, with the method of these sections, all of these issues become special cases of the same analysis. The geometric proof of the Gibbard-Satterthwaite

Theorem is new (and I thank Mark Satterthwaite for discussions about it). The susceptibility to manipulation discussion is a more geometric formulation of ideas first developed in [S10].

While apportionment methods (Sects. 5.4, 5.5) have been widely studied for years, I find the best papers to be Huntington's work from the 1920s – his references [Hu1, 2] are a good place to start. Several papers were published up to the 60s and 70s, but, after the size of Congress was fixed at 435, interest diminished. Then, in 1975, Balinski and Young [BY1] published an entertaining exposition that resurrected interest in the USA and Europe. Also see the book edited by Brams, Lucas and Straffin [BLS].

The presentation about the Alabama Paradox and the method described in the last subsection come from [S2]. In particular, the identification of apportionment and integer programming problems with flows on a torus was first done in [S2]. The material concerning fly-catching leading up to the geometric explanation of the sliding and transition bias is new. Some of the technical support for [Mas] and [Mon] required computer simulations; this new geometric analysis allows for sharper statements that can be obtained in a much easier way.

For the readers interested in creating other apportionment or list approaches, note that the Hamilton method is based on moving a flat object held parallel to the simplices S_h, while the Huntington methods move an orthant in various lagging and sliding ways. These two methods are special cases of moving a cone according to the exact apportionment line – Hamilton's method is where the vertex angle is $\theta = 180^o$ while Huntington is characterized by $\theta = 90^o$. Let an acute cone be where $|\theta| < 90^o$ while an obtuse cone has $90^o < \theta < 180^o$. It is easy to reject the acute cone (it has all the problems associated with requiring values of $\lambda << h$), but what are the properties of the obtuse cones?

REFERENCES

[Ab]   Abbott, E.A., *Flatland; a romance of many dimensions 6th edn.*, Dover Publications, 1952.

[A]   Aizerman, MA, *New problems in the general choice theory: review of a research trend*, Soc Choice Welfare **2** (1985), 235-282.

[Ar]   Arrow KJ, *Social choice and individual values, 2nd edn.*, Wiley, New York, 1963.

[B]   Baker, KM, *Condorcet*, University of Chicago Press, 1975.

[BY1]   Balinski, ML, Young HP, *The quota method of apportionment*, Am Math Mon **82** (1975), 701-730.

[BY2]   Balinski, ML, Young HP, *Fair representation*, Yale University Press, New Haven, 1982.

[Ba1]   Barbera, S, *Pivotal voters: a new proof of Arrow's theorem*, Econ Lett **6** (1980), 13-16.

[Ba2]   Barbera, S, *Strategy-proofness and pivotal voters: a direct proof of the Gibbard-Satterthwaite theorem*, Int Econ Rev **24** (1983), 413-428.

[Bar]   Barthelemy, J-P, *Arrow's theorem: unusual domains and extended co-domains*, Math Soc Sci **3** (1982), 79-89.

[Be]   Benoit, J-P, *Scoring reversals: a major league dilemma*, Soc Choice Welfare **9** (1992), 89-97.

[Bl]   Black, D, *The theory of committees and elections*, Cambridge University Press, London New York, 1958.

[BD]   Blau, JH, and R. Deb., *Social decision functions and veto*, Econometrica **45** (1977), 871-879.

[Bo]   Borda, J-C, *Memoire sur les elections au Scrutin*, Histoire de l'Academie Royale des Sciences (1781).

[Br1]   Brams, SJ, *The AMS nomination procedure is vulnerable to "truncation of preferences"*, Not Am Math Soc **29** (1982), 136-138.

[Br2]   Brams, SJ,, *Spatial Models of Election Competition*, comap, inc., Lexington, MA, 1983.

[BrF1]   Brams, SJ, Fishburn, PC, *Approval voting*, Am Polit Sci Rev **72** (1978), 831-847.

[BrF2]   Brams, SJ, Fishburn, PC, *Approval voting*, Birkhauser, Boston, 1983.

[BrF3]   Brams, SJ, Pishburn, PC, *Manipulability of voting by sincere truncation of preferences*, Public Choice **44** (1984), 397-410.

[BFM]   Brams, SJ, Fishburn, PC, Merril, S III, *The responsiveness of approval voting: comments on Saari and Van Newenhizen*, Public Choice **59** (1988), 121-131.

[BLM]   Brams, S.J. W.F. Lucas, P.D. Straffin, Jr., *Political and Related Models*, Springer-Verlag, Heidelberg, 1983.

[Bro]   Brown, DJ, *Aggregation of preferences*, Quarterly journal of economics **89** (1975), 465-469.

[C]   Chamberlin, JR, *An investigation into the relative manipulability of four voting systems*, Behav Sci **30** (1985), 195-203.

[Ch]   Chichilnisky, G, *The topological equivalence of the Pareto condition and the existence of a dictator*, J Math Econ **9** (1982), 223-234.

[D]   De Grazia, A, *Mathematical derivation of an election system*, Isis **44** (1953), 42-51.

[De]   De Groot, M, *Reaching a consensus*, J Am Stat Assoc **69** (1974), 118-121.

[Do]   Dodgson, CL, *Suggestions as to the best method taking votes when more than two issues are to be voted on*, Oxford, 1874.

[E]   Ellis, GM, *Boso's life of Alexander* III, Rowman and Littlefield, Totawa, New Jersey, 1973.

[EH]   Enelow, JM and Hinich, M (eds.), *Advances in the Spatial Theory of Voting*, Cambridge University Press, 1990.

[F1]   Fishburn, PC, *The theory of social choice*, Princeton University Press, Princeton, 1973.

[F2]   Fishburn, PC, *Paradoxes of voting*, Am Polit Sci Rev **68** (1974), 537-548.

[F3]   Fishburn, PC, *Inverted orders for monotone scoring rules*, Discrete Appl Math **3** (1981), 27-36.

[FG]   Fishburn, PC, Gehrlein, WV, *Borda's rule; positional voting, and Condorcet's simple majority principle*, Public Choice **28** (1976), 79-88.

[Fr]   Francis, MJ, *The Allende victory: an analysis of the 1970 Chilean presidential election*, University of Tuscon Press, Tuscon, 1973.

[FS]   Funkenbusch, WW, Saari, DG,, *Preferences among preferences or nested cyclic stochastic inequalities*, Congressus Numerantium **39** (1983), 419-432.

[G1]   Gehrlein, WV, *Expected probability of Condorcet's paradox*, Econ Lett **7** (1981), 33-37.

[G2]   Gehrlein, WV, *Probability calculations for transitivity of the simple majority rule*, Econ Lett **27** (1988), 311-315.

[GF]   Gehrlein, WV, Fishburn, PC, *Probabilities of election outcomes for large electorates*, J Econ Theory **19** (1978), 38-49.

[Gi]   Gibbard, AF, *Manipulation of voting schemes: a general result*, Econometrica **41** (1973), 587-601.

[GHW]   Gibbard, AF, Hylland, A., Weymark, JA, *Arrow's theorem with a fixed feasible alternative*, Soc Choice Welfare **4** (1987), 105-115.

[H1]   Hansson, B, *The existence of group preferences*, Public Choice **28** (1976), 89-98.

[H2]   Hansson, B, *Voting and group decision functions*, Synthese **20** (1969), 526-537.

[Ha]   Haunsperger, D, *Dictionaries of paradoxes for statistical tests on k samples*, J Am Stat **87** (1992), 149-155.

[He]   Hermens, A., *Democracy and Proportional Representation*, University of Chicago Press, 1940.

[H0]   Horwell, G., *Proportional Representation; its dangers and defects*, George Allen and Unwin LTD, London, 1925.

[Hu1]   Huntington, EV, *The mathematical theory of the apportionment of representatives*, Natl Acad Sci **7** (1921), 123-127.

[Hu2]   Huntington, EV, *The apportionment of representatives in Congress*, Trans Am Math Soc **30** (1928), 85-110.

[KM]   Kalai, E, Muller, E., *Characterization of domains admitting nondictatorical social welfare functions and nonmanipulable voting procedures*, J Econ Theory **16** (1977), 457-469.

[KR]   Kalai, E, Ritz, Z., *Characterization of the private alternatives domains admitting Arrow social welfare functions*, J Econ Theory **22** (1980), 23-36.

[K1]   Kelly, JS, *Arrow impossibility theorems*, Academic Press, New York, 1978.

[K2]   Kelly, JS, *Conjectures and unsolved problems*, Soc Choice Welfare **4** (1987), 235-239.

[K3]   Kelly, JS, *Social choice bibliography*, Soc Choice Welfare **8** (1991), 97-169.

[LS]   Le Breton, M, Salles, M., *On the generic emptiness of the local core of voting games*, Soc Choice Welfare **4** (1987), 287-294.

[LY]   Li T-Y and Yorke, J.A., *Period three implies chaos*, Amer Math Monthly **82** (1975), 985-992.

[M]   Mascart, J, *La vie et les travaux du chevalier Jean-Charles de Borda*, Annales de l'Universite de Lyon **2** (1919).

[Ma]   Maskin, ES, *Implementation and strong Nash-equilibrium*, Aggregation and revelation of preferences (Laffont, J-J, ed.), North-Holland, Amsterdam, 1979, pp. 433-439.

[Mas]   Sec. of Commerce vs. Massachusetts, *US Supreme Court Decision 91-1502* (1992).

[MT]   Merlin, V. and Tataru, M., *On the relationship of the Condorcet winner and positional voting rules*, Preprint (March, 1995).

[Mc]   McLean, I., *The first golden age of social choice, 1783-1803*, Social Choice, Welfare, and Ethics (Barnett, W., Moulin, H., Salles, M., and N. Schofield, N., ed.), Cambridge University Pres, 1995.

[MH]   McLean, I. and Hewitt, F., *Condorcet: Foundations of Social Choice and Political Theory*, Edward Elgar 1994.

[MU]   McLean, I. and Urken, A., *Did Madison and Jefferson understand Condorcet's social choice theory?*, Public Choice **73** (1992), 445-457.

[MS]   Merlin, V., and Saari, DG, *Copeland Method 2; Manipulation, monotonicity, and paradoxes*, NU Center Math Econ Discussion paper 1112 (1994).

[Mo1]   Moulin, H, *Fairness and strategy in voting*, Fair allocation (Young, HP, ed.), AMS, Providence, 1985, pp. 109-142.

[Mo2]   Moulin, H, *Condorcet's principle implies the no show paradox*, J Econ Theory **45** (1988), 53-64.

[Mon]   Montana vs. US Dept of Commerce;, *US Supreme Court Decision 91-860* (1992).

[N]   Nanson, EJ, *Methods of election*, Trans Proc R Soc Victoria **18** (1882), 197-240.

[Ni]   Niemi, RG, *The problem of strategic behavior under approval voting*, American Political Science Review **78** (1984), 952-958.

[NiR]   Niemi, RG, Riker, WH, *The choice of voting systems*, Sci Am **234** (1976), 21-27.

[Nu]   Nurmi, H, *Comparing voting systems*, D. Reidel, Dordrecht, 1987.

[PS]   Packel, EW, Saari, DG, *Strategic equilibria and decisive set structures for social choice mechanisms*, Math Soc Sci **2** (1982), 373-378.

[Pl]   Plott, CR, *Axiomatic social choice theory: an overview and interpretation*, Am J Polit Sci **20** (1976), 511-596.

[P]   Poinchoff, H.,, *The algebraic closing lemma*, Very Unusual Dynamics (Robinson, C., C. Simon, K. Meyer, eds.), Eastern Chicago State Press, 1976, pp. 69f.

[R1]   Riker, WH, *Arrow's theorem and some examples of the paradox of voting*, Mathematical applications in political science (Claunch, JM, ed.), SMU Press, Dallas, 1965, pp. 41-60.

[R2]   Riker, WH, *Liberalism against populism: a confrontation between the theory of democracy and the theory of social choice*, Freeman, San Francisco, 1982.

[R3]   Riker, WH, *The two-party system and Duverger's law: an essay in the history of political science*, Am Polit Sci Rev **76** (1982), 753-766.

[R4]   Riker, WH, *The Art of Political Manipulation*, Yale University Press, 1986.

[S1]   Saari, DG, *The geometry of departmental politics, of the scoring of track meets, and of Arrow's Social Choice Theorem,*, NU mimeo (1978).

[S2]   Saari, DG, *Methods of apportionment and the House of Representatives*, Amer Math Monthly **85** (1978), 792-802.

[S3]   Saari, DG, *Inconsistencies of weighted summation voting systems*, Math Oper Res **7** (1982), 479-490.

[S4]   Saari, DG, *The ultimate of chaos resulting from weighted voting systems*, Adv Appl Math **5** (1984), 286-308.

[S5]   Saari, DG, *Random behavior in numerical analysis, decision theory, and macrosystems: some impossibility theorems*, Dynamics of macrosystems (Aubin, J-P, Saari, DG, Sigmund, K, eds.), Springer, Berlin Heidelberg New York, 1986, pp. 115-126.

[S6]   Saari, DG, *The sources of some paradoxes from social choice and probability*, J Econ Theory **41** (1987), 1-22.

[S7]   Saari, DG, *Chaos and the theory of elections*, Dynamical systems (Kurzhanski, AB, Sigmund, K, eds.), Springer, Berlin Heidelberg New York, 1987, pp. 179-188.

[S8]   Saari, DG, *Symmetry, voting and social choice*, Math Intell **10** (1988), 32-42.

[S9]   Saari, DG, *A dictionary for voting paradoxes*, Jour Econ Theory **48** (1989), 443-475.

[S10]   Saari, DG, *Susceptibility to manipulation*, Public Choice **64** (1990), 21-41.

[S11]   Saari, DG, *The Borda Dictionary*, Soc Choice Welfare **7** (1990), 279-317.

[S12]   Saari, DG, *Consistency of decision processes*, Annals of Operations Research **23** (1990), 103-137.

[S13]   Saari, DG, *Relationship admitting families of candidates*, Soc Choice Welfare **8** (1991), 21-50.

[S14]   Saari, DG, *Calculus and Extensions of Arrow's Theorem*, Jour Math Econ **20** (1991), 271-306.

[S15]   Saari, DG, *Millions of election rankings from a single profile*, Soc Choice Welfare **9** (1992), 277-306.

[S16]   Saari, DG, *Symmetry extensions of "neutrality"* I. *Advantage to the Condorcet loser*, Soc Choice Welfare **9** (1992), 307-336.

[S17]   Saari, DG, *The aggregate excess demand function and other aggregation procedures*, Economic Theory **2** (1992), 359-388.

[S18]   Saari, DG, *Symmetry extensions of "neutrality"* II. *Partial Ordering of Dictionaries*, Soc Choice Welfare (1993).

[S19]   Saari, DG, *Inner consistency or not inner consistency; a reformulation is the answer*, Social Choice, Welfare, and Ethics (Barnett, W., H. Moulin, H. M. Salles, N. Scholfield, ed.), Cambridge University Press, 1995, pp. 187-212.

[S20]   Saari, DG, *Geometry of Voting*, Springer-Verlag, 1994.

[S21]   Saari, DG, *A chaotic exploration of aggregation paradoxes*, SIAM Review **37** (1995), 37-52.

[S22]   Saari, DG, *The generic existence of a core for q-rules*, NU Center Math Econ Discussion paper 1113 (1994).

[S23]   Saari, DG, *Mathematical complexity of simple economics*, AMS Notices **42** (1995), 222 - 230.

[S24]   Saari, DG, *Informational Geometry of Social Choice*, Preprint (1994).

[SM]   Saari, DG and Merlin, V., *The Copeland method 1; Relationships and the dictionary*, NU Center Math Econ Discussion paper 1111.

[SvN1] Saari, DG, van Newenhizen, J, *The problem of indeterminancy in approval, multiple and truncated voting systems*, Public Choice **59** (1988), 101-120.

[SvN2] Saari, DG, van Newenhizen, J, *Is approval voting an "unmitigated evil"? A response to Brams, Fishburn, and Merrill*, Public Choice **59** (1988), 133-147.

[ST]   Saari, DG and Tataru, M., *The likelihood of dubious election outcomes*, Preprint (1995).

[Sa]   Satterthwaite, MA, *Strategyproofness and Arrow's conditions: existence and correspondence theorems for voting procedures and social welfare functions*, J Econ Theory **10** (1975), 187-217.

[SMR]   Sawyer, J. and MacRae, D., *Game theory and cumulative voting in Illinois:1902-1954*, Amer. Political Science Review **56** (1962), 937f.

[ScS]   Schmeidler, D, Sonnenschein, HF, *Two proofs of the Gibbard-Satterthwaite theorem on the possibility of a strategy-proof social choice function*, Decision theory and social ethics, issues in social welfare (Gottinger, HW, Leinfellner, W, eds.), Reidel, Dordrecht, 1978, pp. 227-234.

[Sh1]   Schofield, N., *Social Equiilibrium and cycles on compact sets*, Jour Economic Theory **33** (1984), 59-71.

[Sh2]   Schofield, N., *Social Choice and Demoncracy*, Springer Verlag, 1985.

[ShT]   Schofield, N. and Tovey, G, *Probability and convergence for supra-majority rule with Euclidean preferences*, Mathl. Comput. Modelling **16** (1992), 41-58.

[Se1]   Sen, AK, *The impossibility of a Paretian liberal*, J Polit Econ **78** (1970), 152-157.

[Se2]   Sen, AK, *Social choice theory*, Handbook of Mathematical Economics, vol III (Arrow, KJ, Intriligator, MD, eds.), North-Holland, Amsterdam, 1986, pp. 1073-1181.

[Sm]   Smith, JH, *Aggregation of preferences with variable electorate*, Econometrica **41** (1973), 1027-1041.

[St]   Stavely, ES, *Greek and Roman voting and elections*, Thames and Hudson, 1972.

[Str]   Straffin, P.D., *Topics in the Theory of Voting*, Birkhauser, Boston, 1980.

[T]   Tataru, M., *On growth rates and agenda manipulation*, Preprint (1995).

[T1]   Taggepera, R, *Seats and votes: a generalization of the cube law of election*, Soc Sci Res **2** (1973), 257-275.

[T2]   Taggepera, R, *Reformulating the cube law for proportional representation elections*, Am Polit Sci Rev **80** (1986), 489-504.

[U]   Ullmann, W, *Principles of government and politics in the middle ages*, London, 1961.

[Ur1]   Urken, A., *The Condorcet-Jefferson connection and the origins of social choice theory*, Public Choice **72** (1991), 213-236.

[Ur2]   Urken, A., *Voting methods in context: The development of a science of voting in French scientific institutions, 1699-1803*, Stevens Institute of Technology preprint (1994).

[VN]   Van Newenhizen, J, *The Borda method is most likely to respect the Condorcet principle*, Economic Theory **2** (1992), 69-83.

[W]   Wilson, RB, *Social science without the Pareto principle*, J Econ Theory **5** (1972), 478-486.

[Y1]   Young HP, *An axiomatization of Borda's Theory*, J Econ Theory **9** (1974), 43-52.

[Y2]   Young, HP, *Social choice scoring functions*, SIAM J Appl Math **28** (1975), 824-838.

INDEX

Textbooks from Springer

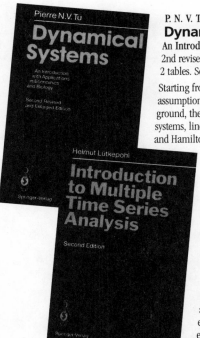

Springer-Verlag
and the Environment

We at Springer-Verlag firmly believe that an international science publisher has a special obligation to the environment, and our corporate policies consistently reflect this conviction.

We also expect our business partners – paper mills, printers, packaging manufacturers, etc. – to commit themselves to using environmentally friendly materials and production processes.

The paper in this book is made from low- or no-chlorine pulp and is acid free, in conformance with international standards for paper permanency.